Constitutional Change in Singapore

Once a ceremonial position modelled after the constitutional monarchy in the United Kingdom, the office of the President of Singapore was transformed from an appointed to an elected one in 1991. As the Head of State, but not the head of government, the Elected President was to have additional discretionary powers involving the spending of financial reserves, appointment of high-ranking public servants and certain ministerial powers to detain without trial. In 2016, a Constitutional Commission was convened to consider further reforms to the office and the elections process. This book explores Singapore's Presidency, assessing how well it has functioned, discussing the rationales for an Elected Presidency and evaluating the Constitutional Commission's recommendations for reforms, including the need for minority representation in the office. In doing so, the book provides important reflections on how the constitutional reform process raises crucial questions about the rule of law and the practice of constitutionalism in Singapore.

Jaclyn L. Neo is an Associate Professor in the Faculty of Law at the National University of Singapore.

Swati S. Jhaveri is an Assistant Professor in the Faculty of Law at the National University of Singapore.

Routledge Law in Asia
Series editors
Randall Peerenboom
Pip Nicholson

11 **Law and Development in Asia**
Edited by Gerald Paul McAlinn and Caslav Pejovic

12 **The Judicialization of Politics in Asia**
Edited by Bjorn Dressel

13 **Juries in the Japanese Legal System**
The Continuing Struggle for Citizen Participation and Democracy
Dimitri Vanoverbeke

14 **Confucian Constitutionalism in East Asia**
Bui Ngoc Son

15 **Religion, Law and Intolerance in Indonesia**
Tim Lindsey and Helen Pausacker

16 **Constitutional Interpretation in Singapore**
Theory and Practice
Jaclyn L. Neo

17 **Politics and Constitutions in Southeast Asia**
Marco Bünte and Björn Dressel

18 **Law and Society in Malaysia**
Pluralism, Religion and Ethnicity
Edited by Andrew Harding and Dian Shah

19 **Judicial Reform in Taiwan**
Democratization and the Diffusion of War
Edited by Neil Chisholm

20 **Constitutional Change in Singapore**
Reforming the Elected Presidency
Edited by Jaclyn L. Neo and Swati S. Jhaveri

Constitutional Change in Singapore

Reforming the Elected Presidency

Edited by Jaclyn L. Neo and Swati S. Jhaveri

Routledge
Taylor & Francis Group
LONDON AND NEW YORK

First published 2020
by Routledge
2 Park Square, Milton Park, Abingdon, Oxon OX14 4RN

and by Routledge
605 Third Avenue, New York, NY 10017

First issued in paperback 2021

Routledge is an imprint of the Taylor & Francis Group, an informa business

Publisher's Note
The publisher has gone to great lengths to ensure the quality of this reprint but points out that some imperfections in the original copies may be apparent.

British Library Cataloguing-in-Publication Data
A catalogue record for this book is available from the British Library

Library of Congress Cataloging-in-Publication Data
A catalog record has been requested for this book

ISBN 13: 978-1-03-208262-2 (pbk)
ISBN 13: 978-1-138-06204-7 (hbk)

Typeset in Times New Roman
by Wearset Ltd, Boldon, Tyne and Wear

Contents

Tables

Contributors

Jaclyn L. Neo is an Associate Professor of Law at the National University of Singapore (NUS). She is a graduate of the NUS Faculty of Law and the Yale Law School. Jaclyn has published in leading journals in her field, including the *International Journal of Constitutional Law* (*I·CON*), *Oxford Journal of Law and Religion*, *Human Rights Quarterly* and the *Singapore Journal of Legal Studies*. She is the sole editor of *Constitutional Interpretation in Singapore: Theory and Practice* (Abingdon: Routledge, 2017); and the co-editor of *Pluralist Constitutions in Southeast Asia* (Singapore: Hart, 2019) and *Regulating Religion in Asia: Norms, Modes, and Challenges* (Cambridge: Cambridge University Press, 2019). She served as a guest editor for special issues of the *Singapore Academy of Law Journal*, the *Journal of Law, Religion, and State*, as well as the *Journal of International and Comparative Law*. Her article on domestic incorporation of international human rights law in a dualist state won the Asian Yearbook of International Law's DILA International Law Prize. In recognition of her research on religious freedom in Southeast Asia, she was awarded the SHAPE-SEA Research Award in 2017. Jaclyn's work has been cited by the Singapore courts and the Supreme Court of India.

Swati S. Jhaveri is an Assistant Professor at the Faculty of Law of the National University of Singapore. Her research areas are constitutional and administrative law, with a focus on the latter. She has published in these areas in *Public Law*, the *Tort Law Review*, *Singapore Journal of Legal Studies*, *Asian Journal of Comparative Law*, *Federal Law Review* and the *International Journal of Constitutional Law*. She obtained her Bachelor of Arts in Jurisprudence and Bachelor of Civil Law from the University of Oxford and is currently a candidate for a DPhil in Law at Oxford. Her thesis looks at developing a positive theory of the executive branch as a constitutional actor/author. She has previously taught at the Faculty of Law at the Chinese University of Hong Kong. At NUS, she has been awarded the Faculty and University's Annual Teaching Excellence Awards for three consecutive years and was placed on the University Honour Roll for Teaching Excellence in 2018. She has also held visiting positions at Melbourne Law School and Columbia Law School.

Maartje De Visser is an Associate Professor of Law and currently also the Associate Dean for (Postgraduate Teaching and Curriculum) at the School of Law of the Singapore Management University. She read for law at Maastricht and Oxford (with distinction), and obtained her PhD (cum laude) at Tilburg University, which was subsequently published as a monograph with Hart. Her main research interests are in the fields of comparative constitutional law and regional integration, and her current work focuses on constitutional interpretation by State institutions other than courts and cross-border judicial networking. Maartje has published widely in these areas, with her work appearing in peer-reviewed international journals including the *American Journal of Comparative Law*, *Global Constitutionalism* and the *Asian Journal of Law and Society*. She has co-edited four books and contributed chapters to more than 20 edited volumes. Her second book, titled *Constitutional Review in Europe: A Comparative Analysis*, was published by Hart in 2014. Maartje is the recipient of two consecutive Lee Kong Chian Fellowships and is a member of the editorial board of the *European Yearbook of Constitutional Law*.

Lam Peng Er is a Senior Research Fellow at the East Asian Institute, National University of Singapore. He obtained his PhD from Columbia University and is a political scientist. His publications have appeared in international journals such as the *Pacific Affairs*, *Asian Survey*, *Asian Affairs*, *Japan Forum* and *Government and Opposition: An International Journal of Comparative Politics*. Lam's latest single-authored book is *Japan's Peace Building Diplomacy in Asia: Searching for an Active Political Role* (New York: Routledge, 2009). Other books include: *Green Politics in Japan* (London: Routledge, 1999); and, as editor, *Japan's Relations with China: Facing a Rising Power* (New York: Routledge, 2006) and *Japan's Relations with Southeast Asia: The Fukuda Doctrine and Beyond* (London: Routledge, 2013). He is an executive editor of the *International Relations of the Asia-Pacific* (A Journal of the Japan Association of International Relations published by Oxford University Press) and *Asian Journal of Peacebuilding* (Journal of the Institute for Peace and Unification Studies, Seoul National University).

Jack Tsen-Ta Lee is the Deputy Research Director of the Singapore Academy of Law, where he works in law reform. He is a graduate of the National University of Singapore Faculty of Law and the University College London Faculty of Laws (on a British Chevening Scholarship), and completed his doctoral dissertation at the Birmingham Law School, University of Birmingham. Called to the Bar in Singapore and on the roll of solicitors in England and Wales, he was formerly a litigation lawyer. He previously taught at the Singapore Management University School of Law, during which he won the School's Most Promising Teacher Award. Among other things, he is currently a member of the International Council on Monuments and Sites (ICOMOS) Singapore; an Expert Member of the ICOMOS International Scientific Committee on Legal, Administrative and Financial Issues (ICLAFI); and the President of the Singapore

Heritage Society. Jack has research interests in constitutional and administrative law, heritage law and media law. He was also a contributor to the first editions of *Halsbury's Laws of Singapore* and the *Singapore Court Practice*, produced by LexisNexis, and is presently contributing to a forthcoming media law title of *Halsbury's Laws of Singapore*.

Eugene K.B. Tan is an Associate Professor of Law and Lee Kong Chian Fellow at the Singapore Management University (SMU) where he teaches at the law, business and social sciences schools. He was also an adjunct faculty between 2015 and 2019 at the Singapore University of Technology and Design, and taught, as a visiting professor in 2013 and 2014, at Yonsei University Law School in South Korea. Eugene's interdisciplinary research interests include constitutional and administrative law, law and public policy, business ethics and corporate social responsibility, and the government and politics of Singapore. An active analyst in the local and international media, Eugene also regularly contributes op-eds to the various Singapore and international media outlets. Between February 2012 and August 2014, Eugene served as a Nominated Member of Parliament in Singapore's twelfth Parliament. Admitted to the Singapore Bar, Eugene was educated at the National University of Singapore, London School of Economics and Political Science, and Stanford University where he was a Fulbright Fellow.

Kevin Y.L. Tan is a Professor (Adjunct) at the Faculty of Law, National University of Singapore (NUS) where he teaches constitutional and administrative law, the Singapore legal system, and law and society, and is Visiting Professor at the S. Rajaratnam School of International Studies, Nanyang Technological University (NTU) where he teaches International Law and International Human Rights. He has published widely in his areas of specialization and has written and edited over 40 books on the law, history and politics of Singapore, including *Managing Political Change in Singapore: The Elected Presidency* (London: Routledge, 1997) (with Lam Peng Er). Kevin has been on the editorial board of several leading legal journals. From 1998–2000, he was also Chief Editor of the *Singapore Journal of International and Comparative Law* and from 2000–2003 was the journal's Adjunct Editor. He was formerly Editor-in-Chief of the *Asian Yearbook of International Law* (2010–2017); and is currently Executive Editor of the *Asian Journal of Comparative Law* (since 2016); and Editorial Board member of the *Korean Journal of International and Comparative Law* (since 2013). Kevin also serves on the Board of Governors of the Human Rights Resource Centre (HRRC).

Li-ann Thio is Provost Chair Professor at the Faculty of Law, National University of Singapore (NUS). She holds a BA (Hons), Oxford University, LLM, Harvard Law School and a PhD, Cambridge University. She is a Barrister (Gray's Inn, United Kingdom), and was a Nominated Member of the Singapore Parliament (2007–2009) and Senior Advisor to the Ministry of Foreign Affairs (2011–2017). She teaches and researches in the fields of constitutional and administrative law, international law and human rights law, with a focus on Asia. A prolific scholar, she has published more than 100 law review articles/ book chapters and her sole authored monographs include *Managing Babel: The International Legal Protection of Minorities in the Twentieth Century* (The Hague: Brill, 2005) and *A Treatise on Singapore Constitutional Law* (Singapore: Academy Publishing, 2012). She has also authored *Constitutionalism in Asia* (with Kevin Y.L. Tan, Wen-Chen Chang and Juinn-rong Yeh) (Oxford: Hart Publishing, 2014); *Constitutional Law in Malaysia and Singapore* (with Kevin Y.L. Tan) (Singapore: LexisNexis, 2010) and *The Evolution of a Revolution: 40 Years of the Singapore Constitution* (Li-ann Thio and Kevin YL Tan, eds) (London: Routledge Cavendish, 2009). She is currently Chief Editor of the *Singapore Journal of Legal Studies* and an Advisory Board Member of the *Max Planck Encyclopedia of Comparative Constitutional Law*; she was formerly General Editor of the *Asian Yearbook of International Law*, Chief Editor of the *Singapore Journal of International & Comparative Law* and Editor, of the *International Journal of Constitutional Law*. She is Editor (with Kevin Y.L. Tan) for the Series on Constitutionalism in Asia (Hart Publishing).

Acknowledgements

This book is a part of a research project funded by the Centre for Asian Legal Studies (CALS) at the National University of Singapore Faculty of Law. We are grateful to Dan W. Puchniak, Weitseng Chen and CALS for supporting this project; Routledge for supporting the publication of this book; and the contributors for their excellent work. We would also like to thank our student research assistants – Louis Lai Wei Kang, Sheiffa Safi Shirbeeni, Shawn Teo Kai Jie, Mao Ning and Zamiq Azmeer Bin Borhanudin. Finally, we are thankful to the National University of Singapore Faculty of Law for its continued support.

Jaclyn L. Neo and Swati S. Jhaveri

Table of cases

Singapore

India

Malaysia

United Kingdom and Privy Council decisions

United States

Table of constitutions and legislation

Singapore

Constitution

Constitutional Amendments

Statutory Instruments

Introduction

Constitutional design and change in 'reforming' Singapore's Elected Presidency

*Jaclyn L. Neo**

I.1 Introduction: designing constitutional change

All constitutions are made;[1] some in an act of revolution, while others follow a more evolutionary path.[2] The making of a constitution may involve codifying pre-existing political norms and socio-political institutions or adopting radically new approaches to constitutional government, or both. They may involve invention, borrowing and/or innovation. In contemporary scholarship, as more is being studied and understood about constitution-making, there is also now a tendency to see constitution-making in terms of 'design'. The term "constitutional design" envisages "a technocratic, architectural paradigm" of constitution-making.[3] It is conceptualized as a purposive exercise aimed to create the 'best' outcomes based on our understanding of how constitutions and governments work. It presumes a *designer* with a master plan as to what the constitution should encompass and how constitutional government should work. Of course, to design something does not mean that one needs to reinvent the wheel. One does not draft a constitution in vacuum. Instead, constitutional design involves "a balance between narrowed models and local tailoring, between conventional choices and creative innovation."[4] Balance may also be necessary in another sense. On the one hand, one might imagine that successful designs need to fit sensibilities in the local context; indeed, constitutions that fail to address deep structural and cultural commitments within the local context are not likely to be effective. On the other hand, constitutions need to overcome the worst excesses of the local context. In particular, in the context of nationally, racially, ethnically, linguistically and religiously divided societies, the focus on constitutional design has long been to try to create institutions and electoral arrangements that could foster peaceful coexistence or, at least, prevent fragmentation and disintegration.[5]

The idea that constitutions are 'designed' has, however, attracted some serious objections. Not only does the idea of 'design' "not easily fit the messy realities of social institutions, especially not the messy process of constitution making",[6] it may also be defeated by other pitfalls like "unanticipated consequences"[7] and self-interest.[8] In addition, as Horowitz points out, any constitutional design exercise is "fraught with the prospect of bias and distortion", including model bias and historical bias.[9] These biases may drive constitution drafters to adopt certain institutions and systems, and to reject others. The purposefulness of the exercise may also belie the reality of constitution-drafting, which often entails compromises and accommodations that result in a document that contains competing, contradictory or even irreconcilable provisions. Indeed, far from being shaped by a fixed range of design principles, constitution-making is more often than not a much more hybridized and perhaps even eclectic exercise that seeks to accommodate a whole range of different interests, both local and international, as well as among different groups.

That said, in the context of Singapore's technocratic style of government, the idea of 'designing' a constitution fits very well with the Government's own narrative about constitution-making. In a speech now well-known to most scholars working on the Singapore constitution, Singapore's first Prime Minister had characterized constitutions as "custom-made" and "tailored".[10] Just as a master tailor carefully measures and plans the making of a suit, this metaphor points to the idea that the constitution is carefully crafted according to the requirements of the society in which it is to operate. Furthermore, it suggests that alterations may be necessary and legitimate to ensure the best fitting.[11] Perhaps no one institution has been subject to more attempts at constitutional design than the Presidency in Singapore. Once a ceremonial office modelled after the constitutional monarchy in the United Kingdom, the President was appointed by the Government and confirmed by the Parliament. As the Head of State, he had a limited range of discretionary powers and was generally obliged to follow the advice of the cabinet unless the constitution specifies otherwise. However, the office was changed to an elected one in 1991 to serve as an additional check on Government. Armed with constitutional discretion to withhold assent to certain parliamentary resolutions relating to fiscal spending and appointments of public servants, the President is envisaged to derive his mandate to check a democratically elected Parliament and Cabinet directly from the people.

The political discourse leading to this fundamental change to the office of the President closely followed the idea of tailoring the constitution not only to respond to present conditions but also to address future anticipated consequences. Indeed, Lee Kuan Yew could be said to be the master architect (or tailor) in creating this constitutional device for fiscal prudence in the form of the Elected Presidency. As Tan and Lam observe, the creation of new institutions and safeguards "promoted the PAP's and probably Lee's vision of a good state".[12] It was meant to guard against a future when "good rulers could not be found to run government".[13] Indeed, the Elected Presidency responds to Singapore's particular political context of a strong political party that has been in government since its independence. This dominance has led to a concentration of power and the political party's dominance over the entire apparatus of government. The new institution is, in some ways, supposed to fill the gap left by the lack of a credible and effective parliamentary opposition and a strong civil society, both of which could serve the function of checking the Government.[14] Remarkably therefore, the Elected Presidency could be seen as the Government designing an institutional change that would serve to limit its own powers. Tasked with implementing Lee Kuan Yew's vision (Lee having stepped down as Prime Minister), the then Prime Minister Goh Chok Tong explained in Parliament that the change "seeks to check and balance the powers of the elected Government" in the specified areas and is "an innovation tailored to meet the unique circumstances of Singapore."[15] Thus, one could conceptualize it as an exercise in constitutionalism; it is an attempt by a dominant government to formalize constitutional devices that would hopefully break the circuit of power and control in the future.

The institution of the Elected Presidency therefore could be seen as a laudable move by a dominant political party to insure against future abuses of power and "to safeguard Singapore's long term future".[16] After all, why would a political party that has been in power for a good 25 years transform a constitutional office that could serve to limit the powers of Parliament and the Cabinet? Perhaps the key lies in the emphasis on the word "future". As Tan and Lam point out, many of the changes instituted by the PAP to constitutionalize political pluralism[17] were "new and often innovative devices [that] were not intended to apply to Lee or his current group of PAP stalwarts for they are 'good rulers'."[18] Indeed, it was intended to guard against "freak election results",[19] understood by many to mean one where the PAP is not returned to power or not returned with a strong governing majority.[20] In more sombre moments, Lee acknowledged that there is also a possibility that future PAP governments may well need to be checked against the temptation to use past reserves for subsidies and to win votes.[21] The intended target government aside, the possibility remains that the Elected Presidency, once created, could take on a life of its own. This is especially since an Elected President could be empowered to criticize or even oppose governmental policies. Even where these do not fall within the scope of his powers, the fact that one is elected as President could have a legitimating effect. Thus, the very fact of the constitutional office may create over time certain expectations about the office and function, as Lutz suggests, like somewhat of a "self-fulfilling prophecy".[22] Indeed, the first Singapore President to be elected through a popular vote, Ong Teng Cheong, took his mandate seriously and used his time in office to 'test' out the system, to the PAP government's consternation.[23] This was despite being seen as the establishment candidate, having previously served in government as a Cabinet Minister.[24] What that showed therefore is that with the innovation of an empowered constitutional office, there could be unintended intended consequences.

What do I mean by unintended intended consequences? There are some consequences which could be intended by those who drafted the constitution to arise under certain expected conditions, however, due to intervening events, these consequences arise but under different conditions. In this case, the PAP had instituted changes to the Elected Presidency in order to guard against future 'rogue' governments, defined primarily as governments not helmed by the PAP. That eventuality did not arise and PAP remained in power. However, Ong Teng Cheong showed the extent to which an independently minded President could use his powers under the constitution to check governmental powers. This was an *intended* consequence, since it was clearly part of the constitutional design to empower the President to check and balance governmental powers. It was however *unintended* as the mechanisms were only meant, in the minds of the PAP government, to check a non-PAP government, or a rogue PAP government.[25]

The unique feature of Singapore, as a country that has never experienced a political turnover and whose government consistently holds more than the requisite proportion of parliamentary seats to amend the constitution, is that any such unintended intended consequences could potentially be managed or even removed via constitutional amendments. Since it was first introduced via a constitutional amendment in 1991, the Elected Presidency has been subject to the most number of constitutional amendments. To be exact, up until the 2016 amendment exercise, which is the focus of this collection, there have been nine constitutional amendment bills directly relating to the Elected Presidency.[26] Thio points out that these amendments have modified the scope of the President's powers which has generally led to a limitation of presidential powers.[27] This latest round of constitutional amendments in 2016 could be said to follow this trajectory, but the changes have been more than just recalibration to remove the President's powers. Instead, these changes are qualitatively different from earlier 'tweaks' as they seek to (re)introduce multicultural representation as a function of the Presidency as well as to shift the balance of powers back to Parliament and to further empower the Council of Presidential Advisers as non-elected technocratic experts in the system. These changes raise the question of whether there is now a reversion back to the former arrangement where the President as Head of State was only meant to play a limited and ceremonial role in Government.

It is the 2016 constitutional amendment process and outcomes that is the focus of this current volume. Unlike in earlier amendments, the Government convened a Constitutional Commission in 2016 to make recommendations for reform. Specifically, the Commission was asked to review:

1 The qualifying process for Presidential candidates, particularly whether the eligibility criteria for such candidates should be updated, and if so how;
2 The framework governing the exercise of the President's custodial powers, including whether the views of the Council of Presidential Advisers can be given more weight, and if so how; and
3 Recommendations to ensure that minorities have the chance to be periodically elected to Presidential office.

The Commission, headed by Chief Justice Sundaresh Menon, is only the second Constitutional Commission to be convened to consider amendments to the Constitution since Singapore's independence. The first being the Constitutional Commission convened in 1965 shortly after Singapore became independent. Similarly headed by the Chief Justice, then Justice Wee Chong Jin, the first Constitutional Commission was tasked to receive and consider representations on how the rights of racial, linguistic and religious minorities can be adequately safeguarded in the constitution.[28]

Against the amendments that were made and the process of constitutional change, this volume seeks to contribute to further understanding of the key changes made to the Presidency as well as provide critical interrogation of the broader constitutional issues implicated. The chapters provide a broad coverage of the reform proposals including those relating to the qualifying criteria for candidacy in presidential elections; the role of the CPA; the need to ensure multiracial and minority representation in politics in Singapore; as well as topics relating to the process of reform and constitutional change in Singapore. It bears noting that many of the contributors to this volume were personally and professionally engaged in the constitutional process having presented written submissions to and made oral submissions before the Constitutional Commission.

In a way, much like the 2016 constitutional amendments, this volume works within the framework of continuity and change. It is the second major collection of essays reflecting specifically from a socio-legal perspective on the office of the Presidency in Singapore. Indeed, it builds on an earlier body of work examining the changes made to the office, notably a set of essays published in *Managing Political Change in Singapore: The Elected Presidency*, which was edited by Lam Peng Er and Kevin Tan.[29] This volume advances the discussion there in two ways. First, it examines how the institution has functioned since it was first introduced in 1991, bearing in mind that many changes have been made to it since *Managing Political Change* was published in 1997, some six years after the conversion of the Presidency to a popularly elected office. As the Introduction of that volume notes, it was focused on the political context for this change at the time and how it was operationalized in the first presidential election in 1993.[30] Second, the discussions in the various chapters examine the impact of the recent reform exercise. Before I go on to examine the 2016 amendments, and identify broadly the contributions in this volume, it is necessary to first examine the initial thinking and structure of this innovative constitutional design in the form of the Elected Presidency.

I.2 The Elected Presidency: evolution of a revolution[31]

I.2.1 Transforming the Presidency

The initial constitutional change to the Presidency from an appointed office to an elected one has been variously described as "momentous",[32] as "an innovative constitutional hybrid",[33] and as "Singapore's most innovative constitutional experiment".[34] Prior to the change in 1991, the Presidency had mainly ceremonial functions with limited discretionary powers over the appointment of the Prime Minister (on condition the Prime Minister commands the confidence of the majority in Parliament),[35] the withholding of consent to a request to dissolve Parliament,[36] and declare the office of the Prime Minister vacant if he is satisfied the Prime Minister has ceased to command the confidence of the majority in

Parliament.[37] Article 21(1) of the Singapore Constitution 'codifies' the Westminster convention that the Head of State must generally exercise his or her functions in accordance with the advice of the Cabinet.

The constitutional changes to the office making it an elective one was transformative in at least three ways. First, the President now no longer performs only ceremonial functions with limited discretionary powers during political transitions, but is endowed under the post-1991 constitutional provisions with more discretionary powers to wield over specific financial decisions that could draw upon the country's past reserves, and to guard against irresponsible appointment of key civil servants. These functions are conceptualized as part of a "two-key safeguard mechanism",[38] whereby both the President and the Government (Cabinet/Parliament) will have to agree before these fiscal or appointment decisions can be made. Besides these, the President was also given discretionary powers to serve as a swing vote where the Cabinet disagrees with its panel of specialist advisory board over detention orders under the Internal Security Act[39] and over restraining orders under the Maintenance of Religious Harmony Act.[40] This means, for instance, that if the advisory board constituted for the purposes of administering the Internal Security Act recommends the release of any person detained under the Act, but the Cabinet disagrees, the President may recommend the person's release if he or she agrees with the board. This applies similarly to decisions made by the Presidential Council for Religious Harmony under the Maintenance of Religious Harmony Act. Lastly, the President is also empowered to authorize investigations by the Corrupt Practices Investigation Bureau, even if the Prime Minister refuses to consent to the investigations.[41]

Second, as an elected office, the President now has a direct democratic mandate from the people. Direct elections were specifically chosen so that the President could claim democratic legitimacy to perform his functions. While this relies on a narrow idea of legitimacy as one based on popular vote, the rationale is simple: the President would need to have "moral authority" since he may, at times, need to disagree with the elected government on spending of reserves, on appointments and on detention/restraining orders.[42] Third, the Presidency is now squarely a political and politicizable office. Exercising his discretion to disagree with an elected government is surely a controversial and political act. This was recognized even by the Government in its White Paper on proposing the change.[43] In addition, the process of elections requires presidential candidates to be subject to public scrutiny and to be able to appeal to voters directly. This politicizes the office as candidates may (naturally) engage in competitive conduct in order to win votes. Thus, while the President could previously be conceptualized, like the Queen in England, as the "dignified"[44] element of the Constitution of the Republic of Singapore, the elections process has weakened, if not removed, this "dignified" aspect. Furthermore, while the President previously was seen as a symbol of unity, the infusion of free elections, especially particularly competitive and divisive ones, may well require a period of political reconciliation in order to vindicate this unifying role. Within Singapore's particular multi-ethnic and multireligious context, it is not only the process of elections that could be divisive, but also the results. Indeed, while the President had previously been informally rotated among the major ethnic groups in Singapore, considerations of electability may discourage candidates from minority groups to put themselves forward.

The amendments are transformative not only in changing the nature of the Presidency, but also in transforming the institutionalization of the separation of powers and the scheme of checks and balances. While previously the principle of collective responsibility meant that it was Parliament that would keep the Cabinet in check, the new scheme meant that the Elected President, as both part of the Executive and the Legislature, would play an additional checking role on the Cabinet. It is in this sense that the Elected Presidency has been called an "intra-branch check".[45] Nonetheless, there is also inter-branch check, insofar as the President also checks the powers of Parliament to authorize spending. Parliament also plays a significant role in checking the President in the exercise of his discretionary powers as they are empowered to override his withholding of assent under certain conditions. The separation of powers and the scheme of checks and balances is further modified by the creation of new expert bodies, as I will discuss in Section I.2.2.

I.2.2 Creating new constitutional bodies

Besides transforming the office of the President, the 1991 changes also created a new constitutional body called the Council of Presidential Advisers (CPA). The CPA advises and makes recommendations to the President.[46] Its initial scope was rather limited. It was only to advise and recommend on matters referred to it by the President and only on matters specifically identified under the relevant provision in Articles 21(3) and (4). The initial scheme was two-pronged – for certain provisions, the President "shall" consult the CPA before exercising his discretion, and for others, the President "may" consult the CPA. Decisions that were subject to mandatory consultation[47] concerned the:

a appointment of public officers;[48]
b appointment of statutory board members as well as budgets and transactions of statutory boards where these draw on their past reserves;[49]
c appointment of government companies' directors as well as budgets and transactions of government companies where these draw on their past reserves;[50]
d withholding of assent to giving of a guarantee and raising of loans by the Government (Article 144(1));[51]
e withholding of assent to any legislative bill passed that provides, directly or indirectly, for the borrowing of money, the giving of any guarantee or the raising of any loan by the Government that will draw on past reserves (Article 144(2));
f withholding of assent to government budget (a "Supply Bill") drawing on past reserves;[52]

g withholding of authorization to additional expenditure prior to the year's budget;[53] and
h withholding of assent to any proposed transactions likely to draw on past reserves.[54]

It should be explained that "reserves" are defined in Article 2 of the Constitution as "the excess of assets over liabilities of the Government, statutory board or Government company". "Past reserves of the Government" are defined in Article 142 as "the reserves not accumulated by the Government during its current term of office".

The functions subjected to the optional consultation requirement[55] concerned:

a the withholding of assent to legislative bills that, directly or indirectly, vary, change or increase the powers of the Central Provident Fund Board to invest moneys in the Fund (Article 22E);[56]
b legislative bills directly or indirectly circumventing or curtailing the President's discretionary powers under the Constitution (Article 22H);
c the exercise of his swing vote on detention orders under the Internal Security Act (Article 151(4));
d the exercise of his swing vote on restraining orders under the Maintenance of Religious Harmony Act; and
e any other function the President is authorized under the Constitution to perform in his discretion.

This scheme of *mandatory* versus *optional* involvement of the CPA may be analysed as corresponding to decisions that went to the core of the Elected Presidency and those that do not. The mandatory consultation covered fiscal decisions that draw upon past reserves as well as appointments of civil servants, statutory board members and directors of government companies who will have significant say over how the Government, the statutory board and government companies are run. In comparison, the optional consultation requirement covered all other functions including his vote on restraining/preventive detention orders as well as on bills affecting his own powers.[57] Thus, generally, where the matter is of greater significance and goes to the core of the Elected President's new functions, consultation with the CPA was mandatory. In matters of lesser importance, in the sense that they do not go to the core of his new functions, consultation is optional. This interjection of the CPA, an unelected body, into the President's decision-making process has led to arguments that the CPA seem to serve as a "de facto Senate";[58] their role is not only to support and lend "collective wisdom"[59] to the President but also potentially to serve as a check against the President when he disagrees with the Cabinet or Parliament. This is especially since, under some provisions covered under the mandatory consulting requirement, the President's withholding of assent may be overridden by Parliament *if* the President's decision was made against the CPA's recommendations. These relate to appointment of public officers (Article 22); the appointment of statutory board members

(Article 22A); the appointment of directors of government companies (Article 22C); and the government budget where it draws down on past reserves (Article 148A). Parliament may then overrule the President by resolution passed by not less than two-thirds votes of the total number of parliamentarians.[60] As long as the PAP has a supermajority in Parliament, this procedural requirement will be easily satisfied. As will be discussed below, the CPA's role was strengthened after the 2016 constitutional amendments.

Another constitutional body created is the Presidential Elections Committee (PEC), whose functions are much more limited though still very important; the PEC is tasked with the function of qualifying the candidates for Presidency and for administering elections. One persistent criticism of the Elected Presidency is that the constitutionally set criteria for eligibility is set so high that it favours establishment candidates. According to Article 19 of the Singapore Constitution, persons qualified to be elected as President must be a citizen of Singapore, not less than 45 years of age, not be a member of a political party at nomination date, and must possess sufficient experience either in the public sector or the private sector as specified. Even after satisfying these fairly demanding experience-based criteria, the candidate still has to satisfy the PEC that he or she is "a person of integrity, good character and reputation".[61]

I.2.3 Post-1991 developments: refining and also reducing the President's functions?

Since its inception, the office has undergone multiple revisions ranging from minor changes to address unforeseen technical issues or to catch up with new developments, to more major ones. Scholars have pointed out that these changes "truncate"[62] the President's fiscal functions and "whittle down" his powers of oversight.[63] A complete list of these amendments is helpfully collated in Li-ann Thio's volume on the Presidency in the *Singapore Chronicles*[64] and in the next few paragraphs, I will highlight only the changes that have had the most impact on the place of the Presidency within the edifice of Singapore's constitutional arrangement.

The first type of change involves the direct removal of certain matters from the President's oversight functions. The most significant change in this regard was the 1995 constitutional amendment, which took away defence and security measures from the President's oversight functions. Critics argue that this change goes against the two-key mechanism since the President would have no role in ensuring that defence and security measures would draw down on past reserves. Under Article 151A, any proposed transactions that may draw down on reserves would be excluded from the President's oversight so long as the Prime Minister and the Minister responsible for defence certifies the transaction as "necessary for the defence and security of Singapore" on the recommendation of the Permanent Secretary of the Ministry of Defence and the Chief of the Defence Force. The insertion of the Permanent Secretary and the Chief of the Defence Force, two high-ranking public officers, was meant to provide additional safeguards in lieu of the President's oversight. Critics argued that the amendment could lead to a loophole in the interlocking scheme of checks and balances that the Elected Presidency was supposed to create.[65] The fall back on "internal checks and balances" and "external auditors"[66] was essentially a reversion to a pre-1991 state of affairs, at least in this area.

Another set of changes removed financial activities from the President's oversight. These were the 1994 and 2002 constitutional amendments, which essentially deemed the mutual transfers of past reserves not to be subject to the President's custodial powers. As discussed earlier, the President's fiscal custodial functions are over *past* reserves held by the Government, statutory boards and listed government companies. These past reserves may exist in various forms and some may be profit-making assets. Under the two-key mechanism guarding the fiscal reserves, every transfer of past reserves will constitute a drawdown, even if it is merely transferred among the Government, the statutory boards or the government companies. Two constitutional amendments in 1994 and 2008, however, changed this, deeming transfer of past reserves among the three entities as not drawdowns requiring presidential assent. Initially, the 1994 amendment only related to the transfer of past reserves to the Government and transfers between statutory boards; such transfers are not considered drawdowns on past reserves, provided the Minister for Finance gives an undertaking in writing to add the transferred reserves to the Government's or statutory boards' past reserves. A 2008 amendment expanded this scheme, allowing transfers from the Government to statutory boards and government companies, as well as between statutory boards and government companies. This change was rationalized as being necessary to allow the Government to undertake "more timely responses to changing economic and business conditions".[67] The only condition imposed is that the recipient will have to give an undertaking or resolution to add the transfers to their past reserves. One might ask why this change is necessary and significant. After all, the overall aggregate of past reserves remains the same. The significance lies in the income that the past reserves, as assets, may generate for the entity it is parked under. Critics question whether this change effectively allows the Government and the statutory bodies to 'subsidize' the government companies and risk subjecting income generated by the Government and the statutory boards to greater financial exposure.[68]

The second type of change involved changing financial definitions, which could take some financial assets/income into or outside the purview of the President. Two amendments addressing the question of whether income generated from past reserves is to be considered past reserves or current reserves may warm the cockles of the most ardent economics and financial adviser, but are likely to appear somewhat daunting to a somewhat financially-literate constitutional lawyer. Nonetheless, a brief explanation is necessary. Between 1994 and 2008, another constitutional amendment (in 2001) clarified that income generated from past reserves, that is, net investment income or NII, was not part of the past reserves and could be spent as part of current income. However, the amendment instituted a rule of fiscal prudence, which was that 50 per cent of NII in any financial year must be added to past reserves. This has been lauded as instituting "a principle of inter-generational equity",[69] striking a fair balance between the claims of the present and the requirements of the future. Later in 2008, not only was the Constitution amended to allow free flow of transfers of past reserves among the three entities, the Government also changed the formula for calculating investment income, renaming it along the way to "net investment returns" or NIR. This had the effect of potentially expanding the amount that could be spent as income on past reserves. The Government argues that such a change is necessary due to an anticipated increase in the Government's social expenditure to cope with problems associated with an ageing society as well as to facilitate further investment in education, research and development, transport and healthcare infrastructure.[70] The NIR is now defined as including capital gains, in addition to income and dividends. Furthermore, investment returns are now to be calculated according to a new formula – long-term real rates of return – which allows income to be calculated on the basis of average returns expected over the next 20 years, rather than on the basis of the historical or even the actual rate of returns. Thus, there is a potentially speculative aspect to such a predictive calculation, and a great reliance on economists and other experts, to determine the long-term real rates of return. This change was, however, justified as necessary to stabilize the rate of returns by spreading them out over a period of time, rather than subjecting Singapore's net income from these past reserves to more volatile short-term market conditions. Nonetheless, the ease with which these amendments are made raises questions about the efficacy of the scheme of checks and balances that the Elected Presidency was supposed to encompass.

I.3 Recommendations of the Constitutional Commission and the Government's response

The rest of the chapters in this volume will carefully parse through and evaluate the various recommendations in the Constitutional Commission's report and the Government's response to it in the form of a White Paper and the resulting constitutional amendment bill. Suffice to say here that the Constitutional Commission addressed the three aspects of its Terms of Reference in the following ways. First, the Commission recommended increasing the stringency of the qualifying process. The recommendations had the greatest impact for potential candidates from the private sector. The previous private-sector criteria was that one must have been chairman of the board of directors or chief executive officer, for not less than three years, of a company in Singapore with a paid-up capital of at least S$100 million. The new criteria states that one must now have been a *chief executive* of at least three years in a company with a shareholder equity of at least S$500 million and the company must have made a profit after tax during his/her time as chief executive.

Second, the Constitutional Commission recommended a streamlining of the framework governing the exercise of the President's custodial powers. Specifically, it recommended that consultation of the CPA is now a general and mandatory duty whenever the President exercises discretionary power except where specified otherwise. Third, the Constitutional Commission recommended a hiatus-triggered elections mechanism or what is more popularly known as the reserved elections whereby a particular election may be reserved for a specified community, if no person belonging to that community has held the office of President for any of the five most recent terms of office of the President.[71]

Three further important areas were identified by the Constitutional Commission for possible reform. The first, which the Constitutional Commission squarely acknowledged fell outside the scope of their Terms of Reference, was whether the office of the President should remain an elective office. Indeed, in their report, the Constitutional Commission gave serious consideration and cautious support to the suggestion[72] that the office should be reverted to the appointed form. The Commission recognized that if the President is to continue to perform his custodial functions over the financial reserves and over the integrity of the public service, it is necessary for the office to remain an elected one. However, there may be competing qualities required for the President to play his custodial role compared to his symbolic unifying role. The Commission thus suggested that there could be an unbundling of the President's symbolic and custodial roles such that the custodial functions could be relocated to an appointed council of experts.[73] This suggestion to rethink the elective nature of the office was however rejected by the Government.[74]

The second further area of recommendation related to the presidential elections process. The Commission suggested various ways to reform the process, to address concerns that presidential candidates may misunderstand or deliberately mislead voters about the role and powers of the President. The Constitutional Commission made it a point to comment on this, observing that there was a mistaken tendency for previous candidates to see the Presidency as "an alternative source of Executive policy-making". To the extent that this is the case, the question was to what extent law should intervene to regulate the conduct of presidential candidates. This raises interesting questions about freedom of speech and political behaviour during campaigning. The Constitutional Commission recommended interventions that include requiring candidates to declare that they understand the President's constitutional role before being issued a certificate of eligibility, such that they could be prosecuted for taking contrary positions. The Commission also proposed that rules be enacted to restrict or exclude acts that might inflame emotions, cause divisiveness or encourage invective. A "white list" of approved campaign methods was also proposed. These measures, if fully embraced, would clearly interfere with candidates' freedom of speech and freedom of association. It is also questionable whether it would unduly interfere with the democratic process, and may reinforce the perception that the Government simply does not trust its people's political maturity, whether rightly or wrongly, to discern credible campaign promises from incredible ones, and to understand how the democratic institutions really work.

Third, the Constitutional Commission suggested that the Government consider whether to bring into force entrenchment provisions that were at the time in the Constitution but not in force (i.e. Articles 5A and 5(2A)). While it did not give a definite view whether to bring into force or continue to suspend the provisions, as it recognized that there were cogent arguments in support of both positions, it did suggest that such indefinite suspension may not be a desirable state of affairs. Instead, the Commission suggested that the Government could take on a partial bringing-into-force by entrenching only those provisions in Part IV of the Constitution relating to fundamental liberties.

The Government accepted most of the Commission's recommendations within its Terms of Reference, but rejected the suggestion to rethink the elective aspect of the Presidency. It also rejected the suggestion to bring into force Articles 5A and 5(2A), whether partially or entirely. Instead, it repealed these two provisions and replaced them with a new and highly complex entrenchment framework that applied only to the Presidency. This meant that while there was previously a possibility that the fundamental liberties chapter could be entrenched beyond the current two-thirds majority vote rule, the chapter is now subject to the ordinary amendment procedure under Article 5 of the Constitution (i.e. two-thirds majority rule). The new entrenchment framework now contains three new provisions (Articles 5A, 5B and 5C), which categorizes the entrenched provisions into two tiers.

Tier 1 covers (a) provisions that are "fundamental to the existence of the Elected Presidency"[75] and the entrenchment framework itself.[76] The "fundamental" provisions are spelled out in Article 5A(7)(b), and include the provisions establishing the President's function as Head of State[77] and his additional function to safeguard the reserves and the integrity of the Public Service;[78] the election of the President;[79] the presidential term of office;[80] immunity from suit;[81] and provisions to do with the vacation or removal from office of the President and the temporary disability of the President.[82] Amendments to these Tier 2 provisions can be introduced in Parliament via one of three ways. First, where the President, acting in his discretion, concurs with the introduction of the amending bill;[83] second, where the President did not concur, but the CPA had recommended to the President that he should concur with the introduction of the Bill;[84] or third, where the Government submits the Bill to a national referendum at which it is supported by more than half of the total number of votes cast by registered electors.[85] Thereafter, regardless of which route is used to introduce the bill, the bill must subsequently be passed by a two-thirds parliamentary majority.[86]

Tier 2 provisions are listed in Article 5B(9) and comprise provisions "relating to more operational aspects of the Elected Presidency and its custodial powers", which may not need to be put to a national referendum.[87] There are two types of provisions protected in Tier 2. The first type comprises Article 17(3) and the provisions mentioned therein.[88] Article 17(3) sets out the provisions which authorize the President to act in his discretion in relation to his custodial role over the national reserves and key appointments,[89] such as the President's discretion to refuse or revoke an appointment to key public offices,[90] the President's discretion to appoint some members of the CPA,[91] and the President's discretion with regard to financial provisions including the withholding of assent to a Supply Bill.[92] Notably, only the specific discretion-conferring provisions of the

Articles listed in Article 17(3), and not the entire Articles, are protected.[93] The second type of Tier 2 provisions[94] are those relating to other aspects of the Presidency such as his access to information,[95] his discretion to withhold assent to any bill (other than one seeking to amend the Constitution) that seeks to circumvent or curtail his discretionary powers,[96] and to the Election Judge.[97] There are four routes by which a bill seeking to amend any of the Tier 2 provisions can be introduced in Parliament. The first three routes[98] mirror the routes under Tier 1. However, the fourth route, as set out in Article 5B(7), permits a bill seeking to amend any of the Tier 2 provisions to be introduced in the ordinary way like other constitutional amendment bills[99] – but it must be passed by a three-quarter parliamentary majority instead of the usual two-thirds majority.

In addition, Article 5C also puts in place a similar entrenchment mechanism for any bill seeking to amend the Constitution (other than a bill to which Articles 5A and 5B apply) if the bill or any of its provisions circumvent or curtail any discretionary power conferred on the President via a Tier 2 provision.[100] The legislative intent behind Article 5C was to cater to situations in which a bill circumvents or curtails the President's discretionary powers without textual amendments being made to the power-conferring provisions.[101] Article 5C(1) permits the President to withhold assent to such a bill. However, the President's withholding of assent may be overruled in two circumstances. First, where the President withholds assent with the CPA's support, he will be deemed to have assented to the bill if (a) the Government submits the bill to a national referendum at which it is supported by a simple majority of registered electors;[102] or (b) Parliament affirms the bill with a resolution passed by a three-quarter majority.[103] Second, where the President withholds assent against the CPA's recommendation, the President will be deemed to have assented to the bill if Parliament affirms the bill by a resolution passed with a two-thirds majority.[104]

There is a further pressure valve in this complex entrenchment framework. The President may, on the advice of the Cabinet, refer the bill to a constitutional tribunal for a decision on whether Article 5C applies to it.[105] If the tribunal is of the opinion that Article 5C does not apply to the bill, the President is deemed to have assented to the bill even if the President had earlier purported to withhold his assent.[106] However, if the tribunal is of the opinion that Article 5C applies to the bill, the President would have basis to withhold his assent[107] and the overruling mechanism in Article 5C(4) will then apply.[108] This complex entrenchment framework is not currently in force.

I.4 Changing landscape and an evolving Presidency

Interestingly, therefore, the 2016 constitutional amendments appeared to be aimed at mitigating some of the transformative impacts of the initial design. The modalities of change have been different. While the 2016 amendments were preceded by the work of a Constitutional Commission, the initial establishment of the Elected Presidency focused more on parliamentary expertise. The idea of changing the office to an elected one was first raised by the then Prime Minister

Lee Kuan Yew in 1984[109] but the process gained momentum only after the first White Paper on the Elected President[110] was issued in 1988. While there was considerable public debate and controversy surrounding the proposal, this first White Paper did not contain many specifics about the institution. It was only in 1990, when the Government released a second White Paper, along with an accompanying Constitutional Amendment Bill, that the specifics of the changes were made known.[111] The White Paper and the Constitutional Amendment Bill were debated in Parliament and thereafter a Select Committee was appointed. The bill was amended and finally passed into law in January 1991.

In both 1990/1991 and 2016/2017, proposed changes to the Presidency were preceded by considerable debate in the parliamentary chambers and the public arena. Prior to the 1990/1991 amendments, the public were invited to make representations. The Select Committee invited written representations on the proposed changes through a press release as well as through advertisements in mainstream papers in the four official languages: the *Berita Harian*, *Lianhe Zaobao*, *Tamil Murasu* and the *Straits Times*. The public was given one month to put in their written representations. In 2016/2017 the Constitutional Commission invited the public to submit written feedback on matters falling within its Terms of Reference. The public also had about one month from the media release to provide their representations.

However, there are some interesting contrasts. First, while the Select Committee played the role of interfacing with the public in 1990, it was the Constitutional Commission that played this role in 2016. These are distinctive institutions, representing differing institutional expertise and functions. The Select Committee is ultimately a parliamentary committee; its members are also parliamentarians.[112] The Select Committee on the Elected Presidency comprised 12 members, including several cabinet ministers and one opposition member. In comparison, the Constitutional Commission is an independent commission and not a parliamentary committee. Its members are not elected Members of Parliament but are chosen, presumably, for their expertise as well as for their ability to represent different constituencies. Besides the Chief Justice, the other eight members of the 2016 Constitutional Commission came from a mix of public-sector and private-sector backgrounds.[113]

Second, public engagement in 2016 far exceeded earlier participation in 1990. In total, the Select Committee received 18 representations. Among these, ten were in favour of the scheme, six opposed the scheme, one expressed no opinion on the scheme but instead proposed a bicameral Parliament, and another stated that the scheme should in any case not take effect until the next general election. From the 18, the Select Committee invited seven representors to make oral representations over two days.[114] In contrast, the Constitutional Commission received a total of 107 written submissions at the close of the consultation period.[115] According to its report, it continued to receive representations even after the consultation period had closed. From the 107 written representations, it invited 20 contributors to make oral representations and 19 of those contributors accepted the invitation. They were heard over four days in public hearings.[116]

Third, arising from the different type of institution involved, there were different degrees of public access to the hearings. The Constitutional Commission's hearings were open to the public and were held at the Supreme Court auditorium.[117] In contrast to Parliament, where Select Committee hearings are heard, the Supreme Court auditorium is generally more accessible since the courts are a space frequently accessed by litigants, lawyers and other interested parties. While there is no data on the number of people who attended these hearings, it would not be far-fetched to think that the space in which they were held could have made a difference.

A comparison between the process of constitutional change in 1991 and in 2016 reflects the politics of their respective times. While the PAP was and is a dominant political party in Singapore, its relationship with the electorate has evolved, not least because the electorate has evolved. With a literacy rate among residents aged 15 years and over of more than 97 per cent as of 2017, and with more than 50 per cent of its resident population aged 25 years and over having post-secondary qualifications, the Singapore electorate has become more well-educated and presumably more politically conscious. To be sure, the rise of a well-educated middle class does not inevitably lead to liberal democracy, but it could lead to a citizenry that is more able to engage in political discourse,[118] especially when such engagement is openly encouraged by the Government. Indeed, the Government's apparent willingness to engage in constitutional discussions in recent years may have also led to a change in attitudes among its citizenry. The political elites appear to recognize that citizen participation could contribute to increased public education about certain issues.[119] Furthermore, broader public exposure may also result in greater acceptance.[120] As such, while most Singaporeans had previously "reacted to constitutional changes rather than participated in them",[121] the 2016 Constitutional Commission process points to increased participation and political consciousness among Singaporeans.

I.5 Constitutional design and constitutional change: overview of the chapters

Against these complex issues of design and redesign, the chapters in this volume address a whole range of constitutional issues arising from the 2016 constitutional amendments. Several of the chapters analyse the impact of the new changes, while others focus not only on the outcome (i.e. the actual amendments), but also on the process and discourse leading up to the amendments. Broadly, one can identify four important themes that emerge from the various chapters.

The first is the practice of constitutional design, or more accurately, redesign. As the Government worked out the Presidency, it seemed unwilling to stop tailor-making the office to address problems that have arisen or may arise, whether because the office worked as it intended or not as it intended. In other words, the alterations address both the unintended consequences and the unintended intended consequences. In order to properly and objectively evaluate the success of the constitutional design, perhaps there needs to be some awareness of the alternatives. It is apt therefore that this volume kicks off with Kevin Y.L. Tan and Lam Peng Er's chapter which contains an overview of the constitutional design choices available to the Government in achieving their aim of stopping a future "profligate government" raiding the past reserves accumulated by past (PAP) governments. They point out that other proposals such as the creation of an Upper House of Senate, rather than relying on one person in office, were simply not given sufficient consideration. Thus, Tan and Lam argue that while some of the issues facing the Presidency, and which the Government has over time repeatedly felt compelled to mitigate or eliminate, are "unintended consequences"; some are actually "design flaws". They argue, therefore, that it may well be necessary to have a complete rethinking of the elected presidential system. From the design perspective, their critique points to a common criticism of constitutional drafting in design terms which is that there is often self or party interest involved which could distort one's capacity to properly identify and evaluate the whole range of possible design choices.[122] Furthermore, Tan and Lam's chapter raises the question of when and how to evaluate whether a design is so flawed that a complete abandonment may be necessary. This resonates with the Constitutional Commission's suggestion to rethink the elective nature of the office, which was rejected by the Government. The Constitutional Commission's willingness to raise foundational design questions is important as a periodic assessment of the system may be necessary to prevent constitutional degeneration.

Still, the question of whether the persistent need to design or redesign the office arises from deep tensions within the very office itself is examined in Chapter 2. Li-ann Thio's chapter in this volume identifies four tensions that appear to animate the Government's repeated alteration of the office. The first tension she identifies is between *efficacy* and *efficiency*; while the Government envisages the President to have powers to be an effective check, it also wants to ensure that there will not be any gridlock in government. Several of the amendments, including the interjection of the CPA in the decision-making process and the provision for the possibility of a parliamentary override, can be analysed as seeking to strike the elusive balance between efficacy and efficiency. The second tension Thio identifies is between *political choice* and *technocratic quality*. This speaks directly to the eligibility criteria for the Presidency. The onerous criteria is meant to ensure that only the most qualified persons can be elected as President. This, however, goes against the broadest idea of political choice as the voters' options are severely restricted from the start. If candidates were colours, this would be akin to voters being asked to choose from multiple shades of blue, but without the option to choose red, black or white, that is, another colour. Thio identifies a third tension as between the unifying *ceremonial* functions and the potentially confrontational *constitutional custodial* powers. The fourth tension she discusses is one only recently raised by the Government in its Terms of Reference to the Constitutional Commission, which is that between *multiracialism* and *meritocracy*.[123] The argument is that a strictly meritocratic system should not use seemingly irrelevant measures such as race/ethnicity in order to determine who should be in office. These tensions, Thio suggests, provide a framework by which to analyse changes to the Presidency. She suggests, however, that there may be ways to mitigate the tensions, and that the recent 2016 amendments constitute attempts to try to strike the proper balance between these various tensions.

One may therefore examine the changes to enhance the role of non-elected expert bodies, such as the PEC and, even more importantly, the CPA, as responding to the anxious balancing of political choice with technocratic quality – between efficacy and efficiency. As Eugene Tan observes in Chapter 4 in this volume on "Perfecting Singapore's system of political governance: privileging elites in the quest for good governance", the office of the Presidency has increasingly become and is best understood as "an elite institution", with the CPA being "an elite body in its own right" whereby good governance is ultimately achieved by ensuring that good men and women are placed in positions of power. This, Tan observes, harks back to the Confucian ethos of political legitimacy and leadership whereby the moral standing of good leaders acting in the collective interest is as important as (if not more important than) the legal and political authority that comes from having an electoral mandate.

The second theme that the amendments and several of the chapters address is the cogency of the claim that the Elected Presidency needs to be underpinned by a democratic mandate. Democracy legitimacy lies at the heart of the Elected Presidency. As Lee Kuan Yew emphasized, the President needs to have "moral authority" to stand up to the elected Prime Minister, and the philosophical foundation he invokes for that power and authority is that of legitimacy through a democratic vote. The initial design justification appeared to prioritize democratic process over mere technocratic qualifications. That said, this was tempered by the inclusion of fairly onerous eligibility criteria that, through the public-sector qualifications, skews access to presidential candidacy in favour of establishment candidates. Kevin Y.L. Tan's chapter argues that the restrictive eligibility criteria has undermined the democratic legitimacy of the President in several ways. Among others, he raises the problem of walkovers, a phenomenon that arises when the eligibility criteria puts off potential candidates from contesting or is used to reject those who come forward.

Jack Lee's chapter critically examines the Constitutional Commission's work on reforming the conduct of the electoral process itself and the resulting changes. From eligibility to candidacy to voting, the whole process of the presidential elections is closely regulated by law. Lee's examination of the legal framework which vests the various committees (the Presidential Elections Committee, the Community Committee and their Sub-Committees) with a high degree of discretion in playing their gatekeeping function should raise important questions as to whether electoral choice is effectively undermined. Indeed, Lee observes that the message being sent appears to be that voters should "trust the authorities to do the right thing, rather than rely on their own discernment to decide whether a candidate is worthy of being elected to the nation's highest office." Further, he notes that the lack of a prohibition against influential and politically linked persons from endorsing candidates may further skew the playing field. These issues go to the integrity of the electoral process. In particular, it raises the question of whether access to political candidacy and choice is unduly affected. Where the rules of the game are skewed so much in favour of establishment candidates, is the institution still democratic?

These discussions in Tan and Lee's chapters implicate a third theme, which is the meaning of democratic legitimacy. In particular, should there be a more multifaceted and more nuanced understanding of democracy and democratic legitimacy. In this regard, Maartje De Visser's chapter provides an important intervention. She shows that the constitutional reform exercise may well enhance our understanding of democracy insofar as the Constitutional Commission sought to engage the people in a very public way. As she highlights, the Constitutional Commission's engagement with the general public could offer a welcome correction to the technocratic tendencies of the dominant party state. It also allows for a more expansive notion of democratic participation beyond the ballot box.

Last is the issue of representation. In her influential theory of representation, Hanna Pitkin defines representing as "acting in the interest of the represented in a manner responsive to them".[124] The questions of who is being represented and how they are to be responded to however could be subject to a variety of responses. Representative democracy, the idea that democratic government is meant to represent its people, could take on multiple forms.[125] While the initial emphasis in changing the Presidency to an elected office was on democratic mandate and legitimacy, the 2016 amendment process however brought a new focus on representation, particularly minority representation. It is this question of representation that occupies the central place in both Eugene Tan and my respective chapters. Eugene Tan examines the rationale for minority representation and situates it within Singapore's social, political and constitutional context. He further examines the claimed tensions between meritocracy and the need to create an inclusive political system for all groups. He suggests that more needs to be done, albeit extra-legally, to educate and encourage voters to make political choices beyond race. Indeed, Tan wisely suggests that the success of the reserved election mechanism should be judged on not whether it produces a President from a minority group but when it is no longer utilized. Along the same vein, my chapter examines the shift in terminology from minority representation and multiracialism in framing the reserved elections. I further argue that the reserved elections mechanism may be a justifiable change to address the need to ensure that minority groups are periodically represented in the office of the President. However, it has brought to fore some difficult questions concerning ethnic identity and inter-ethnic relations, and may well have or will result in the further politicization of ethnicity in Singaporean society.

I.6 Conclusion: looking ahead

In a fascinating study on the *Principles of Constitutional Design*, Lutz pointed out that there are clear gaps between the state of having a written constitution, even one with democratic constitutionalist features, and the actual practice of democratic constitutionalism. Nonetheless, he argues that the fact of a written document may have long-term impact as the constitutional rules may create over time "an expectation of reasonable compliance" among the people. It can function, as mentioned, as a "self-fulfilling prophecy"[126] That said, as Horowitz rightly points out, designs affect the distribution of power, and over time, those who gain power as a result of existing constitutional design may seek to alter the design to favour themselves. Such self-dealing could undoubtedly lead to the problem of constitutional "retrogression".[127] Amid these potential trajectories of constitutional change, constitutional vigilance among the people to ensure government accountability is a necessary constant. Swati Jhaveri's concluding chapter for this volume highlights the power dynamics reflected in the constitutional amendment process and the distribution of powers resulting from the amendments. It shows a need to understand the different roles that the various branches of government play in this scheme of checks and balances, and the need to intersect these roles with citizen participation. After all, coming back to Hanna Pitkin, whom I cited at the start of this chapter:

> … [C]onstitutions are made, not found. They do not fall miraculously from the sky or grow naturally on the vine; they are human creations, products of convention, choice, the specific history of a particular people, and (almost always) a political struggle in which some win and others lose.[128]

Indeed, the practice of constitutionalism should be seen not as merely an implementation of a set of settled normative, analytic and empirical answers but as "an ongoing process of questioning and learning".[129] This volume, with its rich and diverse chapters reflecting upon the 2016 constitutional amendments surrounding the Elected Presidency in Singapore, aims to contribute to that ongoing process.

Notes

* I would like to thank Zamiq Azmeer Borhanudin for his thoughtful research assistance and to Louis Lai for editorial assistance.

1 Hanna Fenichel Pitkin, "The idea of a constitution" (1987) 37 *Journal of Legal Education* 167, 168.

2 For one account of paths of constitution-making and their impact on the development of constitutionalism, see Bruce Ackerman, "Three paths to constitutionalism – and the crisis of the European Union" (2015) 45 *British Journal of Political Science* 705.

3 Tom Ginsburg (ed.), "Introduction", in *Comparative Constitutional Design* (Cambridge: Cambridge University Press, 2012), 1.

4 *Ibid.*, 2.

5 For a review and critique of this exercise, see Donald L. Horowitz, "Constitutional design: proposals versus process", in Andrew Reynolds (ed.), *The Architecture of Democracy* (Oxford University Press, 2002).

6 Ginsburg (n. 3), 1.

7 *Ibid.*

8 See generally Jon Elster, "Clearing and strengthening the channels of constitution making", in Tom Ginsburg (ed.), *Comparative Constitutional Design* (Cambridge: Cambridge University Press, 2012).

9 Horowitz (n. 5), 33–5.
10 *Speech by Prime Minister on the Second Reading of the Constitution of the Republic of Singapore (Amendment) Bill in Parliament* (24 July 1984) www.nas.gov.sg/archivesonline/data/pdfdoc/lky19840724.pdf (accessed 6 March 2019).
11 See Jaclyn L. Neo and Andrea Ong, "Making the Singapore Constitution: Amendments as constitution-making" (2019) 14(1) *Journal of Comparative Law* 72.
12 Kevin Y.L. Tan and Lam Peng Er (eds), "Introduction", in *Managing Political Change in Singapore: The Elected Presidency* (London: Routledge, 1997), 3.
13 *Ibid.*
14 *Ibid.*, 4.
15 Constitution of the Republic of Singapore (Amendment No. 3) Bill Deb, 3 January 1991, vol. 56, col. 717 (as reported from Select Committee).
16 *Ibid.*, (Prime Minister Goh Chok Tong).
17 The Elected Presidency can be analysed in conjunction with several other significant constitutional changes that also depart from the inherited Westminster system, namely, the Non-Constituency Members of Parliament, the Nominated Members of Parliament and the Group Representation Constituency scheme. See Kevin Tan, "The Presidency in Singapore: constitutional developments", in Kevin Y.L. Tan and Lam Peng Er (eds), *Managing Political Change in Singapore: The Elected Presidency* (London: Routledge, 1997), 52.
18 *Ibid.*
19 Constitution of the Republic of Singapore (Amendment) Bill Deb, 28 October 1996, vol. 66, cols 758 and 812 (Prime Minister Goh Chok Tong).
20 Li-ann Thio, *A Treatise on Singapore Constitutional Law* (Singapore: Academy Publishing, 2012), 396.
21 Lee Kuan Yew, "National Day Rally Speech" (19 August 1984) www.nas.gov.sg/archivesonline/audiovisual_records/recorddetails/486d47a6-1164-11e3-83d5-0050568939ad (accessed 7 March 2019).
22 Donald S. Lutz, *Principles of Constitutional Design* (Cambridge: Cambridge University Press, 2006), 5.
23 Ong Teng Cheong, "I had a job to do", *Asia Week* (Singapore, 10 March 2000) http://edition.cnn.com/ASIANOW/asiaweek/magazine/2000/0310/nat.singapore.ongiv.html (accessed 7 March 2019).
24 *Ibid.*
25 Note that in Chapter 1 by Kevin Y.L. Tan and Lam Peng Er, they refer to several unintended consequences.
26 These are:

(1) Constitution of the Republic of Singapore (Amendment) Act 17 of 1994;
(2) Constitution of the Republic of Singapore (Amendment) Act 7 of 1995;
(3) Constitution of the Republic of Singapore (Amendment) Act 41 of 1996;
(4) Constitution of the Republic of Singapore (Amendment) Act 11 of 1998;
(5) Constitution of the Republic of Singapore (Amendment) Act 2 of 2001;
(6) Constitution of the Republic of Singapore (Amendment) Act 24 of 2002;
(7) Constitution of the Republic of Singapore (Amendment) Act 12 of 2004;
(8) Constitution of the Republic of Singapore (Amendment) Act 31 of 2007;
(9) Constitution of the Republic of Singapore (Amendment) Act 27 of 2008; and
(10) Constitution of the Republic of Singapore (Amendment) Act 27 of 2008.

27 Thio (n. 20), 423.
28 See *Report of the Constitutional Commission 1966.*
29 Tan and Lam (n. 12).
30 *Ibid.*, 1.

31 This is a nod to the title of the first critical volume of essays written on constitutional law in Singapore: Li-ann Thio and Kevin Y.L. Tan, *Evolution of a Revolution: Forty Years of the Singapore Constitution* (London: Routledge Cavendish, 2009).
32 Kevin Tan Yew Lee, "The Elected Presidency in Singapore: Constitution of the Republic of Singapore (Amendment) Act 1991" (1991) *Singapore Journal of Legal Studies* 179, 193.
33 Li-ann Thio, "Working out the Presidency: the rites of passage" (1995) *Singapore Journal of Legal Studies* 509, 509.
34 Yvonne C.L. Lee, "Under lock and key: the evolving role of the Elected President as a fiscal guardian" (2007) *Singapore Journal of Legal Studies* 290, 290.
35 See Article 21(2)(a) of the Constitution of the Republic of Singapore ("Singapore Constitution").
36 See Article 21(2)(b) of the Singapore Constitution.
37 See Article 26(1)(b) of the Singapore Constitution.
38 Constitutional Amendments to Safeguard Financial Assets and the Integrity of the Public Services (White Paper, Cmd 10, 1988), para. 20.
39 See Article 151(4) of the Singapore Constitution.
40 See Article 22I of the Singapore Constitution.
41 See Article 22G of the Singapore Constitution.
42 *White Paper on Constitutional Amendments to Safeguard Financial Assets and the Integrity of the Public Services* (n. 38), para. 18(c); see also Thio (n. 20), 399.
43 White Paper on Constitutional Amendments to Safeguard Financial Assets and the Integrity of the Public Services, *ibid.*
44 For this distinction between the dignified and efficient aspects of the Head of State under the British Constitution, see Walter Bagehot, *The English Constitution* (Cambridge: Cambridge University Press, 2001 [1867]), 5.
45 See, for example, Thio (n. 20), 412.
46 Article 37I of the Singapore Constitution.
47 Article 21(3) of the Singapore Constitution: "The President shall consult the Council of Presidential Advisers before performing any of his functions under Articles 22, 22A(1), 22B(2) and (7), 22C(1), 22D(2) and (6), 144, 148A, 148B and 148G."
48 Article 22 of the Singapore Constitution.
49 Articles 22A(1), 22B(2) and 22B(7) of the Singapore Constitution.
50 Articles 22C(1), 22D(2) and 22D(6) of the Singapore Constitution.
51 Article 144 of the Singapore Constitution.
52 Article 148A of the Singapore Constitution.
53 Article 148B of the Singapore Constitution.
54 Article 148G of the Singapore Constitution.
55 The coverage of this optional consultation scheme is rather confusing as it requires one to manually eliminate from a list what had already been included in the mandatory consultation scheme. Article 21(4) of the Singapore Constitution reads: "Except as otherwise provided in clause (3), the President may, in his discretion, consult the Council of Presidential Advisers before performing any of his functions referred to in clause (2)(c) to (i)."
56 The Central Provident Fund is mandatory social security savings scheme funded by contributions from employers and employees.
57 Notably, Article 22H of the Singapore Constitution was interpreted to apply only to legislative bills and not constitutional bills. See *Constitutional Reference No. 1 of 1995* [1995] 1 SLR(R) 803.
58 Thio (n. 20), 411.
59 *Ibid.*
60 See Article 148D of the Singapore Constitution.
61 See Article 19 of the Singapore Constitution.

62 Thio (n. 20), 423.
63 Kevin Y.L. Tan, "State and institution-building through the Singapore Constitution 1965–2005", in Li-ann Thio and Kevin Y.L. Tan (eds), *Evolution of a Revolution: Forty Years of the Singapore Constitution* (London: Routledge Cavendish, 2009), 71.
64 Li-ann Thio, *Singapore Chronicles: Presidency* (Singapore: IPS and Straits Times Press, 2015), 32–44.
65 See, for example, Low Thia Khiang, quoted in "Government not sincere, says Opposition", *Straits Times* (Singapore, 19 August 1999), 29; Constitution of the Republic of Singapore (Amendment No 2) Bill Deb, 25 August 1994, vol. 63, cols 436–8 (NMP Walter Woon).
66 Constitution of the Republic of Singapore (Amendment No 2) Bill Deb, *ibid.*, col. 452 (BG Lee Hsien Loong).
67 Thio (n. 64).
68 For a more detailed analysis, see Lee (n. 34).
69 Thio (n. 64).
70 *Ibid.*
71 This became included as Article 19B of the Singapore Constitution.
72 This suggestion was made by Kevin Tan, who is also a contributor to this volume.
73 Report of the Constitutional Commission 2016 (17 August 2016), paras 7.50–7.52.
74 See Prime Minister's Office, *Review of Specific Aspects of the Elected Presidency* (White Paper, 15 September 2016), para. 124.
75 Constitution of the Republic of Singapore (Amendment) Bill Deb, 7 November 2016, vol. 94 (Deputy Prime Minister Teo Chee Hean).
76 According to Article 5A(7)(a), the entrenchment framework comprises Articles 5A, 5B and 5C, but with the exception of Article 5B(9), which sets out the Tier 2 provisions and is protected under Tier 2.
77 Article 17(1) of the Singapore Constitution.
78 Article 17(2) of the Singapore Constitution.
79 Article 17A of the Singapore Constitution.
80 Articles 20(1) and (2) of the Singapore Constitution.
81 Article 22K of the Singapore Constitution.
82 Articles 22L, 22N and 22O of the Singapore Constitution.
83 Article 5A(1)(a) of the Singapore Constitution.
84 Article 5A(2) of the Singapore Constitution.
85 Article 5A(1)(b) of the Singapore Constitution.
86 Article 5A(5) of the Singapore Constitution.
87 Constitution of the Republic of Singapore (Amendment) Bill Deb (n. 75) (Deputy Prime Minister Teo Chee Hean).
88 Article 5B(9)(a) of the Singapore Constitution.
89 Specifically, the provisions in Articles 22, 22A, 22B, 22C, 22D, 22E, 37B, 37C and 154A and Part XI of the Singapore Constitution that authorize the President to act in his discretion.
90 Article 22(1) of the Singapore Constitution.
91 Such as in Article 37B(2)(a)(i) of the Singapore Constitution.
92 Article 148A(1), which falls within Part XI of the Singapore Constitution.
93 See Constitution of the Republic of Singapore (Amendment) Bill Deb (n. 75) (Deputy Prime Minister Teo Chee Hean).
94 As spelled out in Article 5B(9)(b), these are articles 22F, 22H, 22J, 22M and 93A of the Singapore Constitution.
95 Article 22F of the Singapore Constitution.
96 Article 22H of the Singapore Constitution.
97 Articles 22M and 93A of the Singapore Constitution.

98 Set out in Articles 5B(1), (2) and (5) of the Singapore Constitution.
99 See Constitution of the Republic of Singapore (Amendment) Bill Deb (n. 75) (Deputy Prime Minister Teo Chee Hean).
100 In other words, any provision mentioned in Article 5B(9) of the Singapore Constitution.
101 Constitution of the Republic of Singapore (Amendment) Bill Deb (n. 75) (Deputy Prime Minister Teo Chee Hean).
102 Article 5C(4)(a)(i) of the Singapore Constitution.
103 Article 5C(4)(a)(ii), *ibid.*
104 Article 5C(4)(b), *ibid.*
105 Article 5C(2), *ibid.*
106 Article 5C(3)(a), *ibid.*
107 Article 5C(3)(b), *ibid.*
108 Constitution of the Republic of Singapore (Amendment) Bill Deb (n. 75) (Deputy Prime Minister Teo Chee Hean).
109 Prime Minister's National Day Rally Speech, *The Straits Times* (Singapore, 10 August 1988), 1.
110 White Paper on Constitutional Amendments to Safeguard Financial Assets and the Integrity of the Public Services (n. 38).
111 Safeguarding Financial Assets and the Integrity of the Public Services: The Constitution of the Republic of Singapore (Amendment No. 3) Bill (White Paper, Cmd 11, 1990, presented to Parliament on 27 August 1990).
112 Kevin Y.L. Tan, *The Constitution of Singapore: A Contextual Analysis* (Oxford: Hart Publishing, 2015), 86–7.
113 The other eight members were Justice Tay Yong Kwang (Judge, Supreme Court); Mr Eddie Teo (Chairman, Public Service Commission); Mr Abdullah Tarmugi (former Cabinet Minister, former Speaker of Parliament, and Member, Presidential Council for Minority Rights); Professor Chan Heng Chee (former Ambassador to the United States and current Chairman, Lee Kuan Yew Centre for Innovative Cities, Singapore University of Technology and Design); Mr Chua Thian Poh (Chairman and CEO, Ho Bee Land); Mr Philip Ng (CEO, Far East Organization); Mr Peter Seah (Chairman, DBS Bank); Mr Wong Ngit Liong (Chairman and CEO, Venture Corporation). Walter Sim, "9-member Constitutional Commission formed to review Elected Presidency", *The Straits Times* (20 February 2016) www.straitstimes.com/politics/9-member-constitutional-commission-formed-to-review-elected-presidency (accessed 14 March 2019).
114 Report of the Select Committee on the Constitution of the Republic of Singapore (Amendment No. 2) Bill [Bill No. 41/89] (Presented to Parliament on 15 March 1990).
115 *Report of the Constitutional Commission 2016* (n. 73), para. 1.3.
116 *Ibid.*, para. 1.5.
117 *Ibid.*
118 Keiko T. Tamura, "The emergence and political consciousness of the middle class in Singapore" (2003) XLI-2 *The Developing Economies*, 18.
119 Ho Khai Leong, "Citizen participation and policy making in Singapore: conditions and predicaments" (2000) 40(3) *Asian Survey* 436.
120 *Ibid.*
121 Tan (n. 112), 62.
122 See generally Elster (n. 8).
123 *White Paper on the Review of Specific Aspects of the Elected Presidency* (n. 74), paras 122(a) and 124(d).
124 Hanna Pitkin, *The Concept of Representation* (Berkeley, CA: University of California Press, 1992 [1967]), 209.

125 See, for example, Glenn Patmore, "Making sense of representative democracy and the implied freedom of political communication in the High Court of Australia: three possible models" (1998) 7(1) *Griffith Law Review* 97.
126 Lutz (n. 22), 5.
127 Horowitz (n. 5), 33–5.
128 Pitkin (n. 1), 168.
129 Lutz (n. 22), 215.

1 Looking back at the Elected Presidency

Design choices and unintended consequences

Kevin Y.L. Tan and Lam Peng Er

1.1 Introduction

The Elected President scheme was the product of a panic brought on by the spectre of a 'freak election' in which the ruling People's Action Party ("PAP") is vanquished at the polls. What if a profligate government came to power? Was there anything to stop them from raiding Singapore's considerable financial reserves and send the country down the road to economic ruin? There was really no safeguard against such a scenario since the parliamentary system of government and the single plurality system of voting allowed the party in government to do practically whatever it wanted. Without securing an absolute majority of votes, a political party can come into power and immediately pull on all the levers of power. And there was nothing to stop them from using that power to go on a spending spree, buying votes with populist policies and massive subsidies. In the words of the then Prime Minister Lee Kuan Yew ("Lee"):

> Today, any government elected can get at those reserves and spend it. So you can get a wild offshoot of an election – free bus rides, lower electricity, free water, lower MRT fares, and your reserves will just vanish like that within a few years. Then like Brazil, Argentina and Mexico, we'll be borrowing hundreds of millions of dollars. And we're finished. This place will never get off the ground again.[1]

It appears that the Cabinet began discussing this problem as early as 1982, a year after the PAP was defeated in the by-election for the Anson constituency, its first loss of any seat since 1968.[2] In 1984, at his National Day Rally Speech, Lee made his case for transforming the office of President into an elected one:

> As the Constitution now stands, if there's a freak election result, and a coalition forms the government, all the reserves are available. The larder is wide open. You can raid it! Twenty-five years' work, savings ... You can go on a spending spree for five years and then we are another broken-backed country. We've thought up some mechanisms so that no

> government can spend previously built-up reserves. You build up the reserves, you spend it. You promise free bus rides, you raise the taxes. But you're not spending what we have saved … and I think we should have a President with moral authority to block it. The thing has to be thought out carefully because there's bound to be a row when the President says "No" to a newly-elected Prime Minister. … I think the President has got to be elected by the people, direct vote, not in Parliament. He also has moral authority, preferably he should be an ex-Minister with an understanding of how governments and budgets are run. And there could be a committee too so that he will have the backing of a Special Committee for the Preservation of Reserves. And if the two of them agree, then the Government of the day is blocked.[3]

It was clear from Lee's first soundings of this new scheme that a Parliament of the future would be checked through the office of a *popularly elected* President working in concert with a special council constituted for the sole purpose of protecting Singapore's reserves. Not unexpectedly, Lee's proposal set tongues a-wagging and there was much discussion and speculation about what the new system would look like. It is interesting that much of the discussion focused on the mechanics and personality of who the first Elected President would be – Lee being favoured by most – but hardly anyone asked if this was the best institutional solution to the problem. This article looks at the way in which alternative design choices were proposed and sidelined and how these options came again to the forefront in the course of the Constitutional Commission hearings of 2016.

1.2 Design principles of Lee's original scheme

Lee Kuan Yew's approach to this dilemma of protecting the national reserves from a potentially profligate government and an electorate drunk on political bribes was not to work through parliamentary checks and balances (including an Upper House or Senate), an active civil society or a free press. Instead, he proposed amending the Constitution to transform the office of the President into an elected one. The Elected President ("EP") would then carry the people's mandate to act as a custodian of national reserves and a 'gatekeeper' for the appointment of key office bearers of the State. Lee's assumption was that control should vest in a single PAP-like 'good man' rather than a Council of Ephors (as in Sparta)[4] or Genrō (elder statesmen in Japan)-like system.[5] Lee did not explain how he or the Cabinet arrived at this conclusion or if they had indeed seriously considered any other options.

What seems clear is that Lee's institutional design was premised on an oversimplified 'good versus bad' dichotomy: a Good PAP (type) President versus Bad Opposition Government. In other words, a good President (a person trusted by the PAP establishment) was expected to check a bad Government (formed by an erstwhile opposition party or parties). However, as Lam has previously argued, this

Table 1.1 Alternative scenarios for President–Government checks and balances.

	Good President	*Bad President*
Bad Government	**PAP's Scenario**	**Worst Scenario**
Good Government	**Best Scenario**	**Opposition Scenario**

scenario ignores the possibility of four possible outcomes within this paradigmatic matrix.[6] This is graphically illustrated in Table 1.1. To explain:[7]

1 *PAP's Scenario*: A 'responsible' EP checks an 'irresponsible' government by safeguarding the national reserves, maintaining the integrity of key civil and military appointment, and preventing arbitrary arrests of citizens.
2 *Opposition's Scenario*: An opportunistic and vindictive pro-PAP EP bent on sabotaging a newly elected government formed by non-PAP party or parties. The discrediting of the new government will then result in the PAP regaining power in the next election.
3 *Best Scenario*: A felicitous state of affairs where Singapore is doubly blessed by the presence of a 'good' president and a 'good' government. Since the EP has no need to intervene and exercise his veto against a good and responsible government, the EP will keep a low profile politically and essentially perform a ceremonial role. The EP will continue to act as a sentinel but his veto will not be activated.
4 *Worst Scenario*: A double jeopardy when a 'bad' EP and a 'bad' government collide or collude, thereby spelling disaster for the country. There is nothing in the Constitution to prevent collusion between a venal EP and a corrupt government commanding a parliamentary majority.

Scenarios (1) and (2) above will lead inevitably to clashes between the President and the Government and quite possibly gridlock since the thwarted Government will invariably try its best to either amend the Constitution or have the President removed. This could in turn set in motion a long and ugly political battle that will ultimately devastate the political system and faith in it. Even in the case of the 'Best Scenario', there is no guarantee that the President and the Government will always be *ad idem* on matters invoking the President's discretion. Even when the President had originally been a member of the PAP, a clash between the EP and the Government could still erupt, as in the case with President Ong Teng Cheong, the first EP who served from 1993 to 1999.

The creation and implementation of the EP scheme represented a significant departure from Singapore's erstwhile Westminster constitutional model with a largely ceremonial President as the Head of State and with real political power vested in the Prime Minister and Cabinet drawn from within Parliament. That said, it was not such a major departure in the sense that the President would only have blocking powers and could not initiate policy or legal change.

1.2.1 Other design options

When Lee broached the scheme in 1984, there was little discussion on what possible alternatives the Government had, and it was not until the release of the first White Paper[8] in 1982 that in deciding on the proposed scheme, the Government had:

> considered many alternatives: creating an upper legislative body, reposing the power of veto in the Presidential Council for Minority Rights or some other body analogous to the US Federal Reserve Board, or requiring decisions on financial assets to be subject to the approval of the electorate in a referendum.[9]

The White Paper was introduced by Lim Boon Heng (MP for Kebun Bahru) on 11 August 1988,[10] and in the ensuing debate, several MPs voiced their discomfort with the proposed scheme. Former Cabinet Minister Ong Pang Boon told the House that he harboured "grave reservations" since the idea was first mooted in 1983.[11] He felt that the parliamentary system had worked well and that the "best means of preventing an irresponsible government from coming to power" was to "take positive measures to persuade and convince the people that your policy and actions are in their best interests".[12] Ong further pointed to the danger of allowing "another centre of power" to "emerge around the President, especially if the President had been a towering political leader for a long time" as this would correspondingly reduce the status and power of a future Prime Minister.[13]

Associate Professor Lau Teik Soon ("Lau") (MP for Serangoon Gardens) and Head of the Political Science Department at the National University of Singapore asked the Government for its views on the various alternatives which they considered and why the other options were rejected.[14] He received no answer. Lau nonetheless called upon the Government to "reconsider the option of an Upper House" since an Upper House would "take into account the key considerations" mentioned in the First White Paper.[15] Lau's proposed Upper House or Senate would comprise 10–12 elected members and offered the following useful features:

> Firstly, the country and people will have the valuable services of a group of men and women who will have administrative, management and professional experience at the highest levels of government as well as the public and private sectors. This means that they should possess certain qualifications before they can offer themselves for election. But what you will have, Sir, is a group of men and women with such experience and expertise.
>
> Secondly, their concurrence for any government decision affecting the national reserves and integrity of the civil service will have been arrived at following careful deliberations and debate before the public, since debate in an Upper House should be open to the public. The public will then be aware of the manner in which they have arrived at their decision or concurrence with the government decision.

> Thirdly, there will be a clear division between Parliament and the Senate so that each is independent of the other. No candidate can stand for both Parliamentary and Senatorial elections.
>
> Fourthly, disagreement between the government and the Senate can be resolved by Parliament and the Senate without having to resort to a referendum. For example, let us say that two-thirds of the Senate votes are required for concurrence in these two vital areas. Then if the government fails to get the vote, the matter should be referred to Parliament for further debate. After that the matter can be sent up to the Senate once more. If it fails again, then either the government accepts the decision or resign. Then both parliamentary and senatorial elections can be held and the people can then decide for themselves. That is the usual practice in most parliamentary democracies where there are two Houses of Parliament.
>
> Fifthly, the will of the people will prevail. Both Parliament and Senate members are elected by the people. They are the people's representatives and they should act in the national interest.[16]

Lau's proposal met with a chilling silence. Only Ng Kah Ting (MP for Punggol) argued against it, saying that it was "neither practical nor necessary" for Singapore to have a bicameral system of government because of its "small size".[17] The proposal for an Upper House only attracted the support of one other MP during the debate on the Second White Paper in 1990.[18] Lew Syn Pau (MP for Tanglin) opined that Lau's proposal had "not been given enough serious consideration and study". If it had, then he felt that: "the reasons for discarding other options" were not "made known adequately to the public".[19] Lew was not convinced that if an Upper House or Senate were constituted of between 10 and 20 members, candidates would be difficult to find:

> I think it would not be too difficult to get candidates for this Upper House, as such Members need not shoulder the onerous task of looking after constituents. If their functions are mainly custodial as contained in the Bill, they need not meet as often as Parliament. I believe we have enough prominent politicians, senior civil servants and eminent professionals and businessmen who are capable and willing to discharge these functions with objectivity and dignity. In the long-term, I am not convinced as yet that 10–20 such distinguished members would be inferior to a lone custodian.[20]

In his round-up of the debate at the Second Reading of the Constitution of the Republic of Singapore (Amendment No 3) Bill, the first Deputy Prime Minister Goh Chok Tong ("Goh") finally dealt with the upper house proposal in the context of the proposed Council of Presidential Advisers ("CPA"). Goh likened the CPA to a "de facto Senate", comprising six members, with the EP, and the Chairman of the Public Service Commission and the Prime Minister each nominating two members. The main function of the CPA is to advise the EP in the exercise of "his discretion to approve or veto budgets of the Government, statutory boards and key government companies".[21] Goh however continued to argue that it was impractical to establish a full-fledged Upper House on account of Singapore's small size and corresponding lack of talent:

> We think this scheme is more workable because when you have a Senate, and let us assume it is an elected Senate, first, you have the problem of finding a sufficient number of people to stand for elections to the Senate. You need about 20 to 30 people to make it effective. And secondly, how do we ensure that people who are elected into the Senate have the qualities which we are looking for? There is no control. It is an Upper House which in a sense duplicates the functions of the Lower House. In other words, we should be looking for 20 to 30 senators who are politically superior to Members of this House. Can you find them? If you can, and you are satisfied that these are people who can look after our interests much better than MPs over here, perhaps you can give it a try. But I suggest that for the time being, let us concentrate on a small Upper House, a small Senate with six appointed Council members to advise one elected Senator or the President. We have control over the quality of men or women who will be on the Council and there are certain safeguards to ensure that the person who stands for election as Elected President has the desired attributes.[22]

This is an old argument that no longer holds much water, especially in relation to the lack of talent to constitute an Upper House. The overwhelming number of suitably qualified individuals who regularly put their names forward for the post of Nominated Member of Parliament suggests that there will more than sufficient credible and public-minded individuals to take on this task. The time is ripe to seriously and critically reconsider this question. This is especially the case since the passage of time has shown the severe limitations of the EP scheme, whether due to unintended consequences or design flaws.

1.3 Problems with the EP scheme

1.3.1 Qualifications of EP candidates: illogical proxies for competence

The EP must be one of the most undemocratic 'democratic' institutions in the world. There are probably around 1,000 eligible candidates and most of them are reluctant to run without the blessings and support of the PAP government. Walkovers in EP elections mean that Singaporean voters cannot exercise their rights to choose their preferred president. More significantly, unelected EPs lack a 'positive' electoral mandate.[23] It is not inconceivable that a future unelected EP, not armed with an electoral mandate, will be unable to stand up to a corrupt government.

Second, certain key appointment holders (such as Speaker of the House) who are automatically prequalified to run as EP may lack the financial acumen to understand balance sheets and how national reserves are and should be managed. Is a former Speaker of the House automatically wiser on the national reserves than Singaporeans in most other professions? One can argue that an EP who lacks financial knowledge can be guided by the advice of the Council of Presidential Advisers ("CPA"). If that is the case, then why the need to have managed $500 million to prequalify as an EP candidate? Can an EP who managed a smaller amount, but with other sterling qualities, not be guided by the advice of the CPA?[24] Can we not revert back to the pre-existing system (a parliament-picked president) but equip him/her with limited custodial powers guided by the CPA on national reserves and key appointments?

1.3.2 More locks on the front door ... but the back door is wide open

Another design flaw lies in the assumption that a 'dual key' system is enough to protect the national reserves. The EP does have custodial powers to ensure that the sovereign funds are properly managed. To emphasize the prudent management of sovereign funds, the Singapore Government has indeed highlighted the role of the EP. It would be useful to reproduce the Government's explanation in full:[25]

> First, the appointments to the Board of Directors that oversee each of these investment entities are subject to the concurrence of both the President and Government. Before the President decides on whether to concur, he obtains advice from the Council of Presidential Advisers (CPA), which in turn scrutinises the appointment. The President has discretion to decide whether or not to concur with the appointments after consulting the CPA.
>
> Second, each entity's financial statements are independently audited. The MAS and GIC's financial statements are audited by the Auditor-General, who is an independent organ of state under the Constitution. Temasek's financial statements and those of its subsidiary companies are audited by leading international audit firms.
>
> Third, it is the duty, under the Constitution, for the Auditor-General, Accountant-General, the Board of directors of the Fifth Schedule entities, and their CEOs to inform the President of any proposed transaction that is likely to draw on Past Reserves.
>
> Fourth, the President and the CPA have full access to any information they require from these investment agencies to fulfil their responsibility of safeguarding the reserves. If they suspect any wrongdoings, they can request for further information from the Board of Directors or management of the investment entities.
>
> Allegations of fraudulent reporting by our investment entities are not just baseless but bizarre. It amounts to saying that everyone within the system of safeguards – the President, the members of the CPA, the Cabinet, Auditor-General, Accountant-General, leading international audit firms, members of the boards of the investment entities, and the numerous officers preparing the reports – is collaborating to defraud the public.

It is not inconceivable that the reserves can still be lost through bad investment decisions by Singapore's sovereign funds and not the Government of the day. The analogy is: the padlock to the front door of the national reserves has two keys (Government and EP) but the reserves may still be lost through the back door by poorly managed sovereign funds. At issue is not the EP, the Government and other key appointment holders being in cahoots to loot the national reserves but less than savvy business decisions by managers of the sovereign funds leading to considerable losses of the reserves. Singapore's national reserves have grown exponentially and impressively (see Table 1.1). Obviously, attaining good sustainable returns is a key challenge. The combined assets of GIC (Government Investment Corporation) and Temasek are valued at more than US$0.5 trillion. According to the Monetary Authority of Singapore (MAS), the city-state's total official foreign reserves in 2016 were US$246,575.3 million.[26] Indeed, the imperative remains: the reserves must be safeguarded for future generations of Singaporeans.

Reports show that Singapore has suffered losses in its national reserves despite having a 'dual key' system. Some of Temasek's known investment losses were: Thai telecom Shin Corp,[27] disk drive maker Micropolis,[28] child care operator ABC Learning,[29] Barclays,[30] Bank of America and Merrill Lynch.[31] In the case of GIC, it lost money on UBS[32] but made on Citigroup.[33] One can adopt a philosophical approach and say that in the game of investments, you win some and you lose some; just make sure that you make more than you lose. Arguably, it will be desirable for sovereign funds to be more transparent in their investments including gains and losses. Perhaps Norway's outstanding Sovereign Wealth Fund can be a good reference for other sovereign funds. It appears to strike a good balance between transparency, sustainable returns and ethical investment.

It is unclear whether black swan events like the Asian Financial Crisis and the Post-Lehman American Financial Crisis are a harbinger of things to come for Singapore's sovereign funds. It is not impossible for national reserves to be drained in future by poor investment calls rather than a dishonest government. If the EP scheme were to work well according to design, the President will cast his veto, without fear or favour, against a bad government and save the day. However, the EP's second key was not designed to latch the back door of the treasure house, which can be left wide open by poorly managed sovereign funds. To analyse the role of outstanding sovereign funds and growing the national reserves is beyond the scope of this paper. Nevertheless, a conclusion can be drawn that the role of the EP is insufficient to safeguard our national reserves due to black swan events and the volatility of financial markets. Simply put, the management quality of sovereign funds is most critical.

1.3.3 Gridlock when Executives clash

We are neither clairvoyant nor prescient about the potential for a gridlock between the EP and the Government of the day. However, it is not inconceivable that a future EP and Government may clash because they have different political outlooks, judgements and temperament, and not because they are necessarily corrupt, irresponsible and extravagant. There are at least three hypothetical scenarios, domestic and external, which may lead to a collision between the EP and the Government of the day.

First, in the midst of an uncertain power transition in East Asia (the rise of China and the relative decline of the US superpower), it is possible that a future government may seek to significantly boost defence spending for national security. However, the EP may prefer quiet diplomacy to avoid an arms race and refuse to unlock the national reserves for more armaments. Neither strategy can be said to be clearly right or wrong and hinges purely on political judgement and instinct. Yet, this will invariably lead to a clash between the President and the Government of the day.

Second, is the concern that a Government of tomorrow would give loans to one or more bankrupt and corrupt neighbouring countries in a regional financial meltdown worse than the 1997–1998 Asian Financial Crisis or the 2008 post-Lehman US Financial Crisis. A good loan will be reflected as an 'asset' in the account books but if the borrower defaults on the loan, it will be a clear loss and even a possible drawdown on the reserves. Article 144(1) of the Singapore Constitution only requires the President's concurrence if the Government raises a loan but not when it gives the loan.[34] It is thus possible that a future EP would have to remain silent about a government extending billions of dollars (presumably drawn from the reserves) to other states since he is not constitutionally obliged to exercise his veto or consent over the giving of a loan. However, what if that EP were to have grave misgivings and then expressed his deep concerns openly to harness public opinion against the Government not to 'squander' the reserves? Would that EP be overstepping his circumscribed role (custodial role on taking but not giving loans) to protect the reserves or worse still be regarded as having violated the Constitution thus meriting removal from office? A showdown between the EP and the Government may then be imminent.

Third, is the fact that future governments in Singapore will come under increasing pressure to shoulder a greater social welfare burden for a rapidly ageing society. Governments can hike taxes (which is politically unpopular) or dip into the reserves (which may trigger a presidential veto) to pay for insatiable demands for medical expenses, nursing homes and other social welfare services. What if this long-term trend of ageing and the rising costs for social services coincided with an economic recession and the Government of the day cannot afford to roll out the programme promised in its electoral manifesto? And what if the EP refuses to dip into Singapore's huge reserves to use for a 'rainy day'? Will a populist government mobilize the masses against a conservative EP?

1.4 Unintended consequences

1.4.1 From checking a 'bad government' to checking a 'bad president'

More than two decades ago, we anticipated the scenario of a future 'bad' President and a 'good' government.[35] As pointed out above, the PAP Government created the EP to ensure that there would always be a 'gatekeeper' who was of their ilk; someone cut from the same cloth; an ersatz PAP 'good man'. The qualification requirements for the EP are so onerous that when it was enacted in 1991, it was estimated that no more than 400 persons would qualify for the job. Nonetheless, it was assumed that anyone who could meet these stringent constitutional requirements would be able to perform the EP's constitutional role and could be trusted to do so – obviously not. In 2016, a Constitutional Commission was convened to review the EP scheme generally, and to 'update' the EP's qualification requirement specifically. So, while the original plan was for the EP to check a bad government, it appears now that subsequent constitutional revisions were made to check a potential 'bad' president by making it more onerous to run as a candidate through raising the hurdle to disqualify 'unsuitable' candidates.[36]

There were at least two episodes which led to this change of heart by the PAP government and the more complicated constitutional revisions for the office of the EP. The first was the PAP government's discomfort when the independently minded President Ong Teng Chong wanted greater transparency and financial valuation of the national reserves and assets. The second was the scare of the 2012 Presidential Election when preferred PAP candidate Dr Tony Tan won only by the skin of his teeth. Arguably, it would have been a political nightmare for the PAP government, if a maverick candidate had won instead. This 'design flaw' in the EP scheme that almost led to an 'undesirable' candidate becoming President and possibly checking the 'good' PAP government had therefore to be addressed. However, the 2016 amendments, which raised the qualification bar even higher and also introduced a new reserved election mechanism aimed at periodically ensuring minority representation in the office led to new problems. It limited the pool of eligible EP candidates to around a thousand persons, out of whom there were no more than ten Malays able to run in the 2017 Presidential Election, reserved for Malay candidates.

1.4.2 Loss of President's symbolic role

As Tan pointed out two decades earlier, the transformation of the office the President into an elected one led to the loss of one of its key functions – as a unifying symbolic of the nation:

> In the past the presidency was a semiotic representation of Singapore's multi-racial and multi-religious make up. While Singapore has a predominantly Chinese population, Malays, Indians, Eurasians and other minorities are given due recognition for having members of their communities elected to the post of president …
>
> Under the new scheme, this key function of the president is obliterated. No longer will the currency of race be exploited to unite the nation. The symbol of multi-racial Singapore is now lost. Neither will the president be seen as the benevolent, elder statesman or father figure who soothes the nation over difficult times and patches up family quarrels, bringing diverse factions together for the common good. Indeed, with the office transformed

> into a competitive one, the candidate's personality, promises and outlook will matter more than all else.[37]

However, in the recent 2016 constitutional reform exercise, the Government charged the Menon Constitutional Commission ("Menon Commission") to "consider and recommend what provisions should be made to safeguard minority representation in the Presidency". This was done specifically to avoid locking out Malays and ensuring that there can be a Malay (elected) President. In doing so, the Commission was instructed to take into account: (a) the President's status as a unifying figure that represents multiracial Singapore; and (b) the need to ensure that candidates from minority races have a fair and adequate opportunity to be elected to presidential office.[38]

The Menon Commission noted that the EP's symbolic role demanded "certain traits (largely resting on the ability to connect with and represent the general populace)", which "may not always, or even usually, be found in individuals who also possess the financial qualifications and technical competencies required for the exercise of the President's custodial powers."[39] To solve this contradiction, the Commission proposed "unbundling of the President's custodial role" and devolving it "to a specialist body", which could be operationalized as follows:

> The custodial function over the nation's fiscal reserves and key public service appointments could be vested in an appointed body of experts. The Commission conceptualises such a council of experts as a second chamber of Parliament with the ability to delay measures, force a debate upon them and require the Government to override any objections only with a super-majority. Hence, unlike the Elected President, the council, as an appointed body of experts, would never have the power to absolutely veto or block Government initiatives (as the Elected President presently does when he has the support of the CPA). But through a combination of raising the issue, forcing a debate on the council's objections and requiring a super-majority, a suitable balance could be struck between the need to safeguard our critical assets on the one hand, and, on the other hand, enabling the Government to act.[40]

The Menon Commission went beyond the scope of its Terms of Reference and in effect proposed establishing an Upper House that would take over the custodial role of the Elected President and return the Presidency to a purely symbolic one. In this way, the EP can be rotated among the various ethnic groups without the need for a political contest. However, if this recommendation was unacceptable, the Commission further proposed what it called a "hiatus-triggered" election scheme under which a particular presidential election may be 'reserved' for a particular ethnic community (say, the Malays) if no person from that community has been elected as President for five consecutive terms.[41] This second recommendation of the Commission found favour with the Government, but not the first.

The opposition Workers' Party was, however, in agreement with the Commission's proposal and pushed the Government to establish a Senate but the

Government stuck to its guns, arguing that such a body was inherently unworkable in Singapore.[42] The Senate, as proposed by the Workers' Party, would replace the EP to exercise the powers of the President and the CPA, with pre-qualified Senators to be elected at nationwide General Elections. Under this scheme, if the Senate disagrees with the Government's proposal to draw down on the reserves or make certain key appointments, they will be empowered to reject them. The Senatorial veto could, however, be overridden by a three-quarters majority vote by Parliament.[43] The Workers' Party's Position Paper, released a day after the first day debate on the Second Reading of the Constitution of the Republic of Singapore (Amendment) Bill 2016, did not, however, offer details on the qualification criteria for Senatorial candidates. Law Minister K. Shanmugam launched a blistering cross-examination of the Workers' Party's MPs in Parliament on this lack of details of a proposal he labelled "half-baked" and "absurd".[44]

1.5 Epilogue: Janus – looking back, looking forward

From the then Prime Minister Lee Kuan Yew's first public mooting of the EP idea in 1984 until the 1993 Presidential Election was a span of nine years. In contrast, Prime Minister Lee Hsien Loong ("Prime Minister") rushed to amend the 2016 amendments through in less than a year. In his speech to Parliament on 27 January 2017, the Prime Minister said that it was timely to review the eligibility criteria of the EP. By September 2017, Madam Halimah Yacob became President in a reserved election for Malays without an actual election. Nonetheless, why the 'ungodly' haste?

An argument was made by some that it is perhaps a case of 'killing two birds with one stone' – disqualify an apparently 'undesirable candidate' like Dr Tan Cheng Bock; and elevating Madam Halimah Yacob to become an iconic EP of multiculturalism and feminism in Singapore. It is unclear whether the ruling PAP will actually 'pay a price' for its seemingly high-handed approach (to many Singaporeans) at the next poll. This is because there may be more pressing issues at the next general election and the public may get used to the notion of a Reserved Presidential Election by then.

Looking at the brief history of the EP, it would not be surprising if there are more constitutional amendments to 'fine tune' the institution, should new and unanticipated problems arise. The ruling PAP would say that it is just being pragmatic. Nevertheless, it may unwittingly create a paradoxical institution which does too much and too little at the same time. "Too much" because the President is supposed to safeguard the reserves and the integrity of key appointments, win a contest to gain an electoral mandate and be a rotating symbol of ethnic representation. "Too little" because the EP's second key may be insufficient to protect the national reserves if the back door to the national wealth is left wide open by sovereign funds. Notwithstanding the recurring tinkering to the EP institution, a future political gridlock between an EP and the Government may well happen. Singapore then would be in uncharted political territory.

Table 1.2 Largest sovereign wealth funds (by assets under management).

Name	*Assets in US$ Billions*	*Country*	*Year of Inception*
Government Pension Fund Global	$922.11	Norway	1990
Abu Dhabi Investment Authority	$828.00	UAE	1976
China Investment Corporation	$813.80	China	2007
Kuwait Investment Authority	$524.00	Kuwait	1953
SAMA Foreign Holdings	$514.00	Saudi Arabia	1952
Hong Kong Monetary Authority Investment Portfolio	$456.60	China–Hong Kong	1993
SAFE Investment Company	$441.00	China	1997
Government of Singapore Investment Corporation	$350.00	Singapore	1981
Qatar Investment Authority	$342.00	Qatar	2005
National Social Security Fund	$295.00	China	2000
Investment Corporation of Dubai	$200.50	UAE	2006
Public Investment Fund	$183.00	Saudi Arabia	2008
Temasek Holdings	$180.00	Singapore	1974
Mubadala Investment Company	$125.00	UAE	2002
Abu Dhabi Investment Council	$110.00	UAE	2007
Korea Investment Corporation	$108.00	South Korea	2005
Australian Future Fund	$99.40	Australia	2006
National Development Fund of Iran	$91.00	Iran	2011
National Welfare Fund	$72.20	Russia	2008
Libyan Investment Authority	$66.00	Libya	2006

Source: Reuters Graphics.

Notes

1 "25 Years of hard work could vanish in 25 days of madness", *Straits Times* (Singapore, 16 April 1984), 8.

2 See the White Paper: The President of the Republic of Singapore, *Constitutional Amendments to Safeguard Financial Assets and the Integrity of the Public Services* (Cmd 10, 1988); First Deputy Prime Minister and Minister for Defence Goh Chok Tong, *Singapore Parliamentary Debates: Official Report*, 29 July 1988, vol. 51, col. 479.

3 Lee Kuan Yew, "1984 National Day Rally" (National Archives of Singapore, Singapore, 19 December 1984) www.nas.gov.sg/archivesonline/data/pdfdoc/lky19841219.pdf (accessed 22 August 2018).

4 See C.G. Thomas, "On the role of the Spartan kings" (1974) 23(3) *Historia: Zeitschrift für Alte Geschichte* 257; and P.J. Rodes, "The selection of Ephors at Sparta" (1981) 30(4) *Historia: Zeitschrift für Alte Geschichte* 498–502.

5 The Genrō have been described as a "small group of five outstanding statesmen" and their protégés. See Leon M. Bower, "The Genro of Japan" (1932) 7(4) *Social Science* 406–411; See also, Peter R. Moody Jr, "Genro rule in China and Japan: comparative perspective" (2007) 12(1) *Journal of Chinese Political Science* 29–48.

6 See Lam Peng Er, "The Elected Presidency: towards the twenty-first century", in Kevin Y.L. Tan and Lam Peng Er (eds), *Managing Political Change in Singapore: The Elected Presidency* (London: Routledge, 1997), 200–19.

7 *Ibid.*, 201–3.
8 See The President of the Republic of Singapore, *Constitutional Amendments to Safeguard Financial Assets and the Integrity of the Public Services* (Cmd 10, 1988) (hereinafter referred to as "First White Paper").
9 *Ibid.*, 3–3 [para. 18].
10 *Singapore Parliamentary Debates: Official Report*, 11 August 1988, vol. 51, cols 530–4 (Constitutional Amendments to Safeguard Financial Assets and the Integrity of the Civil Services).
11 *Ibid.*, col. 572.
12 *Ibid.*, col. 574.
13 *Ibid.*, col. 573.
14 *Ibid.*, col. 550.
15 *Ibid.*, cols 550–1.
16 *Ibid.*, cols 551–2.
17 *Ibid.*, col. 556.
18 See The President of the Republic of Singapore, *Safeguarding Financial Assets and the Integrity of the Public Services: The Constitution of the Republic of Singapore (Amendment No 3) Bill* (Cmd 11, 1990) presented to Parliament on 27 August 1990 (hereinafter referred to as "Second White Paper"). This was released along with the Constitution of the Republic of Singapore (Amendment No. 3) Bill (Bill No. 23/90).
19 *Singapore Parliamentary Debates: Official Report*, 5 October 1990, vol. 56, col. 549 (Second Reading of the Constitution of the Republic of Singapore (Amendment No 3) Bill).
20 *Ibid.*
21 Second White Paper (n. 40), 9, para. 30(c). Please see Chapter 4, Eugene K.B. Tan's chapter on the Council for Presidential Advisers in this volume.
22 *Singapore Parliamentary Debates*: Official Report, 5 October 1990, vol. 56, col. 558. (Second Reading of the Constitution of the Republic of Singapore (Amendment No 3) Bill).
23 The matter of mandate has been dealt with in this volume in Kevin Y.L. Tan, "Electing the "Selected President" or selecting the 'Elected President' ".
24 See *ibid.*
25 Government of Singapore, "Factually: is there something wrong with our reserves?" (*gov.sg*, 4 October 2012) www.gov.sg/factually/content/is-there-something-wrong-with-our-reserves (accessed 5 January 2017).
26 See Monetary Authority of Singapore, "Official foreign reserves" (*Monetary Authority of Singapore*, 7 September 2018) www.mas.gov.sg/statistics/reserve-statistics/official-foreign-reserves.aspx (accessed 15 September 2018).
27 See Simon Montlake, "Temasek sells down Thai Telecom asset at loss", *Forbes* (Wall Street, 19 August 2011) www.forbes.com/sites/simonmontlake/2011/08/19/temasek-sells-down-thai-telecom-asset-at-loss/#57999d175396 (accessed 15 September 2018); and P.R. Venkat and Cynthia Koons, "Temasek Looks to sell Shin Corp. stake", *Wall Street Journal* (New York, 18 February 2014) www.wsj.com/articles/temasek-looks-to-sell-shin-corp-stake-1392690440 (accessed 15 September 2018).
28 The *New York Times* reported:

> Temasek's chairman, S. Dhanabalan, a former cabinet minister, asked her to head Temasek in 2002, telling local media at the time that Ho was "the best person for the job", that it had "nothing to do" with her being Lee's wife, and citing "a willingness on her part to take calculated risks". Dhanabalan even referred to ST's purchase of disk drive maker Micropolis, which was liquidated soon afterwards with debts of 630 million Singapore dollars, saying Ho had had the courage to cut the losses.

See Sara Webb, "Temasek's chief, Ho Ching, likes to take risks", *New York Times* (New York, 27 July 2007) www.nytimes.com/2007/07/27/business/worldbusiness/27iht-temasek.1.6862331.html (accesssed 15 September 2018).

29 "Singapore's Temasek tops up stake in ABC Learning". *Reuters* (Sydney, 28 February 2008) https://uk.reuters.com/article/abc/singapores-temasek-tops-up-stake-in-abc-learning-idUKSYD8022320080228 (accessed 15 September 2018).

30 Jane Croft and John Burton, "Temasek faces loss from Barclays stake sale", *Financial Times* (London and Singapore, 4 June 2009) www.ft.com/content/b27b782e-5032-11de-9530-00144feabdc0 (accessed 15 September 2018).

31 Kevin Lim and Saeed Azhar, "Singapore's Temasek defends costly Bank of America exit", *Reuters* (Singapore, 22 May 2009) www.reuters.com/article/us-temasek-bankofamerica/singapores-temasek-defends-costly-bank-of-america-exit-idUSTRE54L17Q20090522 (accessed 15 September 2018).

32 Steve Slater and Owen Wild, "Singapore's GIC faces US$4bn loss on UBS bet", *Reuters* (London, 16 May 2017) www.reuters.com/article/singapores-gic-faces-us4bn-loss-on-ubs-b-idUSL8N1II3TR (accessed 15 September 2018); See also Mayuko Tani, "Singapore fund GIC takes a hit with UBS sell-off", *Nikkei Asian Review* (Singapore, 17 May 2017) https://asia.nikkei.com/Business/Banking-Finance/Singapore-fund-GIC-takes-a-hit-with-UBS-sell-off (accessed 15 September 2018); There is also the claim that GIC suffered substantial losses but it is unclear to what extent these were only 'paper losses'. See Costas Paris and P.R. Venkat, "Singapore's GIC Suffers $41.6 Billion Loss", *Wall Street Journal* (Singapore, 30 September 2009) www.wsj.com/articles/SB125418236117447877 (accessed 15 September 2018).

33 Kevin Brown and Sundeep Tucker, "GIC made $1.6 billion from Citi stake sale", *Financial Times* (Singapore and Hong Kong, 22 September 2009) www.ft.com/content/b8479e9a-a75d-11de-9467-00144feabdc0 (accessed 15 September 2018).

34 See *Jeyaretnam Kenneth Andrew* v. *Attorney-General* [2014] 1 SLR 345.

35 Lam Peng Er, "The Elected Presidency: towards the twenty-fist century", in Kevin Y.L. Tan and Lam Peng Er (eds), *Managing Political Change in Singapore: The Elected Presidency* (London: Routledge, 1997), 202–3.

36 The matter of the onerous qualification requirement has been dealt with by Kevin Y.L. Tan, "Mandates, majorities and the legitimacy of the Elected Presidency" in this volume.

37 Kevin Tan, "The Presidency in Singapore: constitutional developments", in Kevin Y.L. Tan and Lam Peng Er (eds), *Managing Political Change in Singapore: The Elected Presidency* (London: Routledge, 1997), 68–9.

38 Constitutional Commission, *Report of the Constitutional Commission 2016* (2016) (hereinafter referred to as "Menon Commission Report").

39 *Ibid.*, para. 7.45.

40 *Ibid.*, para. 7.48.

41 *Ibid.*, 95–6.

42 *Singapore Parliamentary Debates: Official Report*, 7 November 2016, vol. 94. (Second Reading, Constitution of the Republic (Amendment) Act 2016).

43 The Workers' Party, "Position Paper on the Constitution of the Republic of Singapore (Amendment) Bill 2016" (Workers' Party, 7 November 2016) http://wpge2015.s3-ap-southeast-1.amazonaws.com/wp-content/uploads/2016/11/08171625/Position-Paper-on-the-Constitution-of-Republic-of-Singapore-Amendment-Bill-2016.pdf (accessed 3 January 2017).

44 *Singapore Parliamentary Debates: Official Report*, 7 November 2016, vol. 94. (Second Reading, Constitution of the Republic (Amendment) Act 2016) Please see Chapters 8 and 9 by Maartje De Visser and Swati Jhaveri, respectively, in this volume for analyses of the Workers' Party's proposals.

2 Past imperfect, future tense

The Elected Presidency and the constitutional development of an 'ever evolving hybrid'

Li-ann Thio

2.1 Introduction

The Elected Presidency ("EP") is a unique[1] Singapore experiment in constitutional autochthony. Its primary architect, Prime Minister ("PM") Lee Kuan Yew ("LKY"), first articulated in 1984 the enviable problem of protecting the hard-earned wealth that Singapore had accumulated as it clawed its way from third world to first, shifting from the "politics of poverty and despair" to one "of progress and of hope, not the politics of squatters, but the politics of owners ..."[2]

Two key ideas informed the institutional design. First, the need to cure the perceived accountability deficit, arising from Singapore's version of an 'elective dictatorship'[3] where the Government within a dominant party state (which until 1981 was a de facto one-party state) enjoyed "untrammelled power" which could be abused through fiscal imprudence and nepotistic public office appointments. LKY advocated a reactive "blocking mechanism" through adding discretionary powers to a modified ceremonial presidency. The position would preferably be staffed by an ex-minister familiar with budgets and government operations, perhaps aided by a committee of experts. Second, the President would be directly elected by the people rather than by Parliament. This confers upon the office the moral authority and democratic mandate to say "no" to the Prime Minister, which introduces a dualist democracy.[4] From this early blueprint, three key tensions were wired into the regime, with a fourth recently emerging.

The first tension is between *efficacy* and *efficiency*. It grapples with how strong the EP's powers should be to provide an effective countervailing mechanism to check ministerial decisions while avoiding 'unnecessary' gridlock or intra-Executive confrontations. The second tension lies between *political choice* and *technocratic quality*. This refers to the need for the office to have a popular mandate while ensuring only qualified persons become the President. The third tension is between unifying *ceremonial* and potentially confrontational *constitutional custodial* powers. The fourth tension that has been recently introduced lies between *multiracialism* and *meritocracy*. The 2016 Constitutional Commission and the Government acknowledged these concerns.[5]

These tensions may be the result of the evolution of the EP over time. As a form of "political technology", constitutionalism "attempts to marry power with justice".[6] This is reflected in the design of the EP design scheme, which realigns institutional arrangements to ensure that decision-making over a specified range of matters[7] is subject to multiple actors to mitigate the risk of the injustice of arbitrary decision-making. It applies the separation of powers principle, securing limited Government through intra-executive branch checks and balances operating between the EP and parliamentary executive (Cabinet), with the moderating interposition of non-elected advisory bodies. In this way, the study of the institution of the EP opens a microcosmic doorway into the character and function of a constitution[8] and the nature of the polity it operates within. The EP scheme departed from the traditional ceremonial role the head of state discharges within the Westminster parliamentary system that Singapore inherited from the British (by way of Malaysia, where the Head of State is a constitutional monarch). Accordingly, the unwritten convention that the Monarch generally acts on the advice of the Cabinet[9] was constitutionalized under Article 21(1) of the Independence Constitution. Aside from erecting *constraints* on public powers, a preoccupation of liberal constitutionalism animated by "the liberalism of fear",[10] the development of the EP provides insights into the *legitimating* and *integrative* functions of constitutions[11] and, at least formally, *securing liberty* for citizens.

This chapter posits that these underlying tensions provide a framework by which to understand and analyse changes to the EP scheme as part of the 'living constitution'. Section 2.2 addresses the political environment that makes regular revisions to the EP scheme (and the Constitution generally) possible, and the methods adopted primarily through formal amendment and secondarily through soft constitutional law norms, which generate non-binding expectations and conventions. The approach to constitutional change in Singapore – through conventions and soft constitutional law in addition to formal constitutional change – contributed to the creation of these underlying tensions. Sections 2.3 and 2.4 elaborate upon the nature of the tensions, how the resolution of these tensions have been the focus of constitutional change, and how, moving forward, it may be possible to mitigate the tensions. The discussion focuses on three aspects of the EP scheme which have attracted amendments: first, the scope of its power and the actors involved in the checks and balances scheme, where the EP acts as a 'fire alarm'; second, amendments relating to the presidential elections process in order to 'filter out fools'; and third, amendments designed to promote multiracialism and the 'failsafe' reserved elections mechanism adopted in 2016. Section 2.5 offers concluding observations on the EP scheme's impact on the development of Singapore constitutionalism and good governance.

2.2 Of flexibility and fixity – how the EP as a living institution is developed

Søren Kierkegaard stated, "Life can only be understood backwards; but it must be lived forwards." This sentiment reflects the evolution of the EP as a facet of how the Singapore Constitution is developed, as an 'ever evolving hybrid',[12] not by judicial interpretation, but executive determination.[13] This is facilitated by the reality that constitutional amendment is a political and practical possibility,[14] allowing the Government to periodically adopt 'course corrections'. There has been EP-related constitutional litigation[15] and courts through constitutional interpretation have a role in clarifying the scope or content of powers with an eye to "autochthonous constitutional grounds, informed by our national considerations".[16]

Nonetheless, the parliamentary executive has driven changes to the EP regime propelled by three key influences: how the EP powers had worked in practice, disquiet concerning the 2011 Presidential Elections ("PE"), and a desire to positivize and underscore certain philosophical commitments as a type of constitutional civil religion, such as the principle of multiracialism. These changes take place in the context of Singapore's 'flexible' constitution such that they are achieved not only by formal amendments. Conventions and 'soft constitutional law' are also techniques deployed to change or shape the constitutional office and its modus operandi.

2.2.1 Developing a constitutional institution via constitutional amendment

Unlike non-documentary constitutions, written constitutions are often the products of deliberation that articulate detailed procedure and create institutions. As the changes to the Presidency bring into play complex institutional innovations as well as intricate inter-branch processes, formal constitutional amendments that incorporate precise textual provisions have been primarily utilized. For example, the 2008 amendments embodying Singapore's brand of fiscal constitutionalism[17] introduced complex financial rules through Article 142, which, while not stipulating a balanced budget,[18] defined complex terms like 'net investment income' and 'real rate of return'. An amendment first introduced in 2001 applied the principle of inter-generational equity through a rule capping the financial year's spending limit at 50 per cent of the amount ascertained by applying the expected 'long-term real rates of return', with the remaining sum kept in reserve for future generations.

The ruling People's Action Party ("PAP") government can generally amend the Constitution at will, since the PAP easily commands the two-thirds parliamentary supermajority required by Article 5(2) to pass a constitutional amendment bill. Practically speaking, it is as easy to amend most parts of the Constitution as it is to enact legislation through a simple majority.[19] As such, modifications via constitutional amendment have regularly been made to the EP scheme since its adoption in 1991. This culminated with the latest round of 2016 amendments after the convening of a Constitutional Commission to examine specific aspects of the EP scheme.

Reflecting a pragmatic incrementalism, modifications are made in the light of experience. The genesis of the institution itself was born of the conviction that the proposed EP scheme, novel in conception and untested in practice, was fundamentally necessary. Its authors were determined to see it succeed and specially fashioned strong entrenchment provision to accompany the institution, signifying its importance. Article 5(2A) made it harder for an irresponsible government to remove,[20] by requiring a two-thirds majority at a national referendum to amend specific EP-related provision, *inter alia*, unless the EP acting in his discretion 'vetoes' this requirement. In other words, if the EP agreed with the proposed amendment to an entrenched provision, it only needed a two-thirds parliamentary majority to become law. The special quality of constitutions as higher order laws flow "exclusively in the requirement of a super-majority for amendments".[21] Referenda take an issue out of routine politics by bringing the matter directly to the people.

From the outset, the EP regime was more tightly entrenched under Article 5(2A) than other key co-equal institutions like the Parliament and the Judiciary. The official reason was that the latter was well established and harder to remove.[22] The Government had decided in 1991 not to bring Article 5(2A) immediately into force. This was to keep the Constitution flexible and to permit easy refinements during an initial four year grace period to the EP scheme, which was an experimental work-in-progress. This was continually delayed and ministers declared before Parliament that more time was needed before bringing Article 5(2A) into force as the scheme was "more complex than we originally anticipated",[23] with unforeseen implications.

The fate of Article 5(2A) was to be stillborn, excised in 2016 and replaced by new Articles 5A, 5B and 5C. A quarter decade after 1991, the Government considered that it "remains critical" for the EP scheme to be specially entrenched,[24] making the Constitution 'rigid' insofar as a government commanding a two-thirds parliamentary majority could not automatically effect amendments. Notably, it would have been "virtually impossible"[25] to amend the Constitution had Article 5(2A) been brought into force. Similarly, the new Articles 5A, 5B and 5C have not been brought into force. The Government emphasized the need to let the system "evolve over time". They stated that they might consider bringing into force the revised entrenchment framework "after observing how the wide-ranging amendments in this Bill operate in practice."[26]

Nonetheless, the Government has consistently rejected calls[27] to abolish the EP scheme and return to an appointed ceremonial presidency, which is an option the Constitutional Commission noted.[28] The Government's unyielding faith in the need for the institution is reflected in their commitment to adjust rather than abandon the project, which would "leave ourselves naked and defenceless against all the difficulties which the Elected President enables us to avoid."[29] The 2016 amendments introduced a differentiated and complicated three-tier entrenchment approach towards amending EP-related provisions in the form of Articles 5A, 5B and 5C, which involves not only the President, the Government and Parliament, but also a national referendum that is supported by more than half the total number of votes cast, a new role for the Council of Presidential Advisers, and requirements that certain amendment bills minimally required the support of a three-quarters parliamentary majority. A scheme of a potentially rigid but presently flexible constitution is therefore preserved. This evinces the Government's determination not to have its hands tied by a strict deadline and be unable to further amend the ever-evolving hybrid.

2.2.2 Beyond amendments: conventions and soft constitutional law

Although the EP was a product of conscious deliberation and detailed elaboration, it is apparently accepted that new EP-related constitutional conventions or norms of political morality may emerge. For example, the Government will, absent legal obligation, consult the EP regarding any amendments affecting the Presidency.[30] Adherence to such conventions indicates good faith commitments to follow settled political practice.[31]

The EP institution also develops through 'soft constitutional law' ("SCL").[32] While conventions stem from past practice, SCL norms, which are not legislatively promulgated, enjoy some degree of formality beyond mere policy as executive-articulated declaratory or prospective norms embodied in non-binding documents which are accessible to the relevant parties. These hortatory guidelines, infused with the political weight of a strong executive, frame the expectations of how constitutional actors should conduct themselves and may influence judicial interpretation, akin to the impact of directive principles. SCL norms are flexible, as these are not subject to formal processes, but yet possess some degree of stability and even longevity, as norms are able to regulate behaviour.

SCL was deployed to structure Cabinet-EP interactions. This is contained in the 1999 White Paper on the Principles for Determining and Safeguarding the Accumulated Reserves of the Government and the Fifth Schedule Statutory Boards and Government Companies.[33] These were mutually adopted by the President and the Government after the 'confrontational' media exit interview that President Ong convened in 1999, which criticized embarrassing matters such as encounters with uncooperative government officials and difficulty in securing information on national assets.[34] This public washing of dirty linen prompted detailed ministerial rebuttal of these charges before Parliament. The 1999 White Paper contained principles to facilitate the operationalization of the EP as a fiscal guardian. These principles, which were drawn from the "mutual learning experience"[35] of problems President Ong encountered and "open to future evolution", binds future Presidents and Governments unless one party formally notified the other that it no longer wished to abide by its terms. This 'common understanding' of agreed working procedures would exclude subjective understandings of constitutional requirements and minimize occasion for friction. Aside from technical definitions, stipulated accounting methods, stipulating when the President should receive certain reports, the 1999 White Paper articulated the centrality of cultivating a "harmonious working relationship"[36] between the President and Government. This is in contrast to the "acrimony" arising from Ong's press conference. Notably, subsequent Presidents Nathan, Tan and Halimah Yaacob publicly indicated enjoying a "harmonious" working relationship with the Government. This sets the tone for collaborative cooperation, rather than a belligerent watchdog posture.

Clearly, SCL is a product of political negotiation, with experience being the best teacher. It reflects Karl Llewellyn's realist insight of the Constitution as an institution which is "in essence not a document, but a living institution built in first instance around a particular Document"; the working Constitution "is in good part utterly extra-Documentary", located in "a set of ways of living and doing", given that "people do behave in certain patterns". It involves a study of the "interlocking ways and attitudes of different groups and classes in the community".[37] SCL captures some of these attitudes, actions and reactions, drawn from past experiences from which future prescriptions may emerge. An example of how a specific experience shaped a rule was when President Ong wanted to approve a budget he considered would draw down on past reserves and the Government disagreed with this view and the method of accounting applied. Paragraph 2.3 of the 1999 White Paper stipulates that before the Government proposes to carry out certain financial transactions which the President considers is likely to eat into past reserves, the President "will first inform the Government of his opinion without disapproving the transaction" and provide certain information. This allows the Government to avoid this drawdown by transferring the requisite amount from the current to past reserves equal to what the President thought constituted a drawdown.[38]

2.3 Inherent tensions: a framework for analysis

As discussed, there are at least four tensions underlying the EP institution that continue to shape constitutional changes.

First, *whether the powers of the EP are too weak or too strong* as a countervailing accountability mechanism to check certain ministerial decisions; a related idea is whether to moderate the EP's powers by requiring the EP to act in tandem with another body, rather than alone. This dates back to early suggestions, which were recently revived by the Workers' Party in the 2016 parliamentary debates. They proposed that an elected body such as a group of people or Senate would be better suited to the task, rather than a single person office.[39]

Second, *how important the democratic element of being a popularly Elected President* was to its institutional legitimacy, as opposed to selecting a qualified expert. Some consider the stringent, technocratic pre-selection criteria in Article 19 as being undemocratic. This is exacerbated by the filtering function of the non-elected Presidential Elections Committee ("PEC") which makes non-justiciable decisions[40] (contrary to the rule of law) on who would receive a certificate of eligibility ("COE") and who are not legally obliged to give reasons to applicants.[41] This was criticized as undermining the idea of political equality underlying rights of voting and candidature,[42] central to the theories of democratic legitimacy. An insufficient pool of qualified candidates led to walkovers in 1999, 2005 and 2016, eliciting comments that the President was selected[43] rather than elected. This prompted Government statements, that even if a single eligible candidate was declared elected by default under Section 15(1) of the Presidential Elections Act (Cap. 240A), this would still be legitimate.

It was more important to have a qualified President than presidential elections, the people have been told,[44] to broad disquiet.[45] While the law provides for uncontested elections, to point to this legalism can be alienating, given the felt importance of voting to the citizen as a facet of political participation; it denies the visceral in favour of the cerebral. Elections, as a baptism of fire, have a legitimizing effect; an unelected Elected President may face doubts about his legitimacy from the public at large.[46] If uncontested elections were to become the norm, this would bode ill for the institution, particularly since the 2016 White Paper underscores the importance of a "democratically elected" President as "the most workable and effective solution" such that whether a budget or transaction is vetoed, overridden or agreed with, "it is always an elected institution (President, Government or Parliament) that represents Singaporeans" in making importance decisions concerning national reserves or public service appointments.[47] An Elected President with a "direct mandate" from the People alone will be "seen as legitimately" disagreeing with the elected Government in specific areas.[48]

Notably, the criticism levied against the 2011 Presidential Elections (where COEs were awarded) was not that of a non-election democratic deficit; rather, the surfeit of candidates elicited concerns the PEC had applied pre-qualification criteria too laxly.[49] The 2016 constitutional amendments 'refreshed' these criteria to take into account the changed financial environment, reaffirming the stringent qualifications for the EP that exceeded what parliamentary candidates (from which cabinet, government is formed) must satisfy.[50] The triumph of technocracy over the egalitarian ethos of democracy is evident and has been a consistent feature of the EP regime.

Third, there is a tension between the historical '*ceremonial*' *functions* of the EP as a symbol of unity and the EP's *constitutional functions* as a check or brake on specific cabinet powers, primarily relating to financial policies drawing on past reserves.[51] This flows from fusing these two functions into one office. Accordingly, generating a kind of institutional cognitive dissonance where a popularly Elected President is expected to be "above politics and a symbol of unity while acting simultaneously as check against a democratically elected government", which may be politically divisive.[52]

Where a plurality of competing purposes is built into an institution, the political temper and exigencies of the time will influence which will be accented and which downplayed. In the EP regime's salad days, the emphasis was on the need to constrain a powerful parliamentary executive. This is to correct the perceived deficiencies of a one-man–one-vote system which could, through "freak elections",[53] produce a fiscally irresponsible government who, yielding to populist pressures, would deplete the hard-won national reserves in underwriting social programmes or through imprudent policies. More recently, government rhetoric has focused on the President's traditional, ceremonial roles such as the ability to be the nation's first diplomat and "carry the flag of Singapore high in the international arena"[54] or to promote charity.[55] The pendulum swings and indeed the Government underscored during the 2016 amendments that the EP's symbolic role was "just as important as his custodial role".[56]

A fourth tension emerging recently is that of *multiracialism and meritocracy*, popularly perceived as a tussle between equality and preferential minority group treatment. The Singapore Constitution contains no special rights though Article 152 obliges the Government to protect the interests of racial and religious minorities and to promote the special interests of Malays with indigenous status. This tension ripened when the Government took the "unpopular decision"[57] to amend the Constitution to introduce 'reserved elections' in 2016, to promote multiracialism by ensuring minorities could become President.[58] A presidential election would be reserved for a particular racial group if Singapore has not had a President from that group for five continuous terms (30 years). This recommendation by the 2016 Constitutional Commission sought not to be "overly prescriptive",[59] operating as a failsafe that would not be triggered if minorities were elected to the office in open elections, which is a form of restrained interventionism.

A Westminster Head of State always embodied a "a symbol of national unity and an expression of our national identity".[60] The Queen of England additionally is an Anglican Church Head and *fidei defensor*. On the other hand, Singapore is a Republic and has a non-confessional constitution with no official religion; its national identity is rooted in multiracialism, a fundamental social tenet and feature of its constitutional 'civil religion'. PM Lee stated that having multiracial presidents "is an important symbol of what Singapore stands for, and a declaration of what we aspire to be".[61] Prior to 1991, Parliament took care, as an unwritten convention and not a legal rule, to rotate the Presidency among the different races. The 2016 amendments constitutionalized this convention, not to regulate power, but to shape mindsets and attitudes. Linkages were drawn between this amendment and earlier constitutional experiments like the Group Representation Constituency ("GRC") that seeks to institutionalize multiracial politics by requiring political parties to field multi-member teams with a stipulated minority member.[62] This puts the focus on a multiracial team rather than an ethnic candidate, which a regime based on separate race-based rolls or reserved quotas would do, signalling difference rather than communality. However, vexed questions of defining ethnicity arises; the question of whether the current President Halimah Yacob was 'Malay' (as she had an Indian father) was bandied about before the 2017 Presidential Elections which she won by default.[63] Tensions arise where ethnic-based criteria for contesting reserved elections clash with other constitutional values. The Singapore Constitution does not stipulate, as Article 160 of the Malaysian Constitution does, that a "Malay" is a "person who professes the religion of Islam, habitually speaks the Malay language, [and] conforms to Malay custom." Article 19B(6) borrows the same Article 39 formulation used for GRCs which describes a person belonging to the Malay community as "any person, *whether of the Malay race or otherwise*, who considers himself to be a member of the Malay community and who is generally accepted as a member of the Malay community by that community."[64] While an Indian candidate must be "any person of Indian origin", it appears that 'Malay' in this context is not a racial/biological category but an ethno-cultural term, determined by subjective self-identification and objective community acceptance. This is a pragmatic accommodation of realities that the vast majority of Malays are Muslims,[65] that ethnicity and religious affiliation is conflated insofar as the Malay community will not accept as a Malay a person who was non-Muslim.[66] This view departs in spirit from religious freedom which includes the freedom to choose a religious or non-religious belief system. This pits the ethos behind Article 15 and Article 19B against each other in terms of voluntarist and imputed religious identities. Nonetheless, with economic and human development, it is interesting that the terse Singapore Constitution, typically scant of normative values, is now expected to play a more overt integrative function[67] by promoting intangible values to help form a collective personhood united by shared values. This is a form of non-liberal constitutional patriotism mediated through institutions that shape not just power arrangements, but also political culture.

2.4 Three areas of development: fire alarm, fool filter and failsafe

Having considered the genesis of the various tensions – the modification with the design of the EP over time through formal amendment, conventions and soft constitutional rules – this section turns to consider how these tensions could be mitigated over time.

2.4.1 Fiscal guardianship over past reserves

2.4.1.1 Downsizing the custodial role over public finances – muting the fire alarm?

The EP's muscularity as a fiscal guardian reflects the tension between needing an effective accountability mechanism and the desire to preserve effective governance; this tension operates within a developmentalist state where an instrumentalist rule of law is deployed to secure the political stability needed to facilitate economic development and foreign investment. The creation of the EP was in part to counter the strong state with its efficient and perhaps too effective government; the EP could not stop "fools from being parted with their money" but would serve as a "fire alarm … there's a piece of glass there and knowingly you have put your first through the glass…"[68]

It is apparent from the EP's institutional history that it was not meant to be a second centre of political power, having only reactive "non-executive custodial functions".[69] Unlike executive presidents, the EP would be the second key to a "two-key safeguard mechanism"; the Cabinet held the 'first key' while the EP could concur with or object to a relevant Cabinet decision,[70] serving as "a goal-keeper together with a team of defenders",[71] that is, the Council of Presidential Advisers ("CPA") established under Part VA. Rather than the popular view that the EP is pitted against the PM, the unelected CPA plays a moderating role with respect to the EP who, after 2016, is under a duty to consult the CPA over *all* relevant financial and public appointment decisions: Article 37IA.[72]

It is important to appreciate the scope of the EP's custodial role with particular reference to withholding his assent to budgets and transactions. This is only triggered where 'past reserves' (not accumulated by the sitting government) are implicated; the EP has no say over unwise or financially imprudent decisions drawing on 'current reserves'. Indeed, the buck does not stop with the EP where he exercises his 'veto' over a financial transaction, budget or key public service appointment. Rather, Article 37IF provides that a two-thirds parliamentary resolution overrules the EP's decision over specified matters, when this was contrary to the CPA's recommendation. This subjects the EP as fiscal guardian to checks itself in the form of Parliament as a legislative and deliberative body; it can still, through the public nature of the 'veto' power, sound an alarm, bringing to bear such pressure that public scrutiny exerts on political actors within a democratic polity.

The EP's 'fire alarm' role has been diminished through subsequent constitutional amendments removing the EP's power to concur or withhold assent from transactions involving "past reserves". This is based on reasons of national security or the apparent need to facilitate financial transfers between the Government, statutory boards and Government companies. Article 151A was amended in 1994 to truncate the scope of the presidential veto which no longer applies to "defence spending and measures", as presidential disagreement was considered too great a security risk in this sensitive area which was said to fall within the Cabinet's responsibility. The Government admitted the "significant deviation"[73] from the two-key principle and incorporated replacement safeguards in requiring the Cabinet to obtain certification from two unelected civil servants, the Defence Ministry's Permanent Secretary and Defence Force Chief, that the measures were necessary. Fears were expressed that these two actors could be prey to inducement, unlike the EP as the highest office in the land.[74] Nonetheless, the presidential veto with respect to annual defence budgets drawing down on past reserves remains in place.

Other amendments (in 1994, 2002 and 2004) have scaled back the EP's powers of financial oversight; previously, the EP had a role in relation to transferring reserves between the Government, fifth schedule statutory boards and government companies ("SBGC"). For example, Article 148I provides that the transfer of government reserves to a fifth schedule SBGC is not to be taken into account in determining whether past reserves have been or are likely to have been drawn on. This is provided that the transferee company's board of directors or transferee statutory board adopted resolutions that the transferred reserves be added to their past reserves. Effectively, the transferred past reserves will not be spent, being designated as part of the transferee entity's past reserves. Though unstated, the understanding was, for example, that the 2004 amendments facilitating transferring, sans presidential oversight, government past reserves to government companies like Temasek Holdings would be a capital injection fuelling aggressive investment strategies; this would allow the Government to respond swiftly to "changing economic or business conditions" and opportunities in new growth areas.[75] Government parliamentarians reportedly claimed the two-key principle was not compromised, since the SBGC internal controls remained, urging that the people should have "an implicit trust and confidence" in the government management of reserves.[76] This is contrary to the EP rationale as an external mechanism of accountability, reflecting a swing of the pendulum along the 'too powerful–too weak' axis in terms of presidential powers.

2.4.1.2 Expanding the role of the CPA: moderating the fire alarm (or checking the checker)?

A chief objective of the 2016 amendments was to expand the composition, role and powers of the CPA in relation to the EP's custodial powers, to give its views "more weight"[77] and to include a new role over EP-related constitutional amendments. Just as PM Lee described the EP as an important "long term stabiliser" to the political system,[78] so the CPA as an independent, non-elective advisory body of eight experts variously chosen by the President, Prime Minister and Chief Justice in a staggered fashion[79] was described as providing a "stabilising effect"[80] on the EP. The logic was to ensure the EP's important custodial functions did not solely depend "on the judgement of a single person acting alone".[81] Rather than working solo, having the EP work in tandem with a body of appointed experts or wise elders was the preferred choice over having something akin to an elected senate or Upper House as a corporate fiscal guardian with the moral legitimacy to disagree with the Cabinet.[82]

Article 37I provides that the CPA is to advise the EP and make recommendations on referred matters; Article 37IA places a general duty on the EP to consult the CPA, though this does not apply to traditional discretionary powers such as appointing the PM. This is akin to the moderating influence of the 'decision by committee' model characteristic of Cabinet government. The CPA, which meets in private,[83] plays a role which affects the strength of the EP's veto; where the EP agrees with Cabinet, the CPA's views lack "any legal weight".[84] If the EP's veto has the support of a simple majority[85] of the CPA, which is obliged under Article 37ID to state "the number of votes for and against the recommendation," this is dispositive, although the Constitutional Commission considered this as a "somewhat blunt mechanism" by which a simple majority could "inoculate a Presidential veto from a Parliamentary override".[86]

If the transaction is a supply bill, provision is made for the past year's budget to apply. The EP must provide his reasons and the CPA's recommendation to both the Prime Minister and Speaker for such bills under Article 37IE(b); given the "considerable public signature"[87] of a presidential veto, this process brings to bear the check of publicity, providing citizens with the basis for evaluating their governors. If the EP's non-assent relates to a proposed Article 22B(7) or Article 22(D)(6) transaction, his reasons and the CPA's recommendations are only sent to the Prime Minister under Article 37IE(2)(a). If the EP's decision is contrary to the CPA's recommendation, Article 37IF provides that the Parliament can, by a two-thirds parliamentary majority resolution, overrule the President,[88] who is then deemed to have assented to or not disapproved that transaction. Although one could not assume that this will always be the case, if the matter goes before the current Parliament, the Government of the day will have its way.

The Government rejected the Constitutional Commission's proposal to enhance transparency by requiring the breakdown and publicity of individual CPA member votes and calibrating the size of the parliamentary majority needed for the override, to "more closely reflect the degree of support"[89] the EP has from the CPA. The EP's inability to secure CPA majority support suggests that "his veto may not be based on sufficiently persuasive grounds"[90] such that a simple parliamentary majority should suffice to trigger the override. The Government could proceed with its plans, paying the political cost of public parliamentary debate. Where the CPA was split but the Chair exercised his casting vote in the EP's favour, a two-thirds parliamentary majority would be required. The Government feared this would detract from the CPA's collective judgement, undermining its stature by politicizing how individual CPA members voted.[91]

CPA members as appointed experts or honourable statesmen[92] are expected to act independent of their appointing power, be it the EP, the Prime Minister or the Chief Justice; the staggered terms[93] were thought to "sufficiently secure" this independence.[94] The EP personally appoints three of the eight CPA members, but a "careful balance"[95] has been built into the CPA's composition as "all 3 of the EP's men" need the support of another CPA member to win the day.

The CPA's role as "counterbalance"[96] was extended to apply to the new entrenchment mechanisms under Articles 5A, 5B and 5C. Previously, the CPA had no impact on proposals to amend EP-related constitutional provisions under the pre-2016 Article 5(2A) and 5(A) that involved the EP, the Parliament, and the People through referendum. As the entrenched EP-related provisions concerned areas that could potentially give rise to "sharp and intractable" disagreement between the Government and the President,[97] it was thought that this could be moderated by giving "sufficient weight"[98] to the CPA's collective advice to prevent gridlock and promote systemic stability. The unelected CPA thus is integral to the checks and balances scheme, not in making a decision or being a third centre of power, but in determining the final decision maker over specific matters. This reflects not a trust in an honourable Confucian ruler, but an appreciation of the Madisonian wisdom in needing "auxiliary precautions"[99] beyond bare majoritarian democracy; this is played by the CPA and the EP within a constitutional order where an elected Parliament, or, more precisely, the parliamentary executive is the primary decision maker.

2.4.1.3 Legal and political accountability: defining the roles of constitutional actors

Not all constitutional amendments have truncated presidential powers. Some have committed specific functions to the EP and excluded the involvement of other political and legal actors. For example, Parliament has no role in determining what the "long-term real rates of return" ("LTRRR") to be earned from "relevant assets" under Article 142 is, which is needed to calculate spending limits every financial year. Introduced in 2008, this amendment was designed to make more income available for welfare services.

The EP must concur with the Finance Minister's assessment on what the LTRRR is, which requires a high level of financial literacy that neither the EP nor the CPA members may necessarily possess. The EP and the CPA receive the "full basis" for the Finance Minister's assessment, possessing sufficient market information to make "a well-reasoned assessment"[100] as generalists with related experience. Parliament is kept out of this process, presumably to block out populist pressures, reflecting a reliance on the intra-executive check which is based more on professional than political judgement. In the event of disagreement, the historical rate of return over the past 20 years would be utilized as a "neutral and pragmatic" basis.[101]

Financial decisions are complex and polycentric in nature, and often considered to be ill-suited to judicial review as they concern matters of wisdom rather than legality. This probably explains the thinking behind making the Finance Minister's certification under Article 142(3) of the amount of net investment income of that financial year which is deemed part of the Government's past reserves "final and conclusive evidence". This is presumed to be non-justiciable, a matter for political judgement and accountability. However, the Constitution itself provides for legal checks such as establishing a constitutional tribunal in 1995 under Article 100. It may give advisory opinions on questions affecting constitutional provisions, such as whether a constitutional amendment bill curtails certain presidential powers under Article 5C. Resorting to a legal or quasi-legal forum to resolve such questions, treating them impersonally as questions of law, depoliticizes the subject and removes it from the emotional realm of the political. The shift to the EP as an institutional check marks a shift towards constitutional supremacy and constrained parliamentarianism, though the regime itself deploys a mix of legal and political checks to moderate the exercise of public power.

2.4.2 Upgrading qualifications and regulating elections: filtering fools, depoliticization and the dignity of the office

To imbue the Presidency with democratic legitimacy, the fundamental importance of having a popularly *elected* President was considered integral to the original design. However, insofar as democracy entails a universal franchise and broad rights of candidatures, this was at tension with countervailing non-democratic forces. At the outset, this was located in the form of elitist and stringent rather than egalitarian pre-selection criteria, which an appointed Presidential Elections Committee ("PEC") established under Article 18 had to find satisfied. This is in addition to ascertaining that a candidate was "a person of integrity, good character and reputation",[102] a subjective assessment immune from suit in the absence of malice.[103] Decisions to award certificates of eligibility, which can easily become politically controversial, are non-justiciable.[104]

Proposals for direct popular elections have been consistently rejected, and the democratic imperative has given way to elitist pulls in favour of having a suitably qualified EP, reflecting a form of rule by the learned, virtuous elite. The justification for this lies in the "considerable" power wielded by the EP as a "single individual" and the "complex issues" of a "highly technical nature"[105] which the EP would face, making it "only sensible" that presidential candidates have a record which suggested they possessed "the technical competence and expertise" to discharge the role.[106] The EP would need "a grasp of macro-economic concerns" to understand the budgets of SBGCs, have the wisdom in approving public service appointments, and the ability to deal with the "contrary pulls and pressures"[107] in relation to the security and public order issues related to his powers under the Internal Security Act and Maintenance of Religious Harmony Act. Experience was needed, given that the EP's decision in relation to reserves potentially had "an immense impact and significance on national interests".[108]

In addition, the Constitutional Commission and Government made short shrift of arguments that the qualifications for an EP should be the same for Parliamentarians from whom a Prime Minister is chosen,[109] not more stringent. This is because the process for selecting a PM differed from that of electing an EP as the former would have passed "many stringent tests of leadership",[110] being chosen by and possessing the confidence of his political party that controlled the majority of seats in Parliament. As such, what Parliamentarians know about Prime Ministerial candidates was not comparable to what the average voter would know about presidential candidates from publicly available sources.[111]

The importance of "suitably rigorous" eligibility criteria suited to the "scale and magnitude"[112] of the EP's responsibilities was underscored in 2016 as necessary if the EP were to "continue to function in a meaningful way",[113] enhancing the prospect that only candidates with the "right experience and expertise"[114] should seek election. No changes were made in the round of 2016 amendments to the list of public offices in Article 19(3)(a) such as Ministers, Chief Justices, Speakers and Accountant-Generals, that a candidate must have held for at least three years to satisfy the qualification criteria.[115] Most of the amendments related to expanding the composition and functions of the PEC[116] and 'refreshing' the criteria private-sector presidential candidates must satisfy to reflect the changed economic landscape and expanded size of Singapore reserves such that "the weight of the job has increased".[117]

New performance indicators were introduced relating to the private-sector candidate's position in a company, currency of experience, and the size and complexity of the company itself. Candidates should have the confidence stemming from "familiarity with making decisions involving large sums of money".[118] Thus, a candidate must have served as "chief executive" of a company with a minimum $500 million shareholders' equity for that person's most recent three-year period of service in that position.[119] Otherwise, the PEC has the discretion in ascertaining whether a person who held an office in a private-sector organization has the experience and ability "comparable" to a chief executive, having regard to the office held, nature of the organization, and "any other factors it sees fit to consider".[120] The heightened criteria would not diminish the pool of candidates because more companies would meet the threshold in 2016 than in 1993 when the initial threshold was having $100 million paid-up capital.[121]

The stringent eligibility criteria have been criticized for being too onerous, resulting in only a single COE being granted to aspirant presidential candidates in two of five presidential cycles in 1993 and 2017. The focus on technocratic rather than democratic considerations has disaffected voters[122] denied the dignity of expressing their choice, despite the default provisions for walkovers. The 2017 presidential non-elections was particularly galling after the Government rejected proposals made in 2016 to revert to an appointed President, insisting on retaining a popularly Elected President with a direct mandate.[123] Two other private-sector candidates identifying as Malay,[124] who received certificates confirming membership in the Malay community[125] despite publicly expressed doubts about their ethnicity, were denied COEs, presumably because Mr Salleh Marican and Mr Farid Khan's respective companies, Second Chance ($250 million) and Bourbon Offshore Area ($400 m)[126], did not meet the minimum $500 million shareholder equity threshold. This denotes a strict application of the criteria such that top Malay businessmen did not meet the bar. Nonetheless, Mr Marican's view that the thinking process and evaluation whether for a company worth $250 million or $500 million shareholders' equity "is the same"[127] bears force, particularly since a company CEO will have more financial expertise than certain stipulated public office, such as that of Speaker of the House, the former public office held by President Halimah Yacob who alone received a COE.[128] Indeed, the Constitutional Commission recognized that not all public-sector office holders would have "helmed agencies with large budgets", while all private-sector candidates would have this experience; nonetheless, "no single office" was likely to endow its holder with "all the attributes necessary for him to discharge all the Presidential functions",[129] with public-sector officials bringing to the table the unique skills of "dealing with complex matters having a wide-reaching public dimension"[130] and handling the "contrary pulls and pressures of government decision-making",[131] which private-sector candidates are unlikely to be exposed to.[132] Nonetheless, there is some muting of the argument that candidates need to possess "actual experience in handling the financial affairs of a large entity"[133] in justifying which public offices make the "tightly drawn list"[134] for automatic qualification. This sits uneasily with the view that it is unsatisfactory for the EP to merely rely on the CPA's expertise, as experience in a qualifying office better places an EP to question and evaluate the reasoning of the CPA.[135]

The stringent eligibility criteria, identifying specific public and private-sector offices which serve as a proxy for assumed competence, filter out fools or the unqualified; while this has led to walkovers and a 'selected presidency' where the sole-qualified candidate assumes the office sans contest, the 2011 Presidential Elections may be considered anomalous and, indeed, the experiential driver for corrective changes adopted in 2016. Four COEs were issued, raising concerns that the PEC were too lax in applying the criteria as "candidates who were non-executive chairmen of companies or portfolio managers with no strong solid executive experience..."[136] received COEs. After the divisive 2011 elections, where certain candidates, betraying their lack of constitutional literacy, announced programmes or made promises[137] in the tone of opposition politicians beyond the remit of the EP's constitutional role. Even Government MPs called for a return to an appointed President in the mode of a "senior statesmen" able to heal and unite the country.[138]

Nonetheless, the Government preferred to maintain and refine the EP, arguing that the stringent eligibility criteria could help depoliticize the contests as candidates would not attack each other on grounds of character and qualifications, since all candidates would have passed the PEC's vetting in receiving a COE.[139] To mediate the tension between the historic/unifying and constitutional/contentious functions of the EP, the Government endorsed the Constitutional Commission's vision of presidential elections as being qualitatively different from General Elections. Accordingly, it set about to manage this through rules governing election campaigns[140] to preserve "the dignity" associated with the Presidency, allowing the EP to function as symbol of national unity, above tribal politics, personifying the People.

As the EP has no role in "formulating or initiating national policies" and "no policy agenda to advance", there was no need for a "vigorous contest of ideas" akin to what takes place during parliamentary elections.[141] The Constitutional Commission proposed excluding acts which could "inflame emotions, cause divisiveness or encourage invective",[142] doubted whether rallies were necessary or helpful[143] and urged that candidates campaign "with rectitude and dignity as befits the office"[144] and its unifying role. A new form was made available during the 2017 elections whereby candidates could voluntarily undertake to conduct their campaigns in such a "dignified" manner. Additionally, Section 9 of the Presidential Elections Act was amended to require candidates to make statutory declarations stating their awareness of the EP's constitutional role and limits, indicating that they would not make promises or statements exceeding this role.[145] The EP should be provided platforms to reach out to voters "at a national level" such as increased television airtime, while rallies were discouraged, given their tendency to stir emotions and be divisive.[146]

Thus, the depoliticizing intent of rules governing elections was meant to mitigate tensions between the President's historical and custodial functions; the Government additionally noted that all previous EPs had been able to discharge "these two roles with distinction". Future candidates should aspire to do likewise, "developing rapport with Singaporeans and representing our nation with dignity" while demonstrating "technical competence and expertise" as fiscal custodian.[147]

2.4.3 Failsafe: multiracialism and meritocracy

The final tension relates to a putative tension between the fundamental social value of meritocracy and implicit constitutional norm of multiracialism, as embodied in the GRC scheme and the new Article 19B reserved elections mechanism ("REM").[148] The latter mechanism in seeking to safeguard the EP as the personification of the State and symbol of a multiracial rather than race-based community raised various concerns. This involves the thorny issue of identifying 'race'[149] and how its operation limits democratic choice under certain conditions when candidature is restricted to a specified ethnic community. Its rationale to ensure perceived and actual access to the highest office of the land by all ethnic communities was predicated on the assumption that ethnic minorities, merit aside, would find it harder to be voted EP as "racial factors" still swayed voting choices in Singapore which was not a "post-racial" society.[150] This amendment was designed to correct the under-emphasis regarding the historical and symbolic role of the Presidency,[151] reflecting a form of philosophical praxis in constitutionalizing the ideal of multiracialism, to ensure that directly Elected Presidents will, "over time continue to collectively embody the multi-racialism that symbolizes us as a people and as a country".[152]

Characterized by some as a form of positive discrimination on racial grounds, the REM has been criticized as giving rise to tokenism, contrary to meritocracy. An ethnic Malay lawyer considered that with the REM, "meritocracy has been selectively disapplied", perpetuating the stereotype that Malays required "affirmative action" as they were unable to succeed on their own footing.[153]

The Constitutional Commission affirmed that the eligibility criteria "should not be manipulated" to artificially increase or reduce the pool of potential candidates or achieve other collateral purposes.[154] The Government insisted that "multi-racial representation can be achieved while ensuring that meritocracy is not compromised".[155] Accordingly, guarding against inferior candidates by refusing to compromise and lower standards for any community and subjecting candidates from all ethnic groups to the same eligibility criteria, which serves as a proxy for technical competence and experience. The REM would strike an "appropriate balance"[156] between maintaining the long-term goal of multiracialism while ensuring minority representation in the Presidency en route towards the ideal. It also "carefully balances" "the need for multi-racialism with our meritocratic ideals".[157] The 30-years hiatus model was considered not "too invasive or prescriptive" and the REM could have a "natural sunset"[158] and fade into desuetude eventually.

While an acknowledged imperfect solution, the REM addressed "present realities"[159] as a failsafe if minorities are not elected in open elections, while encouraging the aspiration towards a race-blind society, reflecting a type of principled pragmatism. Requiring the operation of the same 'competence' oriented eligibility criteria in all elections would, in the Government's view, negate any perceptions of tokenism,[160] resolving the tension between multiracialism and meritocracy by increasing the likelihood of competent candidates possessing a baseline of skills and experiences who met the constitutional eligibility criteria; further, the multiracial approach rather than minority quota approach was of significant symbolic importance in underscoring the importance of ensuring "all races", including the dominant Chinese community, are represented in the Presidency. This serves the constitutional 'civil religion' which informs a "shared Singaporean identity",[161] whose chief tenets include that of racial and religious harmony which services the pledge to build a democratic nation, "regardless of race, language or religion".

In a terse constitution not given to the express declaration of ideals, the debates surrounding the EP and REM reflect a continuing shift from the material towards intangibles; the veneration of technocratic rationality will not suffice to foster citizen solidarity in the collective enterprise of nationhood. In an age where Islamic extremism has given rise to concerns over intolerance and government fears that ethnic communities are not mixing, having a tudung-clad 'double minority' female[162] and Muslim President fosters a sense of non-exclusion of the Malay community and may promote social trust. The return to highlighting the President's symbolic, unifying role is meant to buttress political stability; rules to dissuade presidential candidates from engaging in contentious politicking allows the Elected President to be that symbol which 'transcends' the petty and political, which helps forge a national identity and sense of a larger purpose beyond our immediate concerns. To speak of the President in terms of personifying the nation is to invoke a sense of myth and mystery, of continuity associated with what Bagehot termed the "dignified" part of the unwritten English Constitution, the apolitical monarchy, which held the respect of all as a symbol of unity and collective personhood. It foregrounds the integrative function of constitutionalism, which may be considered "the condition for unity and collective action in politics that do not endeavor to eliminate forcibly the plurality of opinions and interests existing within them."[163] This facilitates the process of developing a distinct collective identity, of building "a radically different society in Singapore" compared to other countries where one ethnic group is dominant, as the goal was to be "multi-racial, equal and harmonious".[164]

With the President declared the "key symbol of our multi-racial nation"[165] and with constitutional amendments to promote this, constitutional discourse increasingly embraces not only power arrangements, bureaucratic rationality, and effective governance but also engages values, symbols and identity, the "legal emotions" all law has.[166] In practical and pragmatic Singapore, this may signal a coming of age, although of a peculiarly Singaporean cast, extolling multiracialism, technocratic competence and fiscal conservatism. Idealistic aspiration is married with sober realism.

2.5 Concluding observations: the EP and Singapore constitutionalism

The Singapore Constitution is not a static fossil or revered icon; it is a "living document"[167] which the Government proactively and pre-emptively develops;[168] commanding 83 of 89 parliamentary seats after the 2015 General Elections, its ability to amend EP-related constitutional provisions is a foregone conclusion. An autochthonous creation, the Elected Presidency embodies a set of "novel arrangements without obvious parallel anywhere",[169] designed to address "particular imperatives and vulnerabilities".[170] Yet, specific practices related to the classic Westminster parliamentary system continue to be invoked, such as the continuing and co-equally important ceremonial functions of the Head of State or the workability of the first past the post system as the basis for presidential elections, dismissing suggestions for a 'run-off' system.[171]

In not bringing into force constitutional provisions entrenching the EP regime, the Government in its awareness that the regime "is not a perfect system" adopts an ethos of 'what works' incremental pragmatism[172] towards institution-building. The necessity of the EP institution as a 'second key' over specific matters is not doubted by its authors, reflecting its high standing in the constitutional pantheon; it has for instance been lauded as having the effect of making opposition parties "quite cautious with their spending proposals even during General Elections".[173] The desire to protect the EP scheme from easy removal and amendment is at odds with the desire to keep fine-tuning and adjusting this "important and complex"[174] institution which has operated for 25 years, in the light of experience, trial and error,[175] rather than abstract theory. It is considered an institution which is "very difficult to get right, because the balance is a delicate one",[176] with competing values in tension, in seeking a *via media* between gridlock and a too-powerful 'first key', between "a decisive Executive and having adequate stabilisers."[177] This attitude resonates with Llewellyn's observation that "A constitution begins an experiment; a successful constitution is one that works."[178]

In the latest and probably not last iteration of amendments, a primary concern was to shift the focus back to the historical role of the Presidency where emphasis had been accorded to its custodial functions, to vindicate its "concurrent role as a symbol of national unity".[179] Nonetheless, as an imperfect institution to be continuously improved, it is not "cast-iron and fool-proof" and even with "good people in politics" and "sound institutions", things can go wrong, necessitating reliance on a united citizenry and constructive politics for nation-building to continue to be successful.[180] What is clear is that the Government refuses to return to the status quo ante of a supreme Parliament in the sense of an insufficiently constrained government able to act at will without check.

In terms of the EP's institutional development, the past was imperfect, an indigenous experiment that could go wrong, but could be corrected by constitutional amendment; the future is tense, as it remains uncertain regarding how the refined system will work after the 2016 amendments. Like Article 5(2A), the current Articles 5A, 5B and 5C which regulate the amendment of EP-related provisions are not in force as of 2018, preserving to the Government a relatively free hand to continue developing the institution. The hybrid remains ever evolving.

Notes

1 Constitutional Commission, *Report of the Constitutional Commission 2016* (2016) (hereinafter referred to as "CCR"), para. 7.28.

2 Lee Kuan Yew, "1984 National Day Rally" (National Archives of Singapore, Singapore, 19 December 1984) www.nas.gov.sg/archivesonline/data/pdfdoc/lky19841219.pdf (accessed 22 August 2018).

3 Lord Hailsham popularized the term in a 1976 Richard Dimbleby lecture (*The Listener*:

496–500, 21 October 1976) which refers to the Government's dominance of Parliament. The People's Action Party has been in power since independence and won 83 out of the 89 elective seats in the 2015 General Elections.

4 Lee Kuan Yew, "1984 National Day Rally" (National Archives of Singapore, Singapore, 19 December 1984) www.nas.gov.sg/archivesonline/data/pdfdoc/lky19841219.pdf (accessed 22 August 2018).

5 Prime Minister's Office, *White Paper on the Review of Specific Aspects of the Elected Presidency* (2016) (hereinafter referred to as "2016 White Paper"), paras 122(a) and 124(d).

6 Donald S. Lutz, "Thinking about constitutionalism at the start of the Twenty-First Century" (2000) 30(4) *Publius* 115–35, 129.

7 Drawing down of past reserves, appointment of key public offices, anti-corruption, Maintenance of Religious Harmony Act (hereinafter referred to as "MRHA"), and Internal Security Act (hereinafter referred to as "ISA") powers (hereinafter collectively referred to as "EP's decision-making").

8 See Dieter Grimm, *Constitutionalism: Past, Present and Future* (Oxford: Oxford University Press, 2016).

9 Exceptionally, see Articles 25 and 26 of the Singapore Constitution.

10 Judith N. Shklar, *Political Thought and Political Thinkers*, Stanley Hoffmann (ed.) (Chicago, IL: University of Chicago Press, 1998), 3.

11 Dieter Grimm, "Integration by Constitution" (2005) 3(2)(3) *I·CON* 193–208.

12 V.K. Rajah, "Judicial Review – Politics, Policy and the Separation of Powers" (SMU Lecture, 24 March 2016), para. 23.

13 2016 White Paper (n. 5), para. 131.

14 *Lim Meng Suang* v. *Attorney-General* [2015] 1 SLR 26 [92].

15 *Constitutional Reference No 1 of 1995* [1995] 1 SLR(R) 803; *Ravi s/o Madasamy* v. *Attorney-General* [2017] 5 SLR 489; *Tan Cheng Bock* v. *Attorney-General* [2017] 2 SLR 850.

16 *Comptroller of Income Tax* v. *ARW and another (Attorney-General, intervener)* [2017] SGHC 180 [35].

17 Yvonne Lee, "Under lock and key: the evolving role of the Elected President as a fiscal guardian" (2007) *Singapore Journal of Legal Studies* 290–322.

18 For example, Gonzalo Puig, "Fiscal Constitutionalism and fiscal culture: a comparative study of the balanced-budget rule in the Spanish constitution and the Hong Kong basic law" (2013) 43 *Hong Kong Law Journal* 5–53.

19 This excludes those parts of a constitution which requires a two-thirds vote at a national referendum: Arts 6–8.

20 DPM Teo Chee Hean, "Second Reading, Constitution of the Republic of Singapore (Amendment) Bill" (*Prime Minister's Office Singapore*, 7 November 2016) www.pmo.gov.sg/newsroom/speech-dpm-teo-chee-hean-2nd-reading-constitutional-republic-singapore-amendment-bill (accessed 31 August 2018) (hereinafter referred to as "DPM Teo"), at [192(a)].

21 Dieter Grimm, "Types of Constitutions", in *The Oxford Handbook of Comparative Constitutional Law*, Michel Rosenfeld and András Sajó (eds) (Oxford: Oxford University Press, 2012), 110 (hereinafter referred to as "Dieter Grimm, 'Types of Constitutions'").

22 DPM Teo (n. 20), [192(b)].

23 DPM Lee Hsien Loong, *Singapore Parliamentary Debates: Official Record*, 25 August 1994, vol. 63, col. 421.

24 DPM Teo (n. 20), [192].

25 CCR (n. 1), para. 7.29.

26 DPM Teo (n. 20), [227]; 2016 White Paper (n. 5), para. 143 ("best to let some time past, see how the institution works over time, before entrenchment").

27 Rachel Au-Yong, "Parliament: MP Denise Phua calls to scrap Elected Presi-

dency", *Straits Times* (Singapore, 27 May 2014) www.straitstimes.com/singapore/parliament-mp-denise-phua-calls-to-scrap-elected-presidency (accessed 5 July 2018).

28 CCR (n. 1), paras 7.46–7.53.

29 PM Lee Hsien Loong, *Singapore Parliamentary Debates: Official Record*, 27 January 2016, vol. 94 ("Debate on President's address").

30 S. Jayakumar, *Singapore Parliamentary Debates: Official Record*, 12 February 2007, vol. 82, col. 1239: Whether the Article [5(2A)] is entrenched or not, the Government has *made it a practice to always seek the President's views* whenever it intends to move constitutional amendments that affect the relevant provisions; K. Shanmugam, *Singapore Parliamentary Debates: Official Record*, 4 November 2014, vol. 92: We *consulted the President* on the appointment of International Judges and Senior Judges [and PCMR composition]. The President *is supportive* of these amendments.

31 It is unclear whether the media reported the procedure President S.R. Nathan had adopted in deciding whether to approve a drawdown on national reserves for Budget 2009 sets a precedent. See Li-ann Thio, *A Treatise on Singapore Constitutional Law* (Singapore: Academy Publishing, 2012), 440–1 (hereinafter referred to as "Li-ann Thio").

32 Li-ann Thio, "Soft Constitutional Law in non-liberal Asian Constitutional Democracies" (2010) 8(4) *I·CON* 766–99.

33 The President of the Republic of Singapore, *The Principles for Determining and Safeguarding the Accumulated Reserves of the Government and the Fifth Schedule Statutory Boards and Government Companies* (Cmd 5, 1999) (hereinafter referred to as "The President's Principles for Determining and Safeguarding the Accumulated Reserves").

34 Li-ann Thio (n. 31), 431–2.

35 Dr Richard Hu, *Singapore Parliamentary Debates: Official Record*, 17 August 1999, vol. 70, col. 2019 (in his statement made to Parliament, "Issues raised by President Ong Teng Cheong at his press conference on 16th July 1999") (hereinafter referred to as "Dr Richard Hu").

36 The President's Principles for Determining and Safeguarding the Accumulated Reserves (n. 33), para. 3.

37 Karl Llewellyn, "The Constitution as Institution" (1934) 34 Columbia LR 1 (hereinafter referred to as "Karl Llewellyn, 'The Constitution as Institution'"), 3, 15, 17 and 18.

38 Dr Richard Hu (n. 35).

39 DPM Teo Chee Hean criticized the Workers' Party's proposal for a senate as non-transparent and ill-conceived; it would multiply the difficulties associated with finding a suitable presidential candidate by eight, with attendant operational problems like how to resolve gridlock in the Senate: DPM Teo Chee Hean, "Wrap-up Speech by DPM Teo Chee Hean at 2nd Reading of Constitutional of the Republic of Singapore (Amendment) Bill" (*Prime Minister's Office*, 9 November 2016) www.pmo.gov.sg/newsroom/wrap-speech-dpm-teo-chee-hean-2nd-reading-constitutional-republic-singapore-amendment (accessed on 22 August 2018) (hereinafter referred to as "DPM Teo's wrap up speech").

40 Presidential Elections Act (Cap. 240A) (hereinafter referred to as "PEA"), Section 8C.

41 CCR (n. 1), para. 8.12. Section 8B of the PEA provides only that the PEC must inform the applicant in writing of its decision not to issue a COE by the day before nomination day. See 2016 White Paper (n. 5), para. 60(f).

42 This argument was raised in *M Ravi* v. *AG* [2017] 5 SLR 489.

43 Li-ann Thio, "(S)electing the President of Singapore: diluting democracy?" (July 2007) 5(3) *I·CON* 526–543.

44 Zakir Hussain, "What matters more is a good president, not contest: Swee Say; It's important that those who want to run are up to the task, says minister", *Straits Times* (Singapore, 7 August 2005), 6 (quoting Minister Lim Swee Say) (hereinafter referred to as "Zakir Hussain").

45 Phyllis Lee, "#NotMyPresident trends in Singapore after walkover announced,

Halimah Yacob set to become President" (*The Independent*, 13 September 2017) http://theindependent.sg/notmypresident-trends-in-singapore-after-walkover-announced-halimah-yacob-set-to-become-president/ (accessed 5 July 2018).

46 Valerie Koh, "WP, Aware blame changes to EP scheme for walkover", *Today* (Singapore, 12 September 2017) www.todayonline.com/singapore/many-changes-ep-scheme-led-walkover-lack-voting-opportunity-wp (accessed 5 July 2017).

47 2016 White Paper (n. 5), para. 125.

48 2016 White Paper (n. 5), para. 124.

49 Alvin Yeo, *Singapore Parliamentary Debates: Official Record*, 17 October 2011, vol. 88, cols 73–6 ("Debate on President's Address").

50 Article 44 of the Singapore Constitution, but see the discussion on how the offices of the EP and PM differ, and how the eligibility criteria for these offices are not comparable: CCR (n. 1), paras 4.6–4.17.

51 The Constitutional Commission (CCR (n. 1) 7.43) and the Government both acknowledged this tension: 2016 White Paper (n. 5), paras 124–5.

52 2016 White Paper (n. 5), para. 124(c) notes that all prior Elected Presidents have played these two roles "with distinction", which all presidential candidates should also aspire to do: "developing rapport with Singaporeans and representing our nation with dignity … while simultaneously demonstrating the technical competence and expertise required for his custodial function…"

53 Goh Chok Tong, *Singapore Parliamentary Debates: Official Record*, 28 October 1996, vol. 66, col. 758.

54 Zakir Hussain (n. 44).

55 Tham Yuen-C, "President's 'first and foremost duty to Singapore': Halimah Yacob; President S.R. Nathan set up the President's Challenge which Tony Tan continued", *Straits Times* (Singapore, 11 August 2017) (quoting President Halimah Yacob) www.straitstimes.com/singapore/presidents-first-and-foremost-duty-to-singapore (accessed 5 July 2018).

56 PM Lee Hsien Loong, *Singapore Parliamentary Debates: Official Record*, 8 November 2016, vol. 94 ("Parliamentary Debate on the Constitution (Amendment) Bill") (hereinafter referred to as "PM Lee").

57 Han Fook Wang, "Will reserved election promote multiracialism?", *Straits Times* (Singapore, 3 September 2017) www.straitstimes.com/singapore/will-reserved-election-promote-multiracialism (accessed 6 July 2018).

58 Singapore has "not yet arrived at an ideal state of accepting people of a different race," such that it remains difficult for minorities to win open presidential elections: Tham Yuen-C, "PM Lee spells out why he pushed for reserved election", *Straits Times* (Singapore, 30 September 2017) www.straitstimes.com/singapore/pm-lee-spells-out-why-he-pushed-for-reserved-election (accessed 6 July 2018).

59 Valerie Koh, "Changes to Elected Presidency passed after 3 days of intense debate", *Today* (Singapore, 9 November 2016) www.todayonline.com/singapore/changes-elected-presidency-passed-after-3-days-intense-debate (accessed 6 July 2018).

60 *Tan Cheng Bock* v. *Attorney-General* [2017] 2 SLR 850 [115].

61 Tham Yuen-C, "PM Lee spells out why he pushed for reserved election", *Straits Times* (Singapore, 30 September 2017) www.straitstimes.com/singapore/pm-lee-spells-out-why-he-pushed-for-reserved-election (accessed 6 July 2018).

62 However, if a GRC team loses its minority members, by-elections are not automatically required: s 24(2A) Parliamentary Elections Act (Cap. 218).

63 Nur Asyiqin Mohamad Salleh, "Presidential Election 2017: Question of who is a Malay continues to be raised", *Straits Times* (Singapore, 9 September 2017) www.straitstimes.com/politics/question-of-who-is-malay-continues-to-be-raised (accessed 6 July 2018).

64 This differs from the provision for Indians ("any person of Indian origin") which is explicitly linked to biology, as opposed to a social conception.

65 A figure of 99.6 per cent: Eugene K.B. Tan, "Singapore Country Report", in

Keeping the Faith: A Study of Freedom of Thought, Conscience and Religion in ASEAN (Jakarta: Human Rights Resource Centre, 2015), 7, 424.

66 Siau Ming En and Kelly Ng, "Community committee 'able to deal with evolving concept of race'", *Today* (Singapore, 9 September 2017) www.todayonline.com/singapore/community-committee-able-deal-evolving-concept-race (accessed 6 July 2018): Dr Kevin Tan rhetorically asked at an IPS forum whether a person with an Indian father and Malay mother was "more Malay than a whole-hearted Malay who happens to be a Christian?".

67 Dieter Grimm, "Integration by Constitution" (2005) 3(2)–(3) *I·CON* 193–208 (hereinafter referred to as "Dieter Grimm, 'Integration by Constitution'").

68 EP's decision-making (n. 7).

69 Elgin Toh, "President has no role in policymaking", *Straits Times* (Singapore, 11 June 2011), 1.

70 The President of the Republic of Singapore, *Constitutional Amendments to Safeguard Financial Assets and the Integrity of the Public Services* (Cmd 10, 1988), para. 34.

71 Janice Heng, "Elected Presidency: study on how to give Council of Presidential Advisers greater say", *Straits Times* (Singapore, 28 January 2016) www.straitstimes.com/politics/elected-presidency-study-on-how-to-give-council-of-presidential-advisers-greater-say (accessed 6 July 2018): Goh Chok Tong's analogy, as recounted by PM Lee.

72 This does not apply to ISA and MRHA related decisions: 2016 White Paper (n. 5), paras 90–3.

73 DPM Lee Hsien Loong, *Singapore Parliamentary Debates: Official Record*, 25 August 1994, vol. 63, col. 424.

74 Walter Woon, *Singapore Parliamentary Debates: Official Record*, 25 August 1994, vol. 63, col. 426.

75 DPM Lee Hsien Loong, *Singapore Parliamentary Debates: Official Record*, 19 April 1994, vol. 77, col. 2792.

76 Derrick A. Paulo, "Reserves and loophole fears", *Today* (Singapore, 3 June 2004), 1.

77 2016 White Paper (n. 5), para. 17.

78 PM Lee (n. 56).

79 See Art. 37B.

80 DPM Teo (n. 20).

81 *Ibid.*, para. 168(c).

82 Alan John, "Debate begins on Elected President", *Straits Times* (Singapore, 12 August 1988), 1: MP TS Lau argued that having an elected Senate would allow the President to remain "above politics"; MP K.T. Ng thought Singapore was too small to have a bicameral system.

83 Art. 37J.

84 DPM Teo (n. 20), para. 129.

85 Art. 37IG.

86 CCR (n. 1), para. 6.40.

87 DPM Teo (n. 18), para. 159.

88 See also Article 37IF which requires a fifth schedule SBGC to request that the Government move such an overruling resolution. See also Chapter 4 on the Council of Presidential Advisers by Eugene Tan in this volume.

89 2016 White Paper (n. 5), para. 101.

90 *Ibid.*

91 *Ibid.*

92 Article 37(2)(a)(b), introduced in 2016, provides that when appointing CPA members, the "integrity, good character and reputation" of the candidate as well as whether he/she has relevant "expertise and experience" must be considered.

93 Article 37B(2) provides that CPA members are appointed to six-year terms at a staggered, two-year interval.
94 CCR (n. 1), para. 6.7; 2016 White Paper (n. 5), para. 111(a).
95 DPM Teo (n. 20), para. 167.
96 DPM Teo (n. 20), para. 202.
97 *Ibid.*, para. 203.
98 *Ibid.*, para. 235.
99 PM Lee (n. 56): PM Lee referred to Federalist No. 51 in debating the Presidency in 2016.
100 Tharman Shanmugaratnam, *Singapore Parliamentary Debates: Official Record*, 20 October 2008, vol. 85 ("Second Reading, Constitution of the Republic of Singapore (Amendment) Bill").
101 *Ibid.*
102 Art. 19.
103 Section 8D, PEA.
104 The Constitutional Commission's recommendation that Constitutional Tribunal play a role in relation to PEC determinations was rejected: CCR (n. 1), para. 4.86.
105 CCR (n. 1), para. 4.13.
106 CCR (n. 1), para. 4.12.
107 The phrase was used in the 1988 White Paper (1988) at 18(d), cited in CCR (n. 1), para. 4.13.
108 CCR (n. 1), para. 4.16.
109 Art. 44.
110 CCR (n. 1), para. 4.9, citing the 1990 Select Committee Report, [12].
111 CCR (n. 1), para. 4.10.
112 CCR (n. 1), para. 4.13.
113 CCR (n. 1), para. 4.8.
114 CCR (n. 1), para. 4.31.
115 The Government said it would consider the Constitutional Commission's proposal to remove the Accountant-General and Auditor-General from the list of automatically qualified offices: 2016 White Paper (n. 5), paras 34–5.
116 Arts 18(2); 19(6).
117 2016 White Paper (n. 5), para. 29(c).
118 CCR (n. 1), paras 4.12, 4.18 and 4.58.
119 Art. 19(4)(a). This replaced the previous $100 million paid up capital requirement.
120 Arts 19(4)(b)(ii) and (iii).
121 At least 691 companies (2016) compared to 158 (1993): 2016 White Paper, para. 39(b).
122 Siau Ming En, "People feeling 'muzzled and angry' after walkover: Tan Cheng Bock", *Today* (Singapore, 13 September 2017) www.todayonline.com/singapore/tan-cheng-bock-slams-uncontested-presidential-election (accessed 6 July 2018).
123 2016 White Paper (n. 5), para. 123.
124 Zakir Hussain, "Doubts about presidential hopefuls not being Malay enough are off track", *Straits Times* (Singapore, 20 July 2017) www.straitstimes.com/opinion/doubts-about-presidential-hopefuls-not-being-malay-enough-are-off-track (accessed 6 July 2018): Mr Salleh Marican is an Indian-Malay Muslim while Farid Khan's identity card lists his race as "Pakistani" although he considered himself "Malay enough" to contest the elections. Madam Halimah Yaacob's father was Indian.
125 Charissa Yong, "Halimah Yacob only one to get eligibility certificate, set to be Singapore's next President", *Straits Times* (Singapore, 11 September 2017) www.straitstimes.com/singapore/halimah-yacob-only-one-to-get-eligibility-certificate-set-to-be-singapores-next-president (accessed 6 July 2018) (hereinafter referred to as "Charissa Yong").
126 Faris Mokhtar, "Marine service provider chairman Farid Khan announces presidency bid", *Today* (Singapore, 11 July 2017 www.todayonline.com/singapore/marine-service-provider-chairman-farid-khan-announces-presidency-bid (accessed 6

July 2018). The Elections Department stated the rejected applicants were privately informed why they did not get COEs; applicants are free to publish these reasons: Charissa Yong (n. 125).

127 Danson Cheong, "Businessman Salleh Marican submits application to contest presidential election", *Straits Times* (Singapore, 23 August 2017) www.straitstimes.com/politics/businessman-salleh-marican-submits-application-to-contest-in-presidential-election (accessed 6 July 2018).

128 It was observed that Halimah Yacob "does not have much financial background nor has she headed any ministry as its minister" though she was warm and popular: Han Fook Kwang, "Unique chance for Halimah Yacob to be a different president", *Straits Times* (Singapore, 17 September 2017) www.straitstimes.com/singapore/unique-chance-to-be-a-different-president (accessed 6 July 2018); President Tony Tan in his 7 November 2016 message to Parliament on the constitutional amendments noted that his finance background had help him understand "the technicalities of the Government's proposals" but "good policy acumen" and "sound judgement" was also necessary: President Tony Tan Keng Yam, "Message By President Tony Tan Keng Yam to the Parliament on the Constitutional Amendments On 7 November 2016" (*The Istana*, 7 November 2016) www.istana.gov.sg/the-president/former-presidents/dr-tony-tan-keng-yam/speeches/message-president-tony-tan-keng-yam-the-parliament-the-constitutional-amendments (accessed 28 August 2018).

129 CCR (n. 1), para. 4.25.

130 CCR (n. 1), para. 4.27.

131 CCR (n. 1), para. 4.28.

132 Presumably the Chief Financial Officer, although not at the apex of a Fifth Schedule SBGC, will have more financial expertise than certain public officers.

133 CCR (n. 1), para. 4.58.

134 CCR (n. 1), para. 4.30. The Commission considered that the Auditor-General and Accountant-General office did not merit automatic qualification given the narrower scope of these two offices in not engaging matters with a broad public dimension: CCR (n. 1), para. 4.28.

135 CCR (n. 1), para. 4.17.

136 Dieter Grimm, "Types of Constitutions" (n. 21).

137 2016 White Paper (n. 5), para. 144(b). Some candidates championed a $60 billion job-creating plan and proposed more recognition for military servicemen, the poor and unemployed, which fell with the responsibility of Cabinet government: PM Lee (n. 56).

138 Dieter Grimm, "Types of Constitutions" (n. 21).

139 CCR (n. 1), para. 4.15.

140 2016 White Paper (n. 5), paras 144–148.

141 CCR (n. 1), para. 7.11.

142 CCR (n. 1), para. 7.13.

143 CCR (n. 1), para. 7.13.

144 CCR (n. 1), para. 7.11.

145 Chan Chun Sing, *Singapore Parliamentary Debates: Official Record*, 6 February 2017, vol. 94 ("Second Reading, Presidential Elections (Amendment) Bill").

146 *Ibid.*

147 2016 White Paper (n. 5), para. 124(c).

148 2016 White Paper (n. 5), para. 73.

149 The Wee Commission was hesitant towards the idea of electoral systems involving "the setting up of separate electoral rolls" which would involve "the complicated task of defining the various minority groups"; See Constitutional Commission, *Report of the Constitutional Commission 1966* (Singapore Government Printer, 1966), para. 49.

150 2016 White Paper (n. 5), paras 77 and 79.

151 2016 White Paper (n. 5), para. 71(b)(iii).
152 PM Lee (n. 56).
153 Bhavan Jaipragas, "Why did Singapore PM gamble popularity on 'Double Minority' President Halimah Yacob?", *South China Morning Post* (Singapore, 16 September 2017) www.scmp.com/week-asia/politics/article/2111432/why-did-singapore-pm-gamble-popularity-double-minority-president (accessed 6 July 2018).
154 CCR (n. 1), para. 4.22.
155 DPM Teo (n. 20).
156 2016 White Paper (n. 5), para. 82.
157 2016 White Paper (n. 5), para. 82.
158 2016 White Paper (n. 5), para. 81(b).
159 DPM Teo's wrap up speech (n. 39).
160 2016 White Paper (n. 5), para. 83.
161 PM Lee (n. 56).
162 Lee U-Wen, "I'm a President for all Singaporeans: Halimah", *Business Times* (Singapore, 14 September 2017) www.businesstimes.com.sg/government-economy/presidential-election-2017/im-a-president-for-all-singaporeans-halimah (accessed 6 July 2018). (President Halimah Yacob stated she hoped her status as the first female Head of State would be a "major boost for gender diversity").
163 Dieter Grimm, "Integration by Constitution" (n. 67).
164 PM Lee (n. 56).
165 DPM Teo's wrap-up speech (n. 159).
166 Harold J. Berman, "Law and Logos" (1994), 44 *DePaul Law Review* 143, 159:

> Like religion, law originates in celebration; it reveres the past; it feels bound by authoritative words and symbols; it invokes an all-embracing moral reality. These are legal emotions, legal passions, that may be said to constitute the religious dimension of law.

167 PM Lee (n. 56).
168 PM Lee (n. 56). PM Lee stated that though the EP was working well and there was no pressure to change the system, "it is my Government's duty to review the scheme to make adjustments well ahead of time to enable it to continue to function well."
169 2016 White Paper (n. 5), para. 13.
170 CCR (n. 1), para. 7.28.
171 CCR (n. 1), para. 7.4.
172 Li Xueying, "MM: No need to follow any prescription on democracy", *Straits Times* (Singapore, 24 September 2008), 35. (First PM Lee Kuan Yew stated he was not "following any prescription given me by any theoretician on democracy." Rather he was guided by "first principles" including "social peace and stability within the country, no fighting between the races, between religions, fair shares for all, everybody is a homeowner…").
173 PM Lee (n. 56).
174 DPM Teo's wrap-up speech (n. 39).
175 Including Part IV fundamental liberties under the Article 5(2A) special entrenchment procedure designed mainly for the EP in 1991 was in 2016 considered inapposite, where the entrenchment provision was modified to only encompass EP related provisions. Part IV is now subject to the general Article 5(2) amendment procedure. This reflects a piecemeal approach to constitution-making where changes are first made and later corrected when they make no sense in hindsight: see CCR (n. 1), para. 141.
176 PM Lee (n. 56).
177 *Ibid.*
178 Karl Llewellyn, "The Constitution as Institution" (n. 37), 11.
179 2016 White Paper (n. 5), para. 29(c)(iii).
180 PM Lee (n. 56).

3 Mandates, majorities and the legitimacy of the Elected President

Kevin Y.L. Tan

3.1 Introduction

In 1991, Singapore's Constitution was amended to transform the office of President – hitherto a ceremonial office – into an elected one. While the President had previously been 'elected' by Parliament, there were no real electoral contests since Parliament was only ever offered a single candidate at each 'election'. The purpose of requiring the President to be elected by universal franchise was to invest the elected candidate with legitimacy to check on the Government of the day. The President's legitimacy would thus flow from the fact of his or her election, coupled with the majority received. Legitimacy would thus pivot on two factors – choice and mandate. In this chapter, I consider the evolution of Singapore's presidential office and argue that developments have left the electorate with little or no choice, the candidate with no mandate and the President with no electoral legitimacy.

3.2 Neutralizing a 'freak election'

The creation of the Elected Presidency must be seen as one in a series of moves by Singapore's ruling party – the People's Action Party ("PAP") – to ameliorate the consequences of their worst nightmare – a 'freak election result'. In such an instance, 'irrational' voters might cause a seismic shift in voting patterns to bring into office an irresponsible and profligate government. The Westminster parliamentary system of government, with its fusion of executive and legislative powers, would provide no check on such a government if it had a parliamentary majority. It was thus necessary to create a countervailing force to put the brakes on the excesses of such a government.

Since it won all the seats in the 1968 general election, the PAP has dominated Parliament with near-hegemonic omnipresence. Indeed, from 1968 to 1981, there was not a single opposition Member of Parliament (MP) in the House. This will account for the shock the PAP received when it lost the by-election in Anson constituency in 1981 when the Workers' Party's Secretary-General J.B. Jeyaretnam defeated its candidate Pang Kim Hin. The Anson by-election result represented the largest percentage vote-swing away from the PAP since 1968 – 37 per cent. Three years later, at the general election of 1984, 12.9 per cent of the electorate who previously voted for the PAP, voted for the opposition. It was the largest voter swing since 1972. Table 3.1 shows the percentage of popular votes secured by the PAP over the years, and shows why the 12.9 per cent voter swing in 1984 so alarmed the PAP leadership.

In his 80-minute analysis of the 1984 general election results, former Prime Minister Lee Kuan Yew acknowledged the voters' demands for a more accommodating style and for greater consultation but openly questioned the adequacy and desirability of the one-man, one-vote, first past the post system of government. His key point was that had there been a further 14 per cent shift in the voting pattern, the combined opposition would have captured 40 seats against the PAP's 39.[1] The PAP was sufficiently worried about the election outcome and so established a nine-man task force, headed by Party Chairman Ong Teng Cheong to analyse the results.[2] The 1984 general election presented the PAP with another terrifying spectre – that of a 'freak election result'. In announcing the new Cabinet's new tasks, First Deputy Prime Minister, Goh Chok Tong said:

> This general election has proven to be a little scary in that many of us had misjudged the mood of the population. There was nearly a swing which might result in something all of us did not want – freak election results.[3]

Quite clearly, the Non-Constituency Member of Parliament ("NCMP") scheme that was introduced just before the 1984 general election failed to stem the rising demands for greater oppositional voices in Parliament. The NCMP scheme – unique to Singapore – provided that at least three NCMP seats would be offered to the losing candidates (of parties which did not form the Government) who secured the highest number of votes. In other words, three of the best losers would be offered NCMP seats with all rights and privileges of elected MPs save

Table 3.1 The People's Action Party's popular vote share: 1968–2015.

Year	*Popular vote (%)*	*Percentage swing (%)*
1968	86.7	—
1972	70.4	–16.3
1976	74.1	+3.7
1980	77.7	+3.6
1981 (Anson by-election)	47.1	–37.00
1984	64.8	–12.9
1988	63.2	+1.6
1991	61.0	–2.2
1997	65.0	+4.0
2001	75.3	+10.3
2006	66.6	–8.7
2011	60.1	–6.5
2015	69.9	+9.8

that they were unable to vote on constitutional amendments, Supply Bills and motions of 'no confidence' in the Government of the day.

3.3 Enter the Elected Presidency

At about the same time Lee mooted the NCMP Scheme, he also floated the idea of changing the ceremonial office of President to an elected one.[4] Unsurprisingly, Lee's proposal was in direct response to the looming prospect of a 'freak election result'. If the PAP had been ousted from power in a freak election, there would be nothing to prevent a populist and profligate government from raiding Singapore's foreign reserves, squandering the people's hard-earned resources and filling the top echelons of the civil service with relatives, friends, bootlickers and hangers-on. It was thus necessary to create an institution that could check such a government, even if it was the PAP itself. Lee's proposal was to turn the Presidency into an elected office and increase the President's constitutional powers to act as a 'second key'. Lee put it thus:

> Today, any government elected can get at those reserves and spend it. So you can get a wild offshoot of an election – free bus rides, lower electricity, free water, lower MRT fares, and your reserves will just vanish like that within a few years. Then like Brazil, Argentina and Mexico, we'll be borrowing hundreds of millions of dollars. And we're finished. This place will never get off the ground again.
>
> So perhaps – we've been thinking this one over very carefully – we cannot be sure that even an honest government like the PAP without that will and the resolve will resist pressures, may (not) be tempted to give in to pressure and subsidise. Then you use the reserves surreptitiously. So we said perhaps we should have a blocking mechanism. No reserves should be spent without the President and a special committee to approve it.[5]

However, four years were to elapse before the first White Paper on the Elected President was published.[6]

3.3.1 Qualifying the Elected President

The First White Paper set out in general terms, the rationale for the scheme and more significantly, the "fundamental considerations" in the decision to transform the office of the President into an elected one. We focus on two of these avowed considerations – the need for elections to give the President "moral authority" and the requirement that the President hold ministerial or high executive or administrative experience. First, in relation to elections and moral authority, the First White Paper stated:

> Any disagreement with the elected Government on its proposals to spend reserves and assets will inevitably become a highly controversial and

> politicised issue. Therefore, the official or agency entrusted with the task of exercising such checks must have, and be seen to have, the legitimacy and moral authority to block the Government. *Such authority can only be derived from the will of the people as expressed in an election.* Otherwise, the Prime Minister would insist that his Government's intention must prevail, as it was elected by the people. Officials who have not been directly elected, or non-elected bodies like the Presidential Council for Minority Rights ("PCMR") or the Supreme Court, would be placed in a highly invidious position if they tried to block an elected Government.[7] (Emphasis mine).

And second, in relation to the qualifications of the presidential candidate, the First White Paper stated:

> Whoever is entrusted with the safeguard role must be capable, experienced in public affairs, and have an astute overview of the national interest. He must have the wisdom to judge the Government's actions in the two areas, and the courage and decisiveness to disagree with the Government when national interest so requires. Such a person must himself have exercised authority, preferably in the public sector and have experienced the contrary pulls and pressures of government decision making. He must be able to balance the demands of political expediency and the public interest. The Constitution should require Presidential candidates to have such experience and qualities.[8]

The First White Paper also offered suggestions on the type of public-sector candidates who might qualify to be a presidential candidate: Ministers of Government, Speaker of Parliament, Chief Justice, Judges of the Supreme Court, Attorney-General, Auditor-General, Accountant-General, Permanent Secretaries, Chairmen or Chief Executives of Statutory Boards. For the private sector, the First White Paper only listed Chief Executive Officers of publicly listed companies.[9]

3.3.2 Revisiting the early debates on qualification

At first blush, these two fundamental considerations – the need for legitimizing elections and highly qualified candidates – appear unconnected, but they are not. The need for specially qualified candidates necessarily limits the pool of candidates eligible to contest presidential elections. The narrower the criteria, the fewer the candidates available. Public discussion on the First White Paper was wide-ranging and in some sense speculative since the specific provisions and powers of the proposed Elected President scheme were not explicitly spelt out.

Two Members of Parliament (MPs) thought the proposed criteria to be too stringent. Ibrahim Othman (MP for Tanah Merah) told Parliament that many people told the Ministry of Community Development's Feedback Unit (now renamed REACH) that they felt that the net could be cast wider to "include others who have been successful in life, for example, a successful businessman or an outstanding civil servant".[10] The Singapore Democratic Party's Chiam See Tong (MP for Potong Pasir) felt that the candidacy 'should be open' with the criterion of 'age' as only possible limitation, preferring a candidate of at least 35 years of age.[11] Tan Cheng Bock (MP for Ayer Rajah) did not comment on the proposed requirements, but argued that if the proposed Presidential Elections Committee (PEC) was not impartial, "the people have no free choice".[12] Responding to Ibrahim Othman, First Deputy Prime Minister Goh Chok Tong retorted that the criteria were "not stringent enough":

> If you want to leave open a big hole in which all kinds of candidates can slip through to stand for election, then we are in fact having a worse situation because all kinds of people can become President. It is not an improvement over the present system where all kinds of candidates can stand for elections in a general election. I think this is one of the more innovative features of this elected President which some Members might not have noted, i.e., the quality control over potential candidates for important positions. I wish it could be extended to all candidates standing for election to Parliament ... if you compare the qualifications required for someone to stand for election and the qualifications you would insist upon before you appoint a person an accountant, a SAF officer, a doctor or a lawyer, you will be shocked at the slack and totally non-existent control over eligibility to stand for election to be a Member of this House.[13]

In 1990, a second White Paper[14] was released, along with the Constitution of the Republic of Singapore (Amendment No 3) Bill.[15] Clause 38 of the Second White Paper offered a slightly expanded list for qualification. Presidential candidates had to be citizens of Singapore, and served for at least three years in one of the following capacities:

a Minister, Chief Justice, Speaker of Parliament, Attorney-General, Judge or Judicial Commissioner of the Supreme Court, Chairman of the Public Service Commission ("PSC"), Auditor-General, Accountant-General;
b Chairman or chief executive officer of a company with a paid-up capital of at least $100 million; or
c Chairman or chief executive officer of a key statutory board, namely, Government of Singapore Investment Corporation Pte Ltd; MND Holdings Pte Ltd; Singapore Technologies Holdings Pte Ltd; and Temasek Holdings Pte Ltd.

During the Second Reading of the Constitution (Amendment No. 3) Bill, more MPs voiced their concerns over the stringency of requirements for presidential candidates. The concerns and arguments raised may be divided into two broad categories: (a) that the restrictive criteria limits the pool of eligible candidates; and (b) that there is an overemphasis on particular requirements.

Ibrahim Othman repeated his call to cast the net wider as the proposed eligibility criteria was "too restrictive", had "an elitist bent" and was "loaded in favour of the establishment".[16] Ibrahim was also concerned that with such elitist credentials, the President might "lose touch with the feeling of the people".[17] Given the President's wide-range and scope of powers which required him to be familiar and experienced "in many fields, from law to economics to religion", Chandra Das (MP for Cheng San GRC) wondered if "there will always be a suitable candidate for the post".[18] Das also questioned if all the public officers designated for qualification were indeed suitable. "The Chief Justice", Das said, "may be an expert in law but his understanding of Supply Bills and for him to apply his judgment correctly would be in doubt when he gets elected as Elected President."[19] Finally, he argued that as the presidential candidate was from "the top echelons of the establishment", he or she was unlikely to "stand in opposition to the ruling party".[20] Dr Koh Lam Son (MP for Telok Blangah) argued that it would "seem almost undemocratic if eligibility is confined to a select few, and not thrown open to a wider mass of Singaporeans" and proposed including anyone who has been a Member of Parliament.[21] Dr Aline Wong (MP for Tampines GRC) pointedly observed that the Bill prescribed "two types of qualification" – personal integrity, and financial management experience – expecting them to repose in the same candidate. This, she argued, was "too restrictive" and urged that the pool be enlarged "to include prominent citizens who are known to have made contributions" to Singapore "but who may not have had the requisite experience with financial management, just as in the case of the Chief Justice, Speaker of Parliament, Attorney-General, [and] High Court Judges."[22]

Addressing these concerns, Prime Minister Goh Chok Tong explained that the list in the proposed Bill was "no more than a proxy for the attributes" the Government was looking for:

> We are actually looking for people with competence. They must be competent people before they can stand for election. Secondly, they must be trustworthy. Third, they must have sound judgement. That means, when they look at the situation they can come to the right conclusion. They assess people, they know who are opportunists, who are crooks and who are honest people…
>
> On the suggestion that we should widen the criteria, if you read the clauses carefully, you will notice that, in fact, almost anyone is eligible to stand for election as President, provided he can satisfy the Presidential Elections Committee that he is a person with such experience and qualifications as are necessary for him to carry out effectively the functions and duties of the office of the President.[23]

Following two days of intense debates in Parliament, a Select Committee was appointed.[24] The Select Committee examined the issue of candidate qualification and proposed that the pre-qualification approach should remain, working on the basis that it should not be easier for a person to become a President than a Prime

Minister. Speaking at the Third Reading of the Bill, Prime Minister Goh Chok Tong again dealt with the issue of qualifications for presidential candidates but this time, emphasized the need for candidates to possess "moral stature":

> The President's moral stature is important. If he lacks the necessary experience and stature, he will not have the moral weight to veto the Prime Minister should he hold a contrary view. This moral standing can come only if the President is a man of substance, tested and known for his integrity, objectivity, competence and judgment. It cannot come simply through winning elections.[25]

Dr Koh Lam Son once again objected to these stringent criteria on the basis that it was undemocratic, but more importantly, that too much emphasis had been placed on financial management expertise:

> Mr Speaker, I would also prefer that the pre-qualifications be kept to a minimum so as to increase the pool of talented and capable men from which a President can be elected. I say this because it is the most democratic thing to do. This system has worked well for us, Members of Parliament. The people must have the right and the choice to elect or reject a candidate.
>
> I also feel that as the Bill presently stands, there is far too much emphasis on this expertise on financial management before a person can qualify to be considered a candidate for the post of Elected President. This, to me, is too restrictive. I feel that we would be depriving ourselves of many talented, honest and, in some instances, internationally renowned Singaporeans from standing for the post because of this proviso of financial expertise…
>
> The point, Mr Speaker, is that a man of great leadership abilities with no financial background can safeguard our reserves … So let the very stringent restrictions be removed, and let us allow Singaporeans their democratic right to elect a person they have confidence in.[26]

Koh's democracy argument drew a sharp retort from the Prime Minister:

> So what is democracy all about? It is not the right to stand for election. It is giving the electorate the right to choose good candidates to Parliament. If we do not give the people a choice, then they are choosing between two bad candidates. But if you pre-qualify them, and you allow good candidates to emerge and be chosen, you can be sure that only good ones will be chosen returned to Parliament.
>
> Now, the question is whether the criteria are too stringent or whether we should not lower them to widen the pool, as some Members have argued. I think the present criteria as spelt out are sufficient to draw in good people. They are not so high as to limit the numbers to four or five potential candidates. I think a large number of Singaporeans can meet the criteria…

> We place great store on financial knowledge and expertise because this one key area in which we expect the President to exercise judgment. Unless he has knowledge of finances and is able to evaluate reports, he will not be able to perform his job well. So you have got to ensure that Presidential candidates do have the ability, first, to read accounts, secondly, to understand them, to evaluate them, and most importantly, to make a judgment whether to exercise his veto power or to agree with the government of the day should they wish to draw on reserves for certain well-argued cases.[27]

Several amendments were made to the original Bill although the eligibility requirements were left intact. It was passed into law in January 1991.[28] It should be noted that during the Select Committee hearings, Associate Professor Valentine Winslow not only argued strongly against the stringent criteria but further proposed that like Article 67(3) of the South Korean Constitution,[29] a requirement should be made that in the absence of a contest, the candidate returned should have a minimum receipt of one-third of the total eligible votes.[30]

3.3.3 Implementation of the scheme

I do not propose to go into the intricacies of the many complex details of the constitutional amendments that introduced the Elected Presidency[31] but aspects of the scheme that are germane to our discussion will be highlighted. The presidential candidate must meet two requirements. First, he or she must satisfy the PEC that: "he is a person of integrity, good character and reputation".[32] Second, he or she must also show that for a period of not less than three years, he or she has held office in one of numerous capacities laid down under Article 19(2)(g). Specifically, these offices are:

a Minister;
b Chief Justice;
c Speaker;
d Attorney-General;
e Chairman of the Public Service Commission;
f Auditor-General;
g Permanent Secretary;
h Chairman or chief executive officer of one of the following:
- Board of Commissioners of Currency, Singapore
- Central Provident Fund Board
- Housing and Development Board
- Jurong Town Corporation
- Monetary Authority of Singapore; or Post Office Savings Bank of Singapore.

i Chairman of the Board of Directors or Chief Executive Officer (CEO) of a company incorporated or registered under the Companies Act with a paid-up capital of at least $100 million or its equivalent in foreign currency; or j in any other similar or comparable position of seniority and responsibility in any other organisation or department of equivalent size or complexity in the public or private sector which, in the opinion of the Presidential Elections Committee, has given him such experience and ability in administering and managing financial affairs as to enable him to carry out effectively the functions and duties of the office of the President.

It will be seen that between 1988 and 1991, the eligibility criteria was slightly broadened to include chairmen or CEOs of public companies with a paid up capital of at least S$100 million. The final clause in Article 19(2)(g) gives the PEC the power to qualify "comparable candidates". Under Article 18, the PEC consists of the Chairman of the PSC; the Chairman of the Public Accountants Board; and a member of the PCMR nominated by the Chairman of the Council.

As candidates for the first and second presidential elections had automatically qualified,[33] the PEC was only called upon to seriously exercise this discretion in 2005 in the case of Andrew Kuan, former Group Chief Financial Officer of the Jurong Town Corporation.[34] Kuan was declared ineligible because the PEC assessed:

> the seniority and responsibility of that position as being not comparable to those mentioned in the Constitution and he therefore could not have the experience and ability in administering and managing financial affairs as to effectively discharge the functions and duties of the office of President.[35]

Kuan was once again declared ineligible when he made a second bid for a Certificate of Eligibility in 2011.

Interestingly, the PEC decided that four candidates were eligible to run in the 2011 election. Of the four candidates, only two – Tony Tan and Tan Cheng Bock – qualified automatically under Article 19. Tan was a former Deputy Prime Minister and also served as Chairman of the Oversea-Chinese Banking Corporation and was Chairman of Singapore Press Holdings Ltd at the time of his nomination while Tan Cheng Bock had previously served as Chairman of public-listed Chuan Hup Holdings Ltd. Two other candidates – Tan Kin Lian and Tan Jee Say – were also declared to be eligible. Tan Kin Lian, who was CEO of the highly successful and visible insurance cooperative NTUC Income for 30 years, was expected to qualify since he had grown NTUC Income's assets from $28 million in 1977 to $17 billion in 2007; NTUC Income had a share capital of $500 million. Quite rightly, the PEC felt that NTUC Income was 'comparable in size and complexity' to a company with a paid-up capital of $100 million.[36]

The surprise qualifier was Tan Jee Say, a former Principal Private Secretary to the then Deputy Prime Minister Goh Chok Tong, who, from 1997 to 2001, was Regional Managing Director of AIB Govett Asia, an asset management company. AIB Govett Asia did not have a paid-up capital of $100 million. Nonetheless, the PEC felt that Tan's position was "a position of comparable seniority and responsibility as a CEO" of an organization "of equivalent complexity" to companies in Singapore with a paid-up capital of $100 million.[37]

3.3.4 The Menon Constitutional Commission

On 27 January 2016, during the parliamentary debate on the President's Address, Prime Minister Lee Hsien Loong announced the Government's intention to review the Elected Presidency scheme.[38] The review was not occasioned by "any dissatisfaction with the present working arrangements, or any difference of views between the Government and the President" but "to keep the Presidency a robust and effective institution".[39] Lee highlighted three areas which he thought required review: (a) the qualifying criteria for the President; (b) how to further build up the institution of the Council of Presidential Advisers (CPA); and (c) how to ensure that racial minorities stood a chance of being elected to the office of President.

With respect to the eligibility criteria, Lee felt that it should "be brought up to date" because: (a) the old threshold of $100 million in paid-up capital for public companies was valued in 2016 at $158 million (taking into account inflation), but the value did not reflect how much Singapore had changed since then; (b) Singapore's Gross Domestic Product had risen from $72 billion in 1990 to $400 billion in 2016; (c) Government spending had gone up from $11 billion in 1990 to $68 billion in 2015; (d) CPF balances had increased from $41 billion in 1990 to $275 billion in 2016; and (e) the number of companies with $100 million paid-up capital was 158 in 1993 but 2,100 in 2016.[40] He ended by stating that a Constitutional Commission would be appointed to study the issues raised and to obtain views from the public and recommend improvements to the system.

The nine-member Commission, under the Chairmanship of Chief Justice Sundaresh Menon, was appointed on 10 February 2016 with the following Terms of Reference:[41]

1 To review the qualifying process for Presidential candidacy, particularly the eligibility criteria for such candidates.

   To consider whether the existing provisions in these areas are adequate, taking into account:

   i The President's custodial role in safeguarding our financial reserves and the integrity of our public service; and

   ii The need to ensure that those eligible for candidacy are individuals of character and standing, who possess the experience and ability to discharge these duties and responsibilities of Presidential office with dignity and distinction.

   To recommend any refinements and amendments to the abovementioned areas which are necessary in view of the considerations in (1)(i) and (ii) above.

2 To consider and recommend what provisions should be made to safeguard minority representation in the Presidency, taking into account:

   i The President's status as a unifying figure that represents multi-racial Singapore; and ii The need to ensure that candidates from minority races have fair and adequate opportunity to be elected to Presidential office.

3 To review the framework governing the exercise of the President's custodial powers, particularly the role and composition of the Council of Presidential Advisers.

  To consider whether the existing provisions in these areas are adequate, taking into account:

  i The custodial powers that the President is entrusted with, and the Council of Presidential Advisers' central function as an independent body to counsel and advise the President on the exercise of his powers; and

  ii The need to safeguard our financial reserves and the integrity of our public service, and ensure that decisions in these areas are made with the support of careful consideration given by a group of persons with substantial suitable experience in the public and private sectors.

  To recommend any refinements and amendments to the above-mentioned areas which are necessary in view of the considerations in (3)(i) and (ii) above.

4 To receive and consider representations on (1) to (3) above.

5 To prepare and submit a report of the Commission's proceedings, findings and recommendations to the Prime Minister. In preparing this report, the Commission may seek legal or other professional advice and/or request for information, on any matters within its terms of reference.

The Commission invited the public to submit written feedback on matters falling within the Terms of Reference and a total of 107 representations were received. Twenty contributors were invited to make oral representations to elaborate on or clarify their written submissions, and these hearings were held over the course of four days between 18 April and 6 May 2016. At this point, I must declare my interest in this matter – I was one of the 20 persons who made both written and oral representations to the Commission.

3.4 Selecting the 'Elected' President?

As we saw from the foregoing, the stringent qualification requirements for presidential candidates were controversial from the outset. The MPs' main concerns were that the pool was too small and that 'good' and 'worthy' candidates would be excluded on account of these requirements. However, no one except for Chandra Das appears to have openly questioned the assumed parity in qualification between public- and private-sector candidates who would automatically be qualified. Even so, his critique was couched in terms of finding all the qualities thought necessary in a candidate reposing in any single person. Unfortunately, this assumption – which I challenged – was never overturned during the Constitutional Commission hearings. During the Commission hearings, I pointed out that a candidate whose only experience and skill sets were gained through spending three years as either the Chief Justice, Attorney-General, Speaker of

Parliament or Chairman of the PSC could not possibly be equated with the private-sector candidate (i.e. the Chairman or CEO of a public listed company with $100 million in paid-up capital).

> … it is not entirely clear that the competence and experience required to head up a large corporation can necessarily be equated to someone occupying the office of the Auditor-General or Speaker of Parliament, for example. As a simple matter of comparison, the Auditor-General of Singapore presided over an organisation with a budget of some $32.2 million in FY2015; while the Speaker of Parliament's institutional budget came to $35.1 million in FY2015. These sums are still vast compared to the Public Service Commission's budget in FY2015, which came to just over $2 million. However, the threshold for 'commercial candidates' is $100 million.[42]

Thus, if financial competence, experience and judgement were key to the role of the President, there really is no reason why former Chief Justices, Speakers of Parliament or Chairmen of the PSC should be privileged with automatic qualification. The Commission however dismissed my argument, stating that:

> although the private- and public-sector routes to qualification are both targeted at identifying persons with the relevant skillsets, no single office is ever likely to endow the holder of that office with *all* the attributes necessary for him to discharge *all* the Presidential functions,

and as such, "it may not be correct to compare the two routes as if they are precisely alike".[43]

This is an odd response since I was hardly comparing the 'two routes' for qualification but rather questioning the qualities and qualifications of candidates to *perform the same task* – which is to safeguard Singapore's financial reserves and integrity of the civil service. If the job is the same, why should we continue to countenance, and indeed widen such a wide gulf in experience between public-sector and private-sector candidates? Even so, the Commission recommended the removal of the Auditor-General and Accountant-General from Article 19(2)(g) on the ground that: "the scope of these two offices and the extent of the responsibilities borne by their holders do not … justify automatic qualification" since they are "not necessarily held by civil servants with the rank of Permanent Secretary" and their role in the "delivery of public goods and services" was ancillary and limited.[44] It seems strange that the Commission did not feel the same way about the offices of Chief Justice, Attorney-General, Speaker or Chairman of the PSC had correspondingly limited roles in the delivery of public goods and services.

Instead of proposing the elimination of more public offices by which candidates can automatically qualify, the Commission recommended"'doubling the duration which applicants must have served in the qualifying office, from the current term of 3 years to 6 years" to "capture at least some elements of the applicant's performance" and "filter out those who were either removed or not re-appointed because they had been found wanting".[45] Parliament rejected both of the Commission's recommendations and retained the offices of Auditor-General and Accountant-General in Article 19(2)(g) and kept the period of qualification for public offices at three years. The new Article 19(2)(g)(ii) allows the period of service in a public office to be broken up so that the sum total of service is three years. So, if a person served as Attorney-General for one year and Chief Justice for two years, that would automatically qualify that candidate.

In addition, the new Article 19(3)(c) gives the PEC discretion to consider public officers of 'comparable' experience and ability. It reads:

> 19(3) The public sector service requirement is that the person has –
>
> (*a*) held office for a period of 3 or more years as Minister, Chief Justice, Speaker, Attorney-General, Chairman of the Public Service Commission, Auditor-General, Accountant-General or Permanent Secretary;
> (*b*) served for a period of 3 or more years as the chief executive of an entity specified in the Fifth Schedule;
> (*c*) satisfied the following criteria:
> (i) the person has served for a period of 3 or more years in an office in the public sector;
> (ii) the Presidential Elections Committee is satisfied, having regard to the nature of the office and the person's performance in the office, that the person has experience and ability that is comparable to the experience and ability of a person who satisfies paragraph (*a*) or (*b*); and
> (iii) the Presidential Elections Committee is satisfied, having regard to any other factors it sees fit to consider, that the person has the experience and ability to effectively carry out the functions and duties of the office of President; or
> (*d*) held office or served, as the case may be, for a first period of one or more years in an office mentioned in paragraph (*a*), (*b*) or (*c*) and a second period of one or more years in an office mentioned in paragraph (*a*), (*b*) or (*c*), and the 2 periods add up to 3 or more years.

This additional layer of discretion further complicates the already incoherent relationship between the public- and private-sector requirements. What does it take for a public officer to have experience and ability comparable to the Chairman of the PSC, for example? On what basis can the PEC deal with a claim by say, a former Police Commissioner to be qualified?

Interestingly, the Constitutional Commission noted that only about 70 public-sector candidates automatically qualified under Article 19(2)(g) but expressed grave concerns that the $100 million threshold established in 1991 for private companies was now insufficient given the change in economic circumstances. It noted that in 1991, there were only 158 companies with $100 million in paid-up capital whereas in 2016, the 158th largest company in Singapore had a paid-up capital of $1.6 billion. This represented a 16-fold increase in the capitalization of Singapore's largest companies and this criterion had to be updated to reflect this change of circumstances.

A number of representors discussed raising the bar for private-sector candidates by: (a) substituting "paid-up capital" with "shareholder equity" since the latter better reflected the company's financial well-being than the former; and (b) raising the bar by requiring candidates to have run companies with at least $500 million in shareholder equity. The Commission agreed and their recommendation in this regard was accepted by Parliament. While there is good sense in pegging a company's worth to its shareholder equity rather than its paid-up capital, the raising of the $100 million benchmark is questionable. Is a person who can profitably run a $100 million company qualitatively different from one who can run profitably run a $500 million company? If there is no clear and apparent difference, then the new qualification does little more than to reduce the pool of private-sector candidates.

Beyond the initial qualification requirements under Article 19(2)(g), all presidential candidates must satisfy the PEC that they are persons "of integrity, good character and reputation". Initially, the unelected PEC comprised the Chairman of the PSC, the Chairman of the Accounting and Corporate Regulatory Authority (ACRA) and a member of the PCMR nominated by the Chairman of the Council. With the latest amendments, membership of the PEC has doubled with the addition of: a member or former member of the Council of Presidential Advisers; a person qualified to be a Judge of the Supreme Court appointed by the Chief Justice; and a person from the private sector, who in the opinion of the Prime Minister, has private-sector expertise and experience that is relevant to the functions of the PEC, and is appointed by the Prime Minister.

This enhanced PEC is now required under the new Article 19(4)(a) to determine if a private-sector candidate is "comparable to the experience and ability of a person who has served as a chief executive" of a company with $500 million in shareholder equity. At the same time, a private-sector candidate must satisfy the PEC that "having regard to any other factors" the PEC "sees fit to consider", he or she "has the experience and ability to effectively carry out the functions and duties of the office of President".

Further tightening of the already stringent and restrictive requirements for presidential candidates has further limited of choices available to the voting public. A combination of stringent constitutional requirements and the PEC's screening effectively pre-selects candidates for the office of President. This restriction is even greater with the enactment of a new Article 19B which provides for "reserved elections" for members of different ethnic groups if "no person belonging to that community has held the office of President for any of the 5 most recent terms of office of the President." This new clause operates retrospectively to the time of Singapore's independence in 1965, and as such, the 2017 Presidential Election was reserved for Malay candidates. As such, the amendments further limit voters' choice, which further problematize the claim that elections endow the President with a mandate. Put another way, the harder it is to qualify as a presidential candidate, the less candidates there are likely to be, and this necessarily limits voter choice. Indeed, as seen in the 2017 election, the combination of the stringent requirements and the reserved election qualified only a single candidate resulting in no election, and no mandate for the 'elected' President.

3.5 'Electing' the selected President

Elections are the bedrock of democratic representation and participation. Those elected are presumed to have the mandate of those who elected them, and thus a corresponding legitimacy to undertake whatever their office requires of them. The bigger the majority, the greater the legitimacy and the more secure the mandate. Indeed, it was on this basis that Parliament transformed the office of President into an elected one. As Richard Katz points out, elections function to: (a) legitimize the elected; (b) offer voters selection and choice; (c) create or foster representation; and (d) facilitate popular involvement in the process.[46]

3.5.1 Why elect the President? The problem of walkovers

Prior to 1991, all presidents were nominated and 'elected' by Parliament – there was no real electoral contest in this closed system. Parliament's 'electing' of the President was really a reaffirmation of the Government's choice – nothing more. At the same time, there was an unspoken convention of having the highest office in the land rotate among members of the major ethnic groups in Singapore: Yusof Ishak (Malay, 1965–1970); Benjamin Henry Sheares (Eurasian, 1970–1981); and C.V. Devan Nair (Indian, 1981–1985). The transformation of the office to an elected one, albeit with serious limitations, must be that elections gave holders of the office a majoritarian mandate upon which sat its moral authority to control an elected government. This was emphasized at the inception of the elected office, and again reiterated by Prime Minister Lee Hsien Loong when he announced plans to review the Constitution in 2016. In his speech, the Prime Minister said:

> The President must remain an elected office. If the President is not elected, he will lack the mandate to wield his custodial powers. I have read various op-eds in the newspapers which say we can go back to the old system, just do away with the Elected President and have Parliament elect the President; do not have a national election.
>
> I think the Workers' Party has sometimes espoused this view, too. I think it is most unwise. The President has a role. It is a difficult system to get right, but we have to adjust it and try and get it more right than wrong over a period of time, and not abandon the project altogether and leave ourselves naked and defenceless against all the difficulties which the Elected President enables us to avoid.[47]

The logic of this idea surely lay in (a) giving the electorate a *real choice* in terms of the candidates; and (b) ensuring that the chosen ca ndidate had indeed been put through the rigours of elections and emerged with an undisputed majority. However, provisions in the Constitution and the Presidential Election Act subvert this logic in two ways. First, by severely limiting voters' choice in stipulating the type of candidate who can stand for election based on a mixed criterion of executive experience and financial savvy; and second, by allowing sole candidates to be declared 'elected'.

Any doubt as to whether a candidate succeeded in securing the electorate's mandate is put to rest if he or she obtains an absolute majority during an election. This mandate becomes rather less tenuous if the majority secured is not absolute, and worse still if there is a walkover with no contest. Indeed, a major sticking point concerning the process of electing the President has been Section 15 of the Presidential Elections Act, which stipulates that if, on nomination day, "only one candidate stands nominated" that candidate shall be declared "to be elected to the office of President". A candidate can become President simply through a walkover. This happened thrice, in 1999 and in 2005 when the late S.R. Nathan stood as the sole candidate in both elections, and in 2017 when Halimah Yacob was declared the sole qualified candidate in the reserved election.

The elections of 1999, 2005 and 2017 and that of 2011 bring into sharp relief the fact that none of the winning candidates had an absolute majority of the votes cast. In the case of Presidents Nathan and Halimah, who faced no opponent, it is difficult to ascertain what proportion of the public actually supported them or gave them their mandate to function as President. In such cases, it may well be worthwhile to reconsider the idea of having some kind of endorsement exercise, something akin to the South Korean system of requiring candidates to obtain at least one-third the eligible votes as proposed by Valentine Winslow back in 1990.

3.5.2 Contests, run-offs and absolute majorities

Contrast this with the 2011 election in which President Tony Tan was elected. This election was problematic. Notwithstanding his victory in this four-man race, Tony Tan very narrowly defeated his closest opponent, Tan Cheng Bock, by only 7,382 votes (or 0.35 per cent of the votes cast). Tony Tan's share of 35.2 per cent was just slightly more than a third of all votes cast. Viewed conversely, a large segment of the population – close to 65 per cent of all electors – were actually *not* in favour of Tony Tan. It would thus be difficult to claim the moral high ground to say that such a majority gave him a true mandate from the people to speak and act for them as President.

At the Constitutional Commission hearing, I proposed that in the event of an election involving more than two candidates, a second-round run-off election should be held to give the final winner a clear majoritarian mandate. This system is not new, having been used in countries such as Austria, Brazil, France, Finland and India. The object of this two-round run-off system is to have the second round of voting limited to the top two first-round candidates. Thus, in the case of Singapore's 2011 election, a run-off would have pitched Tony Tan and Tan Cheng Bock against each other. Whoever won that election would have an absolute majority. In addition to ensuring that the winner obtained an absolute majority, the run-off system has the added advantage of forcing the electorate to choose between the top two candidates.

At the oral hearing, I offered the classic example of how effective this system was by looking at the 2002 French presidential election. A total of 16 candidates took part in the election and the top two candidates after the first round of voting were Jacques Chirac (19.88 per cent) and Jean-Marie Le Pen (16.86 per cent). The difference between the two candidates was a mere 3 per cent and their total votes constituted only 36.74 per cent of the vote; the remaining 63.3 per cent being spread between the other 14 candidates. However, after the second round of voting, Chirac won with a majority of 82.21 per cent while Le Pen only secured 17.79 per cent of the vote, just 0.93 per cent more than he won in the first round.[48] If the French had stopped after the first round of voting, Chirac's 19.88 per cent could be interpreted as him having 'lost' the vote of more than 80 per cent of the electorate. However, with the run-off vote, he secured an overwhelming majority and correspondingly, an unassailable mandate to govern.

The Commission was quite adamant in rejecting this suggestion, arguing that it was "wrong to assume that a candidate's legitimacy" was "contingent upon him obtaining the support of an absolute majority of the eligible electorate, or even securing an absolute majority of the votes cast."[49] It said:

> It cannot be the former because if that were the case, nations where voter turnout is poor may be hard pressed to ever claim a legitimate electoral mandate in the majoritarian sense. The Commission also does not agree with the latter proposition. In the Westminster tradition, the first-past-the-post system is a widely-accepted mode of conferring a legitimate democratic mandate on the candidate who emerges victorious at the polls. The question of legitimacy is not a simple numeric exercise of achieving majority support from the voters.[50]

It was the Commission's view that a winner's legitimacy came from "the fact that he has assumed office through a process which is free, open and fair, and which binds all citizens" and the first-past-the-post (simple plurality) system of voting confers as much legitimacy on the candidate as any other system. As such, any insistence "upon an absolute majority or a majority greater than that enjoyed by the Government in Parliamentary elections is, in the Commission's respectful view, simply not warranted".[51]

This logic is difficult to fathom. Electoral legitimacy comes from two things – choice and majorities. Taking the Commission's argument to its logical conclusion, this means that as long as an established process or procedure is carried out freely, openly and fairly, the election is fair and the candidate's legitimacy is secured. Legitimacy often flows from legality, but not always. A procedurally fair election is not necessarily a fair election if substantive unfairness results from it. To take an extreme example – candidacy for the Presidency is limited to former Prime Ministers of Singapore. How much legitimacy would the President have if that requirement reduced the pool of candidates to a single person? In such a case, there would be no choice and no majority, and the Commission would have us believe that such a candidate is as legitimate as one who has won a four-man contest through two rounds of election, securing an absolute majority? The argument applies equally in cases where there is a walkover.

The Commission offered two other reasons for rejecting this proposal: first, that run-off elections would likely be "unnecessarily complex and cumbersome"; and second, that such elections "may worsen the difficulties that candidates from racial minority groups might already face when running for Presidential office", especially in the case where a Chinese candidate is contesting against a candidate from a minority ethnic group as "racial considerations may be brought into sharper relief and may have a much more palpable impact on the outcome of the election." While such a system would certainly involve more time and administrative energy, elections are only held once in six years and the added 'inconvenience' is easily offset by a better system. The last objection cuts both ways. There is nothing to stop candidates in a first-past-the-post system from resorting to ethnic arguments to win votes; and it is conceivable that ethnic considerations could be brought in as sharp relief in cases where there are more than one candidate. Interestingly, at the end of its Report, the Commission nonetheless acknowledged the importance of elections and mandates if the President was to continue in his custodial role:

> The Commission considers that if the President is to continue to perform these custodial functions, the office should remain an elected one. The reasons have already been canvassed above but two bear repeating. First, it would be incongruous to have a second key in the hands of the President, if the holder of the first key (namely, the Government) is to appoint the holder of the second key. Quite apart from whether such a person could or might in fact be an effective check on Parliament, the perceived lack of independence is problematic. Second, the President will likely require a popular mandate if he is to have the authority to act as the custodian of the nation's reserves and be an effective check against governmental action, should the occasion arise. An appointed President is unlikely to have the standing or authority to effectively block a decision made by a democratically elected government.[52]

If elections and mandates were key to the President's legitimacy and authority, surely proposals to strengthen that mandate through a run-off should be taken far more seriously that it currently has.

3.6 Conclusion

With the passage of the Constitution of the Republic of Singapore (Amendment) Act 2016, Parliament lost a wonderful opportunity for rationalizing the Elected

Presidency scheme. Worse still, the Constitution was amended to provide for a 'reserved' election to be held in the event that no candidate from any of Singapore's main ethnic groups – Chinese, Malay, Indian and Others – occupied the Presidency for five consecutive terms. This amendment was brought in to resuscitate the symbolic role of the President, which was lost when the Constitution was amended in 1991. The tension between requiring the President to play two roles – that of financial custodian, and that of symbol and unifier of the state – was recognized by the Commission. Recognizing that this matter lay beyond the scope of its Terms of Reference, the Commission nevertheless felt it necessary to weigh in on the matter:

> The former requires that he be non-partisan and a unifier of the nation, while the latter potentially requires him to confront the Government of the day – a task which is somewhat at odds with the role of a unifier. Furthermore, while the prospect for such confrontation necessitates that the President hold the legitimacy and authority that comes from having an elected mandate, it seems out of place for persons seeking a nonpartisan unifying office to have to go through a national election, which will likely be politicised and divisive.[53]

The solution, thought the Commission, might be the "unbundling" of the President's symbolic and custodial roles and reposing them in two different institutions:

> The Commission suggests that the unbundling of the President's custodial role and its devolution to a specialist body could be operationalized in the following fashion. The custodial function over the nation's fiscal reserves and key public service appointments could be vested in an appointed body of experts. The Commission conceptualises such a council of experts as a second chamber of Parliament with the ability to delay measures, force a debate upon them and require the Government to override any objections only with a super-majority. Hence, unlike the Elected President, the council, as an appointed body of experts, would never have the power to absolutely veto or block Government initiatives (as the Elected President presently does when he has the support of the CPA). But through a combination of raising the issue, forcing a debate on the council's objections and requiring a super-majority, a suitable balance could be struck between the need to safeguard our critical assets on the one hand, and, on the other hand, enabling the Government to act.[54]

This proposal found favour with MPs from the Workers' Party but drew no response from the Government. This is most unfortunate, given that the Commission was the first Constitutional Commission to be convened since 1966. Had the matters been more thoroughly and critically considered, the Constitution could have been amended to give the electorate a real choice and made that choice really count through the ballot box. Instead, it opted to narrow the field and hang onto the first-past-the-post system that cannot vest a candidate with an absolute majority in a contest involving more than two candidates, and giving him or her the true mandate to check on the elected government.

Notes

1 See "PM hints at change in one-man, one-vote system" (*Business Times*, 24 December 1984), 14.
2 Foo Choy Peng, "Goh sets out the two major tasks" (*Business Times*, 1 January 1985), 1; "Task force to study electoral swing" (*Business Times*, 5 January 1985), 1.
3 "Task force" (n. 2).
4 See "A law to protect foreign reserves", *Straits Times* (16 April 1984), 1. According to then First Deputy Prime Minister Goh Chok Tong, the scheme had been discussed by the Cabinet since 1982. See "Constitutional Amendments to Safeguard Financial Assets and the Integrity of the Public Service (White Paper), Statement by First Deputy Prime Minister and Minister for Defence", *Singapore Parliamentary Debates: Official Reports*, 29 July 1988, vol. 51, col. 479.
5 "25 Years of hard work could vanish in 25 days of madness", *Straits Times* (16 April 1984), 8.
6 See Constitutional Amendments to Safeguard Financial Assets and the Integrity of the Public Services, Cmd 10 of 1988 (hereinafter "First White Paper").
7 *Ibid.*, 4.
8 *Ibid.*
9 *Ibid.*, 5.
10 *Singapore Parliamentary Debates: Official Reports*, 11 August 1988, vol. 51, col. 562.
11 *Singapore Parliamentary Debates: Official Reports*, 12 August 1988, vol. 51, col. 591.
12 *Ibid.*, col. 577.
13 *Ibid.*, cols 633–4.
14 See Safeguarding Financial Assets and the Integrity of the Public Services: The Constitution of the Republic of Singapore (Amendment No 3) Bill, Cmd 11 of 1990 presented to Parliament on 27 August 1990 (hereinafter "Second White Paper").
15 Bill No. 23 of 1990 (hereinafter "Constitution (Amendment No 3) Bill").
16 *Singapore Parliamentary Debates: Official Reports*, 4 October 1990, vol. 56, col. 483.
17 *Ibid.*, col. 484.
18 *Ibid.*, col. 468.
19 *Ibid.*, cols 468–9.
20 *Ibid.*, col. 469.
21 *Ibid.*, col. 488.
22 *Singapore Parliamentary Debates: Official Reports*, 5 October 1990, vol. 56, cols 532–3.
23 *Ibid.*, cols 560–1.
24 See Report of the Select Committee on the Constitution of the Republic of Singapore (Amendment No 3), Bill No. 23 of 1990 (Parl 9 of 1990) presented to Parliament on 18 December 1990 (hereinafter "Report of the Select Committee").
25 *Singapore Parliamentary Debates: Official Reports*, 3 January 1991, vol. 56, col. 719.
26 *Ibid.*, cols 726–7.
27 *Ibid.*, cols 746–7.
28 Act No. 5 of 1991, assented to by President Wee Kim Wee on 18 January 1991. The amendments to the Constitution under this Act were not brought into force until 30 November 1991 by GN No. S518/91. An exception was made in respect of the entrenchment provisions under the new Article 5(2A).

29 Article 67(3) provides that: "If and when there is only one presidential candidate, he shall not be elected President unless he receives at least one-third of the total eligible votes."
30 "Report of the Select Committee" (n. 23), B54. See also Valentine S. Winslow, "The Election of a President in a Parliamentary System: Choosing a Pedigree or a Hybrid?", in Kevin Y.L. Tan and Lam Peng Er (eds), *Managing Political Change in Singapore: The Elected Presidency* (London: Routledge, 1997).
31 But see Kevin Y.L. Tan and Lam Peng Er (eds), *Managing Political Change in Singapore: The Elected Presidency* (London: Routledge, 1997). See also, Kevin Tan Yew Lee, "The Elected Presidency in Singapore: Constitution of The Republic of Singapore (Amendment) Act 1991" (1991) *Singapore Journal of Legal Studies* 179; Valentine S. Winslow, "Electing the President: The Presidential Elections Act 1991" (1991) *Singapore Journal of Legal Studies* 476.
32 Article 19(2)(e).
33 The candidates for the inaugural presidential election in 1993 were Ong Teng Cheong and Chua Kim Yeow. Ong had served as Minister and was Deputy Prime Minister while Chua had been Accountant-General and also Chairman of the Post Office Savings Bank of Singapore. The sole candidate in the 1999 election was S.R. Nathan, who had served as Permanent Secretary and had been Chairman of Singapore Press Holdings.
34 "Ex-JTC man wants to run for President", *Straits Times* (5 August 2005), 1.
35 Presidential Elections Committee, "Press Statement by the Presidential Elections Committee on Applications for Certificates of Eligibility" (*Elections Department*, 13 August 2005) www.nas.gov.sg/archivesonline/data/pdfdoc/20050813991.pdf (accessed 1 December 2017). See also, M. Nirmala, "President Nathan poised to serve 2nd term" (*Straits Times*, 14 August 2005), 1.
36 Presidential Elections Committee, "Certificates of Eligibility Issued for Presidential Election 2011" (*Elections Department*, 20 August 2011) www.eld.gov.sg/pressrelease/PreE2011/2011%20-08-11%20Certificates%20of%20Eligibility%20for%20Presidential%20Elections%202011.pdf (accessed 1 December 2017).
37 *Ibid.*
38 *Singapore Parliamentary Debates: Official Reports*, 27 January 2016, vol. 94.
39 *Ibid.*
40 *Ibid.*
41 Constitutional Commission, *Report of the Constitutional Commission 2016* (Singapore Government 2016) (hereinafter "Menon Commission Report").
42 Kevin Y.L. Tan, "Representation on Constitutional Review of the Elected Presidency", 19 March 2016 (on file with the author).
43 Menon Commission Report (n. 41), para. 4.27.
44 *Ibid.*, para. 4.28.
45 *Ibid.*, para. 4.34.
46 Richard S. Katz, *Democracy and Elections* (Oxford: Oxford University Press, 1997), 101–5.
47 *Singapore Parliamentary Debates: Official Reports*, 27 January 2016, vol. 94.
48 See generally, Eric Dubois and Christine Fauvelle-Aymar, "Vote Functions in France and the 2002 Election Forecast", in Michael S Lewis-Beck (ed.), *The French Voter: Before and After the 2002 Elections* (Basingstoke: Palgrave Macmillan, 2004).
49 Menon Commission Report (n. 43), para. 7.4.
50 *Ibid.*
51 *Ibid.*, para. 7.5.
52 *Ibid.*, para. 7.42.
53 *Ibid.*, para. 7.43.
54 *Ibid.*, para. 7.48.

4 Perfecting Singapore's system of political governance

Privileging elites in the quest for good governance

Eugene K.B. Tan

4.1 Introduction

Singapore's institution of the Elected President is often misunderstood. Although it has been part of the system of institutional checks and balances since 1991, a popular misconception is that the President, as Head of State, is a centre of political power unto itself. The President's custodial powers are, however, reactive and blocking in nature, rather than being policy setting and directory.[1] Singapore's system of government remains a staunchly parliamentary one, where the elected government wields executive power exercised primarily by the Cabinet headed by the Prime Minister.[2] This misunderstanding of the constitutional role, power and functions of the Elected Presidency may reside in the fact that the President is popularly elected despite the office being ostensibly designed to be non-partisan and above politics. This lack of understanding of the Elected Presidency can be partly attributed to the fact that of the five presidential elections thus far (namely, 1993, 1999, 2005, 2011 and 2017), only two were contested (1993 and 2011) and they were separated by 18 years.[3]

The Elected Presidency is not a classic inter-branch check-and-balance institution. The classical conception of checks and balances in a constitutional system of government posits the separation of executive, legislative and judicial powers. The Legislature, for example, can hold the Executive accountable for its use of executive power. Through judicial review under constitutional or administrative law, the judiciary can examine and challenge the use of executive power for constitutionality and legality respectively. This is notwithstanding that in a traditional Westminster system of government, it is often said that the legislative and executive powers are "fused" as members of the Executive must first be members of the Legislature and that the Executive dominates or even controls the Legislature.

For some, however, the close link between the executive and legislative branches is apparently inconsistent with the separation of the executive and legislative functions. The so-called strict doctrine of the separation of powers is apparently incompatible with the parliamentary system of government because it requires an absolute separation of persons that constitute the individual branches as well as an institutional separation that permits no connection or linkage between branches. This constitutional orthodoxy is misleading as it suggests that in the exercise of the various aspects of governmental power, a strict separation of powers exists in that each branch of government exercises only its prescribed function. The essential constitutional principle often ignored is that the separation of powers, in essence, requires that legislative, executive and judicial power are not wholly vested in one individual or single institution.

Any theory of responsible government, undergirded by the separation of powers, will entail some measure of both conflict and cooperation, whether one or the other dominates. Tension or conflict between the Executive and Legislature is a necessary and beneficial precondition to limiting and controlling government. This may at times give rise to a gridlock over major policy decisions and governmental initiatives, and potentially making government ineffective. However, the likelihood of tyranny of power is reduced through intervening checks and balances on the power of a single individual or institution. Put simply, the notion of separated powers demands a balance of institutional independence and interdependence. It is not about a strict equality of constitutional power but, rather, an equality of constitutional status among the branches. The different branches of government must be able to both maintain their status as independent constitutional actors and exercise limited (though not determinative) influence over the other branches.

The Singapore Constitution provides the Elected President with executive and legislative powers.[4] Where selected executive power is concerned, Singapore's Elected Presidency system is premised on and envisages an *intra-branch* mechanism to provide a heavily circumscribed and limited check on the Government. It was and remains an institution that is not specifically designed to thwart the will and prerogative of a dominant parliamentary government. Specifically, the use of past national reserves and the appointment of key public-sector office holders are the prerogative of the Government, namely, the Cabinet although they have to be counter-checked and concurred by the Elected President.

Since independence in 1965, Singapore has sought to constitutionally engineer a political system that meets its unique needs and aspirations. Although hewed from the British Westminster parliamentary model, the deliberate and regular institutional redesign of Singapore's electoral and political system has resulted in their evolving away from the original template. For instance, institutional innovations introduced during an intense burst of constitutional engineering between 1984 and 1991 saw the creation of the Non-Constituency Member of Parliament ("NCMP") (introduced in 1984), the Group Representation Constituency ("GRC") (1988), the Nominated Member of Parliament ("NMP") (1990), and culminating with the Elected President (1991) schemes.[5] To be sure, these innovations have been routinely criticized as disingenuous attempts by the ruling People's Action Party ("PAP") to further tilt the political playing field to its advantage and perpetuate its one-party dominance.[6]

Taking advantage of the strong electoral mandate in the September 2015 General Election where the PAP won almost 70 per cent of the popular vote, the PAP Government had embarked on the most significant renovation to the Elected

President framework since its introduction. In his speech on 27 January 2016 during the debate on the President's Address at the opening of the thirteenth Parliament, Prime Minister Lee Hsien Loong noted that the principle of capable and qualified men and women carrying out the custodial duties mandated of the President under the Singapore Constitution remains valid. He observed that, "the details may need to be brought up to date" not just because of inflation but also because "our economy has grown, government spending has gone up, government reserves have accumulated, and the size and complexity of the organisations subject to the second key of the President have grown many fold".[7]

The latest changes to the Elected Presidency were made within a relatively compressed timeline. From start to end, including public consultations and effecting the necessary constitutional and legislative changes, it took about 13 months, with the fifth presidential election a mere seven months later in September 2017. By the end of 2016, the eligibility criteria were updated and enhanced after a process of public consultation, primarily through the Constitutional Commission chaired by Chief Justice Sundaresh Menon. Pre-qualification remains a key feature of the electoral process. The elected post remains an exclusive one limited to an elite group of individuals who meet the stringent eligibility criteria. The Government's stance is that the custodial powers of the Elected President require someone of standing, competence and experience. These changes take place against the backdrop of Singapore being on the threshold of Prime Minister Lee and his so-called third generation (3G) team preparing to hand over the reins of government to the fourth-generation leadership (4G) in a few years' time.

This chapter argues that the office of the Elected President is best understood as an elite institution with eligibility restricted to a select group by a stringent set of criteria for hopefuls from the public and private sectors. The Council of Presidential Advisers ("CPA"), also an elite body in its own right through its membership and the appointment process, advises the Elected President. That the CPA plays a significant role with respect to the triggering of a parliamentary override of a presidential veto reinforces the notion of a highly structured and conservatively calibrated intra-branch check on the Executive. The Elected Presidency, in the ostensible pursuit of good governance, is not conceived or designed as a locus of power unto itself. The institutional design, even in its latest iteration, seeks to reinforce the centrality of good men (and women) in utilizing good institutions to strengthen good governance. The latest set of changes signal a subtle shift in the tripartite relationship comprising the Elected President, the CPA and the Legislature in maintaining financial prudence and stewardship and the integrity of the public sector. With more of the President's discretionary powers subjected to consultation with the CPA, the CPA's reach is also augmented in the latest constitutional review.

This chapter is organized as follows. Section 4.2 examines the considerations behind the changes to the eligibility criteria for persons seeking to contest in the presidential election. The relevance of the Confucian ethos of leaders having a moral duty to act in the collective interest is highlighted as the starting point of the political leaders' moral authority to govern. This moral standing and authority is as important as the legal and political authority that comes with an electoral mandate. Section 4.3 looks at the changes to the Council of Presidential Advisers as part of the overall endeavour to strengthen the Elected President's custodial powers framework while restraining the Elected President from constitutional overreach. In Section 4.4, the implementation of the most significant revamp to the Elected Presidency, including the procedural changes in the electoral process and the election campaigning, and the apparent haste in bringing forth the constitutional revamp, is described and critiqued. Section 4.5 concludes.

4.2 Contesting the Presidency – raising the bar

Given the particularistic neo-Confucian political culture subtly promoted by the Singapore Government, the political leadership valorizes the Confucian precept that leaders have a moral duty to act in the collective interest. It is from this that they derive their moral authority to govern even as the legal and political authority to govern comes from the electoral mandate.[8] This system of government is presumed to be virtuous and so can be trusted. To reinforce its approach to governance, the PAP government gave its imprimatur to and promoted the Confucian notion of good government by good men, incorporating it as a cornerstone of Singapore's political governance philosophy. Thus, the *Shared Values* White Paper declared:

> The concept of government by honourable men (*junzi*) who have a duty to do right for the people, and who have the trust and respect of the population, fits us better than the Western idea that a government should be given as limited powers as possible, and should always be treated with suspicion unless proven otherwise.[9]

In this scheme of things, the *junzi* (君子, Confucian gentleman)[10] and *li* (礼, proper behaviour in sync with societal order and norms through moral propriety) are dominant themes that continue to resonate with the political elites in Singapore.

Although the notion of the Confucian *junzi* is rarely invoked these days, the centrality of good men and women in the political leadership and bureaucracy continues to drive the institutional design, recruitment and promotion, and how governmental power is regulated. This is similarly the case for the Elected Presidency. This precept of good government by good men and women has been reinforced constitutionally with the latest and most extensive changes to the Elected Presidency. This quest to enhance and protect good governance is invariably tied with the political objective of managing the pace of political change.

As an intra-(Executive) branch check in Singapore's system of constitutional government, the President has the constitutional power to veto or disagree with the Government's proposals in the following key areas:

- Use of past financial reserves – that is, reserves not accumulated by the Government during its term of office;

- Appointment and removal of key office holders in the public service and in the statutory boards and government companies listed in the Fifth Schedule of the Constitution;
- Restraining Orders under the Maintenance of Religious Harmony Act (Cap. 167A, 2001, rev edn);
- Continued detention under the Internal Security Act (Cap. 143, 1985, rev edn);
- The Prime Minister's refusal to grant permission for corruption investigations by the Corrupt Practices Investigation Bureau ("CPIB").

The discretionary powers, pertaining to the use of past financial reserves and the appointment and removal of key office holders in the public service which are exercised in consultation with the Council of Presidential Advisers, provide an important check and balance to the parliamentary executive, especially in preventing the misuse of the nation's financial reserves and ensuring the integrity of the public service. Prior to 1991, such a check and balance mechanism was not specifically available at all. While Parliament then was a *de jure* constitutional check on the Executive's exercise of these powers, in reality, this was a very limited check because of the parliamentary majority held and the control of the Legislature by the Executive.

It was this apparent abiding fear of a "rogue government" running the country to the ground through profligate public spending and cronyism and corruption at the highest echelons of the public sector that prompted the search in the 1980s for a more effective checking mechanism resulting in the creation of the Elected Presidency.[11] This checking mechanism has been popularly described as the "second key". For example, to effect a drawdown of the past reserves or to appoint key public officials, both the Cabinet and the President must authorize it. The Prime Minister can no longer act unilaterally in these matters ever since the office of President was converted to an elected one in 1991. Making the Presidency an elected office was to confer on the President the requisite democratic legitimacy and moral authority to disagree with the elected Government's use of its "first key".

Given the significant custodial powers, the Constitutional Commission's key premise was to have "sufficiently stringent" eligibility criteria for presidential candidates.[12] Thus,

> it seems only sensible to require that one seeking to be elected should at least have a record suggesting that he has the technical competence and expertise to discharge the functions and exercise the powers of the Presidency appropriately and effectively.[13]

As such, the criteria had to be "updated periodically to keep pace with changing circumstances".[14] This ensures that only persons with the requisite experience and expertise are eligible to seek election. The White Paper stated that "[q]uantitative thresholds cannot remain fixed in perpetuity, because a country's economic situation does not itself remain static".[15] Given that the original eligibility criteria used in past presidential elections were established in and had not been revised since 1991, an update was merited "to ensure their continued suitability and relevance".[16]

Both the Commission's report and the White Paper relied on the following data to conclude that there had been a sea change in Singapore's economic landscape between 1991 and 2016:[17]

a The original $100 million paid-up capital benchmark for private-sector candidates: in 1993, only 158 companies had at least $100 million in paid-up capital. These companies comprised the top 0.2 per cent of Singapore-incorporated companies.
b If ranked in 2016 by the size of their paid-up capital, the 158th company would have a paid-up capital of approximately $1.6 billion, or 16 times the $100 million threshold in 1991.
c The top 0.2 per cent of Singapore-incorporated companies would number about 600 in 2016, with the smallest of these having a paid-up capital of over $430 million – four times the $100 million threshold.

In addition, the White Paper observed that the size of the Government's reserves, which was the subject of the President's "second key", had also grown substantially over 25 years. In other words, "[t]he weight of the job has increased".[18] This can be usefully summarized in Table 4.1.[19]

4.2.1 From rogue governments to rogue presidents

The Commission was unequivocal that the stringent eligibility criteria for presidential candidates were necessary. Given the "considerable power that is vested in the Elected President",[20] it opined that the President's powers and responsibilities are "far more complex than some assumed them to be".[21] First, the President can single-handedly block the initiatives of the elected Government.[22] Like an elected Government, the President can "cause serious damage to the nation" whenever the President's custodial powers are used indiscriminately or unwisely.[23] This seemed to indicate that the Elected Presidency could, in its workings, transmogrify into a countervailing source of power, or even be a threat to the country. This notion of the "rogue president" arguably resulted in

Table 4.1 Increase in value of national assets between 1990 and 2015 under the President's custodial function.

	1990 ($ billion)	*2015 ($ billion)*	*Quantum of increase (%)*
Gross Domestic Product	71	402	566.2
Central Provident Fund balances	41	300	731.7
Official foreign reserves	48	351	731.3
Temasek's Net Portfolio Value	9	266	2955.6

the latest set of constitutional changes providing the CPA with a bigger say in the Elected President's use of his custodial powers.

Second, in discharging his custodial powers, the President will encounter "complex issues, some of a highly technical nature" and will require "wisdom".[24] These range from the economic case for enormous scale financial proposals to macroeconomic concerns to assessing competency and the character of candidates for key public service appointments to dealing deftly on matters relating to maintenance of security and public order. Given the scale and magnitude of the President's constitutional responsibilities, the Commission observed that, "Discretion in these areas cannot be meaningfully exercised by someone without the requisite experience and expertise".[25]

Third, the Commission opined that stringent eligibility criteria can "help to temper any politicization of the Presidential office and of the election process".[26] Finally, the President should have the "requisite experience to assess the CPA's recommendations and ultimately form his own independent judgment".[27] Responding to the view that the eligibility criteria for the President were far more stringent than the requirements to be Prime Minister, the Commission regarded such a comparison as being "premised upon a false comparison" between the two offices.[28] The Commission noted the following:

> At the outset, it should be noted that the office of Prime Minister is central to the Westminster system of Parliamentary democracy, where it is a cherished value that any adult member of the electorate, who is not subject to a disqualification, is able to run for a seat in Parliament. In the Westminster system, the Prime Minister is selected from among the Members of Parliament so elected. It would not be possible to impose stringent eligibility criteria upon those seeking election to Parliament without doing considerable violence to the Westminster system. The Elected Presidency, on the other hand, is not part of the Westminster system; instead, it was created as a refinement of this model and it was necessitated by our unique circumstances.[29]

This view of the Elected Presidency as not being part of the Westminster system seeks to mark the Elected Presidency as *sui generis*. Consequently, the constitutional norms and conventions that may apply to the Head of State in the Westminster system are arguably not applicable in the Singapore.

4.2.2 Raising the bar: not whether but how much

Having set the context and the rationale for stringency in the eligibility criteria, the Commission noted that such criteria have to be periodically updated "to keep pace with changing circumstances".[30] Coupled with the massive increase in assets that the President had custodial powers over, there was little doubt that the logical conclusion was that the original eligibility criteria had to be updated or risk becoming increasingly unfit for purpose.

Therefore, the question was not *whether* the eligibility criteria should be raised; instead, the pertinent question was *how much* should the criteria be raised. If the bar was raised too significantly, the pool of qualified persons could possibly be reduced significantly. The pool of qualified persons is a limited one since the breadth of skills, knowledge, experience and judgement required of the President under the Constitution is very demanding. From this small pool of qualified persons, those who might be keen to run for public office would naturally be much smaller.[31] And, in the case of a reserved election for the candidates from the Malay or Indian and Others communities, the number of qualified persons and potential candidates would be confined to a very select group.

As such, even as the eligibility criteria are updated and made more onerous in tandem with the significant increase in the value of national assets that the President has to safeguard, they should not result in a dramatic shrinkage in the pool of eligible Singaporeans, especially for the minority races. Consider the following: In the five presidential elections, only nine Certificates of Eligibility were issued.[32] Of these, only three such certificates were issued to non-Chinese – Mr S.R. Nathan in 1999 and 2005, and Madam Halimah Yacob in 2017. In these three elections, there was no contest as no other certificate of eligibility was awarded.

However, as for this concern about a shrinking of the pool of eligible persons to contest, the Commission considered that "an undue focus on the size of the pool [of potential candidates] is a distraction from the real task at hand, which is to ensure that candidates possess the requisite qualifications to satisfactorily discharge the responsibilities of the office".[33] The Commission felt that the eligibility criteria

> should be set at a level where they serve as an effective proxy to best capture individuals who are likely, in fact, to have the requisite experience and expertise. The criteria should not be manipulated so as to artificially increase (or reduce) the size of the pool of candidates, or to achieve any other collateral purpose.[34]

4.2.3 Ringing the changes – cautiously and boldly

> The central purpose of having eligibility criteria is to enhance the prospect that only candidates with the right experience and expertise to ably discharge the exacting responsibilities of the President will be able to seek election. Any revision of the eligibility criteria should be undertaken with this goal in mind.[35]

For the purpose of determining whether they meet the eligibility criteria, presidential hopefuls seeking candidacy were and are categorized either under the public sector or the private sector. In turn, for each category, there are two "tracks": automatic or deliberative. The most significant measure taken in the review and subsequent constitutional amendments was the enhancement of the criteria for those seeking to qualify under the private-sector route. The Commission recommended three changes: (1) The nature of a qualifying company;

(2) The nature of the qualifying position within a qualifying company; and (3) The introduction of performance criteria. Taken together, they point to the need to evaluate whether a person who had helmed private-sector companies is likely to be able to bring a variety of relevant skills to the Presidency. These skills include experience in fiscal matters, management and responsibility for a substantial workforce. Such a skill set would stand the President in good stead as he would be more likely to understand and be able to evaluate the Government's complex proposals involving large sums of money and impacting the country. It would also assist the President "to assess and ask the right questions about persons being considered for very senior appointments".[36]

On the nature of a qualifying company, the Commission recommended that the indicator of paid-up capital be replaced with shareholders' equity. The latter was regarded as a better proxy for a company's size and complexity.[37] The Commission explained that the "shareholders' equity reflects the company's current (and not just its historical) recorded worth".[38] This was a more accurate reflection of the present size or complexity of a company. In this connection, the Commission also proposed that a company's shareholders equity be calculated by taking the average shareholders' equity value for three consecutive financial years.[39]

On the size of a company that is "more likely than not to be sufficiently large and complex", the Commission further recommended that minimum threshold for such a company is one with a shareholders' equity of $500 million.[40] Such companies tended to have substantial cross-border operations, transact significant sums of money, and their leaders making polycentric decisions taking into account diverse strategic and operational considerations.[41] The Commission acknowledged that the $500 million shareholders' equity figure was not derived through a mathematical or formulaic exercise; the threshold could be pegged to another figure within a given range. Instead, the Commission was guided by settling on a threshold that would likely indicate whether a person had the "requisite technical skills, experience and expertise in financial matters"[42] and which would not "dramatically shrink the pool of potentially qualified persons".[43]

On the nature of the qualifying position within a qualifying company, the Commission recommended that only the person holding the "most senior executive position" in the company be eligible.[44] The Commission was concerned that the criteria in the former Article 19(2)(g)(iii) placed "undue emphasis on form rather than substance".[45] Previously, a person who had been the chairman or the chief executive officer of a company of the requisite size requirement would have qualified regardless of his actual scope of responsibility and whether he was actively involved in running the company. Therefore, the Commission proposed that the person must have held the "highest level of executive authority in the company" for at least three years.[46]

These changes point unequivocally to the Commission preferring the eligibility criteria on the qualifying position to focus on the actual nature and scope of a person's work within the company. This ensures that people who merit automatic qualification "have had practical experience in handling fiscal matters of sufficient size or complexity". For the Commission, the person in the most senior executive position "bears the ultimate weight of responsibility for the fate of the company". Through making decisions of scale and magnitude for a company of the requisite size, such a person is deemed to possess: "(a) the financial knowledge to comprehend the intricacies of the various proposals, and (b) the confidence that comes with a certain degree of familiarity with making decisions involving very large sums of money."[47] Referencing two examples of President Nathan approving a drawdown of past reserves in 2008 and 2009 during the "Global Financial Crisis", the Commission observed that "[t]here may be times when the President has to make these large and complex financial decisions on an urgent basis, without the benefit of time for lengthy deliberation and consideration."[48]

The Government agreed with the Commission's recommendations outlined above on the nature of a qualifying company and the nature of qualifying position within a qualifying company. The Government also agreed with the Commission's recommendation to introduce performance criteria for the qualifying company, namely, a record of net profitability and the company not going into liquidation or any type of insolvency process.[49] The Commission noted that these measures were "blunt",[50] but considered it desirable to require applicants to demonstrate that they have displayed an acceptable level of performance of the companies under their charge.[51] With the more stringent requirements for automatic qualification for applicants from the private sector, the bar was similarly and significantly raised for those seeking qualification under the deliberative route. Applicants under this track have to demonstrate that they have held a comparable office and thus possess the requisite expertise and experience to be the President.

4.2.4 A bifurcated approach to eligibility: public versus private

In contrast, for applicants from the public sector, the eligibility criteria underwent minor, if not cosmetic, changes – they were not substantially affected at all. For applicants who qualify automatically, they are deemed to possess the requisite experience and expertise by virtue of having held a stipulated public office for the minimum of three years.[52] Where the applicants do not qualify automatically, they have to satisfy the Presidential Elections Committee that the office they held was of a comparable nature to those held by persons who qualified under the automatic track.[53] For the qualifying public-sector offices, the Commission was of the view that the list was tightly drawn.[54] These offices are taken to indicate that the office holders have managed and led substantial organizations and acquired experience in dealing with complex matters having a "wide-reaching public dimension".[55]

The Commission, however, did recommend the removal of the offices of the Accountant-General and the Auditor-General from the list of tightly drawn qualifying public-sector offices.[56] The Commission's view was that the Accountant-General and the Auditor-General played "an indispensable but ultimately ancillary (and comparatively narrow) role in the delivery of public goods and services." However, they were not required to grapple with the "contrary pulls and pressures of government decision-making".[57] The Government, however, did not agree with the recommendation. It decided to retain both offices as being automatically providing the type of experience and expertise needed for the office of the President.[58]

The Government's approach emphasizes the qualifying criteria for both the public and private sectors as being a set of proxy indicators on whether a person can do the job of the Elected President. However, given the contrasting set of changes for public-sector and private-sector applicants, the eligibility criteria could give a leg-up to public-sector candidates who qualify automatically even if some of the offices may provide much less exposure to financial matters than the private-sector candidates. Nevertheless, these public offices arguably provide the public office holder with the requisite exposure and other attributes, which private-sector candidates may lack, to discharge some presidential functions. As the Commission reasoned, the private- and public-sector routes to qualification while "targeted at identifying persons with the relevant skillsets, no single office is ever likely to endow the holder of that office with all the attributes necessary for him to discharge all the Presidential functions".[59] It was also of the view that "it may not be correct to compare the two routes as if they are precisely alike".[60]

The Commission did not recommend broadening the list of public-sector qualifying offices.[61] It also recommended that only an applicant who has held the most senior executive position in a scheduled statutory board may qualify as a presidential candidate.[62] Previously, Article 19(2)(g)(ii), the equivalent of the current Article 19(3)(b)(ii), provided for "Chairman" or "Chief Executive Officer" as qualifying positions. The current provision provides only for the chief executive of an entity specified in the Fifth Schedule of the Constitution. The Commission felt that only the "most senior" officers in these offices should be eligible. These officers "bear the ultimate weight of responsibility" for their organizations' performance; it is "this unique facet of leadership that qualifies them to hold Presidential office".[63]

Similarly, for private-sector candidates, the Commission persisted in having a person with the "most senior executive position" in the company being eligible. Article 19(10) of the Constitution states that the "chief executive" of an entity or organization "means the most senior executive (however named) in that entity or organisation. Such a person is principally responsible for the management and conduct of the entity's or organisation's business and operations". Furthermore, the Commission proposed that public-sector applicants should not be subjected to a performance assessment, unlike their private-sector counterparts.[64] It argued that the differentiation was due to there being "no *measurable standards* against which their performance may be assessed".[65] It also felt that a subjective assessment of an applicant's performance in public office would detract from the "clear and objective standard that the automatic track" was meant to provide.[66] Instead, the Commission proposed an alternative sift: double the duration public- and private-sector applicants have to hold a qualifying office from three to six years.[67] The Commission agreed with several contributors that three years was too short a period and the duration should be lengthened. It argued that time was needed to "acquire and hone the requisite skills" and that "the length of time one spends in an office can be an indirect indication of that person's success in discharging the responsibilities of that office".[68]

While agreeing that applicants should have spent "adequate time" in a qualifying office, the Government preferred to maintain the original stipulation of three years in a qualifying office for both public- and private-sector candidates.[69] It opined, rather vaguely, that:

> the precise minimum duration to be set is ultimately a question of balance. Given the concurrent changes to other aspects of the eligibility criteria, the Government preferred to adopt a cautious approach, and retain the qualifying tenure at three years at this time.[70]

The Government's bifurcated approach in enhancing the eligibility criteria for private-sector applicants but not the public sector erred on being safe rather than sorry. It also suggests that public-sector applicants may be perceived to be a better fit for the Presidency. Regardless, even as it believed that the pool of eligible persons should be confined to a very select group, it was also concerned that this pool should not be dramatically reduced. With all previous Elected Presidents (namely, Ong Teng Cheong, S.R. Nathan and Tony Tan Keng Yam) hailing from the public sector, the Government adopted a precautionary approach for the public-sector route as compared with the private-sector route. It preferred to maintain the status quo of qualifying public offices since experience suggested that a person being eligible is one thing and whether one is keen to step forth and contest is another thing altogether.

The cautious tack vis-à-vis public-sector applicants demonstrated that the Government preferred the status quo and it would rather move gingerly and not seek to go the full extent that the Commission had recommended, especially on the eligibility criteria for public office holders. This preference for moderation in changes, especially for the public-sector positions, was also manifested by the Government not agreeing with the Commission's recommendation for a look-back period of 15 years for applicants. The Government agreed with the introduction of a currency requirement so that an applicant's experience remains "sufficiently relevant",[71] "given the rapidly evolving environment in which he will have to function".[72] However, the Government considered a longer look-back duration, which falls wholly or partially within the longer period of 20 years of the relevant presidential election, as being "suitably current".[73] Again, the Government was apprehensive about narrowing the field of eligible persons and so decided to "proceed cautiously, particularly as it is a new requirement".[74]

Even as it sought to update the eligibility criteria after 25 years, the overarching theme is the need to proceed with caution in mandating new eligibility requirements, especially for the public sector. This restraint stems from wanting to let time pass and "beta test" the enhanced eligibility criteria.[75] However, where the eligibility criteria for private-sector applicants were concerned, the Government was eager to ring the changes. Such a contrasting approach was perhaps not surprising. To reiterate, since the first presidential election in 1993 to the most recent in 2017, all the Elected Presidents had qualified automatically through the public-sector route. Mindful of the uncertainty on how the proposed changes will work in reality, the Government's overall approach was a veritable mix of cautionary, pragmatic and political considerations. Arguably, the Government did not finely differentiate between these considerations since it had to ensure that whatever changes implemented have to work well, otherwise there will be a political backlash.

The Government preferred treading cautiously and to be able to make changes to the system without the cumbersome requirement of securing the requisite support through a national referendum. This means being able to roll back or go even further depending on how the latest changes work. The Government pointed to the past 25 years of working out the custodial powers framework and processes of the Elected Presidency to justify why it had not brought into force the entrenching constitutional provisions.[76] The aim of entrenching a constitutional provision is to make it more onerous to amend or repeal the provision in question. The requirement of a referendum vests the ultimate say in the people.[77]

4.2.5 Favouring financial and management nous

Raising the stringency of the eligibility criteria is hard to argue against. The value of the assets the President has custodial oversight of has increased many folds since 1991. Yet, it is hard, if not impossible, to devise an all-embracing set of criteria for a person's ability to fulfil the Elected President's full suite of constitutional, ceremonial and community roles. The eligibility criteria are overwhelmingly weighted in favour of financial and management *nous* for applicants from the private sector. For those with a public-sector background, financial and management *nous* is not the most important criterion; it does not occupy the same prominence as political or public-sector experience exemplified through automatic qualification for having held certain public offices.

Considering the President's ceremonial and community roles, judgement, wisdom and empathy are not given similar weight in the evaluation of eligibility.[78] On the one hand, there are the aspirations for the Elected President to be a symbol of multiracialism and a unifying figure to all Singaporeans. This was the whole basis of the reserved election proposal. The eligibility criteria do not at all interrogate whether a presidential aspirant has the ability, the track record or the gumption as an advocate, promoter and practitioner of multiracialism. This contrasts with the near overwhelming expectation that any presidential aspirant possesses the requisite expertise and experience for the custodial functions.

But the eligibility criteria clearly accord different weight to equivalent qualifying requirements for the public and private sectors (including both automatic and deliberative tracks). For persons from the private sector, the emphasis is to throw up a person who has the management and financial *nous*. The raising of the eligibility criteria for a qualifying company and a qualifying position within a qualifying company confirms this. Indeed, the enhanced criteria may further restrict applicants from the private sector, who could very well execute the ceremonial and community roles but do not possess the requisite financial and management know-how.

Ultimately, the fall-back position to the bifurcated approach in determining eligibility of public- and private-sector applicants is that the eligibility criteria serve as a proxy indicator, not a guarantee or fail-proof measure, that a person has the requisite expertise and experience to perform the duties as President. Often, the President has the benefit of the advice of the CPA and the public bureaucracy on competing policy options or why a certain course of policy action should be embarked upon. What is then required is for the President to exercise judgement on the appropriate policy choices for which his custodial powers have to be applied to. All past and present Elected Presidents had spent substantial periods in the public sector. For instance, President Ong Teng Cheong was Deputy Prime Minister (1985–1993). President S.R. Nathan was a senior civil servant. President Tony Tan Keng Yam was Deputy Prime Minister (1995–2005) while President Halimah Yacob was from the trade union movement and Speaker of Parliament.

Given that the President performs custodial, ceremonial and community roles, the enhanced eligibility criteria may appear to be unnecessarily onerous and inordinately limits the pool of eligible persons who could bring to the office desirable attributes that are not or cannot be measured by the eligibility criteria.

4.2.6 Depoliticizing the Presidency

The Commission's conviction that the stringent eligibility criteria for presidential candidates were necessary paved the way for a significant enhancement of the criteria. It also signalled and reinforced the Elected Presidency as an elite institution rather than a popular one, and certainly not a populist institution. This is best exemplified in the measures the Commission proposed (and which were adopted) for candidates campaigning during the election and the undertaking required of candidates during the application process.[79] The goal is to depoliticize the Elected Presidency, understood here as the process of removing or reducing any political character not only of the office but also the decision-making in the exercise of the President's discretionary custodial powers. The effect is that any presidential discretion exercised is one step removed from political agency of the parliamentary executive (the Cabinet). Thus, the Elected Presidency is not an alternative or even a competing centre of power.

This deliberate attempt at depoliticization, however, underestimates that depoliticization is an intrinsically political process in and of itself. Being a popularly elected office inevitably politicizes the Presidency right from the outset. Similarly, having to exercise his discretion in the use of custodial powers, whether or not in alignment with the Government's proposal, renders the President's decision an inherently political one, even if the considerations that undergird the process and decision itself are non-political. The endeavour towards depoliticization reflects the attempt to forge a particularistic narrative of the Elected Presidency as a non-political office. It also seeks to endorse a governance approach in which any over-exuberant expectation of Singaporeans towards the Presidency is appropriately influenced and managed. In particular, that the presidential veto, when exercised, is not intrinsically political in form or in substance. Should the presidential veto be overridden by the executive-controlled Legislature, this legislative decision can also be characterized as non-political as well. However, things may not be so simple. Besides being an elected office, the custodial powers framework has the Council of Presidential Advisers playing a prominent role in the President's use of his veto powers.

4.3 Beefing up the CPA

Unsurprisingly, the third aspect of the Commission's review related to the role and composition of the Council of Presidential Advisers (CPA).[80] The CPA's primary function is to provide the President with the counsel of an independent body of experienced advisers when he exercises his discretionary custodial powers.[81] Although an unelected body, the CPA is an integral part of the Elected Presidency's framework of custodial powers. The President, Prime Minister, Chief Justice and the Public Service Commission Chairman nominate its members.[82]

The Commission noted that the CPA does not have the power to block the President but "plays a significant role in the balance between the President and the Government, where they disagree *on certain matters*".[83] It is this pivotal role the CPA plays in connection with the President's exercise of his discretionary custodial powers that is seemingly at odds with its advisory role and unelected status. The Commission also made the following important observations on the framework governing the President's discretionary powers and the CPA's role:

- The President should in general be advised by the CPA in the exercise of his custodial powers;[84]
- The "two-key" mechanism must be complemented by a political mechanism to resolve differences between the President and the Government;[85] and
- The Elected Presidency was neither intended nor designed to shift the locus of political power. In a situation of impasse, Parliament is the most suitable forum to decide whether the President's decision should be overridden.[86]

Congruent with its unelected status, the CPA has "no power of initiative" with its role "limited only to weighing in on the balance between the President and the Government".[87] Save for certain discretionary powers, the CPA is also Singapore's constitutional response, akin to a tiebreaker, to any potential logjam between the Government and the President on the use of national reserves and key public service appointments. Should the CPA's recommendation on a matter be at odds with the President's veto, Parliament can override the President if no fewer than two-thirds of the total number of Members of Parliament (excluding nominated Members) vote in support of such a resolution.[88] This "secondary role" of the CPA entails that it functions as an independent "counterbalance" should the President exercise his veto against a proposed action of the Government.[89]

The Commission's overall assessment was that the "reforms to the CPA do not appear to have kept pace with changes made to the Presidency".[90] To better aid the CPA in its primary role of advising the President, the Commission proposed additional measures to strengthen and refine the CPA's role and composition, which would augment the CPA's independence. Given the CPA's "pivotal role", the Commission recommended the refinement of the qualification criteria for a person to be appointed to the CPA but it resisted calls to raise the criteria.[91] It recommended that constitutional provisions be enacted to require that certain matters be considered before a person is appointed to the CPA. These matters are: (1) A CPA member must be a person of "integrity, good character and reputation"; and (2) A CPA member "must have relevant expertise that will *inform the exercise of the President's powers*".[92] The Commission opined that the appointment of a CPA member should add to the CPA's "diversity of experience *as a collective body*, so that the CPA as a whole will possess the requisite breadth and depth of experience to better advise the President."[93] The Commission declined to advocate for more prescriptive eligibility criteria as this could result in the exclusion of members "who might otherwise potentially contribute valuable specialist knowledge to the CPA".[94]

To regulate how the CPA can directly influence and affect the parliamentary override, the Commission recommended a finely calibrated approach of requiring different levels of parliamentary override depending on the CPA's degree of support of the veto level.[95] The Government declined to accept this recommendation.[96] It was concerned that such an approach "may unintentionally emphasise or even politicise how individual members of the CPA, particularly its Chairman, had voted, instead of the collective judgment of the Council as a whole."[97] Mindful that the CPA is an unelected body, the Government reasoned that such a calibrated approach would inadvertently politicize how individual CPA members vote. It was concerned that the stature and independence of the CPA be maintained and that it should not descend into the political arena. Given the CPA's intimate connection with the President's exercise of veto powers, compromising the stature and independence of the CPA would detrimentally impact upon the Elected Presidency as well. The Government preferred the long-standing approach of a parliamentary override that is not determined by counting heads (or, the degree of support the President has from the CPA). This means that a parliamentary override is available to the Government where the President's veto was not supported by a simple majority of the CPA. Although adopting different approaches, it was clear that both the Commission and the Government did not wish to see the CPA become a power unto itself.

In the main, the Commission's review of the CPA's role resulted in recommendations to simplify, streamline and to promote consistency in the framework for the President's powers vis-à-vis the CPA. The Commission recommended, and the Government accepted, that the President be constitutionally required to consult the CPA before exercising his discretion in respect of all fiscal matters touching on Singapore's reserves and on all matters relating to key public service appointments.[98] The President's general duty to consult the CPA in the exercise of his custodial powers is now required under Article 37IA(1) of the Constitution. However, the Commission and the Government were in agreement that the President does not need to consult the CPA in the exercise of his protective functions[99] and in the exercise of his historical discretionary powers.[100] As such, these powers are not subjected to a parliamentary override.

Prior to the 2016 constitutional amendments, the President was not obliged to consult CPA before exercising some of the custodial powers.[101] The Commission found this dichotomy in the President's obligation to consult "incongruous" as these matters "may have significant systemic impact and which, for that very reason, have (rightly) been subjected to Presidential oversight".[102] It also saw "no reason in principle" for these powers (and the appropriate scope of parliamentary override) to be treated differently. As such, the Commission recommended that the parliamentary override mechanism should be available so as to avoid the "potentially far-reaching consequences of a logjam affecting decision-making in these areas".[103]

In reviewing the size and structure of the CPA, the Commission made the case for augmenting the CPA with two additional members, one appointed by the President and the other by the Prime Minister. With the scope of parliamentary override expanding, the CPA's workload will increase, justifying the CPA comprising eight members.[104] There is a 1996 precedent when the CPA membership was expanded from five to six when the scope of the parliamentary override was widened. The Commission also expressed confidence that the appointers of CPA members "can be expected to exercise the requisite judgment as to the appointee's suitability and experience before making any nomination".[105] It also noted that CPA members are expected to exercise independent judgement, and not reflect the views of the office holder who had advised the President to appoint them.[106]

The changes to the CPA continue to reinforce the CPA's centrality in the Elected Presidency's framework of custodial powers. As a council of distinguished Singaporeans,[107] the CPA is an important resource and advisory body for the President. The Commission noted that the prospect of impasses was inherent in a system of checks and balances.[108] As such, where an independent body of experts concluded that it could not agree with the President, the Commission concurred that the President's position on that issue "might warrant a second look in Parliament".[109] In the custodial powers framework system design, the Elected Presidency is not conceived nor is it institutionally designed as a locus of power unto itself. The Commission described the CPA's sum total role in rather modest terms of being "limited only to weighing in on the balance between the President and the Government".[110] In contrast, the White Paper went so far as to describe the secondary role of the CPA as a "check".[111] This understates somewhat the CPA's influential role in determining whether a presidential veto prevails or not against the Government. In 1990, the Select Committee had opined that the CPA would over time grow in importance and perhaps evolve into a Council of State.[112] In 1996, when Parliament was asked to widen the scope of the parliamentary override and the Chief Justice was empowered to nominate the sixth CPA member, the then Prime Minister Goh Chok Tong spoke of building up the CPA as "an independent body".[113]

Taken in totality, the latest set of changes, arguably, represents a subtle shift in the tripartite relationship between the Elected President, the CPA and the Legislature. With more of the President's discretionary powers subjected to consultation with the CPA, the CPA's reach appears to be augmented in the latest constitutional review. However, concerns that the CPA is the real power behind the Presidency are exaggerated, and may be mistakenly premised on the view that the Elected President, given his electoral mandate, should be able to exercise his discretionary custodial powers without having to consult an unelected body or for Parliament being able to override a presidential veto.

However, Singapore's system of government remains quintessentially a parliamentary one in which the Cabinet led by the Prime Minister exercises significant grip on executive policy- and decision-making and the day-to-day running of the Government and country. Parliament is the "most important deliberative body"[114] in Singapore and "remains the most suitable forum to decide whether the President's decision should be overridden".[115] Overriding the presidential veto is not without its political risks to the Government of the day. The Commission captured the dynamics of the use of the parliamentary override well:

> The Government must therefore run a political risk should it decide to invoke the Parliamentary override mechanism, as it would have to publicly justify its case for overriding the President's decision and also respond cogently to the arguments raised in opposition to the Government's proposed course of action. If the requisite majority in Parliament is not convinced by the proposal to override the President's decision, the Government will have to bear the political cost of failing to secure the support of Parliament. This ensures that the Government will not lightly invoke the Parliamentary override mechanism and ensures the enduring efficacy of the second key as a safeguard mechanism. It is further strengthened by the existing requirement that a Parliamentary override has to be passed by a super-majority of two-thirds instead of a simple majority.[116]

The parliamentary override mechanism is a political tiebreaker that has to be wielded carefully, even where the Government of the day commands an overwhelming majority in Parliament. There could be potential significant downsides in initiating parliamentary scrutiny, which in turn would invite public scrutiny and debate on the impasse between the Government and the Elected President.[117]

Thus, even with the CPA weighing in on the balance between the President and the Government, the Government has to strategically assess on a case-by-case basis, whether it would be prudent to bring the matter to Parliament to resolve the impasse.

Notwithstanding Lee Kuan Yew's tight grip on the Government during his tenure as Prime Minister (1959–1990), Singapore's system of governance is not reposed on the standing of one person, despite the Prime Minister as *primus inter pares*. By the same token, arguments for the CPA not to get in the way of the Elected President's veto and so risk a parliamentary override cannot but misconceive the manner in which political power, authority and accountability are structured in Singapore. More pointedly, the Elected Presidency, even in its halcyon days when it was touted as a powerful check on the Government, was never designed to supplant the elected Government of the day. Hence, it should not come as a surprise if the (mis-)perception is that the Elected President's custodial powers framework accords significant weight to the CPA to the extent that the President's powers may even be clipped. In making its recommendation on any matter that the President has to consult the CPA, the CPA's ability to set in motion a potential parliamentary override hinges on the President exercising his veto in the first place and it not being aligned with the CPA's recommendation. Put simply, the CPA's role is reactionary and its recommendations do not nullify the presidential veto or prevent the President from exercising his veto in the first place.

To summarize, the 2016 constitutional amendments strengthen the CPA on various fronts. First, the President has a constitutional duty to consult the CPA on all fiscal matters and key public-sector appointments. Second, the CPA increase in its membership, from six to eight, provides it with additional expertise and perspectives to assist the President. Third, the qualification criteria for CPA members were refined in a non-prescriptive way. There were also refinements to the quorum requirements for council meetings[118] as well as staggering the terms and appointment cycles for appointments of CPA members to promote continuity and stability.[119] Additionally, general precepts were provided to guide the President, Prime Minister, Chief Justice and the Public Service Commission chairman for appointments to the CPA. The intent of these refinements seek to enhance the workings of the CPA and to bolster the standing and ability of the CPA to advise the President in his exercise of the discretionary custodial powers. These changes are, nevertheless, more refinements than a substantive reworking of the CPA.

With the latest changes, the custodial powers of the Elected Presidency remain the same even if the instances of the President's general obligation to consult the CPA (and the scope of the parliamentary override) are increased. There is little basis to regard the custodial framework of the Elected Presidency as being a hybrid one comprising the Elected President and the unelected CPA, or even of the CPA being more powerful than the President. The reality remains that the presidential veto, and whether to exercise it, rests entirely with the Elected President. The responsibility and prerogative to challenge the Government resides steadfastly and solely with the President. The President is not obliged to accept the CPA's recommendation (even if the parliamentary override is consequently triggered); he has the final say where the exercise of custodial powers are concerned. In short, the CPA is not another locus of power that competes with the President. Neither is the CPA able to clip the wings of the Elected President who is determined to press the case for his veto. Given that the President is popularly elected, the mandate to decide is far more recognized, accepted and weightier than the unelected CPA.

To be sure, it is the CPA's recommendation that is not aligned with the presidential veto that potentially triggers a parliamentary override. From the inception of the Elected Presidency, the institution design is configured on the basis that the CPA will steward the breaking of any impasse between the Government and the President. In this regard, the CPA is the intervening mechanism rather than a check on the Elected President. The 2016 review of the Elected Presidency does not sharpen but clarifies the intervening sinews of the CPA. The locus of the custodial powers resides firmly with the Elected President.

The "constitutional balance" would have shifted should the CPA drive the exercise of the presidential custodial powers or the President places "excessive reliance on the CPA to make the relevant judgments" when such powers are implicated.[120] This would, as the Commission noted, be "inimical to the framework contemplated in the Constitution, because it will vest considerable power in the hands of an unelected body of members".[121] Regardless of whether the veto prevails or not, the contentious matter is not unilaterally decided by the Cabinet or the President or Parliament. Criticisms of the Elected Presidency hinges on the "pivot" that the CPA is in breaking the impasse between the parliamentary executive and the presidential executive. Depending on whether its recommendation is aligned with the presidential veto or not, parliamentary override may not be invoked. In short, it is not so much whether the veto prevails or not but how the contentious matter is resolved that highlights the saliency of the check and balance on executive decision-making.

At the same time, the CPA as the pivot vis-à-vis the override of the presidential veto may be rationalized on the basis that the CPA collectively has more technocratic ability. It is to be expected that the CPA collectively wields more technocratic ability than the Elected President. After all, the CPA members are appointed on the basis of and for their expertise, experience and judgement. In this regard, a direct comparison of the Elected Presidency and the CPA is somewhat meaningless since they perform separate but interdependent functions within the custodial powers framework.

The Elected President's custodial powers framework is by no means perfect. However, the Elected President office's relevance to good governance is best demonstrated when the Elected President and CPA agree or differ with each other on a principled basis. For instance, if the President exercises his veto and it is aligned with the CPA's recommendation, the Government is "thwarted" since Parliament cannot even override the presidential veto in such a scenario. Similarly, if a simple majority of the CPA recommends against a presidential veto, a logjam is averted if Parliament overrides the veto with a two-thirds majority. Alternatively, the Government may not seek to have Parliament override the presidential veto. In all these instances, the deliberative process of the custodial powers framework is clearly brought into motion as the tripartite partners in the custodial powers framework are engaged with the issue and with the stakeholders.

Just as the eligibility criteria for presidential candidates emphasizes financial and management nous, this theme is repeated for the CPA as well. The CPA provides advice in connection with matters that the President exercises custodial powers. However, in other key areas of the President's discretionary power in relation to the exercise of his protective functions, namely, restraining orders under the Maintenance of Religious Harmony Act, detention under the Internal Security Act and corruption investigations by the Corrupt Practices Investigation Bureau, the President may consult but is under no legal duty to consult the CPA.[122] In these areas, other bodies such as the Internal Security Act advisory board and the Presidential Council for Religious Harmony advise the President.[123] Similarly, the CPA may or may not advise the President on matters pertaining to the President's community and ceremonial functions.

Thus, it should come as no surprise that while the President's functions and roles can be broadly categorized into custodial, ceremonial and community ones, there is a hierarchy of discretionary powers.[124] At the apex is the set of discretionary powers primarily related to his custodial powers where the CPA must be consulted, such as the drawdown of national reserves and key public-sector appointments.[125] This is followed by discretionary powers for which the President may consult the CPA,[126] and where the President is advised, as required by the relevant legislation, by a relevant public body.[127] Finally, there are the discretionary powers where the President has historically acted on his own discretion.[128] The CPA is therefore constituted and more directly connected to the President's custodial functions than other functions. This reflects the importance of the President having the benefit of the advice of the CPA while also subjected to the CPA's weighing in on the balance between the Government and the President should there be a disagreement.

Notwithstanding the above, the CPA's role and advisory jurisdiction is likely to grow. The extent remains unclear. However, one area where the President will likely be required to consult the CPA is the entrenchment of specific constitutional provisions. The purpose in entrenching the Elected President provisions is, *inter alia*, to protect against the abolishment of the Elected Presidency and to "safeguard potential curtailment or circumvention of the President's discretionary powers", specifically over the national reserves and key appointments.[129] The Commission had noted that the indefinite suspension of the entrenchment framework may not be appropriate, and suggested that the Government decides "whether to bring these provisions into force or repeal them in whole or in part".[130] The Commission refrained from taking a view on whether entry into force or repeal of the relevant provisions would be preferable. The Commission emphasized that this was ultimately a matter for political judgement – suggesting that polycentric considerations were involved which the Executive is best placed to work through them.

The Government acknowledged the Commission's view that it was not desirable to have an entrenchment provision held in abeyance indefinitely.[131] Entrenching key constitutional provisions would also provide for stability as well. The Government noted that the entrenchment framework did not accord any constitutional or legal weight to the advice and recommendations of the CPA. In short, "the weight accorded to the President's position on amendments to entrenched provisions does not depend on whether he has the Council's support".[132] For now, the Government opted to repeal the previous entrenchment provisions but did not introduce a new entrenchment regime in their place. The Government indicated that it intended to introduce a:

> recalibrated entrenchment framework that aims for a workable balance between preserving the adaptability of the Constitution to changing circumstances, and providing adequate stability through sufficient rigidity in entrenched areas. *The revised framework will also accord appropriate weight to the advice and recommendations of the Council.*[133]

What this means is that the CPA will play a vital and instrumental role in the further development of the Elected Presidency when the recalibrated entrenchment framework is enacted and brought into force. The Government did not commit to any timeline. With the 2016 review done and changes implemented, the Government indicated that testing and fine-tuning the revised framework will take time. It prefers "to let some time pass, see how the institution works over time, before entrenching".[134] For now, the various provisions on the Elected President can be amended by Parliament where it has been supported by not less than two-thirds of the total number of Members of Parliament (excluding nominated Members) on Second and Third Readings of the amendment bill.[135]

4.4 Implementing the raised bar

4.4.1 Consequential legislative amendments

Beyond the changes to the substantive eligibility criteria for presidential hopefuls, the consequential amendments to the Presidential Elections Act in February 2017 drew to a close the latest round of changes to Singapore's political system to entrench "good politics and leadership".[136] One procedural change was providing more time for prospective candidates to apply for the Certificate of Eligibility and for the Presidential Elections Committee to assess such applications. Another was to make provision for the Community Committee and its Sub-Committees for the Chinese, Malay and Indian and other minority communities to operationalize the hiatus-triggered reserved election mechanism. There were also efforts to improve the election process, including making it more convenient for overseas Singaporeans to register to vote overseas, and the use of a clearer demarcated area on the ballot papers for the voter to indicate his choice of candidate to reduce disputes during the ballot counting process. The law was also changed to provide for the automatic recounting of votes when the difference in votes polled by the top two candidates is 2 per cent or less. Previously, such candidates had to apply for a recount.[137]

4.4.2 Consequential non-legislative changes

Besides these amendments, the debate in Parliament in February 2017 was more notable for the announcement of the non-legislative changes to the presidential elections. The first was the attempt to clearly differentiate the campaigning for the presidential election from the parliamentary election. The Commission noted, "the election process has the potential to become politicised and highly divisive".[138] Given the fundamental differences between the presidential elections and the parliamentary elections, the Government decided that the framework for the presidential election should be non-political and in keeping with the nature of the office as a non-partisan and unifying institution. The new approach encourages the use of platforms and channels that reach out to voters at a national level and which are also more remote in nature. For instance, specific sites for campaign rallies will no longer be designated. However, presidential candidates can still hold rallies if they so wish. They will have to secure the venues themselves, and the requisite police permits. Instead of the outdoor rallies, the preference now is to provide more airtime on television as the Government sought to have candidates shift to television as the primary medium for voter outreach. The use of social media and indoor meetings of targeted group of voters will continue.

These changes come on the back of the combative 2011 Presidential Election, characterized by candidates and voters alike having competing and conflicting visions of the Presidency, which were often at odds with the clear powers of the Elected President provided for in the Constitution.[139] Rallies were seen as being neither necessary to electing a Head of State with custodial, ceremonial and community roles nor were they seen as being helpful in dealing with the divisiveness that often accompanies electoral contests where political parties and candidates alike compete on ideas, policies and ideologies. In its report, the Constitutional Commission stated that: "Presidential candidates should be required to conduct their campaigns with rectitude and dignity as befits the office and comports with the unifying role and purpose of the Presidency."[140] The Government fully agreed, stating that campaigning for the presidential election had to be consistent with the President's status and standing as a symbol of national unity.[141] The Government views presidential elections as polls contested on a national level and not on a local constituency level. Even if they should be competitive, a presidential election should not degenerate into a popularity contest or a political one in which candidates may engage in "constitutional overreach" in order to secure ballots to win. To this end, presidential candidates now have to explicitly declare that they understand the constitutional role of the President before they may be issued a Certificate of Eligibility, in the form of a statutory declaration contained within the application form for the Certificate of Eligibility.[142]

It would appear that the overall approach to the conduct of the presidential election takes its bearings from the *sine qua non* of the President as a symbol of national unity. It is also more in sync with an elitist approach, with a tinge of paternalism, in which the candidates (as elites) and the electorate alike are required to contest within specified confines so as not to descend to an undignified and combative contest that undermines the office of the Elected Presidency and the eventual winner of the presidential poll as President.[143] This also points to the inherent difficulty of reconciling two competing, if not conflicting, imperatives. On the one hand, there is the political imperative to invest the elected office with the requisite mandate and authority and legitimacy to challenge the Government of the day. On the other hand, there is the moral imperative of not debasing the office through a bruising electoral contest especially when the prospective candidates are very likely to hail from the elite class in Singapore society.[144] The Singapore approach points to the bold effort to square the circle – that of having meritorious individuals elected to serve as the President but yet not engaging in the kind of electoral campaigning and behaviour that the public is accustomed to and expects of any competitive poll. As the White Paper put it forthrightly, "a custodial President democratically elected in a national election remains the most workable and effective solution for Singapore for the present".[145]

In a similar vein, another non-legislative change resorted to was the "re-set" of the timing of the presidential election, which had always been held in August every six years since the inaugural presidential election in 1993.[146] The Government explained that this was to avoid the election campaigning coinciding with the National Day celebrations in August each year. Consequently, the fifth presidential election was held in September 2017 instead of August 2017. On this, the Government agreed with the Commission that a clear distinction ought to be drawn in the campaign methods for presidential elections and parliamentary elections. "Campaign methods for the Presidential Elections must not inflame emotions and must be in keeping with the decorum and dignity of the office of the President, given the important unifying and custodial roles of the President."[147] In other words, presidential election campaigning should be depoliticized for the good of the office. To what extent this would help remains to be seen. The country would very much be in election mode even if the election were to be held in September since the main electoral activity in the three months leading to the September poll would be the presidential election.

Besides the legislative changes, Parliament's Standing Orders were amended in May 2017 to improve the parliamentary procedures relating to the Elected Presidency.[148] Under the Constitution, Parliament can overrule a presidential veto that is contrary to the recommendation of the Council of Presidential Advisers. The Standing Orders now require both the President's grounds and the CPA's recommendation to be made available to Parliament at least two days before the motion proposing to overrule the President is debated in Parliament. This is after the Speaker of Parliament has determined and is satisfied that the President's decision in the exercise of his custodial powers was in fact contrary to the CPA's recommendation.[149] Before overruling a presidential veto, the issue must be carefully studied and debated robustly by Parliament. Such an overruling must be done on a principled basis and should have the support of Singaporeans. Otherwise, Parliament's overruling of a presidential veto can be divisive. In this regard, the requirement of a minimum of two days to study the documentation is too parsimonious to fully consider a contentious and weighty issue where public opinion may be split.

4.4.3 More haste, less speed?

Parliament passed the constitutional changes to the Elected Presidency in November 2016. With that, the most significant change to Singapore's Constitution, since the establishment of the Elected Presidency, took less than 12 months from the President's Address at the opening of the thirteenth Parliament in January 2016. In contrast, prior to that the establishment of an "intra-branch check" on the Executive in 1991, the matter of having an intra-branch check was debated at length for at least six years. The 2016 review seemed to have proceeded with relative speed, if not haste. Even as it ramped up its engagement efforts, persuading people that the changes were necessary and not a knee-jerk reaction to the divisive 2011 Presidential Election would take time. Why did the Government not conduct the review earlier between 2011 and 2015? The timing and implementation of the revised eligibility criteria and the reserved election mechanism were crucial. The Government decided to implement them with immediate effect in the 2017 Presidential Election.

While change was needed in due course, the Elected Presidency framework had not irretrievably broken down such that it was in dire need of urgent changes. Implementing the changes in the subsequent election in 2023 would provide more opportunities to further engage Singaporeans. It would not put the Presidency, the Government and Singapore in a worse-off position. This would also be aligned with Singapore's long-standing approach of incremental political change, rather than dramatic changes. It should be emphasized that the previous eligibility criteria were not seen as severely lacking and urgently in need of fixing.[150] And it is also unlikely to be the case that the Elected Presidents had not been equal to the task, requiring urgent changes. This in no way suggests that change was not needed but rather that when to implement the changes matters as much, if not more.

Any change even if it could be justified on rationale and principle must also satisfy the requirement of fairness. This would have reduced the possibility the changes to the eligibility criteria being unnecessarily policiticized.[151] As it turned out, when Parliament made the necessary constitutional changes to the Elected Presidency in November 2016, it was less than twelve months to the 2017 Presidential Election. Although Parliament can amend the eligibility criteria as it deems fit, the impact of any expedient, if not hurried, change would have on the electorate's perception as to the true nature of the review process seemed to be of much less importance.[152]

Moreover, could the changes to the eligibility criteria apply perhaps in the subsequent election, given that changing the rules of the game so late in the presidential electoral cycle would upset legitimate expectations? This would have avoided unnecessarily politicizing the election for a non-partisan office. The changes that the Government made were very substantive ones. Good engagement is not just about intensity but also being patient and persuasive. Singaporeans not only needed time to digest the proposed changes but, more importantly, to be assured that the extent of the changes were necessary and, on balance, would be beneficial to Singapore and Singaporeans.

Rationalizing the changes was the easy part. The Commission and the Government had presented a cogent and persuasive case. However, if the changes were perceived to be hurried through, then the opportunity of sustained engagement and buy-in was less likely. This apparent haste could have resulted in the lack of sustained and patient engagement on the necessity and timing of the changes. Even if the Government held a deep conviction of the necessity and correctness of the changes, the perceived haste with which it effected the changes did not work in favour of the august office of the Elected President. The impact of a hasty engagement of Singaporeans could have affected the legitimacy of the proposed constitutional changes. Further, if Singaporeans were not persuaded, this made it susceptible to conspiracy theories on the *raison d'être* and urgency of the changes. The timing of the implementation of the changes, specifically the combined effect of the enhanced eligibility criteria and the reserved election, rightly or wrongly, breathed life to conspiracy theories that the review and rapid changes were a reaction to the hotly contested and divisive 2011 Presidential Election. This, unfortunately, detracted from the constitutional review, which sought to further perfect Singapore's system of governance.

4.5 Conclusion: elites to the fore, keeping elitism at bay

In the 2017 Presidential Election, which was the first to utilize the enhanced eligibility criteria and the reserved election, only Madam Halimah Yacob, a former Speaker of Parliament (2013–2017) and PAP legislator (2001–2017), obtained a certificate of eligibility via the automatic qualification route for public-sector office holders. This outcome was not surprising at all. On the financial expertise requirement, the other two applicants, namely, Mr Mohamed Salleh Marican and Mr Farid Khan, had to take the more uncertain private-sector deliberative track. Based on the media reports, the companies they led were considerably smaller than the $500 million shareholders' equity that is stipulated in the Constitution. The Presidential Elections Committee ("PEC") was not going to and cannot bend backwards – that would be acting arbitrarily and unlawfully. Contrast this with the online chatter that the PEC could have "bent the rules" to let the other aspirants stand so that the first reserved presidential election would not go uncontested. However, this view stemmed from a fundamental misunderstanding of what the eligibility criteria are supposed to serve and a lack of recognition of the dangers that come with the PEC acting arbitrarily in order to satisfy public expectation.

The Elected President institutional innovation was itself borne out of the nagging fears of a "rogue government" ruining Singapore through profligate spending and unmeritorious key public office appointments. Twenty-five years after its establishment, it was timely to review the institution. Arguably, the substantive changes to the institution in 2016 were ostensibly motivated by the desire to reduce the likelihood of a "rogue president" from upending the parliamentary system of government and to enhance the office as a symbol of national unity. The institution continues to be a work in progress with the latest changes being the most comprehensive and substantive since the Elected Presidency was first introduced.

Like the 1991 changes, the latest changes seek to enable the PAP Government to manage the pace of political change without being dictated to. The adaptation of political institutions and processes is seen as being necessary for Singapore's political survival and prosperity, with a group of elites to develop and shape them to fit the peculiar needs of Singapore. This dovetails with the abiding belief in the 'Singapore way': a model of development that is coterminous with her history, societal values and development objectives, distinct from prevailing Western norms.

Beyond trying to have Presidents from the different races on a regular basis, the review of selected aspects of the Elected Presidency was significant and underlined the idealistic impetus to perfect Singapore's system of governance. It was an ambitious attempt on the part of the Government to "fool proof" Singapore's political governance, promote good governance as well as further promote multiracialism. Central to this institutional design is the importance of good and capable men (and women) to complement good institutions in the quest to sustain good governance. The focus of 2016 review was very much on ensuring that those who seek to be the Elected President, as the constitutional custodian of good governance, have what it takes to keep the Singapore system good and strong. The thinking is that such a talent pool is necessarily limited and pre-qualification of those seeking to become the Head of State is therefore required.

The review of the Elected Presidency in its core aspects confirms that the office is designed to be an elite institution with eligibility restricted to a select group by stringent criteria. The changes to the Council of Presidential Advisers following the constitutional review underscore this critical thrust of having good men and women to support and counsel Singapore's Head of State. It plays a critical role in ensuring that the presidential veto is not exercised without the President having the benefit of the advice and recommendation of his advisers. Clearly, the custodial powers framework of the Elected Presidency institutional design indicates the preference for a highly structured and conservatively calibrated intra-branch check on the Executive. The substantive and procedural changes to the Elected President institution underscore the conscious effort to buttress the understanding that the Elected Presidency is not a locus of power unto itself. Ultimately, the elite governance embodied in the custodial powers framework has to conscientiously manage the possibility of it being seen as an elitist institution. An elitist mode of governance will not be in sync with the Elected Presidency as a symbol of national unity. The ruling PAP's political dominance notwithstanding, the pressure is on the evolving institutional design to become more inclusive, representative, equitable and fair, in tandem with the growing democratic aspirations of Singaporeans.

Notes

1 In the official discourse, especially after 1999, the Elected President is described as having custodial powers rather than executive powers. The intent is not only to differentiate the President's powers from the Cabinet's but also to clarify that the President has no executive powers.
2 Article 24 of the Singapore Constitution (1999 Reprint) (hereinafter referred to as "the Constitution"). Article 23(1) states that: "The executive authority of Singapore shall be vested in the President and exercisable subject to the provisions of this Constitution by him or by the Cabinet or any Minister authorised by the Cabinet."
3 In a crowded race with four candidates and coming on the back of the polarizing General Election in May 2011, the August 2011 Presidential Election was characterized by competing and, at times, conflicting visions of the Presidency. Some candidates showed little regard for the constitutional limits of the presidential office and over-promised what they would do if elected. For instance, one candidate ran his campaign on the platform of being the "voice of the people" while another sought to be the "moral compass", the "conscience" of the nation.
4 Articles 23(1) and 38 of the Constitution.
5 See, further, Eugene K.B. Tan, "Autochthonous Constitutional Design in post-colonial Singapore: intimations of Confucianism and the Leviathan in entrenching dominant government" (2013) 4(2) *Yonsei Law Journal* 273–308.
6 For recent evaluations and critiques of the NMP and/or GRC schemes, see Garry Rodan, *Participation without Democracy: Containing Conflict in Southeast Asia* (Ithaca, NY: Cornell University Press, 2018); Netina Tan and Bernie Grofman, "Electoral rules and manufacturing legislative supermajority: evidence from Singapore" (2018) 56(3) *Commonwealth and Comparative Politics* 273–97; Jaclyn L. Neo, "Navigating minority inclusion and permanent division: minorities and the depoliticization of ethnic difference" (2017) 17 *Jus Politicum* 607–27; Walid Jumblatt Abdullah, "Electoral innovation in competitive authoritarian states: a case for the Nominated Member of Parliament (NMP) in Singapore" (2016) 17(2) *Japanese Journal of Political Science* 190–207.
7 The Prime Minister's speech is available online: PM Lee Hsien Loong, *Singapore Parliamentary Debates: Official Report*, 27 January 2016, vol. 94; and at PM Lee Hsien Loong, "PM Lee Hsien Loong at the debate on President's Address on 27 January 2016", *Prime Minister's Office Singapore* (27 January 2016) www.pmo.gov.sg/mediacentre/pm-lee-hsien-loong-debate-presidents-address-27-january-2016 (accessed 31 August 2018).
8 Singapore's founding Prime Minister Lee Kuan Yew argued that good government was what people want and that cultural values played a constructive role in deciding the political norms of a society; see Han Fook Kwang, *et al.*, *Lee Kuan Yew: The Man and His Ideas* (Singapore: Singapore Press Holdings & Times Editions, 1998), 380.

9 *White Paper on shared values* (Cmd 1, 1991), para. 41.
10 For an elaboration of the classical understanding of the Confucian *junzi*, see W. Theodore De Bary, *The Trouble with Confucianism* (Cambridge, MA: Harvard University Press, 1991).
11 See the White Papers of 1988 and 1990: *Constitutional Amendments to Safeguard Financial Assets and the Integrity of the Public Services* (Cmd 10, 1988), and *Safeguarding Financial Assets and the Integrity of the Public Services: The Constitution of the Republic of Singapore (Amendment No 3) Bill* (Cmd 11, 1990).
12 Constitutional Commission, *Report of the Constitutional Commission 2016* (2016), para. 4.6. The Constitutional Commission's report is abbreviated in this chapter as "CCR" from hereon.
13 CCR (n. 12), para. 4.12.
14 CCR (n. 12), para. 4.18.
15 See Prime Minister's Office, *White Paper on the Review of Specific Aspects of the Elected Presidency* (2016), para. 29(c)(iv). This White Paper is abbreviated as "WP" henceforth.
16 WP (n. 15), para. 29(c)(v).
17 CCR (12), paras 4.45–4.48; WP (n. 15), para. 29(c)(v)(A) to 29(c)(v)(B).
18 WP (n. 15), para. 29(c)(v)(C).
19 See WP (n. 15), 8. (Fourth column is added by the author.)
20 CCR (n. 12), para. 4.12.
21 CCR (n. 12), para. 4.16.
22 CCR (n. 12), para. 4.12.
23 CCR (n. 12), para. 4.12.
24 CCR (n. 12), para. 4.13.
25 CCR (n. 12), para. 4.13.
26 CCR (n. 12), para. 4.14.
27 CCR (n. 12), para. 4.17.
28 CCR (n. 12), para. 4.7. For the requirements to be appointed Prime Minister, see Articles 44 and 45, read with Article 25 of the Constitution.
29 CCR (n. 12), para. 4.8. See also CCR (n. 12), paras 4.9–4.10.
30 CCR (n. 12), para. 4.18. At para. 21, the Commission noted that:

> Quantitative thresholds cannot remain fixed in perpetuity for the self-evident reason that the economic situation in a country, or, for that matter, even the value of money in real terms, does not remain static. A quantitative threshold set some decades ago is simply unlikely to be meaningful today.

31 The Commission stated at para. 4.27 of the CCR that the number of surviving persons who have, since January 2001, held one or more of the qualifying public-sector offices (excluding former Auditors-General and Accountants-General) for at least three years is "around or just over 70".
32 Article 18 of the Constitution read with Section 8 of the Presidential Elections Act (Cap. 240A) (hereinafter referred to as "Presidential Elections Act").
33 CCR (n. 12), para. 4.22.
34 CCR (n. 12), para. 4.22.
35 CCR (n. 12), para. 4.31.
36 CCR (n. 12), para. 4.43.
37 CCR (n. 12), paras 4.49–4.62.
38 CCR (n. 12), para. 4.52.
39 CCR (n. 12), para. 4.54.
40 CCR (n. 12), paras 4.56–4.62. The original minimum threshold was $100 million in paid-up capital.
41 CCR (n. 12), para. 4.59.

42 CCR (n. 12), para. 4.59.
43 CCR (n. 12), para. 4.60.
44 See, generally, CCR (n. 12), paras 4.63–4.65.
45 CCR (n. 12), para. 4.63.
46 See generally CCR (n. 12), paras 4.63–4.65.
47 CCR (n. 12), para. 4.58.
48 CCR (n. 12), para. 4.57. The Commission did not consider whether all the public-sector offices that provide automatic qualification would adequately equip the office holders with such a skillset. For a perspective on what such decisions entail, see S.R. Nathan with Timothy Auger, *An Unexpected Journey: Path to the Presidency* (Singapore: Editions Didier Millet, 2011), 620–7. The 2008–2009 global financial crisis pushed Singapore into its worst recession. President Nathan was called on to make a landmark decision on whether the Government could draw on the national reserves. In October 2008, he agreed for the reserves to be used to back deposits in Singapore's commercial banks, merchant banks and finance companies to prevent a run by investors spooked by the collapse of financial institutions elsewhere, including the United States. Then in early 2009, he agreed to draw $4.9 billion from the reserves to fund schemes to save jobs and ease credit for companies in Singapore.
49 CCR (n. 12), paras 4.66–4.67; WP (n. 15), para. 44.
50 CCR (n. 12), para. 4.67.
51 CCR (n. 12), paras 4.66.
52 CCR (n. 12), para. 4.19(a).
53 CCR (n. 12), para. 4.19(b).
54 Article 19(3)(a) and (b) of the Constitution stipulates that the public-sector service requirement is that the person has held office for a period of three or more years as Minister, Chief Justice, Speaker, Attorney-General, Chairman of the Public Service Commission, Auditor-General, Accountant-General or Permanent Secretary, or served for a period of three or more years as the chief executive of an entity specified in the Fifth Schedule.
55 CCR (n. 12), para. 4.27.
56 CCR (n. 12), para. 4.28 *cf.* WP (n. 15), paras 34–35.
57 CCR (n. 12), para. 4.28. The phrase, "contrary pulls and pressures of government decision-making", was taken from the first White Paper on the Elected Presidency, *Constitutional Amendments to Safeguard Financial Assets and the Integrity of the Public Service* (Cmd 10, 1988), 29 July 1988, para. 18(d).
58 The Government stated that it would like to consider this recommendation more carefully: WP (n. 15), para. 35.
59 CCR (n. 12), para. 4.25. The Commission was responding to the point that not all applicants who qualify through the public-sector route may have managed organizations of considerable size as compared to those qualifying under the private-sector route.
60 CCR (n. 12), para. 4.25.
61 CCR (n. 12), para. 4.29.
62 CCR (n. 12), paras 4.36–4.37.
63 CCR (n. 12), para. 4.30.
64 CCR (n. 12), para. 4.32.
65 CCR (n. 12), para. 4.33 (original emphasis).
66 CCR (n. 12), para. 4.33.
67 CCR (n. 12), paras 4.34–4.73.
68 CCR (n. 12), para. 4.72; see also CCR (n. 12), para. 4.34.
69 WP (n. 15), paras 53–4.
70 WP (n. 15), para. 53.
71 WP (n. 15), para. 58.

72 CCR (n. 12), para. 4.75.
73 WP (n. 15), para. 59.
74 WP (n. 15), para. 59.
75 See WP (n. 15), paras 126–43.
76 The vast majority of the constitutional changes in the last 25 years have centred on the institution of the Elected Presidency. The Constitutional Commission had recommended that the Government make a definitive decision on entrenchment. This is discussed in the CCR (n. 12), paras 7.20–7.31.
77 Prior to the constitutional review in 2016, to amend or repeal an entrenched provision required the support of two-thirds of voters at a national referendum. Note, however, that the constitutional provisions on the Elected President were never brought into force and were held in abeyance for 25 years before being repealed.
78 Judgement, wisdom and empathy are harder to measure, and may defy measurement in the objective sense.
79 See Section 4.4 of this chapter for non-legislative changes adopted.
80 Constitutional provisions relating to the CPA are found in Part VA of the Constitution.
81 Article 37I of the Constitution. The Commission described the CPA as "primarily a body of independent specialist advisors": CCR (n. 12), para. 6.37.
82 Articles 37B and 37C of the Constitution.
83 CCR (n. 12), para. 6.1 (original emphasis).
84 CCR (n. 12), para. 6.1.
85 CCR (n. 12), para. 6.5.
86 CCR (n. 12), para. 2.59.
87 CCR (n. 12), para. 6.7. The Commission added that the CPA is "not an office with ceremonial or symbolic significance": CCR (n. 12), para. 6.37.
88 See Article 37IF of the Constitution generally.
89 CCR (n. 12), para. 6.38.
90 CCR (n. 12), para. 6.1.
91 CCR (n. 12), paras 6.33–6.34.
92 CCR (n. 12), para. 6.35(b) (original emphasis). These are now enacted in Article 37D(2)(a) and (b) of the Constitution.
93 CCR (n. 12), para. 6.35(c) (original emphasis).
94 CCR (n. 12), para. 6.36.
95 CCR (n. 12), paras 6.38–6.45. This also takes into account the extent to which the CPA supported or opposed the presidential veto.
96 WP (n. 15), paras 100–105, especially para. 103.
97 WP (n. 15), para. 103.
98 CCR (n. 12), paras 6.12–6.19; WP (n. 15), paras 90–93.
99 These are the President's discretionary powers in relation to the detention orders under the Internal Security Act, restraining orders under the Maintenance of Religious Harmony Act, and investigations by the Corrupt Practices Investigation Bureau.
100 These are powers that predate the introduction of the Elected Presidency and include the power to appoint or remove a Prime Minister and dissolving or denying a request to dissolve Parliament.
101 See helpful tabulation in CCR (n. 12), para. 3.7.
102 CCR (n. 12), para. 6.13.
103 CCR (n. 12), para. 6.13.
104 CCR (n. 12), paras 6.24–6.28 generally, and WP (n. 15), paras 106–8; See also Article 39B(1) of the Constitution. With the changes, the CPA now comprises three members appointed by the President in his discretion, three members appointed on the advice of the Prime Minister, and one member each appointed on the advice of the Chief Justice and the Chairman of the Public Service Commission.
105 CCR (n. 12), para. 6.34.
106 CCR (n. 12), para. 6.26.

107 It was only in January 2019 that the first woman was appointed to the CPA. Ms Chua Sock Koong was nominated and appointed as an Alternate Member of the CPA by President Halimah Yacob. For a listing of current and past CPA members, see The Istana, "Council of Presidential Advisers" (*The Istana*, 27 August 2018) www.istana.gov.sg/roles-and-responsibilities/presidents-office/council-presidential-advisers (accessed 3 September 2018).
108 CCR (n. 12), para. 6.5.
109 CCR (n. 12), para. 6.39.
110 CCR (n. 12), para. 6.7.
111 WP (n. 15), para. 87(d).
112 *Report of the Select Committee on the Constitution of the Republic of Singapore (Amendment No. 3) Bill* (Parl 9 of 1990, 18 December 1990) para. 31.
113 Prime Minister Goh Chok Tong, *Singapore Parliamentary Debates: Official Report*, 28 October 1996, vol. 66, cols 765–6.
114 CCR (n. 12), para. 6.11.
115 CCR (n. 12), para. 6.5.
116 CCR (n. 12), para 6.6.
117 CCR (n. 12), para. 6.9 and footnote 279; WP (n. 15), para. 111(b).
118 See Article 37IG of the Constitution.
119 See Article 37B of the Constitution.
120 CCR (n. 12), para. 4.17.
121 CCR (n. 12), para. 4.17.
122 See Article 37IA of the Constitution.
123 Under Article 151(4) of the Constitution, where an advisory board recommends the release of any person under any subversion of preventive detention law or ordinance (e.g. the Internal Security Act [ISA]), the person shall not be detained or further detained without the concurrence of the President, acting in his discretion, if the recommendations of the advisory board are not accepted by the authority (usually the Internal Security Department) on whose advice or order the person is detained. See also Sections 12, 13 and 13A of the ISA. Article 22I of Constitution states that the President, acting in his discretion, may cancel, vary, confirm or refuse to confirm a restraining order made under the Maintenance of Religious Harmony Act (MRHA) where the advice of the Cabinet is contrary to the recommendation of the Presidential Council for Religious Harmony. See also Section 12 of the MRHA.
124 By pecking order, it is not suggested that the some discretionary powers are not important.
125 Article 37IA(1) of the Constitution.
126 Article 37IA(2) of the Constitution. See also Articles 25 and 21(2).
127 Article 21(5) of the Constitution.
128 Principally, Article 21(2) of the Constitution. See also Articles 37IA(2), 25 and 21(2) of the Constitution.
129 These provisions (previously Articles 5(2A) and 5A of the Constitution) were enacted in 1991 when the Elected Presidency was created but they were never brought into force. The White Paper explained that this was because the unique nature of the Elected Presidency meant that the flexibility to continually refine and tweak the system was needed: WP (n. 15), para. 126.
130 CCR (n. 12), para. 7.30. See also CCR (n. 12), para. 7.20–7.31.
131 See WP (n. 15), para. 134:

> The Government has therefore proceeded cautiously with regard to the of specific constitutional provisions, in recognition of the careful balance that must be sought between the adaptability of the Constitution to changing circumstances, and the stability afforded by a sufficiently rigid Constitution.

132 WP (n. 15), para. 139.

133 WP (n. 15), para. 140 (emphasis added). For details of the revised framework, see paras 140–2.

134 WP (n. 15), para. 143. The Government noted the previous wisdom of not entrenching the Elected President in the Constitution between 1991 and 2016:

> The fact that there are good reasons for revising the entrenchment provisions now shows that it was wise to have not entrenched them. Likewise, the question of when to bring into force the revised entrenchment provisions should be considered some period after the upcoming set of amendments have been in operation.

135 Article 5 of the Constitution. The ruling People's Action Party has commanded more than 90 per cent of elected parliamentary seats since the 1968 general election.

136 This is a recurrent theme in the Government's characterization of what is needed in the governance of Singapore. See the articulation in the President's Address in 2011, 2014, 2016 and 2018.

137 See Chapter 7 by Jack Tsen-Ta Lee in this volume.

138 CCR (n. 12), para. 4.14.

139 The Commission noted in the CCR (n. 12), at para. 7.11 that a parliamentary election is:

> a contest of ideas and policies, where candidates have to communicate their policies to the electorate and persuade voters as to the strengths of their own proposals as well as the weaknesses of those put forward by other candidates. This clash of ideas and policies makes for a lively but inevitably divisive contest.

140 CCR (n. 12), para. 7.11.

141 See Second Reading Speech on the Presidential Elections (Amendment) Bill 2017: *Singapore Parliamentary Debates: Official Report*, 6 February 2017, vol. 94; See also Elections Department Singapore, "Campaigning Guidelines for the Presidential Election" (*Press Release*, 29 August 2017) www.eld.gov.sg/pressrelease/PreE2017/Press%20Release%20on%20Campaigning%20Guidelines%20for%20the%20Presidential%20Election.pdf (accessed 3 September 2018).

142 See Section 9(3)(c)(iii), Presidential Elections Act which requires a person seeking nomination to make a statutory declaration that: "he understands the President's role under the Constitution, including any particular aspect of the President's role stated in the prescribed form."

143 Given the stringent eligibility criteria which limits the pool to a group of public office and corporate elites and the non-combative nature of campaigning, I have described the presidential contest as one of the "battle of CVs".

144 This has echoes of Shakespeare's tragedy, *Coriolanus*. The following description is taken from an article by Ruth Franklin, "Revisiting Shakespeare's "Coriolanus'" (*New York Times Magazine*, 20 January 2012) (hereinafter referred to as "NYTM article"), which captures well the challenge facing Coriolanus as he transits from soldier to politician in ancient Rome:

> After a military triumph in the city of Corioles, Caius Martius, a respected if not beloved general, is given a new surname – Coriolanus – to honor his achievement, and his friends urge him to stand for election as a senator. But the pride that propelled Coriolanus to triumph in the battlefield makes him reluctant to engage in the kind of vote-mongering niceties that the public expects.

Coriolanus captures well the dilemma of the Elected Presidency as a symbol of national unity but having the person to be chosen through competitive elections. As the NYTM article concludes,

> Perhaps every politician must have a bit of Coriolanus in him: an ego that propels him to believe himself worthy of public service, coupled with the desire to stand unswerving for the rightness of his own convictions. And yet a politician who

wants to win must ultimately subdue his or her inner Coriolanus and "be other than one thing." Victory depends upon a fickle combination of personal merit, political strategizing and the skillful application of flattery. We think of this as cynical and unsavory, a symptom of our own corrupt political climate. However, more than anything else, "Coriolanus" demonstrates that politics has never been pure – and that "May the best man win!" might be its most enduring myth.

The constitutional changes under discussion might suggest the intent to reduce the possibility of the presidential election becoming undignified.

145 WP (n. 15), para. 125; see also Chapter 7 by Jack Tsen-Ta Lee in this volume.

146 Article 17(2)(b) of the Constitution states that the election "must be held" not more than three months before the date of expiration of the term of office of the incumbent. This would mean any time between June and August in a presidential election year. With the advice of the Attorney-General, the Government, however, took the view that Article 22N of Constitution was applicable and could be resorted to in the plans to re-time the presidential poll. The Attorney-General was of the view that there could be an interval between the expiry of the incumbent's term and the assumption of office by the new President: see Second Reading Speech by Minister Chan Chun Sing on the Presidential Elections (Amendment) Bill 2017 at *Singapore Parliamentary Debates: Official Report*, 6 February 2017, vol. 94. Article 22N(1) states that:

> If the office of President becomes vacant, the Chairman of the Council of Presidential Advisers or, if he is unavailable, the Speaker shall exercise the functions of the office of President during the period between the date the office of President becomes vacant and the assumption of office by the person declared elected as President.

Note that Article 22N of the Constitution was inapplicable as the Presidency was not vacant at the relevant time. In this case, President Tony Tan's term was allowed to lapse deliberately. The apparent incongruence between Article 17(2)(b) and Article 22N was not dealt with by the Government.

147 See Second Reading Speech on the Presidential Elections (Amendment) Bill 2017 at *Singapore Parliamentary Debates: Official Report*, 6 February 2017, vol. 94.

148 Standing Orders (hereinafter abbreviated to "SO") are the written rules of procedure that regulate Parliament's proceedings. Article 52 of the Constitution empowers Parliament to "make, amend and revoke Standing Orders for the regulation and orderly conduct of its own proceedings and the despatch of business".

149 See SO 44A.

150 As Prime Minister Lee Hsien Loong recounted in January 2016, Mr Eddie Teo, chairman of the Presidential Elections Committee (2011 and 2017) and Public Service Commission chairman (2008–2018) had written to him after the 2011 Presidential Election recommending that the qualifying criteria for candidates to be president should be reviewed. Mr Teo had written that: "The criterion of $100 million paid-up capital … was set more than 20 years ago. It is, therefore, unclear whether or not with inflation, the threshold continues to reflect the original intent of the requirement." Mr Eddie Teo has been the Chairman of the CPA since January 2019.

151 There was also the legitimate expectation of presidential candidates who had obtained certificates of eligibility in previous Presidential Elections being rendered ineligible in the 2017 election. To be clear, this is not a matter of legitimate expectations under the law but one of not unnecessarily politicizing the changes to the Elected Presidency and the Presidential Election.

152 Popular coffee shop talk had it that the changes were designed to prevent Dr Tan Cheng Bock, who lost very narrowly in the 2011 Presidential Election, from contesting.

5 Constitutionalizing minority representation

The reserved elections mechanism and the politicization of ethnicity in Singapore?

*Jaclyn L. Neo**

5.1 Introduction

We are multiracial. Multiracial, why must reserve the election for them?[1]

Ensuring minorities can be represented in the office of the President is a "very necessary symbolism" of Singapore as a multi-ethnic society and not a form of "tokenism".[2] This was the key message that Prime Minister Lee Hsien Loong ("Prime Minister Lee") conveyed in an exclusive television interview to Channel NewsAsia (a main broadcasting channel) in September 2016. The Prime Minister had appeared in the interview to explain a range of proposed constitutional amendments, which include the institution of the hiatus-triggered mechanism to reserve certain presidential elections for underrepresented ethnic groups in Singapore. In his speech in Parliament initiating the constitutional reform process, Prime Minister Lee stated that it was "important that minorities have a chance to be elected President, and that this happens regularly".[3]

Ensuring minority representation was only one of three issues that engaged the constitutional reform process. Other aspects of the Presidency were also identified for reform. The Constitutional Commission, helmed by the current Chief Justice Sundaresh Menon, was also asked to review the qualifying process for presidential candidacy and to review the framework governing the exercise of the President's custodial powers. As other chapters in this volume show, changes to these two other aspects of the Presidency arguably narrowed access to non-elite, non-establishment candidates, recalibrated how powers are separated in Singapore and affected the scheme of checks and balances. Accordingly, from the perspective of constitutionalism, the changes in these two aspects have greater systemic impact.

However, it was the issue of minority representation that dominated most of the public imaginary and discourse during this process of constitutional reform. The Constitutional Commission received representations from the public and conducted a series of public hearings before rendering its report on 7 September 2016. On the question of safeguarding minority representation, the Constitutional Commission received a large number of suggestions, which it grouped into five categories – group-representation models, pre-assigned cycles, hiatus-triggered safeguards, hybrid models, as well as other models.[4] Having examined all the proposals, the

Constitutional Commission proposed the hiatus-triggered model of elections, whereby certain elections would be reserved for candidates from specified ethnic backgrounds. Specifically, this means that if there has not been an office holder from an ethnic group for more than five consecutive terms, then the next election would be reserved only for candidates from that particular group. This would ordinarily translate to a 30-year interval since each term of office is six years, unless the President resigns or is prematurely removed for cause. For ease of reference, this chapter will refer to this model as the *reserved elections mechanism*, as this is what it has become popularly known.

Just as the public's focus was on issues of minority representation, much of the public's attention following the Constitutional Commissions' report was on the reserved elections proposal. That certain presidential elections would be reserved for minorities became a flashpoint for debate in Singapore. The Prime Minister's remarks in the Channel News Asia interview sought to respond specifically to criticism that minorities did not want to be represented in the office of the President by a candidate who is seen as "having an easy ride into the Istana".[5] He acknowledged the inconsistency between the reserved elections mechanism and another systemic value that the Government has consistently promoted – meritocracy. He nonetheless argued that the criticism arises as a result of "the success of our meritocracy" that the Government itself strongly propounds where "people want to succeed on their own merits". This "meritocratic" culture strongly resists the perception that "standards have been lowered for a particular race".[6] As such, while there is broad consensus that minorities should periodically become President, and not be seen to be left out of the political office, serious reservations were raised about the way this was to be achieved. Furious debate emerged over news media and social media, as well as in Parliament and in other public forums about the necessity and desirability of the reserved elections mechanism.

This chapter examines the range of criticism of the reserved elections mechanism and seeks to identify the basis for the discontent. Greater focus, where possible, will be given to criticism raised by those speaking from the perspective of the Malay community since, as will be explained further below, they are seen as the primary beneficiary of the reserved elections mechanism. The premise for giving especial attention to the Malay voice, though without excluding other voices, is that it provides important insights into how minority groups view the State's proclaimed efforts to include them in the political process. This chapter also observes the shift in terminology from 'minority representation' to 'multiculturalism', and argues that this is a change of substance that better reflects the aims of the mechanism. Nonetheless, the chapter argues that the shift to multiculturalism could not avoid the politicization of ethnicity as an unintended consequence of the reserved elections mechanism.

At this juncture, it should be explained that this chapter prefers the term "ethnicity" as opposed to "race" as this is a category that more accurately refers to the various communities in Singapore. However, the terms "race" or "multiracialism" and their likes, do appear in this chapter where they are direct quotes. This itself reflects significant slippage in the use of these terms where they are often used interchangeably in public discourse in Singapore. Section 5.2 contextualizes this chapter's critique by providing a broad overview of the Government's official account of why there is a need to ensure minority representation. Section 5.3 identifies the range of criticisms against the reserved elections. Section 5.4 examines the shift in terminology from minority representation to multiculturalism, and suggests why this is more than a symbolic change in terms. Section 5.5 nonetheless argues that despite the Government's best efforts, the reserved elections mechanism could be counterproductive as a mode of preserving multicultural coexistence as it has politicized ethnicity, albeit unintentionally. Section 5.6 concludes.

5.2 The need for the reserved elections: the official account

5.2.1 From ethnic equality to ethnic representation

The 2016/2017 exercise was only the second time the constitution was amended to institutionalize measures for ethnic representation. The first was when the electoral system was changed to introduce in 1988 the Group Representation Constituency ("GRC") scheme, which required that certain constituencies be designated as group representation constituencies and be contested by a team of candidates, one of which must be a minority candidate. There are two categories of group representation constituencies – those designated for at least one Malay candidate and those designated for at least one Indian or other minority candidate.[7] Until the GRC, constitutional law in Singapore tended to emphasize ethnic equality over measures that singled out minorities for protection. The Wee Constitutional Commission, the first constitutional commission convened in Singapore, solidified the view that the best way to protect racial, religious and linguistic minorities was to ensure equal protection of fundamental liberties for all. Proposals that explicitly used ethnicity as a basis for eligibility for political participation were rejected on the basis that this would entrench differences rather than encourage integration.

Specifically, the Wee Commission rejected a proposal that there be a Committee of (Minority) Representatives which would be entitled to elect three persons from among its members to represent minorities in the elected chamber in Parliament. The Commission took the view that any participation in the elected chamber of Parliament by persons *appointed* to represent minorities would be "inappropriate" and "retrograde".[8] The Commission also rejected the alternative proposal that there be an Upper House in Parliament consisting of, or at least, including members elected or nominated to represent the racial, linguistic and religious minorities in Singapore. It argued that such an Upper House would "perpetuate racial and other differences" but also require and involve "the complicated task of defining the various minority groups."[9]

In the end, the only institution proposed by the Wee Commission was for the creation of a Council of State with a small number of members chosen irrespective of race, colour or creed who would scrutinize all proposed legislation to ensure that they are not "discriminatory of racial, linguistic or religious minorities."[10] This was incorporated in the Constitution as the Presidential Council of Minority Rights. As per the Wee Commission's proposal, this Council serves as an advisory body to scrutinize parliamentary bills for what is called "differentiating measures". What is interesting is that differentiating measure is not defined as measures discriminating against the minorities, as was suggested in the Wee Commission report. Instead, the Constitution defines "differentiating measure" as:

> any measure which is, or is likely in its practical application to be, disadvantageous to persons of any racial or religious community and not equally disadvantageous to persons of other such communities, either directly by prejudicing persons of that community or indirectly by giving advantage to persons of another community.[11]

In other words, the focus is on the differential treatment of groups, and not merely on the protection of minorities from discrimination.

5.2.2 Ethnic classification and ethnic thinking in Singapore

Like the GRC, the reserved elections mechanism modifies the majority principle in electoral systems. Such modifications may be seen as a way to accommodate minorities and could be necessary to prevent permanent disenfranchisement.[12] As Horowitz observes, in certain societies "severely divided by ethnicity, race, religion, language, or any other form of ascriptive affiliation, ethnic divisions make democracy difficult, because they tend to produce ethnic parties and ethnic voting."[13] This would ordinarily mean that unmitigated majority rule would result in the domination of the political system by one ethnic party/group.[14] While Singapore is not a severely divided society, it is a society that is ethnically divided, in terms of demography as well as in its self-conscious sociopolitical image. Its population is broadly divided into 76 per cent ethnic Chinese, 15 per cent ethnic Malays and 7 per cent ethnic Indians. The remaining 2 per cent are composed of diverse ethnic groups, including a well-established group known as the Eurasians.

The Chinese, Malay, Indian and Other ("CMIO") classification underpins governmental policies towards ethnicity in Singapore, pervading Singaporean society. It is used to classify the population and this has ramifications on the rights and privileges of the people. One instance of application is in the public housing's ethnic integration policy whereby there are broad limits to the proportion of ethnic groups that can occupy a particular public housing development. This inevitably impacts the property owners' right of property and freedom to contract. Andreas Ackermann has also argued that "ethnic thinking" is prevalent in Singaporean society and that the classification scheme reinforces ethnic stereotypes.[15] That aside for now, the integrality of the CMIO scheme in state and social thinking has meant that the political system is evaluated through those differentiated lenses. In other words, the success or failure of Singapore's representative democracy has become closely related to ensuring that the democratic institutions are representative of these different ethnic groups. As it stands, the reserved elections mechanism extends this existing ethnic classification scheme to the formalized process of presidential elections.

Indeed, the reserved elections mechanism appears to attempt to approximate a convention of rotation among the four major ethnic groups that was practised before the office was changed to an elected one. Between 1965 and 1991, Singapore had four Presidents who were from Malay, Eurasian (classified under 'Other'), Indian and Chinese ethnic backgrounds. After 1991, with the injection of elections for the Presidency, Singapore has had three Elected Presidents from a Chinese background, and one Elected President from an Indian background. There has not been any *democratically elected* Malay President since. Notably, there has also not been any elected Eurasian President but presumably since the Eurasian community is not often seen as an underprivileged community, and it is a much smaller community than the Malays (i.e. less than 1 per cent of the population), there may be less concern that there has not been an elected Eurasian President. Consequently, when the suggestion first came up to ensure that ethnic minorities can be represented in the office of the Presidency, it was clear that the main concern was perceived underrepresentation within the Malay community. By the 2017 Presidential Elections, it had been 46 years since President Yusof Ishak, Singapore's first President, who was also the first Malay President, passed away in office in 1970.

5.3 Reservations about the reserved elections

While there was widespread support for the ideal of multiculturalism and multi-ethnicity/multiracialism, various issues have been raised about the reserved elections mechanism. In particular, critics question the efficacy and need for such a mechanism to correct perceived ethnic underrepresentation. Within the Malay community, especially, this prompted a period of community self-examination. The reaction within the community was mixed. Some consider the Government's plan as a form of tokenism, "akin to letting Malays win a runners-up medal since no one from the community is capable of competing in an open and fair election against other ethnic groups."[16] Others however "embrace[d] the amendments with open arms" and stated that they "cannot wait to see another president emerge from the community".[17] Indeed, this conflict between an almost visceral objection towards preferential treatment and the desire for representation is at the heart of the debate within the Malay community, and in its interlocutors' engagement with broader society. This section identifies four types of arguments raised against the reserved elections as a form of preferential treatment for the Malay community.

5.3.1 The Malay community does not need a Malay President

The first type of argument challenges the idea that it is necessary to have a Malay President. As Member of Parliament Rahayu Mahzam puts it, "we would like our Malay representative to be selected because he or she is the best person, and not just because he or she is a Malay. We do not want the selection to be merely a symbolic one."[18] Indeed, as the Government itself acknowledged, there was no "groundswell" within the Malay community for a Malay President.[19] In a public forum, the Minister for Law acknowledged that the Malay community "generally felt" the absence of a Malay President, but there was "no groundswell of clamour".[20] He explained that the Government was being pro-active and wants to "move ahead of the problems".[21] Notably, discussion about having a Malay President also did not appear in parliamentary debates between 1991 and 2016, and only started to be debated in Parliament in 2016 after the Prime Minister's speech in January that year. The one reported public discussion about the need to have a Malay President was in 2005, when the Singapore Malay National Organization ("PKMS") – the only ethnic-based political party in Singapore – started to highlight the lack of Malay representation in the office of the President. PKMS proposed that "[t]he next Elected President should be a Malay, as no Malay has held the post for more than 30 years".[22] It is not entirely clear if PKMS was seeking a change in the electoral system for the Presidency to ensure this outcome through reserved seats, or if it was encouraging qualified Malay candidates to contest.

Furthermore, some critics argue that it is a fallacy to think that only persons from a Malay background can represent the interests of the Malay community. The President is meant to be a symbol of unity and multiracialism, and that it should not matter which community the President hails from. A more trenchant version of this line of argument suggests that the interests of the community in general might be better protected by a competent and effective President, rather than a President that looks like us.[23] This criticism rejects the salience of identity-based representation in the Presidency and, interestingly, was the prevailing position until recently. When commenting on PKMS' statement about the lack of an elected Malay President in 2005, then Minister of State for Foreign Affairs Zainul Abidin Rasheed emphatically stated that "Singapore will choose the best candidate possible within the system we have collectively chosen", thus suggesting that having a good candidate as President is more important than having one from any particular community.[24] Some therefore suggest that the reserved elections was a "major step backwards", and that "most Malays are willing to wait patiently for our next Malay President to be voted into office based on his own merit and in a contest against other capable Singaporeans of different races or creeds, however long it takes."[25]

5.3.2 Reserving elections not necessary to ensure minority President

The reserved elections essentially changes the rules of the game in order to overcome perceived underrepresentation within a particular group. A second type of criticism posits that the mechanism is not necessary for a minority President to be elected. To be sure, modifications of the majority principle are not uncommon amid claims that a formally neutral system of representative government fails to recognize and correct systemic discrimination faced by historically disadvantaged groups such as ethnic, religious and gender minorities. Preferential policies ensure access to underrepresented groups on the assumption that they would otherwise not be able to access it. This supports a narrative that has emerged over the years and which grounds the initiative to change the laws to ensure minority representation.

However, some challenge this underlying assumption of *ethnic preferential voting* which posits that Malay candidates are unlikely to win any open presidential elections because the majority Chinese and perhaps even the other minority groups would not vote for them. However, the Constitutional Commission observed that Singapore was not yet a "post-racial" society.[26] The Government has also emphasized that "race remains a significant factor for many Singaporeans, and that voting choices can, and are, swayed by racial factors, quite apart from the merit of candidates."[27] Great reliance was placed on a survey commissioned by Channel NewsAsia ("CNA") and administered by the Institute of Policy Studies ("IPS").[28] This is a survey of about 2,000 respondents (Singapore citizens and Permanent Residents), weighted for ethnicity. The survey results suggest that while most respondents strongly agree that one's ethnicity does not affect one's life chances or success, there is a high degree of "in-group preference". With respect to political office, respondents in fact were asked about their ethnic preference for President and the results show that Chinese respondents had a much stronger in-group preference than the other groups. Table 5.1 is reproduced from the report.[29]

As can be seen, Chinese respondents diverge the most in their rates of acceptances between a Chinese President and a President from a minority group. There is a difference of 37 percentage points between their rate of acceptance of a Chinese President versus that for a Malay President and a difference of 28 percentage points for an Indian President. In contrast, Malay respondents only show a differential of 10 percentage points for a Chinese President and 19 percentage points for an Indian President. Indian respondents show similarly lower in-group and out-group preference differentials – there is a 5 percentage point differential for a Chinese President and a 20 percentage point difference for a Malay President. The survey shows that the Chinese have greater in-group preference for the office of the President. To the extent that this is the best evidence we currently

Table 5.1 Racial preference for President.

To be President of Singapore	*Acceptability by Race (%)*		
	Chinese	*Malay*	*Indian*
Chinese Respondents	96	59	68
Malay Respondents	84	94	75
Indian Respondents	87	72	92
Other Respondents	84	84	69

have about electoral preferences, it suggests an ethnic-bias among Chinese voters, and less so among non-Chinese voters. Coupled with other parts of the study which indicate that ethnic minorities tend to perceive more instances of negative (differential) treatment on the basis of their ethnicity, there is some evidence that social, economic and political behaviour in Singapore remains ethnicized.[30] The survey further shows that perceptions of negative treatment stem from different causes. A larger proportion of Malays think that they were treated negatively on the basis of their religion and income or education, while Indians feel that they have been treated negatively because of their skin colour.[31]

However, there is a danger in relying too much on a sample survey like this. Asking voters an abstract question about "acceptability" of a Chinese, Indian or Malay President is not sufficiently indicative of voting patterns. There is no evidence that the survey tries to bracket out qualification differentials such that race/ethnicity is the only differentiating factor. As Cherian George observes, "[i]t is one thing to ask survey respondents to react to a hypothetical, nameless, faceless candidate of a given race. It's another thing entirely to ask voters to consider a specific, real-life individual."[32] More quantitative and qualitative studies are needed to better understand the role of ethnicity in political behaviour, although surveys can never fully predict the myriad of factors that affect political behaviour and choices. At best, such surveys show that ethnicity *could be* a relevant factor.

5.3.3 Instrumentalization of minorities

A third type of criticism is a more insidious one and this doubts the authenticity of the Government's stated motivations for changing the system. Critics argue that the constitutional reform exercise and the resultant change was brought about because the Government wanted to further entrench its party dominance.[33] The background to this argument is a suspicion, which the Government has strenuously denied, that the constitutional changes were instituted to thwart the presidential bid of a strong contender who is not endorsed by the PAP.[34] Even in a crowded race, Tan Cheng Bock lost the last presidential elections in 2011 by only a narrow margin to Tony Tan who became President. Indeed, the former parliamentarian and former presidential candidate has questioned the reserved elections as a way to "disqualify him from contesting".[35] This is especially after the Government decided to start counting the five continuous terms from the term of the first President vested with the powers of the Elected President but who was not democratically elected; then President Wee was already in office when the changes to make the Presidency an elected office came about. Tan Cheng Bock's constitutional challenge to the counting of the presidential terms was not successful.[36]

The authenticity criticism appears to be further supported by an observation that the issue of Malay representation in the office of the President was never put forth as a pressing issue until 2016 even though there have been four presidential elections since the office was made an elected one. That "the establishment has never put forth a Malay candidate" for any of the last four presidential elections"[37] exacerbates this discomfort that critics have with the reserved elections. In the context of Singapore's dominant party state, where the ruling Peoples' Action Party ("PAP") has formed the Government after every General Elections since Singapore's independence, ethnic power-sharing has been greatly influenced and even driven by the party. Since the establishment candidate has always won the presidential elections, the fact that the Government has not proposed or put its weight behind a Malay candidate has meant that there was never an opportunity for Singaporeans to elect one. In this regard, it is difficult to evaluate the implicit suggestion that a Malay candidate has a lower chance to win in an open presidential elections.

5.3.4 Sending the wrong message: perpetuating the stereotype of the underachieving community

The last and arguably most salient type of criticism is that the reserved elections may perpetuate the stereotype that the Malay community is less capable and less able than the other communities. This concern was echoed by several Malay parliamentarians and Malay elites. Parliamentarian Zaqy Mohamad points out that although the Malay community welcome the certainty of a Malay President, they are "worried that the selection will not be based on merit".[38] Indeed, others have pointed out that the very concept of an election reserved for the Malay community gives them "an unfair shot at the office of the president".[39] Furthermore, in mass media, others suggest that this "risks being read as a vote of no confidence in the community".[40]

In raising these objections to a mechanism that essentially is a form of preferential treatment, critics are worried about the perception that is being perpetuated about the minority group. Within the context of Singapore's strong narrative of meritocracy,[41] modifying the rules of the game for a minority group may send the message that they are unable to compete on equal footing. Furthermore, there are worries that it may feed into stereotypes and prejudices against the Malay community as being in need of assistance. Speaking in parliament, Yaacob Ibrahim, who had been the Minister in charge of Muslim Affairs, explained that the Malay community already carry the "historical burden" of being perceived as "an underachieving community".[42] This stereotyping has strong roots within the region; cultural-ethnic factors have been used to explain why the Malay community is disadvantaged.[43] One argument, for instance, that the late former Prime Minister Lee Kuan Yew suggested in a different context is that Malays have different cultural values and are "less predisposed to the pursuit of material wealth" as compared to the other ethnic groups.[44]

There is also criticism that changing the rules of the game to ensure minorities can have a chance "would tacitly validate the racial dominance of the majority"[45] since it suggests that minority candidates need assistance, whereas majority candidates are self-reliant and do not. This may result in further marginalization of the community,[46] especially since the reserved elections' focus on the Malay minority fits within a persistent narrative of underrepresentation and underperformance within the community. In an analogous situation, when the GRC was first mooted, the Government was explicit that its foremost concern was representation from the Malay minority.[47] The initial scheme was to twin Malay candidates with a non-Malay candidate for certain twinned constituencies. The Malay Members of Parliament, however, vehemently rejected this proposal, calling it retrogressive for sending the wrong signal that Malay candidates could not win elections on their own.[48] The resulting change was for a GRC scheme, which aimed at minority representation generally.[49]

It is significant therefore that, with regards to the reserved elections, the Constitutional Commission opted to couch its proposal in ethnicity-neutral terms, presumably to de-emphasize majority–minority differences in favour of equal coexistence. It is interesting to note the strategy ultimately adopted in both the GRC and the reserved elections scheme to remove focus on their primary target group and to broaden the schemes. The GRC became a general minority representation scheme whereas the reserved elections mechanism was recrafted from a "minority representation" scheme to a "multi-ethnic" scheme.[50] Thus, as it stands, it is possible that a presidential election could even be reserved for Chinese candidates should the community not be represented in the office for six terms. In practical terms, based on current political conditions, the likelihood that a presidential election would be reserved is the lowest for Chinese candidates. This is particularly since Indian and other minorities are grouped into one constitutional category for the purposes of determining whether a reserved election is necessary.

The Government has further sought to counter perceptions that the reserved elections mechanism is necessary to overcome under-achievement by pointing out that the same qualifying criteria would apply for reserved elections such that only eminently qualified candidates could stand for presidential elections, even in a reserved election. Notably, the Prime Minister's interview referenced at the start of this chapter was clearly aimed at defending against charges of tokenism.[51] However, despite the Government's best efforts, the fact that the 2017 Presidential Elections did not result in a contest may have perpetuated the problematic image that there are indeed very few qualified Malay candidates who Donald could run for the Presidency. This is especially if one contrasts this with the previous presidential election, which was a tight race among four (male) Chinese candidates.[52] Thus, while the institution of special procedures can ensure that minorities are included in important political positions, it may however be counter-productive to inter-ethnic relations insofar as such procedures accentuate ethnic difference and signal that minority groups are less capable.

5.4 From minority representation to multiculturalism: changing the terms of discourse

Against this backdrop of criticism, it is interesting to analyse the impact of changing the terms of discourse from minority representation to multiculturalism. The initial focus of the reform was "minority representation", as the Prime Minister mentioned in his 2016 parliamentary speech prefacing the appointment of the Constitutional Commission. Furthermore, the Terms of Reference to the Constitutional Commission made clear reference to "minority representation". It bears reproducing this second term in full here:

> To consider and recommend what provisions should be made to safeguard *minority representation* in the Presidency, taking into account: (i) The President's status as a unifying figure that represents multi-racial Singapore; and (ii) The need to ensure that candidates from minority races have fair and adequate opportunity to be elected to Presidential office.[53]

While there was also an emphasis on the President as a "unifying figure" or in other parlance, as a "symbol of unity", this was clearly subject to the first ideal of minority representation. However, over time, the Constitutional Commission changed the terms of the debate to focus more on multiculturalism than minority representation. This is a significant distinction.

To talk about minority representation is to emphasize the identity of representatives and the relevance of identity in representation. Identity-based representation posits that a person's identity is a relevant factor in politics and in representing the interests of a group. In what Anne Phillips calls the "politics of presence", representatives are to "mirror" the characteristics of the person or people they represent.[54] There are many reasons for advocating that a person's ascriptive identity should be taken into account in representative institutions. On one level, identity-based representation is meant to send a signal of inclusiveness; it is aimed at making under-represented groups feel included in the political process. To see 'someone like me' in political office can be empowering for under-represented groups, especially those who may have felt consistently disenfranchised by the lack of representation in the highest office(s). Indeed, ensuring representation of conventionally under-represented groups has become a flashpoint for debate not only in politics but also in other arenas including popular culture.[55]

On another, more substantive level, identity-based representatives are assumed to be better able to give voice to the assumptions and priorities of under-represented, and often underprivileged groups.[56] Indeed, Melissa Williams argues that it is crucial to include minority groups (or their identitarian representatives) in decision-making bodies as it is more likely that their interests would be overlooked if they were not present in the final decision-making arena.[57] Thus, identity-based representatives can help to overcome the tendency to exclude social groups based on their race/ethnicity, religion or gender that tends to occur in non-identitarian politics.[58] This is especially since it has been observed that facially neutral political processes could and often do function to reproduce existing patterns of social inequality along group lines.[59] Identity-based representation thus puts forward the claim that identity has political salience in decision-making. It posits that "the range of political ideas and preferences is seriously constrained by the characteristics of the people who convey them".[60] Not only that the acts and choices of representatives are influenced by their identity, but that voters are motivated by identity. In other words, democratic choices are "bound up with both how people identify themselves and what they therefore want".[61]

Strictly speaking, however, the reserved elections, as well as the GRC, do not provide 'mirror' representation in that the minority representatives are not really 'ethnic' representatives. Minority representatives in these schemes merely provide *corporatist representation*; they increase political representation of people from minority groups, but these representatives are not meant to provide a definitive voice of their group or be presumed to be solely qualified to speak on their group interests. The Chinese/Malay/Indian/Eurasian President is expected to serve as the President of Singapore, just as the Malay/Indian/Eurasian parliamentarian remains a national parliamentarian, that is, a Member of the Parliament of Singapore. Once s/he assumes office, his/her ethnic identity is supposed to become secondary or even irrelevant to how s/he performs his/her function. These representatives are not expected to represent or advocate their "group interests", which means that they could be less effective in achieving the substantive aims of identity-based representation. That said, corporatist representation can achieve some of the aims of having minorities in positions of power, particularly in the symbolic sense of seeing "someone like me" in important positions. Furthermore, corporatist representation may be less likely to give rise to a criticism against minority representation which is that it tends to mask internal disagreements and give select representatives an oversized influence over the group.[62]

In comparison to minority representation, multiculturalism here looks upon minority inclusion as necessary to reflect the diversity of society. While minority representation focuses on the interests of the minority, multiculturalism focuses on ensuring that policies reflect the multi-ethnic nature of the population. Ethnicity is relevant only insofar as it reflects the diverse nature of society. This focus better coheres with the early emphasis that the symbolic nature of the Presidency. Prior to the 1991 changes, the emphasis has always been on the President as a "symbol of unity of people of various races"[63] or a "symbol of unity among our multi-racial, religious and cultural communities".[64] For instance, during his third re-appointment as President, it was remarked that President Yusof Ishak "always remained the Head of the nation as a whole – not the representative of any particular community, race, class or religion."[65] One's ethnic identity is de-emphasized, even while his/her ethnic identity is relevant in his/her nomination.

Thus, even when Yusof Ishak was nominated to be President for the third time, a Malay parliamentarian made it a point to emphasize that his nomination was based on his qualities, and not merely based on his ethnicity:

> Though as a Malay I am gratified that a member of my community is being nominated for the third time to be the Head of our Republic, it would, nevertheless, be unfair to Inche Yusof and even to my community to say that he has been nominated to this office simply because he is a Malay. I find greater pride in the fact that he is being nominated for no other reason than that we believe him to be the Singaporean with all the qualities necessary to hold this

> responsible office. It is his qualities as a man and a citizen of Singapore and nothing else which recommend him for this high office.[66]

Further, another parliamentarian in Parliament emphasized the fact that President Yusof Ishak is "by accident of birth a Malay" and that "nobody, as far as I know, thinks of him as Malay Head of State."[67]

The discourse on ethnicity and the Presidency therefore has always reflected an attempt to blunt the significance of ethnicity, while never escaping or rising above the ethnic frame. This ethnic frame continues to shape minority–majority relations. This is reflected interestingly in a speech by a Malay parliamentarian Yatiman Yusof at the appointment of President Wee Kim Wee, the first person of Chinese ethnicity to become President. Yatiman observed that this "marks an important change in the history of Singapore" and "reflects the maturity of thought on the part of the multi-racial people of Singapore."[68] This presumably refers to Singapore's position within the Malay archipelago and as formerly part of the Malay sultanate of Johor. This history is reflected, for instance, in the adoption of Malay language as the national language and the designation of Malays as the indigenous people of Singapore in the constitutional text. These constitutional provisions, however, exist within a social-political context in which English, not Malay, is the main working language of Government, and where it is the Chinese, not the Malays, who are the majority ethnic group. Thus, what Yatiman is suggesting, it seems, is that the appointment of an ethnic Chinese President represents an acceptance among (indigenous) Malays of the multi-ethnic complex of Singapore. Ethnic representation in Singapore thus must be understood as responding to an intricate confluence of historical contingencies and social facts.

5.5 Unintended consequences: politicizing ethnicity and ethnic relations

The shift from the tropes of minority representation to multiculturalism however could not avoid the politicization of ethnicity. Despite the best efforts of the Government, the reserved election has, perhaps inadvertently, politicized ethnicity. To the extent that the changes were aimed at maintaining peaceful coexistence among different ethnic groups, the reserved elections risks being counterproductive. Politicization arises as one's ethnic identity becomes central to political status and choices, or when political access and benefits depends on ethnicity. Politicization is different from social relevance; ethnicity is socially relevant when people notice and condition their actions on ethnic distinctions in everyday life. Thus, ethnicity can be socially relevant without it being politicized in a significant way.[69] The reserved elections also raises fraught questions of inclusion and exclusion. This was manifest in the 2017 reserved elections, which surfaced difficult questions about ethnicity, including how to define them and, even more controversially, who would be considered a proper or authentic member of a racial/ethnic community. The reserved elections also gave cause to the question of whether 'multiculturalism' is essentially a way to perpetuate ethnic hierarchy in Singapore. More worryingly, the proposal surfaced latent racism among certain groups in society.

5.5.1 Who is a Malay? Politicizing ethnic definition

Legally, the 2016 amendments to the Presidential Elections adopted the GRC's twofold test of self-identification and community acceptance to determine whether a candidate is from a relevant minority background. It stipulates that a person is from the community if he/she considers himself/herself to be a member of that community ("self-identification") and if he/she is generally accepted as a member of the community by that community ("community acceptance"). Community Committees were set up to decide on the latter. Presumably, this twofold test, which focuses on the process of determination, seeks to avoid any controversy that would arise if Parliament were to legislate a substantive definition of ethnic identification.

However, the task of defining ethnicity is a difficult one, fraught with political and social minefields. The first Constitutional Commission, tasked in 1966 to consider how to ensure adequate safeguards for the rights of racial, linguistic and religious minorities, declined to incorporate a definition of Malay into the Singapore constitution. A proposal had been made to include a definition of Malay based on Article 160(2) of the Malaysian constitution, which states that: "Malay means a person who professes the Muslim religion, habitually speaks the Malay language and conforms to Malay custom". The Commission found the definition over-inclusive because it would include all persons who satisfied those criteria but who are not of the Malay race. It was also under-inclusive because it would exclude persons of the Malay race who choose to renounce Islam. In the end, no definition was included in the Constitution. It was only in 1988, when the Constitution was amended to include the GRC scheme, that a formula was included to determine whether a person belongs to the Malay (as well as Indian or another) community.

In the lead-up to the 2017 Presidential Elections, which was reserved for Malay candidates, one of the most common questions raised was who is Malay. How is Malay-ness to be defined?[70] The Constitution's twofold definition as based on self-identification and community acceptance did not entirely obviate the need for clarity on this issue. Article 19B, defined a "person belonging to the Malay community" as "any person, whether of the Malay race or otherwise", who "considers himself to be a member of the Malay community and who is generally accepted as a member of the Malay community by that community". The reference to the Malay race or *otherwise* is interesting, and appears to be directed at extending the category beyond racial groups that have been more traditionally associated with the Malay community. It is furthermore interesting that slightly different terms are used in defining other groups. The definition for a "person belonging to the Indian or other minority communities" refers to "any person of Indian *origin*" (emphasis added). A new definition for persons belonging to the Chinese community had to be formulated since the GRC scheme did not require such a definition. This new definition makes no similar reference to "race" or "origin". It merely refers to "any person" who considers himself to be a member of the Chinese community and is generally accepted as a member by that community. The use of these different terms – "race", "origin" and "community" – is fascinating, and may point to differing conceptions of ethnicity even among the different groups.

The thorny question of who is Malay was raised not only in online discussions but also in public forums. The question of whether someone is an authentic Malay was also raised.[71] One proposal suggested a definition of Malay as someone who speaks the Malay language, practises Malay culture and practises Islam, that is, a definition identical to the one rejected by the 1966 Constitutional Commission. This definition – based on religion, language and culture – is touted as being inclusive as it would have encompassed all three potential Malay candidates in the 2017 elections. Ultimately, even if such a definition was accepted, it did not resolve the under-inclusive problem, which the 1966 Constitutional Commission raised and that is whether a person who speaks the Malay language and practises Malay culture but is not Muslim can be considered Malay. Or as Kevin Tan asked during an IPS Forum, would a person born into a Malay family but who leaves Islam be accepted as a Malay?[72] This problem of under-inclusivity could presumably be addressed through the second limb of the definition, that is, community acceptance. As Norshahril Saat stated at the same forum, the Malay community, in his view, is not ready for a view of Malayness without Islam.[73] This of course implicates crucial questions concerning religious freedom to choose one's religion as it ties one's religious identity to one's ethnicity and thus political eligibility.

While issues of definition have not been publicly controversial under the GRC scheme, the potential for contestation and politicization may be higher in the context of the Presidency. This is because the reserved elections mechanism raises the stakes on ethnic identity; there is only one office of the President, and therefore one position to vie for. If one does not qualify as an ethnic candidate in a reserved election, one would be precluded from that election cycle and would have to wait for the next cycle or later to contest the Presidency.[74] In comparison, there are multiple seats in any one general elections and if one was not able to qualify as a minority candidate to run in a GRC, one could always run as a non-minority candidate in that constituency or in another. There is no need to wait for the next parliamentary elections to contest. Relatedly, the process of obtaining an eligibility certificate for the reserved election is more public since there is only one position to contest. Potential presidential candidates also receive greater media coverage and more public attention since potential candidates must appeal to all voters in a country, rather than to just a small proportion living in a particular constituency as in a parliamentary contest.

5.5.2 Who is an authentic Malay?

Ethnicity was also politicized when commentators started debating as to who is more Malay. Much of this was played out over social media where commentators questioned whether candidates for the Presidency were "truly Malay" or were the "most authentic" Malay. This is because even though the three potential candidates declared themselves members of the Malay community, one had Pakistani listed as his race in his identity card, while the other two had fathers of Indian origin.[75] One candidate was also criticized for not being fluent in Malay after he fumbled during a Facebook Live interview about his candicacy.[76] Even though several community leaders and observers say the critics' obsession with authenticity and purity flies in the face of a more "open, inclusive view of race that many Malays have adopted in welcoming new members to the community, which includes a wide range of admixtures and ethnicities",[77] the debate shows that the reserved elections have the potential to open a Pandora's box of contested claims of ethnic authenticity. Indeed, several commentators suggest that the "ideal theoretical situation" entails having "a pure Malay or Melayu Asli" as President, with the suggestion that the three declared candidates, all of whom have parental origins in the Indian subcontinent, could not be considered authentic Malays.[78]

Further politicization of ethnicity was, to a large extent, avoided in the 2017 elections since only the former speaker of Parliament, Halimah Yacob received a certificate of eligibility and the election went uncontested.[79] The other two candidates who declared themselves to be from the Malay community did not satisfy either the public-sector or private-sector requirements. Notably, they were not denied certificates on ethnic grounds. Two additional applicants did not receive certificates of eligibility because they did not declare themselves to be members of the Malay community. Nonetheless, as long as ethnic identity remains a criterion for political eligibility, there remains a strong likelihood that such difficult questions concerning ethnic definition and difference will crop up in future reserved elections.

5.5.3 Multiculturalism and latent ethnic hostility

This intra-Malay debate challenges the stated claim of ensuring peaceable inter-ethnic coexistence, often encapsulated in the term 'multiculturalism'. Indeed, as the terms of the debate evolved from minority representation to ensuring multiculturalism, the Government repeatedly emphasized that the reserved election is necessary to enhance multiculturalism or multiracialism in Singapore. However, political contestation about ethnic identity has however also surfaced latent inter-ethnic hostility in Singapore. Cherian George observed that the reserved elections "unleashed a social media flurry of racist remarks in the guise of political comment, injuring the very harmony that the government claimed it was trying to promote."[80] Furthermore, there is suggestion of discontent among the Chinese community. For instance, a survey conducted after the proposal for reserved elections was put forward showed that public opinion was split along majority-minority lines on whether the reserved election was necessary. The poll showed that only 36 per cent of Chinese respondents found the changes "absolutely necessary" or "good to have", as compared to 56 per cent of Malay respondents and 57 per cent of Indian respondents.[81]

Furthermore, as suggested earlier, there is criticism that the claimed ideal of multiculturalism may in fact perpetuate ethnic hierarchy in Singapore. Michael Barr and Zlatko Skrbis, for instance, has previously criticized the Singapore system of multiracialism for having evolved from being primarily concerned with inter-communal tolerance into "an aggressive program of assimilation of the racial minorities into a Chinese-dominated society."[82] According to them, while the initial focus was on the creation of a civic-national identity, this later moved towards an ethnic-centred idea of ethno-national identity. They referred to the increasing references to Singapore as a Confucian society, and various policies that privileged Chinese education, Chinese language and Confucian/ Chinese values as evidence of this move towards ethno-nationalism.[83] A recent debate in Singapore on "Chinese privilege" further reveals certain discontent and anxieties concerning systemic everyday discrimination in Singapore.[84] This includes claims of discrimination on the rental market[85] and in employment. Rental racism involves situations whereby "owners of private residential properties routinely exclude individuals from tenancy based on ethnicity, even explicitly stating in advertisements that requirements are 'no Indians/PRC' (PRC stands for People's Republic of China) or 'no Malay'."[86] On employment, Malay and Indian applicants report being discriminated against when applying for jobs. The reported figures are not high; in 2016, the Minister of State for Manpower stated that about 10 per cent of complaints of alleged discriminatory workplace practices between 2011 and 2015 relate to race and religion.[87] However, anecdotal accounts of employment racism periodically surface over social media, sparking debate over "casual racism"[88] and majority privilege.[89]

Incidences of racist remarks being directed at the Malay minority directly related to the reserved elections have also surfaced. For instance, a Facebook post was picked up by an online news outlet, where a Malay woman wearing a hijab was referred to as "Halimah":

> I was at the fitness corner at Bishan Park doing my workout and minding my own business when a senior citizen remarked jokingly and loudly, "Halimah coming! Halimah coming!" I was the only 'Malay' there.[90]

A member of the group further voiced unhappiness about the reserved elections, invoking multiculturalism: "We are multiracial. Multiracial why must reserve the election for them?"[91] This reflects, at the very least, how multiculturalism itself can become a placeholder for contradictory positions about minority–majority coexistence.

5.5.4 Charges of tokenism

Lastly, the politicization of ethnicity has also resulted in serious discussions about the treatment of minorities and raised some of the community's ire against tokenistic measures. There are several ways to understand "tokenism". The *Oxford English Dictionary* defines "tokenism" as "[t]he practice or policy of making merely a token effort or granting only minimal concessions, esp. to minority or suppressed groups." The *Merriam-Webster Dictionary* is more explicit about the underlying problem with tokenism, which it defines as "the practice of doing something (such as hiring a person who belongs to a minority group) only to *prevent criticism* and *give the appearance* that people are being treated fairly."[92] Measures are "tokenistic" when individuals from minority backgrounds are given prominent positions but do not necessarily perform influential roles beneficial to the group and nor does their presence truly reflect social parity among minority–majority groups.[93] Measures that are tokenistic do not adequately address the underlying causes of under-representation or even discrimination. In fact, such measures may sometimes be used to deflect criticism that a particular organization is not sufficiently representative and inclusive of minority groups.

Tokenism is broadly considered a pejorative term used to describe a social situation whereby minorities are utilized for "display" purposes.[94] It refers to the creation of the impression that "the rhetoric of racial equality is being adhered to by powerful interests", when in fact it is not, at least not on a sufficiently substantive manner. Thus, tokenistic arrangements could be used to perpetuate conditions where social and/or political spaces continue to be dominated by powerful ethnic interests.[95] These arrangements could excuse hierarchical relations or relations of domination, as well as neutralize efforts for full integration.[96]

There were two broad responses to the tokenism criticism in relation to the reserved. The first was to deny that it is tokenistic since candidates in reserved elections have to meet the same eligibility criteria as other candidates in open elections.[97] However, as tokenism broadly refers to practices or policies that grant minimal concessions, including in the form of prominent positions, to a minority or suppressed group, it is not necessary to lower the standards of entry or eligibility in order for a measure to be tokenistic. The key critique is that it is used to deflect criticism of systemic discrimination. For instance, using an example of company hiring, candidates from minority backgrounds could be hired in a company with the same or similar qualifications as others hired for the same position, but could nonetheless be treated as the "token minority" if s/he was hired to "prevent criticism and give the appearance that people are being treated fairly".[98]

Furthermore, even if someone is hired or selected on the same basis, that does not detract from the more insidious effect sometimes associated with tokenism, which is that it perpetuates ethnic hierarchy within the system whereby dominant groups continue to control the agenda. What the "tokenism" criticism tries to strike at is the lack of true "social parity" among minority–majority groups, despite certain prominent measures.[99] As such, this argument that the reserved election is not "tokenistic" because candidates still have to satisfy the same eligibility criteria as others may not be adequate.[100] The second response was to accept that reserved elections *are* tokenistic but that it is a "necessary tokenism".[101] This is because, as Norshahril Saat argues, "there is a risk that if there is no president from a particular racial group for a long time, the issue could be politicised should some claim that discrimination is at play."[102]

Indeed, the reserved elections could be criticized as tokenistic if it is meant to ensure minority representation and political inclusion. This is because it does not seek to address the question of why there has not been any candidate from the Malay community. Of course, several possible reasons could be at play. The first and the most simplistic one is that the eligibility criteria are set so high that there are too few possible Malay candidates. Even before the 2016 changes, a person could only stand as a candidate for President if s/he had held high public office (Minister, Chief Justice, Speaker, Attorney-General, Chairman of the Public Service Commission, Auditor-General, Accountant-General or Permanent Secretary), or had been at the helm of a private company with paid-up capital of at least S$100 million for at least three years. While the criteria based on public-sector experience remains largely unchanged,[103] the eligibility criteria based on private-sector experience was significantly raised such that only those who have been in a chief executive position in a company of at least S$500 million in shareholder equity can qualify.[104]

With respect to public-sector qualification, the number of eligible candidates from the Malay community is comparatively low. There has not been a Malay Chief Justice, Attorney-General, Chairman of the Public Service Commission, Auditor-General or Accountant-General. As of 2017, there had only been six Malay full Cabinet Ministers and two Malay Speakers of Parliament since independence (one of whom was also a Cabinet Minister). As for private-sector qualifications, there is not enough data to conclude whether it is actually true that there are not enough eligible Malay candidates. Being a minority group that occupies only about 15 per cent of the population, it may be that there are proportionately fewer eligible candidates compared to the majority Chinese community, which stands at about 72 per cent of the total population. However, it appears that there could even be disproportionately lower number of eligible candidates from the Malay community.[105] Any perception of a lack of eligible candidate is sometimes accentuated by the fact that no Malay candidate has contested in the last four presidential elections and in the last open elections in 2011, all four candidates contesting were ethnic Chinese.

A second possible reason for the lack of Malay candidates is that even if they were eligible, Malay candidates would not want to contest in the presidential elections because they are not confident of winning because of ethnic voting. This is where the Government's constant reiteration of ethnic preferential voting may be counter-productive in encouraging minorities to come forward to participate in elections. If the Government is right, and there is a need for remedial measures, then this may further undermine ethnic minority candidates' confidence in putting themselves forward. The thinking is: why fight a losing proposition?

5.6 Conclusion

The "hiatus-triggered" or reserved election is a uniquely Singaporean innovation. The "natural sunset" mechanism suggests that despite present assumptions about ethnic voting and ethnic thinking, there remains a deep-seated aspiration that such ethnic differences could be overcome in the future. As the Constitutional Commission puts it, a presidential election will only be reserved when "there has been an exceedingly long period of time during which no member of a particular ethnic minority has occupied the Presidency."[106] Thus, "if free and unregulated elections produce Presidents from a varied distribution of ethnicities, the requirement of a reserved election will never be triggered."[107] In the meantime, the impact of a measure that puts ethnicity at the forefront of political discourse will continue to reverberate.

In general, Singapore's approach towards ethnic relations has been described as "interactionist", as opposed to integrationist or assimilationist as it acknowledges social heterogeneity and views the population as comprising of distinct races.[108] Consequently, policies in education, employment, housing, immigration and national security are designed to allow each ethnic group to retain and perpetuate its distinctiveness within a general framework of national interests.[109] This inherently involves a balancing exercise, as the preservation of ethnic distinctiveness inevitably undermines a broad commitment to ethnic equality (guaranteed under the Singapore Constitution and recited in the national pledge) and national unity. The Elected Presidency, with its emphasis that ethnic candidates also have to meet the stringent requirements like any other candidate, seeks to preserve this broad commitment to equality. However, as academic Kenneth Paul Tan observed, the reserved election also reflects "the bleak realism of Singapore's government" and its belief that "racial feelings are such that you have to design things around them, rather than trying to transform them."[110] The Government's tight management of ethnic relations may well become increasingly fraught as it seeks to introduce ethnic-based measures while trying not to open the door to communalism or ethnic politics.

Ultimately, this critique of the reserved election mechanism in ensuring periodic minority representation is not meant to suggest that electoral changes should not be made to address and improve ethnic relations and minority interests. In some ways, the reserved elections is an important symbolic nod to the importance of ethnic equality and coexistence. However, more will be needed to address the root causes of racialized-thinking/ethnicized-thinking and to overcome ethnic voting. This would require more broad-based efforts at addressing systemic causes of under-representation among minority groups in all areas, public and private.

Notes

* I would like to thank Donald Horowitz for his comments on an earlier draft and Zamiq Azmeer B. Borhanudin for his research assistance.

1 These were statements made (in Singlish) by a group to a Malay lady shortly after the first Malay woman President was appointed in a reserved elections: Fasiha Nazren, "Woman referred to as 'Halimah' at Bishan Park just because she's Malay & wearing tudung: Only Halimah can be Malay and wear tudung is it?", *Mothership* (20 September 2017) https://mothership.sg/2017/09/woman-referred-to-as-halimah-at-bishan-park-just-because-shes-malay-wearing-tudung/ (accessed 30 April 2018).

2 "Ensuring minority representation in Elected Presidency not 'tokenism': PM Lee", *Channel NewsAsia* (Singapore, 4 September 2016) www.channelnewsasia.com/news/singapore/ensuring-minority-representation-in-elected-presidency-not-token-7818436 (accessed 28 September 2018).
3 *Singapore Parliamentary Debates: Official Report*, 27 January 2016, vol. 94.
4 Constitutional Commission, *Report of the Constitutional Commission 2016* (2016) (hereinafter referred to as "Constitutional Commission Report 2016"), 88.
5 "Ensuring minority representation in Elected Presidency not 'tokenism' " (n. 2).
6 *Ibid.*
7 Article 39A(2) of the Singapore Constitution.
8 *Constitutional Commission Report 1966*, [47].
9 *Ibid.*, [49].
10 *Ibid.*, [51].
11 See Article 68 of the Constitution of the Republic of Singapore.
12 See Jaclyn L. Neo, "Navigating minority inclusion and permanent division: minorities and the depoliticization of ethnic difference" (2017) 17 *Jus Politicum* 607–27.
13 Donald L. Horowitz, "Ethnic power sharing: three big problems" (2014) 25(2) *Journal of Democracy* 5, at 5.
14 *Ibid.*
15 Andreas Ackermann, " 'They give us the categories and we fill ourselves in': ethnic thinking in Singapore" (1997) 4 *International Journal on Minority and Group Rights* 451.
16 Norshahril Saat, "Elected Presidency changes: necessary tokenism to boost long-term multiracialism", *The Straits Times* (Singapore, 15 November 2016) www.straitstimes.com/opinion/necessary-tokenism-to-boost-long-term-multiracialism (accessed 28 September 2018).
17 *Ibid.*
18 Rahayu Mahzam, *Singapore Parliamentary Debates: Official Report*, 9 November 2016, vol. 94, 71.
19 See also Nizam Idris, "Elected Presidency changes: big step backwards for Malay community", *The Straits Times* (Singapore, 15 November 2016) www.straitstimes.com/opinion/big-step-backwards-for-malay-community (accessed 28 September 2018).
20 Kelly Ng, "Race matters to voters, Govt had to make 'judgment call' for reserved election: Shanmugam", *TODAY* (Singapore, 9 September 2017) www.todayonline.com/singapore/race-matters-voters-govt-had-make-judgement-call-reserved-election-shanmugam (accessed 28 September 2018).
21 *Ibid.*
22 "PKMS calls for Malay President", *The Straits Times* (Singapore, 10 June 2005), 15.
23 In his usual trenchant terms, playwright Alfian Sa'at says: "I would rather have a Chinese Elected President who can act as an effective check on the government than a puppet Malay President holding a golden rubberstamp", Alfian Sa'at, "We've had four presidential elections (of which two went uncontested)", *Facebook* (22 August 2016) www.facebook.com/alfiansaat/posts/10153733229682371 (accessed 3 February 2018).
24 *Ibid.*
25 Nizam Idris, "Elected Presidency changes: big step backwards for Malay community", *The Straits Times* (Singapore, 15 November 2016) www.straitstimes.com/opinion/big-step-backwards-for-malay-community (accessed 28 September 2018).
26 *Constitutional Commission Report 2016* (n. 4), para. 5.15. See also the White Paper on *Review of Specific Aspects of the Elected Presidency: The Constitution of the Republic of Singapore (Amendment) Bill* (2016), para. 78 (hereinafter referred to as "White Paper").
27 *Ibid.*, para. 79.
28 The CNA-IPS Survey on Race Relations can be found at Mathew Mathews, "Channel NewsAsia-Institute of Policy Studies (CNA-IPS) Survey on Race Relations",

Lee Kuan Yew School of Public Policy (19 August 2016) http://lkyspp.nus.edu.sg/docs/default-source/ips/CNA-IPS-survey-on-race-relations_190816.pdf (accessed 28 September 2018).

29 *Ibid.*

30 For instance, 67 per cent of Indian and Malay respondents think that they have been treated negatively because of their ethnicity: *ibid.*

31 *Ibid.*

32 Cherian George, "The Singapore presidential (s)election: a monumental miscalculation", *Mothership* (15 September 2017) https://mothership.sg/2017/09/a-monumental-miscalculation/ (accessed 28 September 2018).

33 "I don't want us minorities to be used, once again, as a pretext to devise a system which will allow the PAP to entrench power", Alfian Sa'at (n. 23).

34 Linette Lim, "On Tan Cheng Bock, mixed-race candidates: Singaporeans ask tough questions on the Elected Presidency review", *Channel NewsAsia* (15 September 2016) www.channelnewsasia.com/news/singapore/on-tan-cheng-bock-mixed-race-candidates-singaporeans-ask-tough-q-7788466 (accessed 7 October 2018).

35 Tham Yuen-C, "Tan Cheng Bock questions presidential election changes", *The Straits Times* (Singapore, 1 April 2017) www.tnp.sg/news/singapore/tan-cheng-bock-questions-presidential-election-changes (accessed 28 September 2018).

36 See Swati Jhaveri's Chapter 9 in this volume.

37 This was stated in a Facebook post made by former Non-Constituency Member of Parliament Yee Jenn Jong and reproduced in The Online Citizen: "If we want a Elected Presidency, stop changing rules when they make you uncomfortable", *The Online Citizen* (7 September 2017) www.theonlinecitizen.com/2017/07/09/if-we-want-a-elected-presidency-stop-changing-rules-when-they-make-you-uncomfortable/ (accessed 28 September 2018).

38 Zaqy Mohamad, *Singapore Parliamentary Debates: Official Report*, 8 November 2016, vol. 94, 51.

39 Nur Asyiqin Mohamad Salleh, "Singapore's next president set to be Malay: mix of cheer and concern in Malay community", *The Straits Times* (Singapore, 9 November 2016) www.straitstimes.com/singapore/mix-of-cheer-and-concern-in-malay-community (accessed 17 April 2018).

40 Nizam Idris (n. 19).

41 See Teo You Yenn, *This Is What Inequality Looks Like* (Singapore: Ethos Books, 2018).

42 Yaacob Ibrahim, *Singapore Parliamentary Debates: Official Report*, 7 November 2016, vol. 94, 81.

43 Political leaders such as Malaysia's Mahathir Mohammad and Singapore's first Prime Minister Lee Kuan Yew has pointed to cultural-ethnic factors for the performance differential among the various ethnic groups, particularly to explain the uneven economic achievements between the Chinese and Malay communities. Mahathir Bin Mohamad, *The Malay Dilemma* (Singapore: Asia Pacific Press, 1970); Han Fook Kwang, Warren Fernandez and Sumiko Tan, *Lee Kuan Yew: The Man and His Ideas* (Singapore: Marshall Cavendish International Asia, 2015) in the chapter on "The difference between the Malays and the Chinese".

44 Speech to the Southeast Asia Business Committee Meeting Dinner, at Hotel Singapura on 12 May 1968, reproduced in Han Fook Kwang, Warren Fernandez and Sumiko Tan, *Lee Kuan Yew: The Man and His Ideas* (Singapore: Marshall Cavendish International Asia, 2015) in the chapter on "The difference between the Malays and the Chinese".

45 Eugene Teng, "Majority race must be wary of false sense of entitlement", *TODAY* (Singapore, 1 December 2016) www.todayonline.com/singapore/majority-race-must-be-wary-false-sense-entitlement (accessed 28 September 2018).

46 See further Lily Zubaidah Rahim, *The Singapore Dilemma: The Political and Educational Marginality of the Malay Community* (Kuala Lumpur: Oxford University Press, 2001).

47 Goh Chok Tong, *Singapore Parliamentary Debates: Official Report*, 11 January 1988, vol. 50, cols 182–186.
48 *Ibid.*, cols 180–1.
49 See Article 39A of the Singapore Constitution.
50 On the GRC, see Goh Chok Tong (n. 47), cols 187–8; and on the reserved elections, see *Constitutional Commission Report 2016* (n. 4), para. 5.37.
51 "Ensuring minority representation in Elected Presidency not 'tokenism' " (n. 2).
52 That turned out to be a close fight between Dr Tony Tan and Dr Tan Cheng Bock, who obtained 35.2 per cent and 34.85 per cent of votes respectively. Norshahril Saat, "Elected Presidency changes: necessary tokenism to boost long-term multiracialism", *The Straits Times* (Singapore, 15 November 2016) www.straitstimes.com/opinion/necessary-tokenism-to-boost-long-term-multiracialism (accessed 29 September 2018).
53 "Constitutional Commission to review specific aspects of the Elected Presidency", *Prime Minister's Office Singapore* (10 February 2016) www.pmo.gov.sg/newsroom/constitutional-commission-review-specific-aspects-elected-presidency (accessed 28 September 2018) (emphasis added).
54 Anne Phillips, "Dealing with difference: a politics of ideas or a politics of presence?" (1994) 1(1) *Constellations* 76.
55 See for instance debates in Hollywood about Asian representation: Hua Hsu, "Crazy Rich Asians and the end point of representation", *The New Yorker* (New York, 20 August 2018) www.newyorker.com/culture/cultural-comment/crazy-rich-asians-and-the-end-point-of-representation (accessed 28 September 2018).
56 Iris Marion Young, *Justice and the Politics of Difference* (Princeton, NJ: Princeton University Press, 2011), 185.
57 Melissa S. Williams, *Voice, Trust, and Memory: Marginalized Groups and the Failings of Liberal Representation* (Princeton, NJ: Princeton University Press, 2000), 78.
58 Phillips (n. 54), 77–8.
59 Williams (n. 57), 78.
60 Phillips (n. 54), 85.
61 Amy Gutmann, *Identity in Democracy* (Princeton, NJ: Princeton University Press, 2003), 15.
62 Anne Phillips, *The Politics of Presence: The Political Representation of Gender, Ethnicity, and Race* (Oxford: Oxford University Press, 1995).
63 Speech by Senior Parliamentary Secretary to the Minister for Education (Encik Sidek bin Saniff) on the "Re-election of Wee Kim Wee", in *Singapore Parliamentary Debates: Official Report*, 31 August 1989, vol. 54, col. 493.
64 This was emphasized by a Malay MP in the 're-election' of Dr Benjamin Sheares as President: Speech by Encik Rahmat Bin Kenap Al-Haj, on the "Election of President of Republic of Singapore", in *Singapore Parliamentary Debates: Official Report*, 6 November 1974, vol. 33, col. 1083.
65 Speech by Inche Rahamat Bin Kenap (Geylang Serai) on the "Election of President of Republic of Singapore", in *Singapore Parliamentary Debates: Official Report*, 30 November 1967, vol. 26, col. 413.
66 *Ibid.*
67 Speech by the Parliamentary Secretary to the Minister for Finance (Mr S. Ramaswamy) (In Tamil) on the "Election of President of Republic of Singapore", in *Singapore Parliamentary Debates: Official Report*, 30 November 1967, vol. 26, col. 418.
68 *Singapore Parliamentary Debates: Official Report*, 30 August 1985, vol. 46, col. 320.
69 James D. Fearon, "Ethnic mobilization and ethnic violence", in Donald A. Wittman and Barry R. Weingast (eds), *The Oxford Handbook of Political Economy* (Oxford: Oxford University Press, 2008), 853.
70 Nur Asyiqin Mohamad Salleh, "Presidential Election 2017: question of who is Malay continues to be raised", *The Straits Times* (Singapore, 9 September 2017)

www.straitstimes.com/politics/question-of-who-is-malay-continues-to-be-raised (accessed 28 September 2018).

71 Bhavan Jaipragas, "In Singapore, how Malay is Malay?", *South China Morning Post* (Hong Kong, 29 July 2017) www.scmp.com/week-asia/politics/article/2104516/singapore-how-malay-malay (accessed 28 September 2018).

72 Nur Asyiqin Mohamad Salleh (n. 70).

73 *Ibid.*

74 Jaclyn L. Neo, "Constitutional change in Singapore's Elected Presidency: navigating questions of ethnic identity and representation", *IACL-AIDC Blog* (30 November 2017) https://blog-iacl-aidc.org/test-3/2018/5/17/constitutional-change-in-singapores-elected-presidency-navigating-questions-of-ethnic-identity-and-representation?rq=jaclyn%20neo (accessed 6 October 2018).

75 Zakir Hussain, "Doubts about presidential hopefuls not being Malay enough are off track", *The Straits Times* (Singapore, 20 July 2017) www.straitstimes.com/opinion/doubts-about-presidential-hopefuls-not-being-malay-enough-are-off-track (accessed 28 September 2018); Nurulkhasanah Agost, "'Bapa saya tidak pernah tahu cakap Tamil' – Halimah Yacob perjelas faktor identiti", *Berita Mediacorp* (Singapore, 30 August 2017),online:https://berita.mediacorp.sg/mobilem/singapore/bapa-saya-tidak-pernah-tahu-cakap-tamil-halimah-yacob-perjelas/3812074.html (accessed 6 October 2018).

76 Zakir Hussain, *ibid.*

77 *Ibid.*

78 Bhavan Jaipragas (n. 71).

79 Charissa Yong, "Halimah Yacob only one to get eligibility certificate, set to be Singapore's next President", *The Straits Times* (Singapore, 11 September 2017) www.straitstimes.com/singapore/halimah-yacob-only-one-to-get-eligibility-certificate-set-to-be-singapores-next-president (accessed 28 September 2018).

80 Cherian George, "The Singapore presidential (s)election: a monumental miscalculation", *Mothership* (15 September 2017) https://mothership.sg/2017/09/a-monumental-miscalculation/ (accessed 28 September 2018).

81 Bhavan Jaipragas (n. 71).

82 Michael D. Barr and Zlatko Skrbis, *Constructing Singapore: Elitism, Ethnicity and the Nation-Building Project* (Copenhagen: Nordic Institute of Asian Studies 2008), 87.

83 *Ibid.*

84 Walter Sim, "The race issue: how far has Singapore come?", *The Straits Times* (Singapore, 8 November 2015) www.straitstimes.com/politics/the-race-issue-how-far-has-singapore-come (accessed 28 September 2018).

85 For instance, some landlords have explicitly refused to rent to Indian tenants because of an existing stereotype that they tend to do a lot of heavy cooking and use a lot of spices in their cooking. Helier Cheung, "'No Indians No PRCs': Singapore's rental discrimination problem", *BBC News* (Singapore, 1 May 2014) www.bbc.com/news/world-asia-26832115 (accessed 28 September 2018).

86 Nyshka Chandran and Michelle Loh, "Even in weak market, racial bias trumps profit for many Singapore landlords", *CNBC* (Asia-Pacific, 2 March 2017) www.cnbc.com/2017/03/02/singapore-rental-racism-prc-and-indian-tenants-often-deemed-undesirable.html (accessed 28 September 2018). Among the prejudice is that PRCs do not give sufficient regard to the upkeep of properties, that Indian tenants do not sufficiently clean up after cooking South Asian cuisine, and that Malay tenants are often errant in paying rent.

87 Olivia Ho, "Parliament: less than 10% of complaints on work discrimination to do with race, religion", *The Straits Times* (Singapore, 11 July 2016) www.straitstimes.com/singapore/manpower/parliament-less-than-10-of-complaints-on-work-discrimination-to-do-with-race (accessed 28 September 2018).

88 Chua Mui Hoong, "Is it time to bring racism out of the closet?", *The Straits Times* (Singapore, 3 June 2017) www.straitstimes.com/opinion/is-it-time-to-bring-racism-out-of-the-closet (accessed 28 September 2018).

89 For instance, in 2016, a bakery chain was taken to task for a job interview where the interviewee of Malay ethnicity experienced outright racism; she was told that Malays overpromise and tend to disappear after two days of employment. According to the interviewee's Facebook post, the head of department told her:

> From what I see, and the way you look, and not trying to be racist ah, but you Malay, I think you cannot la. You know ah, Malays ah they over promise, promise I can do this I can do that, in the end, cannot make it, after 2 days disappear.

Olivia Ho and Aw Cheng Wei, "PrimaDeli apologises, sacks staff for making racist remarks to job interviewee", *The Straits Times* (Singapore, 29 April 2016) www.straitstimes.com/singapore/manpower/primadeli-apologises-sacks-staff-for-making-racist-remarks-to-job-interviewee (accessed 28 September 2018).

90 Fasiha Nazren, "Woman referred to as 'Halimah' at Bishan Park just because she's Malay & wearing tudung: Only Halimah can be Malay and wear tudung is it?" *Mothership* (20 September 2017) https://mothership.sg/2017/09/woman-referred-to-as-halimah-at-bishan-park-just-because-shes-malay-wearing-tudung/ (accessed 30 April 2018).

91 *Ibid.*

92 Emphasis added.

93 James Jennings, "Tokenism", in Ellis Cashmore, *Dictionary of Race and Ethnic Relations*, 4th edn (London: Routledge 2002), 363.

94 Notably, tokenism as an idea has been developed within the context of black–white relations in the United States whereby scholars have even described tokenism as "a political resource of powerful white interests, both in the public and private arena of the USA." James Jennings, "Tokenism", in Ellis Cashmore (ed.), *Encyclopedia of Race and Ethnic Studies*, 4th edn (London: Routledge, 2004), 421.

95 *Ibid.*, 422.

96 *Ibid.*

97 Nur Asyiqin Mohamad Salleh (n. 39).

98 Emphasis added.

99 Jennings (n. 92), 363.

100 Nur Asyiqin Mohamad Salleh (n. 39).

101 Norshahril Saat (n. 16).

102 *Ibid.*

103 The Constitutional Commission proposed no changes to the list of qualifying offices except for the removal of the offices of Auditor-General and Accountant-General from the list of public offices through which applicants could qualify. *Constitutional Commission Report 2016* (n. 4), para. 8.3(a).

104 *Constitutional Commission Report 2016* (n. 4), para. 8.3(c).

105 Dr Norshahril Saat highlighted that it maybe a little more difficult to field more Malay candidates given the more stringent criteria and that it is not clear how many potential candidates exists in the private sector but for the public sector, there's one former Minister and the then Speaker of Parliament. Emillia Amin, "Dr Norshahril: Peruntukan calon Melayu untuk Pilihan Raya Presiden demi penyatuan Negara", *Berita Mediacorp* (Singapore, 8 November 2016) https://berita.mediacorp.sg/mobilem/singapore/dr-norshahril-peruntukan-calon-melayu-untuk-pilihan-raya/3271644.html (accessed 17 April 2018).

106 *Constitutional Commission Report 2016* (n. 4), para. 5.36.

107 *Ibid.*

108 Sharon Siddique, "The phenomenology of ethnicity: a Singapore case study" (1990) 5(1) *Sojourn: Journal of Social Issues in Southeast Asia* 35.

109 Netina Tan, "Multiracialism and politics of regulating ethnic relations in Singapore". Paper presented at the annual meeting of Canadian Political Science Association, Victoria, British Columbia, Canada, 4–6 June 2013, www.cpsa-acsp.ca/papers-2013/Tan2.pdf (accessed 29 September 2018).

110 "Singapore expands its paternalistic policy on race", *The Economist* (USA, 15 December 2016) www.economist.com/asia/2016/12/15/singapore-expands-its-paternalistic-policy-on-race (accessed 28 September 2018).

6 Squaring the circle

The President as a symbol of multiracialism and national unity

Eugene K.B. Tan

6.1 Introduction

On 14 September 2017, Halimah Yacob was sworn in as Singapore's eighth President. She is the first woman to hold office as Singapore's Head of State. She is also the first Malay President since President Yusof Ishak, who had passed away in office in November 1970. Halimah Yacob was elected unopposed in the presidential election that was reserved for candidates from the Malay community. This reserved presidential election mechanism was instituted following the enactment of the 2016 constitutional amendments.[1] The 2016 changes were easily the most significant set of changes to Singapore's system of government since the 1991 constitutional amendments, which had provided for the conversion of the Presidency from an appointed and ceremonial office to an elected one with significantly enhanced "custodial powers". This reconfigured the institution as an intra-branch check and balance.[2]

A key objective of the 2016 amendments is to ensure that the Presidency remains accessible to persons from all the major racial communities in Singapore. Through a "hiatus-triggered" mechanism, where a major race had not been elected in five presidential elections, the reserved election is designed to obviate the need to mechanically rotate the Presidency among the major racial groups as was the case prior to 1991.[3] Having granted the democratic franchise to Singaporeans to vote for their Head of State, it was impossible to revert, without severe political repercussions, to the original position of the President being elected by Parliament and performing a largely ceremonial role.[4] Further, given the critical custodial powers vested in the President, it was incongruent for Parliament to elect the President to check on the Cabinet and the Legislature. To do so would gravely affect the legitimacy of the Presidency, especially in the exercise of custodial powers, which may extend to overriding the decisions of the elected parliamentary government.[5]

Earlier in September 2016, the Constitutional Commission, chaired by Chief Justice Sundaresh Menon, proposed a "hiatus-triggered" reserved election mechanism to safeguard representation of all major racial groups, namely, Chinese, Malay, Indian and other communities. The Constitutional Commission's starting premise was that the Presidency has a crucial role as "a symbol of unity and the personification of the state" right from the time the office was created at independence.[6] In its report, the Commission stated that there was a pressing need to ensure that "no ethnic group is shut out of the Presidency … lest the office of President lose its vitality as a symbol of the nation's unity."[7]

For the People's Action Party ("PAP") government,[8] multiracialism – a core tenet of Singapore's governance system – is premised on the adequate representation of the minorities in key institutions such as the Legislature.[9] As Singapore had not become a "post-racial" society,[10] ensuring minority representation is not only compatible with multiracialism, but is also mutually constitutive of it. Much was made of a key finding in a Channel NewsAsia ("CNA") and the Institute of Policy Studies ("IPS") study that Singaporeans still "found a member of their own race more acceptable to be the President and the Prime Minister over other races."[11] While the Government did not take the position that a minority candidate was unelectable, it argued that: "race remains a significant factor for many Singaporeans, and that voting choices can, and are, swayed by racial factors, quite apart from the merit of candidates."[12]

The very notion of racial representation in the Presidency is inherently cleaved from the 'Chinese-Malay-Indian-Others' or 'CMIO' categorization of Singapore society. Under this relatively rigid, largely state-assigned racial classification system, every person whose birth is registered in Singapore is racially designated, primarily based on one's patrilineage.[13] The intent of having minority Presidents periodically is laudable. However, the reserved election mechanism is, in essence, electoral affirmative action. It has the potential to strike at the heart of Singapore's system of multiracialism and meritocracy. It could also undermine the ability of the electorate to elect the best person for the office but for the restrictions on candidature. On the other hand, it can be a powerful statement of multiracialism for a Chinese-majority nation-state to have a non-Chinese elected by popular mandate as Head of State.[14] But *how* minority Presidents are elected is crucial, since it comes with potentially significant ramifications for the standing and legitimacy of the office and the office holder and the robustness of Singapore's multiracialism.

Unless measures are taken to deal with the electorate voting along racial lines – which was presented as the root of the problem of inadequate minority representation – then even a reserved election which shoehorns the election of a minority race President would be a sure way to undermine the standing and legitimacy of the Elected Presidency. This is not to deny or underestimate race, religion and language as fault lines in Singaporean society. Neither does it make light of the primordial or essentialist loyalties that markers of ethnicity can induce, arouse and mobilize in the different communities.

That said, constitutional design should not pander to these centrifugal forces. Instead, institutional designers must endeavour to rise above society's prejudices, stereotypes and weaknesses. The electoral system can and should play a key part in racial integration and lead change in electoral behaviour. Ultimately, the goal is to reduce the salience of ethnic markers in politics and governance. This is notwithstanding that any measure that seeks to promote and safeguard adequate minority representation in key state institutions is arguably aligned with Article 152 of the Singapore Constitution,[15] which exhorts the Singapore Government to "constantly to care for the interests of the racial and religious minorities in Singapore" and to "recognise the special position of the Malays".

Yet, constitutional engineering cannot remove a racial or even a racist mindset and disposition in electoral behaviour. All it can do is to try to reduce the centrifugal tendencies while seeking to generate centripetal forces. As part of the schema of institutional design, the electoral system must play a central role in the larger effort to design and engineer desired constitutional outcomes. Specifically, what an electoral system can and should do is to "nudge" and provide "incentives" for candidates and the electorate to think of how their electoral behaviour, principally through their votes and the election campaigns, can be advantageous to them individually and collectively, while enhancing multiracialism.

This chapter considers the rationale for minority representation in the office of the Elected President. It examines the official discourse on the Head of State as a symbol of multiracialism and national unity. This chapter argues that even as Singapore has had its first reserved presidential election, it is important to educate and encourage voters to look beyond their navels and to consider whether a candidate, regardless of his or her race, is an exemplary practitioner and promoter of multiracialism and of national unity. Such a consideration should go into a voter's assessment of a candidate's merit, especially in an "unreserved" or open election.

Even as it seeks to emplace the Presidency as a symbol of Singapore's national unity and multiracialism, the paradoxical challenge of the reserved election mechanism is to avoid triggering it. The success of the reserved election mechanism is not whether it produces a minority race President but for it not to be utilized. This means Singaporeans electing minority race candidates in open elections, where all qualified candidates are able to contest, regardless of their race. Constitutional fiats are often unsustainable and the long-term effects of the reserved election mechanism on race relations will not be known for decades.

The discussion in this chapter is organized as follows. Section 6.2 overviews the importance of institutional design, including constitutional frameworks, in heterogeneous post-colonial nation-states in order to maintain social harmony. Section 6.3 examines the 2016 Constitutional Commission's considerations in designing the reserved election safeguard to ensure minority representation in the Presidency. Section 6.4 considers the notion of minority representation within Singapore's multiracial framework, and also explores the effort to influence electoral behaviour in the cause of race-blindness. Article 152 of the Constitution is also examined in the context of whether the reserved election is another manifestation of the Government looking after the interests of the minorities. Section 6.5 describes the recriminations from the 2017 uncontested reserved election and how that could impact the President's execution of the constitutional, community and ceremonial duties.[16] Section 6.6 concludes.

6.2 The challenge and limitations of institutional design

6.2.1 Institutional design in ethnically diverse societies: making moderation pay-off

Institutional design plays a fundamental role in the attainment of constitutional ideals and imperatives and the well-being of societies such as the promotion of the rule of law. Furthermore, the democratic process can facilitate a viable system of governance that is inclusive and gives effect to the political aspirations of the people. In plural post-colonial societies, the role of such a constitutional regime takes on greater importance as it is expected to provide a framework for the "forging of a common political identity ... by creating the institutional spaces for shared decision making".[17] The development of a shared experience of belonging and the crystallization of a shared identity and community are not only necessary but also onerously demanding in the nation-building journey. Electoral systems "represent, perhaps, the most powerful instrument available for institutional engineering, with far reaching consequences for party systems, the composition of legislatures, and the durability of democratic arrangements."[18] The literature has evolved and extended beyond Arend Lijphart's influential theory of consociation (or 'power sharing')[19] to discussing the suitability of majoritarian system vis-à-vis those employing proportional representation, and whether an electoral system can generate mass support for the political system – especially from the minorities.[20]

Proponents of electoral integration champion the creation of an electoral system that is configured to generate inducements for moderate behaviour and cross-cutting loyalties. In order to secure as many votes as possible in order to win, politicians seeking public office have to reach out to voters across ethnic lines. In the main, electoral system reform and innovation for plural societies strives to "engineer" a system of political competition that fosters the development of cross-cutting cleavages and inter-ethnic cooperation. They also seek to establish a political structure that provides incentives for political moderation and inter-ethnic appeal between elections. This lends critical support to the virtues of moderation and racial non-partisanship, as well as to the development of inter-ethnic ties and trust in the politics and policy-making of any modern society.[21]

Where an electoral system is staunchly centred on electoral integration, political parties and electoral candidates cannot afford to marginalize any segment of the electorate. Candidates must instead have a broad-base appeal that transcends ethnic lines. Racial chauvinism and extremism would gain no traction with large swathes of the electorate.[22] Subsequently, political representation is endowed with substantive purpose and meaning rather than mere tokenism.[23]

The forging of a common political identity is an imperative for a polyglot nation-state like Singapore. A multi-ethnic, multireligious and multilingual polity would arguably require a constitutional framework and ethos that is able to provide a shared understanding of inclusive governance amid diversity and difference, buttressed by trust and confidence in the institutions, the laws and the policies. This would naturally extend to necessitating a process for such objectives. Thus, institutional design for the management of heterogeneity within nation-states, including the regulation of ethnic conflict, results in significant attention being given to the role that electoral systems can play as part of perpetual constitutional quest to harness the polity's better angels.[24]

Singapore has been fortunate to have party politics and a system of government that is not organized and competed along racial lines. Right from the late 1950s when the British colonial authorities began to encourage limited political participation in preparation for the movement towards self-government and eventual independence (albeit as part of the Malayan Federation), the electoral landscape has seldom seen political parties organized and seeking political power along racial lines.[25] This has certainly provided a strong measure of stability to the political system. Emotive and sensitive issues of race, religion and language are strenuously excluded from the hustings. In part, this can be attributed to the leadership of the dominant political party, the PAP, since it won the first elections in 1959 upon Singapore attaining self-governance.[26]

The heterogeneity of Singapore requires careful attention be given to the design of institutions if multiracialism is to be sustained. As John Ikenberry observes generally of plural nation-states, "[e]thnic divisions put at risk the nation-state, but they also provide a powerful incentive for the designing and building of state institutions."[27] In order to sustain multiracialism, the PAP Government believes that the workings of the electoral system should result in the minority races being adequately represented in the Legislature, especially in an ethnically Chinese-dominant Singapore. Adequate representation of the component groups of a nation-state is not only of symbolic importance but can help ensure that the needs, concerns and views of the minority races are not ignored or neglected.

6.2.2 Voting consciously with race?

Despite political parties not organized and competing against each other along racial lines, the Government has long claimed that the Singaporean electorate adopts a racial approach in the electoral process in choosing the candidates in parliamentary elections and, more recently, in the presidential elections.[28] It is said that Singaporeans, especially young voters, have a tendency of voting along racial lines and of "preferring candidates who were best suited to their own needs without being sufficiently aware of the need to return a racially balanced slate of candidates."[29] This, the Government argued, would particularly threaten the representation of the ethnic Malay community, the most significant minority race community in Singapore.[30]

This racial identification between the electorate and the electoral candidates prompted the Government to engage in extensive constitutional engineering, ostensibly with the purpose of ensuring adequate representation in Parliament of legislators from the Malay and Indian and other minority communities.[31] The election laws were amended in 1988 to provide for the Group Representation

Constituency ("GRC") system, a cornerstone of Singapore's electoral integration effort. The GRC electoral division is now the dominant electoral division in Singapore's electoral landscape with almost 85 per cent of all elected parliamentary seats being GRCs.

Under the GRC scheme, voters in a multi-member enlarged electoral district elect a team of legislators rather than an individual legislator. The "one person, one vote" electoral model was retained under the GRC scheme: each vote was cast for one of the competing multiple-member teams in an electoral district. A political party contesting in a GRC has to field a multi-member team of three to six candidates, of which one candidate must be a member of a designated minority race.

The reserved presidential election draws inspiration from the workings of the GRC system. It is a significant extension of the principle of adequate representation of the Malay and Indian and other minority communities in Singapore's political system. Much faith is now placed by the Singaporean political leadership in the reserved presidential election mechanism to reinforce the *raison d'être* of the Elected Presidency as a key institution of multiracialism and national unity. However, in transforming the Presidency from a ceremonial to an elected office in 1991, this important quality of the Presidency appeared to have been de-emphasized since the rotation of the major races in the Presidency could no longer be guaranteed or maintained as an attribute of the office. Both the GRC and reserved presidential election systems are geared towards electoral integration, and each leverages on the concept of substantive equality. The overarching concern is that the political branches of government must be – and seen to be – representative of Singapore's racial composition.[32]

Much as multiracialism is a core tenet in Singapore's constitutional system of government, the abiding concern is still whether it is robust enough to withstand the pressures of centrifugal fears even as it embraces centripetal hopes. Even if the reserved election framework safeguards minority representation in the Presidency, it also has within it the potential to undermine multiracialism and national unity.

To reiterate, electoral integration aims at nurturing a system of healthy political competition that also facilitates the development of cross-cutting cleavages and encourages inter-ethnic cooperation while making racial chauvinism and extremism politically counter-productive. This approach lends critical support to and emphasizes the virtues of moderation, racial non-partisanship and the development of inter-ethnic trust and cooperation. In essence, electoral integration revolves around the search for a framework to manage differences through constitutional arrangements, political norms and a consensual ethos that promote integration as well as accommodation. Integration of different communities in a nation-state is closely tied to equal citizenship, which entails either turning a blind eye to ethnic difference for public purposes or privatizing these differences. In a multiracial polity, group-based partisanship in political institutions is detrimental to social cohesion as some groups would be excluded or marginalized.[33]

On the other hand, accommodation requires the recognition of multiple racial, religious, linguistic and cultural communities within a nation-state. As such, coexistence is a powerful theme in accommodation given that ethnic identities can be enduring and powerful mobilizers. To cater to integrative and accommodationist impulses and imperatives, institutional design of the electoral process has to be structured towards "making moderation pay off". This may be achieved by nudging politicians to seek inter-ethnic support and to adopt a pan-ethnic appeal, rather than pandering to a single community.

The reserved election is a variation from the pre-1991 arrangement where the President was elected by Parliament. Where a conscious effort was made to "rotate" the Presidency among the different racial communities, there was no real concern of inadequate representation of the different major races in the Presidency. All the Presidents elected by Parliament prior to 1991 came from the major races: Malay (President Yusof Ishak, 1965–1970, who was previously *Yang di-Pertuan Negara* from 1959–1965), Eurasian (President Benjamin Henry Sheares, 1971–1981), Indian (President Devan Nair, 1981–1985) and Chinese (President Wee Kim Wee, 1985–1993). However, with the Presidency reintroduced as an elected office in 1991, it was no longer possible to ensure representation of the major races with the same deliberateness.

Since the first presidential election in 1993, no candidate from the Malay community had been elected as President until 2017 when Madam Halimah Yacob was elected in the first reserved election, which was also uncontested. Her predecessors as Elected Presidents were either ethnic Chinese or Indian: Wee Kim Wee (1991–1993; ethnic Chinese),[34] Ong Teng Cheong (1993–1999; ethnic Chinese), S.R. Nathan (1999–2011; ethnic Indian) and Tony Tan Keng Yam (2011–2017; ethnic Chinese). The quest for some degree of deliberateness and certainty in having non-Chinese Singaporeans elected as Presidents led to Prime Minister Lee Hsien Loong establishing a Constitutional Commission in early 2016, which eventually recommended the hiatus-triggered reserved election referred to above.

6.3 Reviewing the Presidency: the Constitutional Commission

At the opening of the thirteenth Parliament in January 2016, then President Tony Tan Keng Yam highlighted the need to "ensure our politics continues to work for the long-term good of Singapore". He noted that through the specific custodial powers, the office of the President fostered "resilience and stability" in Singapore's political system. He indicated that the Government would review the political system. Even as it had "delivered stability and progress for Singapore," the system "must be refreshed from time to time, as our circumstances change".[35]

Speaking during the debate on the President's Address, Prime Minister Lee Hsien Loong elaborated that specific aspects of the Elected Presidency would be reviewed and that a Constitutional Commission would be appointed to study and make recommendations on aspects of the Elected Presidency. On having minorities elected to the Presidency, he expected future presidential elections to "more likely to be contested, even hotly contested," which would make it "much harder for a minority President to get elected".[36] On 10 February 2016, Prime Minister Lee appointed nine distinguished Singaporeans to the Constitutional Commission. This was only the second time in independent Singapore's history that a Constitutional Commission was appointed.[37]

Chaired by Chief Justice Sundaresh Menon, the Commission was tasked to review three selected aspects of the Elected Presidency. The first was the qualifying process for potential presidential candidates. In particular, it was to consider whether existing provisions were adequate, taking into account the President's custodial role in safeguarding financial reserves, and the need to ensure that eligible candidates are individuals of character and standing. Second, the Commission was to review the framework governing the exercise of the President's custodial powers, particularly the role and composition of the Council of Presidential Advisers (CPA), an independent body that advises the President on the exercise of his custodial powers. Third, the Commission was to make recommendations to "safeguard minority representation in the Presidency", taking into account the President's status as a unifying figure that represents multiracial Singapore, and the need to ensure minority candidates "have fair and adequate opportunity to be elected to Presidential office".[38] It is noteworthy that the Commission was not tasked with examining whether there ought to be provisions made to safeguard minority representation but rather "what provisions should be made to safeguard minority representation in the Presidency".

6.3.1 Innovation of a hiatus-triggered mechanism

After public consultations and hearings in April and May 2016, the Commission considered and deliberated on the more than 100 submissions. The Commission studied the evolution of the Presidency over the last five decades and noted that the President embodied the nation,[39] symbolized Singapore's multiracial community[40] and expressed Singapore's national identity. With the Presidency becoming an elected office with custodial powers in 1991, the Commission observed that the President's crucial symbolic role was consequently overlooked. It was necessary to refocus the understanding of the Presidency, especially its ceremonial and symbolic roles, as a "multifaceted institution".[41]

The Commission concluded that there were "strong justifications … to ensure that the highest office in the land is not only accessible, but *is seen to be accessible*, to persons from all the major racial communities in Singapore."[42] The Commission considered several models put forth by the contributors and explained why some were "not optimal". The various models can be broadly classified into the "group representation models, pre-assigned cycles, hiatus-triggered safeguards, and hybrid models".[43]

The Commission was guided by three key principles in designing a suitable safeguard. The first principle was the requirement of minimum intervention to achieve the aim of ensuring that all racial groups are represented in the Presidency.[44]

Second, the safeguard should have an in-built mechanism to enable it to "recede in significance over time", even ceasing to be needed.[45] Third, the eligibility criteria for presidential candidates must not be compromised.[46]

The Commission favoured and proposed a hiatus-triggered reserved election mechanism, which the Government accepted.[47] When a member from any racial group (namely, the Chinese, Malay, Indian and other communities) had not occupied the President's office after five continuous terms, the next presidential election will be reserved for a candidate from that racial group. The hiatus-triggered model was preferred because it was "race-neutral",[48] posed the "lowest degree of intrusiveness … [and] enables the representation of *all* racial groups in the Presidency in a meaningful way while being minimally prescriptive."[49] When a reserved election is triggered, it "will likely encourage candidates from that group to step forward and contest the next election".[50] The Commission also emphasized its conviction that the eligibility criteria must not be lowered "under no circumstances".[51]

The reserved election holds promise as a constitutional safeguard for multiracialism. The requirement of a generational "hiatus" or "an exceedingly long period"[52] without a President from a specified race avoids reverting to the former system of rotation among the major races. It also contains a natural sunset mechanism: should unreserved or open elections result in Presidents from the three major racial groups, then a reserved election will not be invoked.[53] This would help to ameliorate the perception that a reserved election is an affirmative action electoral vehicle. The Commission also did not specify that the reserved election was meant only for the non-Chinese minorities. The Government agreed that the reserved election mechanism should apply to all races – that is, a "race-neutral" safeguard.[54]

However, the challenge lies in demonstrating that the reserved election is for the benefit of not just the minority communities but is equally beneficial to the Chinese majority. The likelihood of an overwhelmingly Chinese-majority Singapore electorate not electing a Chinese candidate in five elections is very low – although, if it comes to pass, that in itself could very well be unequivocal testimony that Singaporean multiracialism had reached a state of enlightenment. The White Paper noted the balance afforded by the hiatus-triggered reserved election: maintaining the "ultimate long-term goal of multi-racialism, and ensuring the representation of minority races in the Presidential office as we progress to that ideal." It also "carefully balances the need for multi-racialism with our meritocratic ideals".[55]

At face value, the hiatus-triggered reserved election mechanism is not conceived as a form of affirmative action for the racial minorities. Furthermore, minority representation through the reserved election mechanism is designed to not compromise the quality of the candidates. The Commission and the Government were conscious that it was crucial not to lower the eligibility criteria for candidates in a reserved election. Both agreed that reserving elections for particular races would not undermine meritocracy, as the eligibility criteria were not lowered for any candidate, regardless of whether they belonged to a minority race. While the bar is not lowered for minority candidates, a legitimate argument can be made that the meritocratic principle is not exercised in its full measure because a reserved election is only open to those of a specified race, rather than all persons being eligible. The Commission also acknowledged the legitimate concern expressed by several contributors that a President elected via the reserved election might be viewed as "a token President who lacks legitimacy". But it ultimately agreed with the view that it is for the President, "upon taking office, to conduct himself with the dignity and gravitas which befits the Presidency and thereby earn the respect of the electorate."[56]

Ultimately, it is a question of balancing the imperative of minority representation in the Presidency and having the best person for the job. To be clear, the two objectives are not mutually exclusive even though they may compete against each other from time to time. It cannot be denied that the reserved election could deprive the country of the services of someone who can be a good President – perhaps one better than the winner of a reserved election.[57]

In any case, no amount of constitutional engineering can remove a racial or even a racist mindset and disposition in electoral behaviour. The reserved election is not the silver bullet in Singapore's quest to ensure that no ethnic group is shut out of the Presidency. It helps ensure that the Presidency is not only accessible, but is seen to be accessible to all the major racial communities in Singapore. It functions as an inter-generational safeguard for minority representation, while not mechanically rotating the Presidency among the major races – the latter of which may be suggestive of tokenism and affect the legitimacy of the President's decisions in the exercise of his custodial powers.

Hence, if properly approached by the candidates and electorate, the reserved election can be the platform by which candidates and the electorate alike can be nudged and incentivized to think of how their electoral campaign and behaviour can further the cause of multiracialism in Singapore. The reserved election should be seen not as an end in itself, but rather as a means of recognizing and strengthening Singapore's racial diversity and its resilience. This also means that it is not solely the responsibility of each community, but also that of the nation as a whole to identify and encourage suitable individuals to consider putting themselves up for election. A reserved election cannot function as one that is about a specific community in question; it must concern the larger collective called the nation-state.

6.3.2 Putting in motion the first reserved election

In February 2017, Parliament amended the Presidential Elections Act,[58] which among other things determined that the presidential terms counted for the purposes of the reserved elections would commence with President Wee Kim Wee, who served as Head of State between 1985 and 1993.[59] President Wee had exercised the powers of the Elected President from 1991 when the Elected Presidency was first instituted.[60] Prior to the 2017 poll, five presidential terms had passed without a Malay being elected as President, thus triggering the reserved election in 2017.[61]

There was much anticipation in the lead-up to the 2017 Presidential Election – the fifth since the first presidential election in 1993. There was no contest for the office in 1999 and 2005, and by the time of the 2011 election, almost two decades had gone by since Singaporeans last cast their ballots in the presidential poll. Hence, it was no surprise that the 2011 election, which had a record four candidates on the ballot sheet, was characterized by competing and, at times, conflicting visions of the Presidency. Some candidates showed ignorance or little regard for the constitutional limits of the presidential powers and over-promised what they could and would do if elected. For instance, one candidate ran his campaign on the platform of being the "voice of the people" while another sought to be the "moral compass", the "conscience" of the nation. The 2011 election was also the most keenly contested. Dr Tony Tan Keng Yam, a former Deputy Prime Minister, narrowly edged out Dr Tan Cheng Bock, a former PAP Member of Parliament. The former won with 35.2 per cent of the popular vote against the latter's 34.85 per cent.[62]

Alas, the first reserved presidential election in 2017 came to an anti-climactic and abrupt end on the eve of Nomination Day.[63] Although there were five applications, three applicants declared that they belonged to the Malay community and applied for Malay Community Certificates. The Presidential Elections Committee awarded only one certificate of eligibility to Madam Halimah Yacob, a former PAP Member of Parliament, who had resigned her parliamentary seat and position as Speaker of Parliament to contest.[64] The public expectations of a contest were high in the lead-up, even though the reality was that the potential field of eligible persons was relatively small, and that the likelihood was low that there would be a contest between two candidates formerly from the ruling party.

Had a contest materialized, it could have gone a long way towards sensitizing Singaporeans on the centrality of the Elected President in Singapore's system of constitutional government.[65] A contest would also boost the legitimacy of the Presidency since it would manifest the exercise of democratic choice by Singaporeans. In previous editions of the presidential election, where there was only one eligible candidate, questions had arisen as to the President's political authority, legitimacy and standing.[66] What more for a minority candidate elected unopposed in a reserved election? If it is perceived that a leg-up to the highest office had been given to the minority candidate, this could potentially compromise his or her ability to properly execute his constitutional, community and ceremonial duties upon election.[67]

Furthermore, as the 2017 election was the first-ever reserved election, it could have contributed immensely towards the understanding and appreciation of how the reserved election enhances multiracialism in Singapore. The opportunity for Singaporeans to specially consider a candidate's commitment and contributions to multiracialism was, unfortunately, not afforded. In a reserved election, this consideration would very likely have been part of the electorate's assessment of a candidate's overall merit and suitability to be an elected Head of State, in addition to his or her professional qualifications, expertise and experience.

The salient emphasis to "safeguard minority representation in the Presidency" was premised on the President's status as a unifying figure who represents multiracial Singapore. However, this stance affirmed in the Commission's Terms of Reference presupposes that only a minority race President can be a symbol of Singapore's much-vaunted multiracialism. While it is a very powerful symbol to have the office of the Elected President occupied by a Singaporean from a minority race, it does not automatically endow the office as a symbol of multiracialism. It was what Singapore's past Presidents did to promote, and further the cause of multiracialism that Singaporeans identified them as symbols of multiracialism. They infused into the Presidency the spirit and soul of multiracialism in Singapore.

For instance, Singapore's first President Yusof Ishak, a Malay, utilized the "soft power" of the office of the President through his actions, which enabled him to successfully transform the head of state office into a symbol of multiracialism. President Yusof Ishak went out of his way to interact with people of all races to promote multiracialism in Singapore and to help restore trust and confidence among the different racial groups after the 1964 riots.

There is no concatenation of events that would render a non-Chinese Singaporean automatically becoming a symbol of multiracialism. If that were the case then, an ethnic Chinese President cannot possibly be a symbol of multiracialism. Such thinking would set Singapore back in terms of her nation-building efforts as well as trying to write that grand narrative of multiracialism of Singapore. To be sure, there was the constitutional intent of the head of state office being a symbol of multiracialism. Singapore's founding fathers determined that appointing Yusof Ishak as *Yang di-Pertuan Negara* was important at Singapore's founding constitutional moments, namely, when Singapore became self-governing in 1959 and when independent Singapore came into being in the throes of her traumatic departure from Malaysia on 9 August 1965. This strategic and pragmatic thinking set the tone for multiracialism and non-discrimination in Singapore.

The appointment of Yusof Ishak as *Yang di-Pertuan Negara* and President was a brilliant masterstroke of the fledgling government and for a country suddenly thrust into nationhood amid racial suspicion, tension and violence. As Singapore's first Prime Minister, Lee Kuan Yew recounted, "We wanted a distinguished Malay in order to show the Federation that Singaporeans were willing to accept Malays as their leaders…"[68] It was a powerful symbol of the fledgling nation-state's commitment to inclusiveness and multiracialism. That remains as pertinent today as it was then.

But the Presidency did not automatically become a living embodiment of multiracialism merely because the Head of State was a member of the Malay community, who were first constitutionally recognized by the State of Singapore Constitution as the indigenous people of Singapore (and remains so under Article 152(2)). Instead, it was President Yusof Ishak's actions that infused the institution of the Head of State with the spirit and soul of multiracialism in Singapore. Similarly, President Wee Kim Wee, a Peranakan-Chinese, was much beloved and respected by all Singaporeans, demonstrating that being from the majority race is not a barrier to one being a symbol of multiracialism.

What is common among the past Presidents is that they were active and exemplary practitioners and promoters of multiracialism. It was what they did for multiracialism as President that made the difference; it was not the colour of their skin that automatically endowed them as symbols of Singapore's multiracialism. The 2016 constitutional changes seemed to have overstated the importance of race vis-à-vis the President being a symbol of multiracialism. As indicated earlier, the requirement of a five presidential term hiatus in a specific racial representation in the Presidency before the reserved election mechanism is triggered can go some way in ameliorating the concerns that the reserved election goes too far.

Notwithstanding the virtues of the hiatus-triggered reserved election, the reality is that a person elected as President in a reserved election will have to bear the burden of showing that he or she is deserving of being Head of State. While it might be considered unfair, nagging doubts from the "but for" question will always remain: but for the reserved election, would that person have become President? Thus, it becomes important that every community spares no effort in encouraging eligible and suitable persons to consider putting themselves up for election. If a person has a proven track record, then it is less likely that there will be such doubts prevailing upon him or her. Such a person will have to show that she has a record of being a practitioner and promoter of multiracialism. Each candidate will also have to manage expectations from his or her own community. This is where it also becomes important to educate Singaporeans so that they can appreciate that a President elected through a reserved election is still a President for all Singaporeans.[69]

6.3.3 But who is a Malay?

In the September 2017 reserved presidential election for Malay candidates, presidential hopefuls had to submit to the Community Committee a community declaration stating that they considered themselves to be a member of the Malay community,[70] in addition to obtaining a certificate of eligibility from the Presidential Elections Committee. Similar to the race requirement for the GRC in parliamentary elections, a person belonging to the Malay community is "any person, whether of the Malay race or otherwise, who considers himself to be a member of the Malay community and who is generally accepted as a member of the Malay community by that community."[71]

The Malay Community Sub-Committee, a constituent part of the Community Committee, will determine if the applicant does indeed belong to the Malay community. The law requires that the Sub-Committee be guided by the merits of the case without regard to legal forms and technicalities.[72] The Sub-Committee must consider whether the person considers himself to be a member of the Malay community ("self-definition") by examining the evidence put forth on his way of life. The Sub-Committee will also have to consider whether the Malay community would regard the applicant as one of their own ("community regard"). In short, whether one belongs to a particular community or not is a two-fold inquiry of fact: the candidate must first consider himself or herself to be a member of that community, and the community must likewise consider the candidate as one of their own. For the Malay community, a Malay presidential hopeful is probably expected to be a Muslim as well given that Malay identity is almost coterminous with being a professed believer and practitioner of Islam.[73] In contrast, religious affiliation will not feature for the Chinese and Indian communities. Where the Sub-Committee concludes that the applicant belongs to the Malay community, it must issue a community certificate to that effect.[74]

Having secured both the eligibility and community certificates, such a person is eligible to be nominated as a presidential candidate on Nomination Day. If there is a contest, there will be nine days of campaigning followed by a cooling-off day. The number of people eligible to contest in the first reserved election was thought to be relatively small such that the likelihood of a contest was reduced. Nevertheless, Singaporeans looked forward to a contest. Such a contest would have gone a long way towards educating Singaporeans on the centrality of the Elected President in Singapore's system of constitutional government.

However, the lead-up to the first reserved election was dogged early on by questions of whether the three aspirants, Mr Farid Khan, Mr Salleh Marican and Madam Halimah Yacob, were "Malay enough".[75] Mr Khan is classified as a Pakistani. Madam Halimah is classified as Indian, while apparent concerns were raised about Mr Marican's proficiency in the Malay language. The presidential hopefuls, especially Mr Farid Khan, pointed out that they have adopted the Malay culture and practices and considered themselves Malays. Madam Halimah referred to her long-standing association with Malay and Muslim organizations. In contesting in the general elections of 2001, 2006, 2011 and 2015, she had obtained the requisite certification to contest as a Malay candidate in a GRC. In any event, all three presidential hopefuls received the requisite community certification as persons belonging to the Malay community.

The question of "are you (insert relevant race) enough?" is more likely to arise when someone is not officially classified as being of that race. To the average person on the street, it raises the question of whether "self-definition" should suffice for the purposes of the law and for community acceptance of belonging. In some respects, the reserved election for Malay candidates opened a can of worms. Not only did the presidential hopefuls have to assure the other communities that they will represent all Singaporeans, they also had to establish to Malay community that they were community stalwarts. As it turned out, the reserved election mechanism can potentially make a community more "possessive" and judgemental as to who is of the community and who is not. The first reserved election drew the attention of the Malay community to the "Malayness" of presidential hopefuls. It will likely have the same effect on other communities when it is their turn for the reserved election.

But what exactly is "Malayness"? Is it race, language, religion (Islam), culture?[76] When does a non-Malay "*masuk Melayu*" (that is, embracing Malayness, adopting Malay culture, customs and practices)? When is a classified Malay not "Malay enough"? The legal provisions are of little assistance here as the Singapore Constitution defines a Malay for the purpose of the presidential election as "any person, *whether of the Malay race or otherwise*, who considers himself to be a member of the Malay community and who is generally accepted as a member of the Malay community by that community".[77]

The CMIO racial classification masks the inherent heterogeneity of each community. The classification homogenizes the heterogeneity and diversity within each community. The reserved election mechanism inevitably prioritizes the question of race, while a candidate's qualifications are rendered secondary. So even as one community frets over whether a hopeful is sufficiently of the community, the other communities might be concerned whether such a person is sufficiently representative of all others! Will someone who is regarded as being "very Malay", for example, be seen as inadequately representative of the non-Malay communities? The reserved election, while racial in one dimension, requires the electorate to think beyond race and to determine how a candidate can be a symbol, promoter and practitioner of multiracialism. The first reserved election, however, did not show that consideration coming to the fore. Instead, there was an over-indulgent focus on who is Malay.

It is therefore imperative that the reserved election mechanism does not result in Singaporeans getting too fixated over the race of a candidate such that it detracts from the *raison d'être* of the Elected Presidency and of the Elected President as a symbol of Singapore's multiracialism. Is there empirical evidence to make the case that Singaporeans do vote along racial lines? It has been repeatedly asserted that Singaporeans tend to vote along racial lines. Prime Minister Lee Hsien Loong himself observed,

> in future … I believe it will become much harder for a minority President to get elected. It is the same problem with the parliamentary elections which led us to create GRCs, to ensure a minimum representation of minority race MPs in Parliament.[78]

The view that Singaporeans tend to vote along racial lines can be traced back to the introduction of the GRC scheme in 1988. However, without empirical evidence of this alleged voting behaviour, this view risks perpetuating a political myth of racial exclusiveness in elections. It also perpetuates the belief that the majority of Chinese Singaporeans discriminate against non-Chinese Singaporeans, even for the august office of the Head of State. Worse still, it might even result in inappropriate counter-measures. Looking at the 2015 general election results, PAP GRC teams helmed by minorities have held their own, including Deputy Prime Minister Tharman Shanmugaratnam's Jurong GRC team being the best PAP election performer. Likewise, prior to the introduction of the GRC in 1988, minority candidates demonstrated that they could win even single-member seats where the majority of the electorate were ethnic Chinese.

Perhaps, all things being equal, a Singaporean voter may prefer someone they could identify with in terms of ethnicity. I would, however, argue that in most instances Singaporeans would vote along meritocratic principles. In other words, they would vote for a candidate or a slate of candidates who they think would best represent them in Parliament. As it has been demonstrated in the general elections, most Singaporeans have no problems voting for whom they regard as being the best candidate (in a single-member constituency) or best team (in a group representation constituency) regardless of their race.[79]

To be sure, race, religion and language remain fault-lines in Singapore society as the Government reminds Singaporeans ever so often. But it is crucial that Singaporeans do not pander to these centrifugal forces. Instead, Singaporeans should endeavour to rise above their prejudices, stereotypes and weaknesses. The electoral system can and should a play a part in this regard.

If Singaporeans do vote along racial lines, then the appropriate response is to work towards encouraging Singaporeans to abandon that behaviour so that minority candidates can compete on an even footing with ethnic Chinese candidates. To give in to racial discrimination would be an indictment of the national ethos of meritocracy and multiracialism. Efforts should also be made to encourage suitably qualified minorities to step forward and seriously consider running for the Presidency.

6.3.4 Whither group rights?

With the reserved election mechanism, would the minority groups see having a minority President from their race as a right of their group? Singapore's constitutional system and government is not premised on group rights but rather on individual rights. It is instructive to bear in mind what the 1966 Constitutional Commission noted in its report of a non-racial approach to tackling problems in a polyglot society:

> We find also in the years succeeding the Second World War the growth of a national spirit amongst the many peoples of many races who now regard Singapore as their home if not the home of their forefathers and we believe there is a growing awareness and acceptance amongst these peoples that in spite of their different origins, their destinies and that of their children are all inextricably intertwined, intermixed and interwoven and *that their future and the future of the nation lies in a non-racial approach to all problems under a form of government which would enable the growth of a united, multi-racial, free and democratic nation in which all its citizens have equal rights and equal opportunities*.[80]

The 1966 Constitutional Commission added that Singapore should avoid creating group rights. It was of the view that "the best and most appropriate way of safeguarding the rights of the racial, linguistic and religious minorities in the Republic would be specially to entrench in the Constitution the fundamental rights of both the individual and the citizen..."[81]

Although the Government did not accept the 1966 Commission's proposal to entrench Part IV of the Constitution on fundamental liberties then, the Commission's rationale for proceeding on the basis of individual rather than group rights is cogently articulated in paragraph 12 of its report:

> We believe that a person, whether he is a citizen or not, who belongs to a racial or a linguistic or a religious minority in Singapore will have all his rights as a member of such racial or linguistic or religious minority safeguarded if his fundamental rights as an individual, and as a citizen if he is one, are entrenched in the Constitution, and if those fundamental rights are enforceable by the Courts.

Even if the reserved election of a minority race President may not crystallize the recognition of group rights, such a racial approach is likely to unwittingly bring race into the presidential election, which the 2017 reserved election so vividly demonstrated. Should the putative notion of group rights crystallize, then the cause of multiracialism will be further set back as consciousness of racial identity is not only reinforced but asserted. Thus, the need to be careful in managing expectations flowing from the reserved election is an important one.[82]

The other implication would be the possibility of Singaporeans becoming motivated to vote along racial lines. Voters from each major race could think and act along the lines that since each race will have their turn of one of their own becoming President through a reserved election, each race should support a candidate who is of the same race in a non-reserved election. This would be a sure way to trigger a reserved election with a certain regularity since the non-reserved elections will likely result in a Chinese candidate being elected. This electoral behaviour would also marginalize the principle of meritocracy and, worse, reinforce the tendency of people to think and vote along racial lines.

When Singaporeans start to think along those lines, then Singaporeans would have put themselves on the slippery slope and would be undercutting what it means to be a multiracial society, a meritocratic society and the Elected Presidency as a race-neutral institution. If it comes to pass that, the Presidency is premised on racial lines of voting, would Singaporeans be able to look up to and respect and recognize the Presidency as a very powerful symbol of multiracialism? Thus, even as the ideal of having a minority President elected on a regular basis is provided for in the reserved election, the very foundation on which the Singapore society is built on would be undermined if the reserved election does not result in electoral integration and race blindness and meritocracy being the main criteria in presidential elections.

6.4 Minority representation and multiracialism: reserved election as manifestation of Article 152 of the Constitution?

One way of understanding the Government's concern with ensuring minority representation in the Elected Presidency, especially of the indigenous Malay community, is by analysing its belief that the reserved presidential election would enhance Singapore's multiracialism and ensure that a key institution of state is not foreclosed to the minority communities. This concern seeks to go beyond formal equality by boosting substantive equality. While there was clearly formal equality in terms of eligibility to contest in the presidential election prior to the 2016 constitutional amendments, the reality was that there was no Malay candidate in all the presidential elections between 1993 and 2011. The last time a Malay was President was between 1965 and 1970, and 47 intervening years went by without a Malay President until Madam Halimah Yacob's election in 2017. The reserved election might thus be regarded as promoting substantive equality for the Malay community in terms of their representation in the Presidency.

The centrepiece of Singapore's attempt at inclusive citizenship is Article 152 of the Singapore Constitution, which predates Singapore's independence and the drafting of the present Constitution. Article 152(1) states that: "It shall be the responsibility of the Government constantly to care for the interests of the racial and religious minorities in Singapore." Article 152(2) specifically states that:

> The Government shall exercise its functions in such manner as to recognize the special position of the Malays, who are the indigenous people of Singapore, and accordingly it shall be the responsibility of the Government to protect, safeguard, support, foster and promote their political, educational, religious, economic, social and cultural interests and the Malay language.

Article 152 recognizes the "special position of the Malays" by virtue of their being the indigenous people of Singapore.[83] Furthermore, it legitimizes and constitutionally protects minority claims to cultural diversity and autonomy in Singapore. The Singapore Government's approach to the management of ethnic relations comports with these principles. Additionally, Article 153 reinforces the special position status of the Malays by providing that the Legislature "shall by law make provision for regulating Muslim religious affairs and for constituting a Council to advise the President in matters relating to the Muslim religion."[84] Put simply, the Singapore Constitution enshrines formal equality of all races, but also provides for substantive equality in specified aspects even if the measures are not specifically mentioned.

This distinction between formal and substantive equality is important. The reserved election is, in effect, an attempt at substantive equality for the minority races, especially the Malays, in a Chinese-dominant nation-state. In rebutting the notion of a strict and uncompromising racial equality in the Singapore Constitution, Singapore's founding Prime Minister Lee Kuan Yew stated robustly in his last parliamentary speech in 2009 that formal equality has its inherent limitations:

> We explicitly state in our Constitution a duty on behalf of the Government not to treat everybody as equal. [Formal racial equality] is not reality, it is

> not practical, it will lead to grave and irreparable damage if we work on that principle. So this was an aspiration. ... You suggest to the Malays that we should abolish these provisions [that is, Articles 152 and 153] in the Constitution and you will have grave disquiet. ... The American Constitution does not say that it will treat blacks differently but our Constitution spells out the duty of the Government to treat Malays and other minorities with extra care. ... And I thought to myself, perhaps I should bring this House back to earth and remind everybody what is our starting point, what is our base, and if we do not recognise where we started from, and that these are our foundations, we will fail. ... Today, 44 years later, we have a Malay community, I believe, at peace, convinced that we are not discriminating against them, convinced that we are including them in our society.[85]

Articles 152 and 153 elevate the principle of minority protection into one of salutary constitutional importance, but not as a prescriptive constitutional guarantee that could lend itself to significant contestation. As such, Article 152 is more of a political shield, rather than a legal sword that the minorities can assert collectively against the Government of the day if it fails to care adequately for the minorities. The constitutional and political reality, however, is that no Singaporean Government of the day can legislate against the interests of the racial and religious minorities without being subject to judicial scrutiny via constitutional review, or incurring a high political price. Put simply, multiracialism is a constitutionally entrenched obligation and a political imperative for Singapore.[86]

The direct linkage between the reserved elections mechanism with Article 152 of the Singapore Constitution was never relied upon by the Government nor alluded to by the Constitutional Commission. Nonetheless, the reserved election can be regarded not only as compatible with, but also giving effect to Article 152. In a similar vein, the GRC system is largely driven by such considerations of preserving substantive equality.

The virtue of Article 152 and related provisions in the Singapore Constitution is that they constitutionally recognize the ethnic minorities in Singapore. Recognition extends to their having distinct cultures, religions and languages with the state's tacit support. It also extends to protecting, safeguarding, supporting, fostering and promoting their political interests. Such affirmative support for adequate political representation of the minorities is also very much about duly recognizing the different racial communities in Singapore.

More specifically, such recognition helps to reduce political contestation and uplifts political enfranchisement. This recognition of minorities as equal citizens, in form and in substance, helps ensure that the right of membership in a nation-state is substantively endowed, expressed purposefully and honoured meaningfully. At its heart, it is about being recognized by others as an equal, treated by the same standards and values, and accorded the same level of respect and dignity as all other members of that community. Any benefits, policy exceptions, preferences and the like, when provided, are carefully structured to avoid any sense of entitlement or legal rights.[87] Despite the constitutional safeguards for the ethnic minorities, expectations have been structured towards one of emphasizing interests rather than rights.[88]

6.5 Recriminations from uncontested 2017 reserved election

Following the Presidential Elections Committee's award of only one certificate of eligibility, the groundswell of public opinion was rapid, robust and rumbustious. This was not entirely unexpected since there was so much hype, publicity and official commendation for the first reserved election. The uncontested reserved presidential election was an anti-climactic end to a long-drawn process that started with the opening of the thirteenth Parliament in January 2016 when Prime Minister Lee Hsien Loong first intimated on ensuring minority representation in the Presidency. Singaporeans felt let down that they could not exercise their democratic choice. But the ferocity embraced with a vengeance by a vocal cross-section of society was less expected. The Government had expected that a no-contest would be disappointing to most Singaporeans, but it probably did not anticipate the extent and depth of the public sentiment even though it knew that the reserved election mechanism was unpopular and could even adversely impact voting behaviour at the next parliamentary elections. Even though it would cost the ruling party votes at the next general election, Prime Minister Lee Hsien Loong said that he had proceeded with the reserved presidential election because he "strongly believed, and still does, that this is the right thing to do".[89] In its judgement, the Government probably took the position that the backlash would be a short-term phenomenon. The Government was hoping that the constitutional changes made to institute a reserved election would be well received and seen as the right thing to do. Prime Minister Lee, in addressing the public unhappiness for the first time after the presidential election, said Singapore had "not yet arrived at an ideal state of accepting people of a different race".[90]

It appears that the Government misapprehended public sentiment and miscalculated as to whether there would be a backlash. Would the negative sentiments, which appeared to be directed towards Halimah Yacob, affect her Presidency? It was a start that no president would wish for, but the negativity towards her would quickly subside. She will also win over the doubters and critics. Given her track record, humility, empathy and determination to make her Presidency different, Singaporeans have already warmed up to her.[91] She has embraced the challenge of defining her Presidency as one that seeks to unify Singapore. In some respects, the initial backlash against the no contest was unfair to President Halimah Yacob. Many Singaporeans within and beyond the Malay community had said they would be willing to vote for her even in an open election. It was unfortunate that she had to bear the brunt of the unhappiness and pointed criticisms since it was never within her power to ensure an electoral contest. Unfortunately, President Halimah Yacob had become the proverbial lighting rod. The criticism were not so much directed at her, but rather at the electoral process and at the Government which was seen as being exclusive and disenfranchising.

The Government could have done more to prevent or pre-empt the extent of backlash. Arguably, a more accurate assessment of ground sentiments could have been made, rather than moving hastily to affect the constitutional and legislative changes to the Elected Presidency. After all, the former system was not demonstrably broken.[92] It was also within the Government's prerogative, as it had done so in previous presidential elections, to encourage eligible individuals to run in the presidential election so that there would be a contest. This would still be in keeping with the growing expectations of formal and substantive enfranchisement in the electoral process. Had more time been devoted to consultation, especially after the Government had accepted the Commission's recommendation on the reserved election mechanism, it could help Singaporeans gain a better understanding of what was at stake and to acquire an affinity to the significant changes. Charges that the changes were more self-serving than altruistic were elicited because of the haste with which the major changes were put in place.

Going forward, it is clear that there is a pressing need to nurture an ethos of public service that would encourage eligible men and women to step forward and run for the office of the Head of State. Second, the actual ability to vote is a growing demand and the electoral process must be one that balances the need for stringent criteria for eligibility while giving effect to the citizens' right to vote and the imperative for enfranchisement. In tandem with a maturing polity, Singaporeans did not want to feel or, worse, be disenfranchised. The right to vote is cherished and must be given effect to, lest people lose faith in the electoral process and instead use it primarily to vent their unhappiness.[93] Above all, fidelity to the form *and* substance of political franchise manifested in the right and opportunity to vote is what Singaporeans hope to see endowed in the country's institutional design and political process.

Second, the Government must shed a paternalistic mindset so that they can better engage, talk with, rather than talk to, Singaporeans. This also means not infantilizing Singaporeans even on issues like race and religion and on the right persons to vote for in parliamentary and presidential elections. Third, greater recognition and confidence should be given to Singaporeans for their commitment to multiracialism and meritocracy and support for good governance. In my view, the so-called lost opportunity to vote was disappointing because many Singaporeans wanted to demonstrate their commitment to multiracialism and meritocracy.

There is no shortage of eligible men and women to be Singapore's Head of State. The right lessons have to be learnt so that the Elected Presidency and reserved election mechanism are strengthened, and to secure the trust and commitment of Singaporeans to the mechanism. But if there is a silver lining, it is that Singaporeans are demonstrating that they have internalized multiracialism and meritocracy and are keen to do their duty as citizens through exercising their right to vote. There is a more engaged citizenry even if they may be less enthusiastic of or receptive to the Government's views of race relations in Singapore. Singapore is not "post-racial" yet, but the idea that Singaporeans will set aside multiracialism and meritocracy when it comes to voting is probably an exaggeration as well.

Going beyond the form of regular minority representation in the Presidency, the reserved election mechanism will have to entrench multiracialism as an integral part of a candidate's overall merit. Such an approach would then be sustainable, authentic and meaningful. Only then can the reserved election be a shining symbol of Singapore's multiracialism rather than a crutch to prop up an enervated multiracialism. How a candidate is viewed as a symbol of multiracialism (that is, as a promoter and practitioner) will count towards a candidate's meritorious standing, in addition to his or her professional achievements and career highlights.

In constitutional engineering, the aspiration should be to design an election process in which candidates and the electorate alike consider how their electoral behaviour and their votes would be in the individual and collective self-interest, thus entrenching multiracialism. It is in this way that the Presidency can continue to be a true symbol of national unity and make multiracialism sustainable, rather than one that is artificially supported and imposed by constitutional fiat.

6.6 Conclusion

> [A] race-blind society is the only legitimate aspiration for Singapore; but there is a pressing need to ensure that no ethnic group is shut out of the Presidency even as progress is made towards that ideal, lest the office of President lose (sic) its vitality as a symbol of the nation's unity. Singapore cannot yet be considered a post-racial society: this is a reality that must be faced even if it is one that is not to be endorsed.[94]

It is fair to say that Singaporeans would not disagree with minorities being the Elected President from time to time. The concern that Singaporeans have, regardless of their race, is how that ideal is realized. Given the Elected President's custodial powers, the electoral system must enable all who are qualified (and keen) to contest. The demands of the office require that the best person do the job. In making the Presidency an elected one, one significant trade-off is that the office could no longer be rotated among the different races as deliberately as it was in the past. Is this a circle that cannot be squared? As the Presidency is an office elected by universal franchise and functioning as an intra-branch check, merit arguably must come ahead of race if the Presidency is to command authority, authenticity and respect.

So entrenched is the commitment to meritocracy and the aversion to a race-based electoral system, that any overt policy of affirmative action for the minorities will be beleaguered with the need to find real and deep support among Singaporeans. This is not surprising. Singaporean society has long been socialized into treating policies of affirmative action (for the minorities) and preferential treatment (for the majority) as undermining the self-worth of the very group they were supposed to help and politically untenable for being inimical to multiracialism and meritocracy. Likewise, Singaporeans also perceive such policies as reinforcing racial stereotypes and prejudices.

Nevertheless, the hiatus-triggered reserved election holds promise as a constitutional safeguard and an institutional mechanism to promote multiracialism. The requirement of five continual terms (or 30 years) without a President from a particular race obviates the need to revert to the former system of mechanical rotation. To use race as a pre-qualifying condition to contest in a reserved election is akin to effecting affirmative action. However, the hiatus of 30 years is sufficiently long to reduce the sharp edge of affirmative action, if any. In a situation of two competing public good and ideals – meritocracy and multiracialism – there will be the rare occasion when the latter must be given priority over the former. This is not to suggest that meritocracy and multiracialism are diametrically opposed, but that where both ideals cannot be attained conjunctively, then prioritization is inevitable for the greater good. The reserved election is a manifestation of this. It can be justified on the basis that the long-term stability of Singapore's multiracial society requires that the Presidency be sustained as a symbol of multiracialism and a unifying figure for multiracial Singapore. This means having a mechanism by which minority races have fair and adequate opportunity to be elected to the Presidency.

In an extended report, the Presidential Council for Minority Rights (PCMR) in considering the Constitution of the Republic of Singapore (Amendment) Bill 2016 noted that the reserved election "applies equally" to the Chinese, Malay and Indian and other minority communities, and that each community is "not advantaged or disadvantaged vis-à-vis the other communities".[95] It also noted that the purpose of the reserved election is "not discriminatory" and that the measure "is borne out of a recognition that, while race neutrality is and remains a Singaporean ideal, active measures must from time to time be taken to foster multiracialism."[96] It observed that the reserved election mechanism was "minimally intrusive" and was meant to be a "long-stop measure, triggered by a five-term hiatus" with the default position being open elections.[97] As such, the PCMR concluded that the reserved election mechanism, if enacted, would not be a differentiating measure under Article 68 of Constitution.[98] It added that the Government's announcement that the 2017 Presidential Election which would be reserved for the Malay community did not detract from the points above.[99]

The challenge of the reserved election mechanism, even as it seeks to position the Presidency as a symbol of Singapore's national unity and multiracialism, is to avoid triggering its coming into operation. Constitutional fiats are often unsustainable, and the long-term effects of the reserved election mechanism will not be known for a few generations. It remains to be seen if there will be a reserved election in 2041. This will occur if no member from the Indian or other minority community is elected as President between now and then. To avoid triggering a reserved election requires candidates from the three major racial communities to be elected in open elections. It is a very powerful message should a minority race candidate be elected to the highest office of the land. But that message is only powerful and would only resonate with Singaporeans and reinforce her multiracialism if such an achievement was earned through merit, rather than affirmative action. This means the reserved election mechanism must develop and be integrated into the meritocratic framework in Singapore.

The reserved election is not the silver bullet in the quest to ensure that no racial group is precluded from the Presidency. Hence, the reserved election should instead function as a "nudge" in encouraging candidates and the electorate alike to think of how their electoral behaviour and their votes can entrench multiracialism. In a Chinese-majority Singapore, to have a minority race President would be a very strong testament to the success of a multiracialism because it would show that even a Chinese-majority Singapore is able to go beyond race and elect a non-Chinese candidate to be President.

From its inception, the Presidency has been a powerful symbol of the fledgling nation-state's commitment to inclusiveness and multiracialism – first, on attaining self-government from the British in 1959 and, then, in the throes of Singapore's traumatic separation from Malaysia in 1965. Encik Yusof Ishak, a Malay, Singapore's first *Yang di-Pertuan Negara* and first President played a pivotal role in her early journey of multiracialism.

The reserved election seeks to ensure that multiracialism continues to thrive. But it must also be a measure of last resort. Will Singaporeans and their Government resolve to make the 2017 reserved presidential election the first and the last reserved election in Singapore's history? If that comes to pass, Singapore would have succeeded immensely in entrenching multiracialism and meritocracy as abiding tenets of faith in Singapore. The circle would then be squared.

Notes

1 Constitution of the Republic of Singapore (Amendment) Bill, No. 28/2016. The Bill was first read on 10 October 2016 and passed on 9 November 2016.

2 On the Elected Presidency as an intra-(Executive) branch check and balance, see my Chapter 4, in this volume. "Custodial powers", instead of executive power, is the preferred term the Singapore Government uses for the check-and-balance powers of the Elected President. For a multi-disciplinary perspective on the Presidency and its evolution, see Kevin Y.L. Tan and Lam Peng Er (eds), *Managing Political Change in Singapore: The Elected Presidency* (London: Routledge, 1997). A useful description and discussion of the Elected Presidency between 1991 and 2015 can be found in Li-ann Thio, *Singapore Chronicles: Presidency* (Singapore: Institute of Policy Studies and Straits Times Press 2015). See also Chapter 2 of the *Report of the Constitutional Commission 2016* (17 August 2016), which traces the evolution of the Presidency in post-colonial Singapore.

3 In this chapter, race/racial group is distinguished from and used in preference to ethnicity/ethnic group when referring to the group classifications assigned by the Singapore state to its citizens. Ethnicity is used to refer to the collective attributes of race, religion, language and culture.

4 On the historical powers of the President, see *Report of the Constitutional Commission 2016* (17 August 2016), paras 2.9 and 2.10 (henceforth, the Constitutional Commission's report is referred to as "CCR"). See also Huang Jianli, "The Head of State in Singapore: an historical perspective", in Kevin Y.L. Tan and Lam Peng Er (eds), *Managing Political Change in Singapore: The Elected Presidency* (London: Routledge, 1997).

5 See also Chapter 1 by Kevin Y.L. Tan and Lam Peng Er in this volume.

6 CCR (n. 4), para. 2.8.
7 *Ibid.*, para. 5.15.
8 The PAP has governed Singapore since she gained self-government from the British in 1959 and independence from Malaysia in 1965.
9 See Jaclyn L. Neo, "Navigating minority inclusion and permanent division: minorities and the depoliticization of ethnic difference" (2017) 17 *Jus Politicum* 607; Eugene K.B. Tan, "Multiracialism engineered: the limits of electoral and spatial integration in Singapore" (2005) 4(4) *Ethnopolitics* 413.
10 CCR (n. 4), para. 5.15. See also the White Paper on *Review of Specific Aspects of the Elected Presidency: The Constitution of the Republic of Singapore (Amendment) Bill* (2016), para. 78 (henceforth, the White Paper is referred to as "WP" in this chapter).
11 WP (n. 10), para. 79. The CNA-IPS Survey on Race Relations as delivered by Mathew Matthews on 19 August 2016 can be found at http://lkyspp.nus.edu.sg/docs/default-source/ips/CNA-IPS-survey-on-race-relations_190816.pdf.
12 WP (n. 10), para. 79.
13 The CMIO classification is used for a variety of purposes including the choice of mother tongue language instruction in schools, ethnic quotas in public housing, opportunities within military service (whether conscript or professional), and eligibility to contest as a Malay, Indian or other minority candidate in parliamentary and presidential elections. See further, Sharon Siddique, "Singaporean identity", in Kernial Singh Sandhu and Paul Wheatley (eds), *Management of Success: The Moulding of Modern Singapore* (Singapore: Institute of Southeast Asian Studies, 1989). Limited racial self-definition, through 'double-barrelled race options', was permitted from 2011. See Singapore's Immigration and Checkpoints Authority's press release of 29 December 2010: "Greater flexibility with implementation of double-barrelled race option from 1 January 2011". For relevant Government policies and the collection of statistics, the first component of a hyphenated race will be used. For example, a person who is classified as "Chinese-Malay" will be treated as Chinese for relevant official purposes and data gathering.
14 According to the Singapore Government's *Population in Brief 2017* (September 2017), Singapore's citizen population of 3.44 million as of June 2017 comprised 76.1 per cent Chinese, 15.0 per cent Malay, 7.4 per cent Indian and 1.5 per cent Others. The report is available at www.strategygroup.gov.sg/docs/default-source/default-document-library/population-in-brief-2017.pdf.
15 Constitution of the Republic of Singapore (1999 Reprint) ("Singapore Constitution").
16 The official President's website (at www.istana.gov.sg) broadly categorizes the Singapore's Head of State's roles and responsibilities into three broad pillars: constitutional, community and ceremonial. "Istana" means palace in Malay. The Istana is the official residence of the President of Singapore.
17 Sujit Choudhry, "Bridging comparative politics and comparative constitutional law: constitutional design in divided societies", in Sujit Choudhry (ed.), *Constitutional Design for Divided Societies: Integration or Accommodation?* (New York: Oxford University Press, 2008), 6.
18 Pippa Norris, *Electoral Engineering: Voting Rules and Political Behavior* (Cambridge: Cambridge University Press, 2004), 209.
19 Arend Lijphart, *Democracy in Plural Societies: A Comparative Exploration* (New Haven, CT: Yale University Press, 1977). See also Arend Lijphart's stout defence of power sharing and group autonomy in his "Constitutional design for divided societies" (2004) 15(2) *Journal of Democracy* 96.
20 For a succinct discussion and a helpful list of references, see Pippa Norris, *Electoral Engineering* (Cambridge: Cambridge University Press, 2004), 209–29.
21 See, for example, Donald L. Horowitz, *Ethnic Groups in Conflict* (Berkeley, CA: University of California Press, 1985), especially Part III, and 628–52; Donald Horowitz, "Electoral systems: a primer for decision makers" (2003) 14(4) *Journal of Democracy* 115. See

also Andreas Wimmer, *Nation Building: Why Some Countries Come Together While Others Fall Apart* (Princeton, NJ: Princeton University Press, 2018).

22 However, where the electorate is overwhelmingly dominated by one particular racial group, then chauvinism in favour of the dominant group may provide electoral dividends unless the electorate has internalized the virtues of non-discrimination.

23 Please see Jaclyn Neo's "Constitutionalizing minority representation: the reserved elections mechanism and politicization of ethnicity in Singapore", Chapter 5 in this volume.

24 Andrew Reynolds (ed.), *The Architecture of Democracy: Constitutional Design, Conflict Management, and Democracy* (Oxford: Oxford University Press, 2002); Timothy D. Sisk and Andrew Reynolds (eds), *Elections and Conflict Management in Africa* (Washington, DC: United States Institute of Peace Press, 1998); Benjamin Reilly, *Democracy and Diversity: Political Engineering in the Asia-Pacific* (Oxford: Oxford University Press, 2007); Benjamin Reilly, *Democracy in Divided Societies: Electoral Engineering for Conflict Management* (New York: Cambridge University Press, 2001).

25 The PKMS (*Pertubuhan Kebangsaan Melayu Singapura*, or Singapore Malays National Organisation) is the only political party that is ostensibly organized along racial lines but it has consistently contested in general elections as a member of an election alliance comprising of political parties not organized along racial lines.

26 On the PAP's taming the combustible mix of race, language and religion in Singapore, see Sonny Yap, Richard Lim and Leong Weng Kam, *Men in White: The Untold Story of Singapore's Ruling Political Party* (Singapore: Singapore Press Holdings, 2010), Ch. 35 – "Lee: You Are Equal to Me". See also Diane K. Mauzy and R.S. Milne, *Singapore Politics Under the People's Action Party* (London: Routledge 2002), Ch. 8.

27 G. John Ikenberry, "What states can do now", in T.V. Paul, G. John Ikenberry and John A. Hall (eds), *The Nation-State in Question* (Princeton, NJ: Princeton University Press, 2003), 356.

28 The Government has not proffered a basis for its stance that Singaporeans tend to vote along racial lines. Since voting is secret and no opinion polls are allowed before or after elections, the assertion her deserves but lacks further substantiation. See Section 78D of the Parliamentary Elections Act which prohibits exit polls on polling day.

29 *Singapore Parliamentary Debates: Official Report*, 11 January 1988, vol. 50, no. 3 at col. 180.

30 The Malay community (almost all of whom are Muslims) has a significant influence despite constituting only 14 per cent of Singapore's population. Singapore is surrounded by substantive Malay- and Muslim-majority Malaysia and Muslim-majority Indonesia. The Malays are constitutionally recognized as the indigenous people of Singapore: Article 152, Constitution of the Republic of Singapore (n. 15).

31 Article 39A(1), Constitution of the Republic of Singapore (n. 15).

32 In *Wong Souk Yee* v. *AG* [2018] SGHC 80, the applicant sought, *inter alia*, mandatory orders requiring that the MPs for the Marsiling-Yew Tee GRC vacate their seats in Parliament and that the Prime Minister advises the President to issue a writ of election for the GRC. The action was founded on the basis that a vacancy had arisen in the Marsiling-Yew Tee GRC when one of its MPs and the minority race MP, Halimah Yacob, vacated her seat in Parliament on 7 August 2017 to contest in the 2017 Presidential Election. In essence, the applicant argued that Article 39A(2) of the Constitution required a GRC to be represented by an MP belonging to a minority community during the term of Parliament. Therefore, when the minority MP vacated the seat midway through the term, the *raison d'être* for the GRC was not given effect to and hence a by-election was necessary. The Singapore High Court dismissed the lawsuit The Court of Appeal also dismissed the applicant's appeal: see *Wong Souk Yee* v. *AG* [2019] 1 SLR 1223.

33 For a comprehensive discussion, see John McGarry, Brendan O'Leary and Richard Simeon, "Integration or accommodation? the enduring debate in conflict regulation",

in Sujit Choudhry (ed.), *Constitutional Design for Divided Societies: Integration or Accommodation?* (Oxford: Oxford University Press, 2008).

34 Mr Wee Kim Wee assumed the office and exercised the powers of the Elected President when the office was established in 1991. He was the last President to be elected by Parliament (1985–1991).

35 See President Tony Tan Keng Yam, Opening of the Thirteenth Parliament Address, www.istana.gov.sg/the-president/former-presidents/dr-tony-tan-keng-yam/speeches/opening-the-thirteenth-parliament-address-president-tony-tan-keng-yam (accessed 8 September 2018).

36 Transcript of Prime Minister Lee Hsien Loong's speech on 27 January 2016, www.pmo.gov.sg/newsroom/pm-lee-hsien-loong-debate-presidents-address-27-january-2016.

37 The first Constitutional Commission, comprising 11 members, was chaired by then Chief Justice Wee Chong Jin. Appointed in December 1965, the Commission was tasked to propose ways for the rights and interests of racial, linguistic and religious minorities to be safeguarded in the Constitution. Public hearings were held at which the commission received and considered representations.

38 Prime Minister's Office, "Constitutional Commission to review specific aspects of the Elected Presidency", 10 February 2016, www.pmo.gov.sg/newsroom/constitutional-commission-review-specific-aspects-elected-Presidency.

39 CCR (n. 4), para. 5.5.

40 *Ibid.*, paras 5.5 and 5.16.

41 *Ibid.*, paras 5.4 and 5.6.

42 *Ibid.*, para. 5.16 (emphasis in the original).

43 *Ibid.*, para. 5.18. The elaboration of these various models is at paras 5.19–5.39.

44 *Ibid.*, para. 5.17(a).

45 *Ibid.*, para. 5.17(b).

46 *Ibid.*, para. 5.17(c).

47 *Ibid.*, paras 5.27, 5.36–5.40; WP (n. 10), paras 82–3.

48 The Commission recognized race neutrality as not singling out any one ethnic group for protection: see CCR (n. 4), para. 5.36.

49 *Ibid.*, para. 5.36 (emphasis in the original).

50 *Ibid.*, para. 5.40.

51 *Ibid.*, para. 5.41.

52 *Ibid.*, para. 5.36. Five continuous terms (six years each), if fully served, would be 30 years. The Commission described such a scenario where a particular racial group has not occupied the Presidency for "an exceedingly long period of time" as "worrying".

53 *Ibid.*, para. 5.36: "if free and unregulated elections produce Presidents from a varied distribution of ethnicities, the requirement of a reserved election will never be triggered".

54 WP (n. 10), para. 83. A legal challenge was mounted against the reserved election mechanism as set out in Articles 19 and 19B of the Constitution in *Ravi s/o Madasamy* v. *Attorney-General* [2017] 5 SLR 489 (HC). The plaintiff's primary arguments were that the qualification requirements for presidential candidates in Article 19 were contrary to Article 12 as it deprived citizens of the equal right of candidature to stand for the office of the Elected Presidency. Second, the 2016 amendments to institute the reserved election framework, namely, Article 19B was also inconsistent with Article 12, by discriminating on the basis of race and thus being contrary Article 12(2) of the Constitution. The High Court dismissed the constitutional challenge.

55 WP (n. 10), para. 82.

56 CCR (n. 4), para. 5.42. The Commission also observed that the "perceptions of tokenism may persist to varying degrees, regardless of how the electoral system is structured".

57 The Commission observed of another scenario of the "temporary" "loss of talent" when an incumbent President is barred from seeking re-election because the reserved election has been triggered: *ibid.*, para. 5.38.

58 Cap. 240A, 2011 rev edn.

59 Presidential Elections (Amendment) Bill (Bill No. 2 of 2017). First read on 9 January 2017, it was passed on 6 February 2017.
60 Presidential Elections Act (n. 58), s 5A.
61 However, this interpretation of Article 19B of the Constitution (which provides for reserved presidential election) that the hiatus had been triggered was challenged by Dr Tan Cheng Bock, runner-up in the 2011 presidential candidate, challenged the Government's interpretation: see *Tan Cheng Bock* v. *Attorney-General* [2017] 2 SLR 850 (HC); [2017] 5 SLR 424 (CA). See the analysis of this case by Li-Ann Thio in "Administrative and constitutional law" (2017) 18 *Singapore Academy of Law Annual Review* 1. An e-publication of this is available at https://journalsonline.academypublishing.org.sg/Journals/Singapore-Academy-of-Law-Annual-Review-of-Singapore-Cases/Current-Issue/ctl/eFirstSALPDFJournalView/mid/497/ArticleId/1313/Citation/JournalsOnlinePDF.
62 The other two candidates were Tan Jee Say and Tan Kin Lian. They polled 25.04 per cent and 4.91 per cent of the popular vote respectively. The election results are available at the Elections Department website www.eld.gov.sg/elections_past_results_presidential.html#Y2011 (accessed 8 September 2018).
63 The headline of an online *New York Times* article headline 12 September 2017 captured it well: "Singapore has a new president, no election needed" (by Richard C. Paddock, *New York Times*, 12 September 2017) www.nytimes.com/2017/09/12/world/asia/singapore-president-yacob.html (accessed 8 September 2018). The print edition's version of the article carried the headline, "Lack of vote tarnishes a milestone in Singapore", *New York Times* (New York, 13 September 2017), A10.
64 See Elections Department's press release of 11 September 2017, "Issue of Certificate of Eligibility and Malay Community Certificate for Presidential Election 2017", www.eld.gov.sg/pressrelease/PreE2017/Press%20Release%20on%20Issue%20of%20Certificate%20of%20Eligibility%20and%20Malay%20Community%20Certificate%20for%20Presidential%20Election%202017.pdf (accessed 8 September 2018). The press release did not identify the five applicants and the sole applicant awarded both the Certificate of Eligibility and the Malay Community Certificate.
65 It could also help correct the aberration that the 2011 Presidential Election was.
66 Li-ann Thio, "Singapore: (S)electing the President – diluting democracy" (2007) 5(3) *I·CON* 526.
67 Garry Rodan, "Singapore's Elected President: a failed institution" (2018) 72(1) *Australian Journal of International Affairs* 10; see also Mohamed Nawab Mohamed Osman and Prashant Waikar, "The People's Action Party and the Singapore Presidency in 2017: understanding the contradictions between state discourse and state practice" (2019) 59(2) *Asian Survey* 382.
68 See Kevin Y.L. Tan, *Puan Noor Aishah: Singapore's First Lady* (Singapore: Straits Times Press, 2017), 56.
69 This was a point that Madam Halimah Yacob emphasized shortly after she was elected unopposed as President: "I want to be president for all: Halimah", *The Straits Times* (Singapore, 14 September 2017), A1. The article is also available at www.straitstimes.com/politics/i-want-to-be-president-for-all-halimah (accessed 8 September 2018).
70 Presidential Elections Act (n. 58) s 8F.
71 Article 19(B)(6) of the Singapore Constitution. Note the differences in the definition of a Chinese person and Indian or other minority person: a "person belonging to the Chinese community means any person who considers himself to be a member of the Chinese community and who is generally accepted as a member of the Chinese community by that community". Similarly, a "person belonging to the Indian or other minority communities" means

> any person of Indian origin who considers himself to be a member of the Indian community and who is generally accepted as a member of the Indian community

by that community, or any person who belongs to any minority community other than the Malay or Indian community.

The proviso, "whether of the Malay race or otherwise", is not stipulated for the Chinese and Indian and other communities.

72 Under the Presidential Elections Act (n. 58), s 8G(4)(b), the Sub-Committee "must be guided by the merits of the case without regard to legal forms and technicalities, or to whether the evidence before it is in accordance with the law of evidence or not."

73 This will very likely conflict with Article 15 of the Constitution, which guarantees the freedom of religion.

74 Presidential Elections Act (n. 58), s 8G(4)(c); see s 8H(4)(c) in the case of non-reserved elections. The certificate must be issued no later than the day before Nomination Day; *ibid.*, s 8I(b)(i).

75 The debacle on whether the three candidates identified sufficiently with the Malay race, and were "Malay enough", was evident across multiple news reports. For instance, see Faris Mokhtar, "Reserved presidential election casts spotlight on 'Malayness'", *Today* (Singapore, 15 July 2017) todayonline.com/singapore/reserved-presidential-election-casts-spotlight-malayness (accessed 8 September 2018); and Zakir Hussain, "Doubts about presidential hopefuls not being Malay enough are off track", *The Straits Times* (Singapore, 20 July 2017) www.straitstimes.com/opinion/doubts-about-presidential-hopefuls-not-being-malay-enough-are-off-track (accessed 8 September 2018).

76 The position in Singapore can be contrasted with that under Article 160 of the Constitution of Malaysia 1967, which defines a Malay primarily as "a person who professes the religion of Islam, habitually speaks the Malay language, conforms to Malay custom…"

77 The clause "whether of the Malay race or otherwise" is unique to the description of a person belonging to the Malay community.

78 A transcript of Prime Minister Lee's speech at the debate on the President's Address on 27 January 2016 is available at www.pmo.gov.sg/newsroom/pm-lee-hsien-loong-debate-presidents-address-27-january-2016.

79 Eugene K.B. Tan, "Multiracialism engineered: the limits of electoral and spatial integration in Singapore" (2005) 4(4) *Ethnopolitics* 413.

80 *Report of the Constitutional Commission 1966* (27 August 1966), para. 10 (emphasis added).

81 *Ibid.*, para. 11.

82 The Commission noted that, "the notion of group rights is inconsistent with our constitutional framework": CCR (n. 4), para. 5.14. See also Li-ann Thio's "Past imperfect, future tense: the Elected Presidency and the constitutional development of an 'ever evolving hybrid'", Chapter 2 in this volume for a further and insightful discussion of whether the reserved election manifests a putative development of group rights or merely group-differentiated rights, or group-based management of politics.

83 The Singapore Constitution does not define who a Malay is. In contrast, Art 160(2) of the Malaysian Constitution defines a "Malay" as: "… a person who professes the religion of Islam, habitually speaks the Malay language, conforms to Malay custom."

84 Islam is the only religion mentioned in the Constitution. The overwhelming majority of Malays are Muslims.

85 *Singapore Parliamentary Debates: Official Report*, 19 August 2008), vol. 86 at col. 1145ff. (Lee Kuan Yew, Minister Mentor).

86 See Chan Sek Keong, "Multiculturalism in Singapore: the way to a Harmonious Society" (2013) 25 *Singapore Academy of Law Journal* 84.

87 See further, Eugene K.B. Tan, "Racial politics and imperatives and the constitutional special position of the Indigenous Malays in a new society: asserting interests and the non-contestation of rights in Singapore's Communitarian Constitutionalism", in

Marco Bünte and Björn Dressel (eds), *Politics and Constitutions in Southeast Asia* (London: Routledge, 2017).

88 See also Eugene K.B. Tan, "The imperative of integrative pluralist constitutionalism: going beyond formal equality, eschewing rights, and accommodation of differences in Singapore", in Jaclyn L. Neo and Bui Ngoc Son (eds), *Pluralist Constitutions in Southeast Asia* (Oxford: Hart Publishing, 2019).

89 "PM Lee spells out why he pushed for reserved election", *The Straits Times* (30 September 2017), A1. See also, "PE2017 will affect voting at next GE: Tan Cheng Bock", *The Sunday Times* (Singapore, 17 December 2017), A15.

90 "PM Lee spells out why he pushed for reserved election", *The Straits Times* (Singapore, 30 September 2017), A1, www.straitstimes.com/singapore/pm-lee-spells-out-why-he-pushed-for-reserved-election (accessed 8 September 2018).

91 President Halimah Yacob's first public event after her inauguration was to visit a centre that prepares people with intellectual disabilities for employment. See Nur Asyiqin Mohamad Salleh, "President Halimah visits special needs centre", *The Straits Times* (Singapore, 16 September 2017), A6, www.straitstimes.com/singapore/president-halimah-visits-special-needs-centre (accessed 8 September 2016).

92 The present author had previously suggested, in his written submission and oral testimony, to the Constitution Commission that any change be implemented in the subsequent presidential election (that is, in 2023).

93 That the 2017 Presidential Election will weigh on the minds of voters when the next general election is held (by April 2021) was expressed by Dr Tan Cheng Bock, a long-time PAP MP and the runner-up in the 2011 Presidential Election: "PE2017 will affect voting at next GE: Tan Cheng Bock", *The Sunday Times*, (17 December 2017), A15.

94 CCR (n. 4), para. 5.15.

95 Report of the Presidential Council for Minority Rights on the Constitution of the Republic of Singapore (Amendment) Bill (Bill No. 28/2016), Pres. Co. 21 of 2016, 25 November 2016, para. 4. The chairman of the Presidential Council for Minority Rights is Chief Justice Sundaresh Menon.

96 *Ibid.*, para. 5.

97 *Ibid.*, para. 6.

98 The PCMR has the general function of considering and reporting on "matters affecting persons of any racial or religious community in Singapore'" as may be referred to it by Parliament or the Government. Its particular function is to draw attention to any Bill or to any subsidiary legislation if the Council deems them to be a differentiating measure. See, generally, Part VII of the Constitution. A differentiating measure is:

> any measure which is, or is likely in its practical application to be, disadvantageous to persons of any racial or religious community and not equally disadvantageous to persons of other such communities, either directly by prejudicing persons of that community or indirectly by giving advantage to persons of another community.
>
> (Art. 68, Singapore Constitution)

99 *Ibid.*, para. 8.

7 From eligibility to election

The mechanics of the presidential poll

Jack Tsen-Ta Lee[1]

7.1 Introduction

On 9 November 2016, Parliament enacted the most significant constitutional amendment in the twenty-first century thus far, making wide-ranging changes to the Elected Presidency scheme. These amendments were preceded by a detailed examination of aspects of the scheme by a Constitutional Commission chaired by Chief Justice Sundaresh Menon which rendered its report on 17 August,[2] and a White Paper issued by the Government in response to the report on 15 September.[3] Most of the debate on the constitutional amendment bill[4] that took place in Parliament on 8 and 9 November concerned major alterations that were proposed. These were the increase in the minimum qualifying financial value of a company from $100 million in paid-up capital to $500 million in shareholders' equity for a prospective candidate seeking a certificate of eligibility under what is now termed the private-sector service requirement,[5] and the introduction of elections from time to time reserved for members of particular ethnic communities.[6]

In the end, the 2017 Presidential Election – the first to which the changes mentioned above applied – turned out to be largely a non-event, as it was won by Halimah Yacob by a walkover on nomination day. Two others who had thrown their hats into the ring were determined by the Presidential Elections Committee (hereafter "PEC") not to have met the private-sector service requirement, and were not issued the requisite certificate of eligibility for the election. Although there was thus no opportunity to observe in full the mechanics of the presidential poll, this chapter considers some of the changes to the procedure proposed by the Constitutional Commission and given legal effect by the Parliament. Specifically, it looks at the process for obtaining certificates of eligibility and community certificates, and the reviewability of decisions of the PEC, the Community Committee (hereafter "CC") and the CC's Sub-Committees. In addition, some elements of the campaigning process will be examined, namely, how candidates can conduct their campaigns, limitations on what candidates and voters can communicate electronically on cooling-off day and polling day, and whether Ministers and Members of Parliament should be allowed to endorse or criticize candidates.

The examination reveals that the legal framework vests the various committees mentioned above with a high degree of discretion to determine whether persons are eligible to contest presidential elections. Yet, due to various mechanisms including finality and conclusive evidence clauses, limited recourse is provided for ensuring accountability for the decisions made. The message sent appears to be that voters should trust the authorities to do the right thing, rather than rely on their own discernment to decide whether a candidate is worthy of being elected to the nation's highest office. Additionally, because campaigning rules do not prohibit influential, politically linked persons from endorsing candidates, voters' opinions may be skewed in favour of these candidates, thus creating an uneven playing field.

7.2 Qualifying for an election

One of the key features of a presidential election that distinguishes it from a parliamentary election is the need for people who wish to take part to undergo a qualification procedure. To contest, candidates must obtain certificates of eligibility from the PEC and, in a reserved election, community certificates from the CC declaring that they are from the community to which the election is confined. Thus, these committees are reposed with much discretion. Where, as we shall see, the exercise of such discretion can only be independently reviewed in very narrow circumstances, the perception that the committees are making decisions in a partisan manner may be hard to dismiss.

7.2.1 Certificate of eligibility

7.2.1.1 Issuance

The qualifications to be a presidential candidate are set out in Article 19 of the Constitution; in particular, an application must be made to the Presidential Elections Committee for a certificate of eligibility,[7] which will be issued if the PEC is satisfied that the applicant is "a person of integrity, good character and reputation"[8] and meets the potentially complex public- or private-sector service requirements set out in the Constitution.[9]

To enable the PEC to assess these requirements, the Constitutional Commission recommended that each applicant should submit a self-disclosure form containing information relevant to character and reputation, such as whether the applicant has a criminal record, or has been bankrupt or subject to disciplinary proceedings.[10] In view of the more stringent private-sector service criteria, applicants relying on this eligibility route should be required to provide detailed information about their business affairs.[11]

Moreover, the Commission felt that the PEC should be entitled to seek further information from prospective candidates.[12] This recommendation was given effect by Regulation 6 of the Presidential Elections (Certificate of Eligibility) Regulations 2017:[13]

> 6. (1) The Committee may, for the purposes of deciding an application –
>   (a) require the applicant or any referee of the applicant to provide further information;

(b) interview the applicant or any referee of the applicant;
(c) inform itself on any matter; or
(d) consult any person.

(2) The Committee may reject an application if the applicant or any referee of the applicant refuses to provide any information required by the Committee or to be interviewed by the Committee.

This provision does not appear to have addressed the issue of whether the Committee should be impressed with a duty to consider matters brought to its attention by candidates.[14] It may be recalled that during the 2005 Presidential Election, one applicant for a certificate of eligibility, Andrew Kuan, was subject to what has been called a 'trial by media' – it was reported in the news that his work performance had been less than satisfactory, that he had allegedly been ousted as chairman of his condominium management committee, and that he faced a defamation suit. The PEC reportedly asked the Jurong Town Corporation, one of Kuan's former employers, to provide a report on his character and tenure as the statutory board's chief financial officer, but did not ask Kuan for his response to the various allegations against him. Kuan was subsequently denied a certificate of eligibility on the ground of insufficient financial and managerial ability. Due to the absence of any other qualified candidates, S.R. Nathan was declared re-elected as President on nomination day without a poll.[15]

The present situation, therefore, does not adequately ensure that the PEC has before it the best information available to determine whether a person is qualified to seek the highest office in the land. It may even be that applicants are effectively denied the right to be heard, which is one of the pillars of natural justice, before decisions are made as to whether they should be issued certificates of eligibility.[16] It is submitted that a provision should be introduced to give applicants the right to provide the PEC with additional evidence, and requiring the PEC to take this evidence into consideration.

An example that might be followed is a procedure applicable in the planning law context. Under the Planning (Master Plan) Rules,[17] when the Master Plan is sought to be amended, the Urban Redevelopment Authority is required to invite the public to submit objections to and representations concerning the proposed amendment. Thereafter, unless the Minister for National Development is of the view that an objection or representation is "of a frivolous nature", the Minister

> *shall* afford to any person whose objection or representation was received by him [...] an opportunity of appearing before and being heard by a person or persons appointed by the Minister for the purpose, or cause a public inquiry to be held [...]".[18]

The Minister is under a legal duty to consider the objections and representations, and the findings of the hearing or public inquiry, when deciding whether to approve the proposed amendment.[19]

By referring to the planning procedure, I do not intend to suggest that all of its elements are appropriate to presidential elections. Whether the PEC should receive representations from members of the public and hold public hearings, for example, are issues requiring further consideration. While public hearings can promote transparency and democratic participation on the part of the public,[20] they may politicize the process to an undesirable extent. However, the modest proposal of enshrining in legislation the right of applicants to place additional evidence before the PEC and the duty of the PEC to take such evidence into account in its decision-making, it is argued, would go some way towards redressing the imbalance of power between the Committee and potential candidates.

7.2.1.2 Effect of false or misleading statements

A further recommendation of the Constitutional Commission was that the PEC should have the power to revoke a certificate of eligibility if the application form on which it was based is found to contain material false declarations. This would be so even if the candidate has been elected as President, thus resulting in the office of President being vacated and another election being held. The Commission suggested that: "to safeguard the President from potential abuse, any such determination by the PEC directed at an incumbent President should be open to challenge by the President before a Constitutional Tribunal."[21]

The Government decided to implement this recommendation differently. Within 21 days of the publication of the result of a presidential election in the *Government Gazette*,[22] the PEC[23] may apply to an Election Judge for a candidate's election as President to be declared void on the grounds:

> that the candidate intentionally or knowingly made a materially false or misleading statement of fact, or intentionally or knowingly failed to state a material fact, to the Presidential Elections Committee for the purpose of demonstrating his eligibility to be elected as President.[24]

The terms 'materially false or misleading statement of fact' and 'material fact' could be points of contention; the Act provides no guidance as to their meaning. (Another ground for a declaration of invalidity is "that the candidate was at the time of his election a person disqualified for election as President".[25] Such applications can be made by a voter, someone claiming that he or she should have been returned or elected at the election, or someone claiming to have been a candidate at the election.)[26] An Election Judge is the Chief Justice or a Judge of the Supreme Court nominated by the Chief Justice who is constitutionally empowered to determine all proceedings relating to a presidential election.[27] Decisions by an Election Judge are expressed to be final.[28]

Once the 21-day window referred to above has closed, any allegation that the President has intentionally or knowingly stated materially false or misleading facts or failed to state material facts to the PEC has to be dealt with by what is essentially a process of impeaching the President under Article 22L(3)(e) of the Constitution.[29] The process must be initiated by the Prime Minister or not less than a quarter of the total number of elected Members of Parliament (MPs) and Non-constituency Members of Parliament (NCMPs) giving notice of a parliamentary motion alleging misconduct on the President's part.[30] If the motion is adopted by at least half of the elected MPs and NCMPs, the Chief Justice is to appoint a tribunal[31] comprising not less than five Supreme Court Judges to inquire into the allegations.[32]

What is interesting about this procedure is that if the tribunal reports to the Speaker of Parliament that it is of the opinion the President is guilty of the allegations levied, the Parliament has a choice whether or not to act on the report: Article 22L(7) states that: "Parliament *may* by a resolution passed by not less than three-quarters of the total number of Members of Parliament (excluding nominated Members) remove the President from office" (emphasis added). One may wonder whether this provides a lacuna for political considerations to sway the decision. For example, if the President was formerly a member of, or otherwise associated with, the political party forming the Government of the day, the Government might be reluctant to procure the impeachment of someone who used to be 'one of its own'. Nonetheless, the risk of this happening is probably outweighed by the fact that it would not be politically astute for the Government to exhibit partiality in this way.

7.2.2 Community certificate

Under the reserved election scheme which came into force on 1 April 2017,[33] a presidential election is reserved for a particular ethnic community if no one from that community has held the office of President for any of the five most recent terms of office.[34] The term *community* is defined as meaning the Chinese community, the Malay community or the Indian or other minority communities,[35] the latter being treated as a composite group. I have described these as ethnic rather than racial communities, because a "person belonging to the Malay community" is specifically defined as "any person, *whether of the Malay race or otherwise*, who considers himself to be a member of the Malay community and who is generally accepted as a member of the Malay community by that community."[36]

While members of the Chinese community and Indian community are similarly defined by reference to self-identification and community acceptance, there is no mention of race in those definitions – a 'person belonging to the Chinese community' means 'any person who considers himself to be a member of the Chinese community' while a person belonging to the Indian community is 'any person of Indian origin who considers himself to be a member of the Indian community', provided that their respective communities accept them as members thereof. It is unclear why members of the Indian community must be 'of Indian origin' while there is no analogous requirement for people claiming membership of the Chinese community to be of Chinese origin. Likewise, where a person belonging to some other minority community is concerned, the only requirement is that he or she 'belongs to any minority community other than the Malay and Indian community'.[37]

It is patent that the definitions of persons belonging to the Malay community and Indian and other minority communities were borrowed from definitions laid down earlier for the Group Representation Constituency (hereafter "GRC") scheme;[38] indeed, Deputy Prime Minister Teo Chee Hean said as much in Parliament during the Second Reading of the Constitution of the Republic of Singapore (Amendment) Bill that established reserved elections.[39] Under the GRC scheme, electoral divisions designated as GRCs are contested by groups of candidates rather than individual candidates, and each group is required to have at least one candidate from a designated minority ethnic community to ensure representation of these communities in Parliament.[40]

The report of the select committee[41] convened to examine the GRC scheme before its introduction in 1988 sheds light on the definition of a 'person belonging to the Malay community'. The Constitution of the Republic of Singapore (Amendment) Bill and Parliamentary Elections (Amendment) Bill had specifically included people of Arab, Boyanese, Bugis and Javanese descent in the definition. This was deemed unacceptable to some individuals who had made representations to the select committee on the ground that other groups from the Malay Archipelago were not mentioned in the definition.[42] Their understanding of the Malay community was clearly quite broad. The Select Committee agreed that it would be undesirable to "lay down prescriptive criteria as to who does or does not belong to the Malay community", and that this was a matter to be determined by the community. It thus recommended the current definition.[43]

With the advent of reserved elections, it became necessary to create a mechanism for determining which ethnic community a prospective presidential candidate belongs to. The 2017 amendments to the Presidential Elections Act established a Community Committee with a chairman and five members each from the Chinese community, Malay community and Indian or other minority communities.[44] The five members from each group then form a sub-committee: for example, the five members belonging to Indian or other minority communities constitute the Indian and Other Minority Communities Sub-Committee.[45] A prospective presidential candidate is required to submit a community declaration to the CC either stating that he or she belongs to the Chinese community, Malay community, *etc*, and wishes to apply for a community certificate confirming this, or that he or she does not consider himself or herself as a member of any of the communities.[46] The period for making a community declaration begins three months before the expiry of the incumbent President's term (or the date when the office of the President falls vacant, if this happens prior to the term expiring), and ends five days after the date of the writ of election.[47]

Community declarations are required to be made whether or not a forthcoming election is a reserved election. This is because it is necessary to know which ethnic community, if any, the person elected as President belongs to for the purpose of determining whether a future election is to be a reserved election or not.[48] Where a non-reserved election is involved, in the general case the CC will accept a community declaration and refer it to the relevant Sub-Committee for the latter to determine whether the declarant does in fact belong to the community that he or she declares himself or herself to belong to.[49] If the Sub-Committee agrees with the declarant, the CC must issue a community certificate to the declarant stating that he or she belongs to that community.[50] In the event a declarant says he or she does not belong to any of the communities specified in the law, or if the Sub-Committee concludes that the declarant does not belong to the community as the declarant claims, the CC may invite the declarant to submit another declaration.[51] If the declarant then declines to do so, in the former scenario the CC must accept the community declaration, whereas in the latter scenario it must reject the application for a community certificate.[52]

However, when a reserved election is due to be held, the CC must reject community declarations in which the declarants state that they do not consider themselves as members of the community or communities to which the election is reserved.[53] Declarations that are not rejected for this reason are, as before, referred to the Sub-Committee for the community to which the election is reserved.[54] Depending on the Sub-Committee's view, the CC must either issue a community certificate to the declarant stating that he or she belongs to the relevant community, or reject the declarant's application for a community certificate.[55]

Sub-Committees are accorded much leeway in determining whether declarants are members of the communities they claim to belong to. They "must be guided by the merits of the case without regard to legal forms and technicalities, or to whether the evidence before it is in accordance with the law of evidence or not."[56] As the law provides virtually no guidance to Sub-Committees, they may potentially take into account factors that some may regard as irrelevant, unexpected or unfair. For instance, Salleh Marican, a prospective candidate for the 2017 Presidential Election, was criticized by some members of the public for his lack of fluency in speaking the Malay language;[57] he responded by saying he was taking regular Malay language lessons.[58] Would a Sub-Committee be justified in taking an applicant's language ability into account?

At a forum on the reserved election scheme organized by the Institute of Policy Studies on 8 September 2017, in response to a question on whether a person who was born into a Malay family but had decided to leave the religion of Islam would be accepted as a Malay, one speaker posited that being Muslim might be a requirement for being regarded as belonging to the Malay community.[59] This is not specified in the Presidential Election Act, and is in fact inconsistent with views expressed by legislators when the definition of a "person belonging to the Malay community" was adopted for the GRC scheme. The select committee examining the scheme said:

> [A]s Singapore is a democratic secular state, and as the Constitution recognises the right of individuals to profess any religion of their choice, it is neither prudent nor appropriate for legislation to prescribe that a Malay must also be a Muslim in order to stand as a candidate for election. It will

> set an invidious and dangerous precedent to have in our laws a provision to single out a particular religion for special treatment.[60]

This recommendation was accepted by the Government during the Third Reading of the Parliamentary Elections (Amendment) Bill in Parliament on 18 May 1988, the first Deputy Prime Minister and Minister for Defence commenting:

> Several Malay representors and witnesses submitted that to qualify as a member of the Malay community, that person must be a Muslim. The Select Committee, however, concluded that as a secular State, the laws should not prescribe any religion for any individual as the Constitution recognizes the right of individuals to profess any religion of their choice. Anyway, whether a person is a member of the Malay community or not, it is for that person and the community to decide.[61]

The Malay Community Sub-Committee itself has not commented publicly on whether it took into account the applicants' language ability and religion during the 2017 Presidential Election.

When introducing the Constitution of the Republic of Singapore (Amendment) Bill during its Second Reading in Parliament, the Deputy Prime Minister said: "It is useful to note that the 'other minority communities' refers to groups that have some degree of history, permanence, and established presence in Singapore, such as the Eurasian community."[62] As this limitation is not mentioned in the law, presumably the statement made in Parliament might be relied on to interpret the phrase "person belonging to the Indian or other minority communities" in Article 19B(6) of the Constitution.[63] However, this might work unfairness on prospective candidates of less traditional descent.

While one can understand the Government's desire to accord the CC and its Sub-Committees broad flexibility in determining the sensitive matter of which ethnic community a prospective candidate belongs to, for the avoidance of doubt it may be preferable for the issues highlighted above to be clarified in the legislation. As the GRC select committee stated, it is submitted that religion should be excluded as a factor to be considered in determining a person's membership of a community; to hold otherwise would be to impair the right to profess one's religion guaranteed by Article 15(1) of the Constitution. The possible limitation of "other minority communities" to those that have an "established presence" in Singapore adds a layer of complexity which might usefully be eliminated.

When prospective candidates of mixed ethnicity apply for community certificates for a reserved election, another peculiarity in the law becomes evident. The likelihood of this occurring is not slim. In the 2017 Presidential Election, the main prospective candidates were Halimah Yacob and Salleh Marican, whose fathers are Indian and mothers are Malay; and Farid Khan Kaim Khan who is of Pakistani descent.[64] All of them made community declarations that they belonged to the Malay community, and the CC issued community certificates to them in those terms.[65] It might be said that the CC and the Malay Community Sub-Committee heeded the Government's call for an "inclusive approach" to be adopted when determining if a person is a member of a community.[66] In the end, the PEC determined that Salleh Marican and Farid Khan did not meet the private-sector service requirement (certainly a less controversial conclusion), with the result that Halimah Yacob was declared elected as President without the need for a poll.

In the community declarations made by prospective candidates for a particular election, the law restricts each of them to making "one (and only one)" statement that they either consider themselves as belonging to one of the three specified communities and wish to apply for a community certificate to that effect, or that they do not consider themselves to be of any of the specified communities.[67] In a reserved election, the CC will reject a community declaration if the declarant did not state that he or she belongs only to the ethnic community to which the election is reserved.[68] The law does not allow a person to state in a declaration that he or she belongs to more than one ethnic community – such a person must either aver that he or she belongs to one of the "other minority communities" in Singapore or, paradoxically, none of the communities. Depending on the declaration, the person would only be entitled to participate in an election reserved to the Indian and other minority communities, or a non-reserved election.

However, the law does not appear to expressly prevent a person of mixed ethnicity who has been issued a community certificate for a particular community, but who has been unsuccessful in a reserved election, from seeking to contest an election reserved for another community by making a fresh declaration that he or she is a member of that community. Although the earlier community certificate would be conclusive of the fact that the person belongs to one community,[69] when considering a subsequent community declaration a Sub-Committee is, as we have seen, not to be bound by legal forms and technicalities and evidence law.[70] One could argue that the law does not unambiguously require a person to claim for all time that he or she is a member of only one community and no other. It would be up to the Sub-Committee of the second ethnic community to decide whether to also recognize the declarant as a member of that community as well. In reaching its decision, the Sub-Committee would no doubt take the first community certificate into account, but would it be fair for the Sub-Committee and CC to hold that a person can only be a member of one community for the purposes of a presidential election in the absence of any express legal prohibition?

In Parliament, the Deputy Prime Minister expressed the view that the combination of self-identification and community acceptance "has proven to be capable of handling situations involving persons of mixed heritage" in the GRC context,[71] and so presumably would not pose a problem for reserved elections either. Nonetheless, by effectively compelling a prospective candidate to choose between denying an aspect of his or her ethnic heritage and being disentitled from participating in a reserved election highlights a matter going to the heart of the scheme:[72] do reserved elections reinforce an unrealistic conception of ethnic uniformity, and the mistaken idea that a community cannot be properly represented in the office of the President by a person of mixed heritage?

7.2.3 Justiciability of decisions by the Presidential Elections Committee and the Community Committee

7.2.3.1 Effectiveness of finality and conclusive evidence clauses

Decisions by the Presidential Elections Committee as to whether a prospective candidate is a person of "integrity, good character and reputation" and satisfies the private-sector or public-sector service requirements, and by the Community Committee and its Sub-Committees as to community declarations, are expressed to be "final and [...] not subject to appeal or review in any court" by Article 18(12) of the Constitution[73] and Section 8J(1) of the Presidential Elections Act[74] (hereafter "PEA") respectively. Moreover, certificates of eligibility issued by the PEC and community certificates issued by the CC are declared to be "conclusive of the matters" certified and also "not subject to appeal or review in any court" by Sections 8C and 8J(2) of the PEA.

The extent to which the finality or ouster clauses are effective in ousting judicial review is uncertain in Singapore.[75] According to the High Court in *Stansfield Business International Pte Ltd* v. *Minister for Manpower*,[76] such a clause must be construed strictly, and does not prevent judicial review if the decision-making body has "acted without jurisdiction" or "done or failed to do something in the course of the inquiry which is of such a nature that its decision is a nullity", as the House of Lords put it in *Anisminic Ltd* v. *Foreign Compensation Commission*.[77] However, the clause is effective if the decision-maker has "merely made an error of law which does not affect its jurisdiction, and if its decision is not a nullity for some reason such as breach of the rules of natural justice."[78]

In contrast, in the later case of *Borissik* v. *Urban Redevelopment Authority*,[79] the High Court held that the effectiveness of a finality clause no longer depends on whether an error is jurisdictional or not, but on "practical matters" including:

> [...] the need in the circumstances for legal certainty and the need for finality on which the affected person may rely; the degree of expertise of the decision-making body; the esoteric nature of the traditions or legal provisions decided by the decision-making body; and the extent to which interrelated questions of law, fact and degree are best decided by the body which hears the evidence at first hand, rather than the courts on judicial review. In particular, account will be taken as to whether there has been previous appropriate opportunity for the claimant to challenge the relevant decision.[80]

A difference of opinion thus exists as to whether the Singapore courts understand the reference in *Anisminic* to acting without jurisdiction or doing or failing to do something that causes a decision to be a nullity in the expansive way that the United Kingdom courts have done in cases like *O'Reilly* v. *Mackman*[81] and *R* v. *Lord President of the Privy Council, ex parte Page.*[82] In *Page*, for instance, Lord Browne-Wilkinson expressed the view that *Anisminic* had "rendered obsolete the distinction between errors of law on the face of the record and other errors of law by extending the doctrine of ultra vires", with the effect that "in general any error of law made by an administrative tribunal or inferior court in reaching its decision can be quashed for error of law."[83] The High Court was invited to rule on this issue in *Nagaenthran a/l K Dharmalingam* v. *Attorney-General,*[84] but decided to refrain from reaching a firm conclusion on the matter.[85] It noted, though, that if the concept of jurisdictional error were understood broadly, this "would not appear to be aligned with the 'green-light' approach towards administrative law, which is presently the most accurate reflection of the socio-political attitude in the existing Singapore milieu."[86]

The matter may have been implicitly clarified by the Singapore Court of Appeal in *Per Ah Seng Robin* v. *Housing and Development Board.*[87] The Court acknowledged that commentators have opined that ouster clauses that seek to prevent courts from reviewing "*justiciable* matters" or to "take away the judicial power of the court where its supervisory jurisdiction is concerned"[88] are incompatible with the rule of law since it is the courts' duty to declare the limits of discretionary powers,[89] and may even be inconsistent with the vesting of judicial power in the courts by Article 93 of the Constitution.[90] However, as the respondent had not relied on Section 56(6), the ouster clause in the Housing and Development Act,[91] the Court declined to reach a firm conclusion on whether the clause prevented judicial review of the executive decision in question.[92] Indeed, it is submitted the issue did not arise on the facts of the case as Section 56(6) merely states: "The decision of the Minister shall be final and not open to review or challenge on any ground whatsoever." As *Stansfield* and other cases indicate, clauses of this nature do not oust judicial review completely.

The Court went on to assume that Section 56(6) did not prevent the decision made by the Minister for National Development from being reviewed, and regarded the issues raised in the case as "eminently justiciable".[93] It then assessed the actions of the Minister on the traditional broad categories of grounds of judicial review in administrative law – illegality, irrationality and procedural impropriety. The Court's conclusion was in line with its judgements in *Chng Suan Tze* v. *Minister for Home Affairs* and *Tan Seet Eng* v. *Attorney-General.*[94] While these cases involved subjectively worded executive discretion rather than finality clauses, the Court held in the cases that executive decisions to detain persons without trial for national security reasons under the Internal Security Act,[95] and for "public safety, peace and good order" under the Criminal Law (Temporary Provisions) Act,[96] were respectively subject to objective judicial review on traditional administrative law grounds.[97] Reference may also be had to *Yong Vui Kong* v. *Attorney-General,*[98] where the Court of Appeal inferred that since the Constitution requires the Cabinet to consider certain materials when deciding how to advise the President to exercise the power of clemency,[99] this implies that the Cabinet has a constitutional duty to act impartially and in good faith.[100] If the Cabinet fails in this regard the court must be able to intervene, otherwise "the rule of law would be rendered nugatory".[101]

It is submitted that *Per Ah Seng Robin* may confirm that when interpreting finality clauses that do not seek a complete ouster of judicial review, the Singapore courts, like those in the United Kingdom, will examine all possible errors of law rather than adhering to the old distinction between jurisdictional and non-jurisdictional errors. Indeed, when the Government sought to have Parliament amend the Criminal Law (Temporary Provisions) Act in February 2018 by inserting a clause stating that detention decisions by the Minister for Home Affairs are "final",[102] it affirmed the Court of Appeal's ruling in *Tan Seet Eng* and said the new clause was not intended to, and indeed could not, alter the legal position regarding the reviewability of such decisions by the courts.[103]

As for the conclusive evidence clauses in the PEA, it appears they are capable of precluding judicial review of certificates of eligibility and community certificates to a greater extent than finality clauses.[104] In *R* v. *Registrar of Companies, ex parte Central Bank of India*,[105] the Court of Appeal of England and Wales said that a clause containing words excluding the admission of evidence rather than excluding the courts' jurisdiction to grant judicial review is unaffected by the *Anisminic* rule.[106] It described the rationale underlying such clauses as the desirability of obviating the need for proof of statutory requirements which could be "so difficult as to be impossible",[107] and to accord certainty to transactions based on the certificates issued by the public authority.[108] While the Singapore Court of Appeal has accepted the rule,[109] it has ameliorated its strictness to a degree by accepting in *Teng Fuh Holdings Pte Ltd* v. *Collector of Land Revenue*[110] that a conclusive evidence clause will not prevent judicial review if there is proof that the public authority has acted in bad faith.[111]

It is incongruous, though, that while Article 18(12) probably does not prevent decisions of the PEC on a prospective candidate's good character and satisfaction of the public- or private-sector service requirements from being challenged on traditional administrative law grounds, the conclusive evidence clause in Section 8C of the PEA seems to do so. Since Section 8C is thus partially inconsistent with Article 18(12), it would appear to be void to the extent of the inconsistency.[112]

Of course, as mentioned earlier, it is possible that the finality and conclusive evidence clauses in the PEA may also be inconsistent with the vesting of judicial power in the courts by Article 93 of the Constitution and with the constitutional doctrines of the rule of law and separation of powers. When the time comes for the Court of Appeal to address this issue squarely, given its generally cautious and deferential approach towards judicial review,[113] in all likelihood it would hold that Article 93 and the rule of law principle require recognition of the UK position concerning ouster clauses, but not to the extent of rendering such clauses entirely ineffective. This would also avoid a clash between Article 18(12) and Article 93, which, both being constitutional provisions, the court would strive to read harmoniously.[114]

This position has been foreshadowed by *Nagaenthran*, which held that Section 33B(4) of the Misuse of Drugs Act,[115] insofar as it ousts judicial review of non-justiciable determinations by the Public Prosecutor,[116] is not a violation of Article 93 or the constitutional doctrines mentioned above. The High Court said that judicial deference should be shown to the Legislature's decision to enact the provision "by dint of the constitutional doctrine of the separation of powers" and "the relative institutional competence of the executive in respect of decisions that concern issues that judges are ill-equipped to adjudicate".[117] In any case, the ultimate position taken by the Court of Appeal towards finality or ouster clauses should similarly apply to conclusive evidence clauses as they serve essentially the same purpose and are often coupled with ouster clauses.[118] It is paradoxical "that the strongest form of ouster clause may fail to protect some ultra vires decision or act whereas the weaker one [the conclusive evidence clause] may succeed in doing so."[119]

In addition, finality clauses cannot prevent the court from looking into alleged unconstitutional conduct by the Executive. In *Cheong Chun Yin* v. *Attorney-General*,[120] the High Court examined how Section 33B(4) of the Misuse of Drugs Act should be interpreted. The section states:

> The determination of whether or not any person has substantively assisted the Central Narcotics Bureau in disrupting drug trafficking activities shall be at the sole discretion of the Public Prosecutor and no action or proceeding shall lie against the Public Prosecutor in relation to any such determination unless it is proved to the court that the determination was done in bad faith or with malice.

The High Court accepted that even though unconstitutionality of the Public Prosecutor's determination is not expressly mentioned in the section, it is a ground on which judicial review can be sought.[121] This position was confirmed by the Court of Appeal in *Muhammad Ridzwan bin Mohd Ali* v. *Attorney-General*[122] on the basis that since

> the Constitution is supreme and all governmental powers are ultimately derived from and circumscribed by the Constitution [...] all executive acts must be constitutional and the court is conferred the power to declare void any executive act that contravenes the provisions of the Constitution.[123]

It therefore stands to reason that the fundamental liberties in the Constitution cannot simply be deemed irrelevant by finality and conclusive evidence clauses that exist in ordinary legislation.

Apart from the approach the courts might take towards the ouster and conclusive evidence clauses in the Constitution and the Presidential Elections Act, is there a case for them to be done away with? The Constitutional Commission disagreed with suggestions that judicial review of the PEC's decisions either on the merits or on the grounds of legality should be available. It felt that the Judiciary would be asked to make decisions "which are, in substance, political", and this would be "an undesirable derogation from the principle of the separation of powers under the Constitution". Furthermore, it "would not be desirable to encourage collateral litigation connected with the office of President". The PEC was "uniquely qualified to decide whether the requirements set out in Art 19(2) are met", and it would be more "efficient and expeditious" to ensure legal propriety in the PEC's decision-making process by having a legally qualified person serve as a member of the PEC.[124]

In connection with this, the Commission proposed adding three members to the PEC in addition to the existing three.[125] This recommendation was adopted by Parliament. The new members are a current or former member of the Council of Presidential Advisers, to be appointed by the Chairman of the Council;[126] a person, to be appointed by the Prime Minister, with expertise and experience acquired in the private sector, who would be able to provide insights as to whether prospective candidates satisfy the private-sector service requirements;[127] and a person, to be appointed by the Chief Justice, who is qualified to be or has been a Judge of the Supreme Court.[128] The Commission said the latter person would be able to assist the PEC in ensuring the legal requirements of Article 19(2)(g) are satisfied, and that its decisions are reached in a procedurally fair manner.[129]

It is certainly not disputed that the PEC's legally qualified member would indeed be well positioned to advise the Committee on these matters.[130] The CC is not statutorily required to have a legally qualified member, though presumably it may consult someone with legal expertise if it deems necessary.[131] Nevertheless, the benefit of allowing decisions of the PEC, and the CC and its Sub-Committees, to be judicially reviewable is to provide public assurance that the decisions are subject to an independent legal check. In fact, despite the Constitutional Commission's view, the current state of the law suggests that the finality clause applying to certain decisions of the PEC does not prevent the courts from exercising judicial review on the ground of legality. Going a step further, it might be said that the decisions made by the various committees are more factual than 'political' in nature. For example, a prospective candidate seeking a certificate of eligibility from the PEC based on the private-sector service requirement must provide a plethora of financial information about the private-sector organization which the person has served as chief executive of.[132] A court is manifestly capable of determining if the PEC has properly evaluated such data and drawn correct inferences therefrom. Hence, there is no reason why decisions of the PEC and CC should not be appealable to the courts on both issues of law and fact.

Rather than derogating from the separation of powers doctrine, an appeal (or, at least, judicial review) would give effect to the concept of checks and balances that is a crucial and inseparable part of the doctrine. It is also, as has been pointed out earlier, consistent with the rule of law and the vesting of judicial power in the courts. If court review is unavailable, perceptions that the various committees are making determinations in a partisan and politicized manner may be difficult to dispel. It is not surprising the view has been taken that the non-reviewability of the PEC's decisions "poses problems for the practice of constitutional government, not to mention for the principles relating to the transparency and accountability of decision makers when exercising public power."[133]

7.2.3.2 Procedure for judicial challenges

In view of the foregoing, under the law as it stands there are at least some situations where decisions of the PEC, CC and Sub-Committees of the CC are subject to judicial review. Despite the applicable finality clauses, such decisions are probably at least challengeable before the courts on the grounds of illegality (including acting in bad faith), irrationality and procedural impropriety. Non-compliance with any statutory procedure could be considered either a form of illegality or procedural impropriety. In contrast, the PEA provisions declaring certificates of eligibility and community certificates to be conclusive of the matters they certify are effective in preventing the courts from examining whether the certificates breach administrative law rules, unless it can be shown that the body issuing a certificate acted in bad faith.

However, it is submitted that finality and conclusive evidence clauses cannot prevent the courts from considering if any decisions of the PEC, CC and Sub-Committees of the CC infringe constitutional rights. In connection with this, it should be noted that Article 19B(5) does not prevent decisions of the CC and its Sub-Committees as to whether a person is a member of a particular ethnic community from being disputed before the courts as contrary to Articles 12(1) and (2) of the Constitution; for example, it could be alleged that the person has been discriminated against on the ground of race or descent. Article 19B is the constitutional provision establishing reserved elections, and clause (5) of the Article states: "No provision of any law made pursuant to this Article is invalid on the ground of inconsistency with Article 12 or is considered to be a differentiating measure under Article 78." Yet, this only immunizes from incompatibility with the Constitution's equality clause the reserved election scheme as a whole,[134] and not the decisions by the CC or any Sub-Committee. Nonetheless, it would be an uphill battle for a prospective candidate to succeed in proving a violation of equality as the legal test is difficult to satisfy.[135]

We should not overlook the fact that only decisions of the PEC as to whether a person is of "integrity, good character and reputation" and satisfies the private-sector or public-sector service requirements are subject to a finality clause.[136] There is no bar against an applicant for a certificate of eligibility challenging the PEC's refusal to issue the certificate due to, say, a mistaken belief that the applicant is an undischarged bankrupt or holds an office of profit.[137]

The procedure for judicial challenges would benefit from some clarification. Article 93A(1) of the Constitution states that "[*a*]*ll proceedings* relating to the election of the President" shall be heard by an Election Judge,[138] which seems to require a person seeking to challenge a decision of the PEC, CC or a Sub-Committee to apply to an Election Judge rather than to the High Court, which would be the usual procedure. However, a number of things point to Article 93A having a narrower application. For one, the heading of the Article reads: "Jurisdiction to determine questions as to validity of Presidential election". While a provision's heading "is intended only to summarise the contents of sections for ease of reference, and is not always exhaustive or precise", and therefore cannot "control or limit the operation of the plain words" in the provision,[139] Article 93A(2) goes on to provide that the Election Judge "shall have the power to hear and determine and make such orders as provided by law on proceedings relating to the election of the President." The PEA, which is the relevant law, essentially provides that an Election Judge is empowered to determine if an election should be invalidated on specified grounds, including corrupt and illegal practices by a candidate or his or her election agents, and proof that the candidate was disqualified from standing in the election.[140] The Act says nothing about an Election Judge playing any role in judicially reviewing the decisions of the PEC, CC or a Sub-Committee. Thus, it is submitted that such applications must be brought before the High Court in the normal way.

The timeframes set out in the legislation do not contemplate any legal challenges being brought. The latest time that the PEC can issue a certificate of eligibility to an applicant or notify the applicant that a certificate will not be issued is the eve of nomination day.[141] The CC must adhere to the same deadline when informing declarants if their community declarations have been accepted, and issuing community certificates to them or notifying them of the rejection of their applications for certificates.[142] This means that a person aggrieved by the PEC and CC's decisions may well have less than a day to file a lawsuit and have it heard by the High Court, much less to appeal the matter to the Court of Appeal. The PEA provides for nomination day and polling day to be postponed for reasons such as riots, storms and floods, health hazards, fires and "difficulties in the physical conduct" of nomination proceedings or polling,[143] but not because of pending legal proceedings.

Thus, it would be apposite for adjustments to be made to the relevant legislation clarifying the role of the Election Judge, requiring the PEC and CC to notify prospective candidates whether their applications for certificates of eligibility and community certificates are successful, and providing an expedited procedure for judicial review cases to be heard and appealed.

7.3 The conduct of election campaigns

Moving from the prerequisites for candidacy in a presidential election to the campaigning period between nomination day and cooling-off day, it will come as no surprise that the latter is also quite heavily regulated in Singapore, with rules ranging from the maximum amount that candidates can spend on their campaigns[144] to the sizes of posters.[145] In principle, the law should strive to accord candidates and voters freedom to share information and views that may help voters to decide how to mark their ballots, while preventing opinions from being unduly skewed by highly influential voices. In this respect, it might be said that the balance between these factors could be better struck.

7.3.1 The conduct of candidates during campaigns

The 2011 Presidential Election was the first to have been contested by four qualified candidates. A controversy arose over statements made by some of these candidates concerning the President's role and what the President can publicly say without the advice of Cabinet. For example, Tan Kin Lian said that the President "represents the views of the people", and that if many people have views on an issue they regard as important and the Government has not addressed it, the President "should bring these to the Government's attention and have a dialogue with the Government".[146] Tan Jee Say, on his part, expressed the view that the President possesses 'moral power' to air views in public on 'issues of conscience' such as the building of casinos.[147] On the other hand, Law Minister K. Shanmugam observed at a forum organized by the Institute of Policy Studies that while the President may privately offer advice to the Prime Minister, the Constitution requires that he or she only act and speak as the Cabinet advises.[148]

Commenting on this, the Constitutional Commission said:

> [T]o the extent candidates in the last Presidential elections appeared to misstate what they could or would do if elected, this may have stemmed from a failure to understand the proper remit of the Presidency and in particular, the tendency to see it, mistakenly, as an alternative source of Executive policy-making power.[149]

It proposed that the law should require candidates to declare that they understand the President's constitutional role before being issued a certificate of eligibility; that it should be an offence for candidates to make promises or take positions incompatible with the office of the President; and that the sanctions could range from criminal liability, to declaratory reliefs issued by an Election Judge, and, in "appropriate extreme cases", revocation of a certificate of eligibility.[150]

The Government decided against amending the law along these lines, resolving instead to require each candidate to make a statutory declaration in the nomination paper to be submitted to the Returning Officer on nomination day that he or she "understands the President's role under the Constitution, including any particular aspect of the President's role stated in the prescribed form."[151] Section B of the nomination paper now requires a candidate to declare that:

> (d) I have read the explanatory material provided by the Returning Officer and understand the President's role under the Constitution, and in particular that –
> (i) the President is the Head of State and the symbol of national unity;
> (ii) it is also the function of the President to safeguard the reserves of Singapore and the integrity of the Public Services of Singapore, in accordance with the specific discretionary powers conferred on the President by the Constitution; and

> (iii) the President must exercise his functions according to the advice of the Cabinet, except where the Constitution otherwise provides.
>
> And I make this solemn declaration by virtue of the Oaths and Declarations Act (Cap. 211), and subject to the penalties provided by that Act for the making of false statements in statutory declarations, conscientiously believing the statements contained in this declaration to be true in every particular.[152]

Hence, the possibility of criminal liability has not entirely disappeared. Under Section 14(1)(a) of the Oaths and Declarations Act, it is an offence for a person to make:

> in a statutory declaration a statement which is false, and which he knows or has reason to believe is false or does not believe to be true, touching any point material to the object for which the declaration is made or used.[153]

It may be asked whether the chance that a candidate may inadvertently make comments inconsistent with the declaration in the nomination paper has a chilling effect on what candidates say while campaigning. The imposition of criminal liability seems unnecessary when the inaccuracy of any statement can simply be pointed out and the facts clarified, as the Law Minister did during the 2011 election, and voters trusted to decide for themselves how credible the candidate making the statement is.

The Government took a lighter approach when responding to another of the Constitutional Commission's recommendations. The Commission had suggested that,

> with a view to tempering the divisiveness of the election process and ensuring that campaigning remains consistent with the role of the President as a symbol of national unity and which preserves the dignity associated with the highest office in the land,

rules should be enacted "to restrict or exclude acts that might inflame emotions, cause divisiveness or encourage invective. Such rules could also prescribe a 'white list' of approved campaign methods, such as televised debates or speeches." It was not clear to the Commission that holding election rallies was "either necessary or helpful in this context".[154]

The Government decided against disallowing candidates from holding rallies. Instead, during the 2017 Presidential Election the Elections Department, departing from previous practice, announced that it would not designate any rally sites for candidates to book, leaving it to them to make their own arrangements if they wished to hold rallies.[155] (No rallies were eventually held as Halimah Yacob was elected as President unopposed on nomination day.) Neither did the Government issue regulations banning particular campaigning methods. Instead, the Returning Officer introduced a voluntary undertaking that candidates could make, to be submitted on nomination day and publicly displayed on a notice board together with the nomination paper and associated documents.[156] The undertaking was that a candidate would "campaign for election as President in a manner that is dignified, decorous and consistent with the President's position as the Head of State and the symbol of national unity."[157] It is submitted that an addition to the voluntary undertaking in the form of a statement concerning a candidate's understanding of the President's constitutional role is preferable to requiring candidates to make a statutory declaration to that effect in their nomination papers.

7.3.2 Sharing of information through the Internet

All election advertising, including advertising on the Internet, is regulated by the Presidential Elections Act and the Presidential Elections (Election Advertising) Regulations[158] issued thereunder.[159] The regulations relate to particulars that must be provided together with the advertising,[160] the content of the advertising,[161] and various other requirements (for example, the sender of an email or electronic message must cease sending such messages if requested to do so by a recipient,[162] and discussion fora must be moderated).[163]

In 2010, the concept of making the eve of polling day a 'cooling-off day' was introduced in both parliamentary and presidential elections.[164] The idea was to provide voters with an opportunity to reflect on how to exercise their vote without being bombarded by messages sent on behalf of candidates. Restrictions on election advertising that had applied on polling day were extended to cooling-off day.[165] However, "the telephonic or electronic transmission by an individual to another individual of the first-mentioned individual's own political views, on a non-commercial basis", was exempted from the restrictions.[166]

What is somewhat uncertain is whether this exemption includes electronic messages that are sent by one person to a number of recipients, for example, by email or a messaging app such as WhatsApp, or on social media such as Facebook or Twitter. This interpretation was given credence by a press release issued by the Elections Department during the 2015 general election which stated that "transmission of personal political views by individuals to other individuals, on a non-commercial basis, using the Internet, telephone or electronic means" on cooling-off day and polling day was permissible.[167] The use of the phrase *by individuals to other individuals* suggested that the exemption applied to communications from a single sender to multiple recipients, rather than being limited to communications from one sender to one recipient at a time.

On the other hand, speaking in Parliament on 27 April 2010, the Minister for Law explained the analogous provision in the Parliamentary Elections Act[168] – Section 78B(2)(c) – differently during the Second Reading of the amendment bill leading to the inclusion of the provision in the Act.[169] (An identical change was debated and made to the Presidential Elections Act on the same day).[170] Initially, he said:

> [I]nstead of allowing only individual transmission of personal political views on the Internet (on a non-commercial basis), we have widened the exception to cover any form of telephonic or electronic transmission of personal political views *by individuals to other individuals* (on a non-commercial basis). This is to take into account new forms of individual personal communication.[171]

This is essentially the same as the statement put out by the Elections Department in 2015. However, he subsequently clarified:

> [I]ndividual-to-individual transmission of personal political views, on a non-commercial basis, is not caught by the prohibition on Cooling-Off day and Polling Day. So, if a person posts a message on his blog or on a website which everyone can read, asking readers to vote for a particular party or candidate, that would probably be election advertising. But if he sends an email or SMS to a friend to share his personal political views about the election and provided he does not collect money for doing so, then that would not be caught.[172]

Thus, it appears that while one-to-one electronic communications made on cooling-off day and polling day are allowed, one-to-many communications are not. Given how widely messaging apps and social media are used these days, it may be asked if it is worth making such activities criminal offences. A halfway house might be to prohibit official representatives of candidates from communicating with multiple recipients while allowing voters to do so, though admittedly it would be quite hard to determine whether someone is communicating on behalf of a candidate or not. On balance, it may be better not to have a rule that is simply a trap for the unwary and probably upheld more in its breach than adherence, and to simply accord voters greater freedom to communicate with each other on political and electoral matters, even on cooling-off day and polling day.

7.3.3 Endorsement and criticism of candidates

As the President is supposed to be politically neutral, he or she is barred from being a member of a political party and, if formerly a Member of Parliament, must vacate his or her parliamentary seat.[173] A candidate for the office cannot be a member of any political party on nomination day,[174] and the Elections Department advises that "[p]olitical parties should not be involved in campaigning using their party names and symbols in support of a candidate".[175] Nonetheless, it has been pointed out that the Constitution does not prevent political parties, the Government or non-governmental bodies with close government ties from endorsing – or, indeed, criticizing – candidates.[176]

I proposed to the Constitutional Commission that Ministers and MPs should be barred from endorsing candidates, whether in their personal or official capacities. The Commission did not see the need for this requirement on the ground that political parties are "are likely to have strong and potentially relevant views on the merits or demerits of Presidential candidates" which voters may wish to consider.[177] It is submitted, though, that the expression of positive or negative views by influential members of political parties may be unfair to candidates because of the undue effect they may have on voters, and conflicts with the non-partisan nature of the office of the President reflected in the law and the Elections Department's policy. It has also been pointed out that prohibiting such persons from expressing these views would "preserve the objectivity and integrity" of the PEC's work in vetting prospective candidates and "ensure it is not prematurely politicized", as well as dispel public perceptions that this may be happening.[178]

7.4 Concluding thoughts

This chapter has examined a number of issues relating to the mechanics of how presidential elections are conducted. Concerning the qualification process for becoming a candidate, it has been argued, among other things, that the Presidential Election Committee should be impressed with a legal duty to consider evidence that applicants for certificates of eligibility may wish to place before it. It has also highlighted the lack of statutory guidance given to the Community Committee and its Sub-Committees when it comes to deciding whether a person who has applied for a community certificate belongs to a particular ethnic community. Moreover, it seems that persons of mixed ethnicity may find themselves in the invidious position of choosing between denying one aspect of their ethnic background and being unable to participate in a reserved election.

There are finality and conclusive evidence clauses in the Constitution and the Presidential Elections Act that seek to prevent decisions of the PEA, CC and the latter's Sub-Committees from being challenged in court. At the time of writing, such clauses do not operate to prevent judicial review where the committees have acted unconstitutionally or where jurisdictional errors of law have occurred. It may well be that the concept of a 'jurisdictional error of law' should now be understood broadly, with the result that courts may review all situations where an error of law, however characterized, has occurred. It remains undetermined whether ouster clauses are in fact entirely unconstitutional; the Court of Appeal has suggested they may be if they seek to prevent the courts from reviewing the legality of executive action.[179] It has been submitted that such clauses are unnecessary, and that the committees' decisions should be made appealable to the courts on both law and fact. This would arguably provide an avenue for independent scrutiny that aggrieved prospective candidates could avail themselves of, and help to dispel perceptions that the committees are arriving at determinations in a partisan and politicized manner.

During the campaigning period between nomination day and polling day, it is submitted that some of the applicable rules tend to slant public debate in favour of the views of highly influential persons such as Ministers and MPs. For instance, the possibility that presidential candidates who accidentally comment on the President's role in a way inconsistent with the statutory declaration in the nomination paper may find criminal charges brought against them may have a chilling effect on what they speak about. Moreover, it seems that on cooling-off day and polling day, voters are prohibited from electronically sharing information and opinions to multiple recipients by email or through a messaging app or social media. On the other hand, political parties, the Government, and non-governmental bodies with close government ties are not enjoined from criticizing or endorsing candidates. The rules could do with some rebalancing.

It is hard to escape the sense that underlying the various rules examined in this chapter seems to be a persistent belief that voters may not be trusted to properly assess whether candidates merit being elected to the nation's highest office. Thus, prospective candidates need to be pre-screened by various committees whose decisions are expressed to be final and probably only reviewable by the courts on narrow grounds, and what is said during election campaigns need to be carefully cabined. It is worth asking ourselves whether this fundamentally underestimates the electorate's powers of discernment. Ultimately, the procedures for electing the President should treat prospective and actual candidates even-handedly, and promote public confidence in the integrity of the process.

Notes

1 I thank Swati S. Jhaveri, Jaclyn L. Neo and other participants of a workshop on the Elected Presidency held on 10 January 2018 for their helpful comments.

2 *Report of the Constitutional Commission 2016* [Chairman: Chief Justice Sundaresh Menon] (The Commission, 17 August 2016) www.gov.sg/~/media/elected%20presidency/files/report%20of%20the%20constitutional%20commission%202016.pdf (accessed 29 July 2017); archived at https://web.archive.org/web/20170729025724/www.gov.sg/~/media/elected%20presidency/files/report%20of%20the%20constitutional%20commission%202016.pdf (hereafter *Constitutional Commission Report*).

3 *White Paper on the Review of Specific Aspects of the Elected Presidency* (Cmd 7 of 2016) (Government of Singapore, 15 September 2016) www.parliament.gov.sg/lib/sites/default/files/paperpresented/pdf/2015/Cmd.7of2016.pdf (accessed 14 November 2016); archived at https://web.archive.org/web/20161114084734/www.parliament.gov.sg/lib/sites/default/files/paperpresented/pdf/2015/Cmd.7of2016.pdf (hereafter *White Paper*).

4 Constitution of the Republic of Singapore (Amendment) Bill 2016 (No. B28 of 2016).

5 Constitution of the Republic of Singapore (1985 rev edn, 1999 Rep) (hereinafter "Constitution"), Arts 19(4)–(10), as amended by the Constitution of the Republic of Singapore (Amendment) Act 2016 (No. 28 of 2016) (hereafter CAA 2016), in force with effect from 1 April 2017 except for a number of provisions. See generally the chapter by Eugene Tan on eligibility and the Council of Presidential Advisers, Chapter 4 in this volume.

6 Constitution, *ibid.*, Art. 19B, as inserted by the CAA 2016, *ibid.*

7 The period for applying starts three months before the incumbent President's term expires (or, if the office has fallen vacant before the expiry, the date when that occurred), and ends five days after the writ of election has been issued by the Prime Minister: Presidential Elections Act (Cap. 240A, 2011 rev edn) (hereafter "PEA"), as amended by the Presidential Elections (Amendment) Act 2017 (No. 6 of 2017), s 8(2).

8 Constitution (n. 5), Art. 19(2)(e).

9 *Ibid.*, Arts 19(2)(g) and 19(3)–(7): see the PEA (n. 7), s 8A.

10 *Constitutional Commission Report* (n. 2), [4.78]–[4.80], implemented by the Presidential Elections (Certificate of Eligibility) Regulations 2017 (S 263/2017), reg 3 read with the Schedule, Form 1, Annex C.

11 *Ibid.*, [4.82], implemented by the Presidential Elections (Certificate of Eligibility) Regulations 2017 (S 263/2017), reg 3 read with the Schedule, Form 1, Annex B5 and note Part 3 of the Regulations ("Further Provisions on Private Sector Service Requirement").

12 *Ibid.*, [4.85].

13 Presidential Elections (Certificate of Eligibility) Regulations 2017 (n. 11).

14 A point previously raised by Li-ann Thio, "Singapore: (S)electing the President – Diluting Democracy?" (2007) 5 *International Journal of Constitutional Law* 526, 538–9.

15 Thio, "(S)electing the President", *ibid.*, 534–7. President Nathan was elected for the first time in 1999, also in an uncontested election.

16 *Ibid.*, 537.

17 Cap 232, R 1, 2000 rev edn.

18 *Ibid.*, r 6(1) (emphasis added).

19 *Ibid.*, rr 6(2)(c) and (d).

20 Li-ann Thio has suggested that:

> since the PEC may potentially impugn the character of possible candidates by their findings, these candidates should have the right to respond to negative findings in a public setting, with broadcast media in attendance, as is the practice for vetting high administrative officials in the United States. [...] Such reform would enhance transparency and afford citizens a role in a more democratized process, open to public scrutiny.

See Thio, "(S)electing the President" (n. 14), 540–1.

21 *Constitutional Commission Report* (n. 2), [4.86]. Under the Constitution (n. 5), Art. 100(1),

> [t]he President may refer to a tribunal consisting of not less than 3 Judges of the Supreme Court for its opinion any question as to the effect of any provision of this Constitution which has arisen or appears to him likely to arise.

The Constitutional Commission proposed that the remit of the Constitutional Tribunal be expanded to enable it to decide if the PEC has correctly determined that an application for a certificate of eligibility contains material falsehoods: *Constitutional Commission Report*, *ibid.*

22 PEA (n. 7), s 77(1).

23 *Ibid.*, s 73(b).

24 *Ibid.*, s 71(f). Presumably the phrase "materially false or misleading" in the provision should be read as "materially false or materially misleading", as it would make no sense for a statement of fact that was misleading but not material to an applicant's eligibility to be a presidential candidate to lead to an election being annulled.

25 *Ibid.*, s 71(e).

26 *Ibid.*, s 73(a).

27 Constitution (n. 5), Art. 93A(1).

28 *Ibid.*, Art. 93A(2).

29 The word *impeachment* is not used in the Constitution.

30 Constitution (n. 5) Art. 22L(3)(e).

31 *Ibid.*, Art. 22L(4).

32 Unless the Chief Justice otherwise decides, he or she is one of the members of the tribunal: *ibid.*, Art. 22L(5).

33 The pros and cons of the reserved election scheme are discussed in detail in Eugene Tan's Chapter 6 and Jaclyn Neo's Chapter 5 in this volume.

34 Constitution (n. 5), Art. 19B(1).
35 *Ibid.*, Art. 19B(6).
36 *Ibid.*, (emphasis added).
37 *Ibid.*
38 *Ibid.*, Art. 39A(4), and see also the Parliamentary Elections Act (Cap. 218, 2011 rev edn) s 27A(8).
39 Teo Chee Hean (Deputy Prime Minister), speech during the Second Reading of the Constitution of the Republic of Singapore (Amendment) Bill, *Singapore Parliamentary Debates: Official Report*, 7 November 2016, vol. 94: "The definitions for the Malay, Indian and other minority communities are identical to those adopted in the GRC context." The Constitutional Commission also suggested adapting the GRC scheme's definitions of the communities for the reserved election scheme: *Constitutional Commission Report* (n. 2), [5.37].
40 Constitution (n. 5), Arts 39A(1) and 39A(2)(a).
41 *Report of the Select Committee on the Parliamentary Elections (Amendment) Bill [Bill No 23/87] and the Constitution of the Republic of Singapore (Amendment No 2) Bill [Bill No 24/87]* (Parl 3 of 1988) (hereafter *GRC Select Committee Report*).
42 *Ibid.*, [39].
43 *Ibid.*, [41]–[42]. The recommendation was accepted by the Government: Goh Chok Tong (first Deputy Prime Minister and Minister for Defence, speech during the Third Reading of the Parliamentary Elections (Amendment) Bill (as Reported from Select Committee), *Singapore Parliamentary Debates: Official Report*, 18 May 1988, vol. 51, cols 24–25.
44 PEA (n. 7), s 8E(1).
45 *Ibid.*, ss 8E(3)–(5).
46 *Ibid.*, s 8F(1).
47 *Ibid.*, s 8F(3).
48 Once the Returning Officer declares a person to be elected as President, he or she must add the person, and the community (if any) that the person belongs to, to the Schedule to the PEA, which is then used for determining whether an election is reserved under Article 19B(1) of the Constitution: *ibid.*, ss 5A(1) and (2).
49 *Ibid.*, ss 8H(2) and (3).
50 *Ibid.*, s 8H(4)(c).
51 *Ibid.*, ss 8H(2)(b) and (4)(d)(ii). Only one such invitation may be issued: *ibid.*, s 8H(7)(c).
52 *Ibid.*, ss 8H(8).
53 *Ibid.*, s 8G(2).
54 *Ibid.*, s 8G(3).
55 *Ibid.*, ss 8G(4)(c) and (d).
56 *Ibid.*, ss 8G(4)(b) and 8H(4)(b). In addition, when determining whether a declarant belongs to a community, a Sub-Committee may:

> (a) require the declarant to provide further information; (b) interview the declarant; inform itself on any matter; and (d) consult any person, and may take into account any refusal by the declarant to provide further information or to be interviewed.

Presidential Elections (Community Declaration and Community Certificate) Regulations 2017 (S 264/2017) reg 5(1).
57 Zakir Hussain, "Doubts about Presidential Hopefuls Not Being Malay Enough are Off Track", *The Straits Times* (Singapore, 20 July 2017) www.straitstimes.com/opinion/doubts-about-presidential-hopefuls-not-being-malay-enough-are-off-track (accessed 27 April 2018); archived at https://web.archive.org/web/20170823055603/www.straitstimes.com/opinion/doubts-about-presidential-hopefuls-not-being-malay-enough-are-off-track).

58 Safhras Khan, "Salleh Marican: I am taking Malay lessons ahead of Presidential Election 2017", *Yahoo! News Singapore* (19 June 2017) https://sg.news.yahoo.com/salleh-marican-taking-malay-lessons-ahead-presidential-election-2017-102557004.html (accessed 27 April 2018) (archived at https://web.archive.org/web/20180206193220/https://sg.news.yahoo.com/salleh-marican-taking-malay-lessons-ahead-presidential-election-2017-102557004.html).

59 Nur Asyiqin Mohamad Salleh, "Presidential Election 2017: Question of Who is Malay Continues to be Raised", *The Straits Times* (Singapore, 9 September 2017) www.straitstimes.com/politics/question-of-who-is-malay-continues-to-be-raised (accessed 8 January 2018) (archived at https://web.archive.org/web/20180108033511/www.straitstimes.com/politics/question-of-who-is-malay-continues-to-be-raised); see also Siau Ming En and Kelly Ng, "Community Committee 'Able to Deal with Evolving Concept of Race'", *Today* (Singapore, 9 September 2017) www.todayonline.com/singapore/community-committee-able-deal-evolving-concept-race (accessed 8 January 2018) (archived at https://web.archive.org/web/20170911115450/www.todayonline.com/singapore/community-committee-able-deal-evolving-concept-race).

60 *GRC Select Committee Report* (n. 41), [40].

61 Goh, speech during the Third Reading of the Parliamentary Elections (Amendment) Bill (n. 43), col. 25.

62 Teo, speech during the Second Reading of the Constitution of the Republic of Singapore (Amendment) Bill (n. 39).

63 Pursuant to the Interpretation Act (Cap. 1, 2002 rev edn) ss 9A(2) and (3)(c).

64 Nur Asyiqin Mohamad Salleh, "Presidential Election 2017: question of who is Malay continues to be raised" (n. 59); see also Faris Mokhtar, "Reserved Presidential Election casts spotlight on 'Malayness'", *Today* (Singapore, 15 July 2017, updated 16 July 2017) www.todayonline.com/singapore/reserved-presidential-election-casts-spotlight-malayness (accessed 8 January 2018) (archived at https://web.archive.org/web/20170719124842/www.todayonline.com/singapore/reserved-presidential-election-casts-spotlight-malayness).

65 "Press Release: Issue of Certificate of Eligibility and Malay Community Certificate for Presidential Election 2017", Elections Department, Prime Minister's Office (11 September 2017) [4] www.eld.gov.sg/pressrelease/PreE2017/Press%20Release%20on%20Issue%20of%20Certificate%20of%20Eligibility%20and%20Malay%20Community%20Certificate%20for%20Presidential%20Election%202017.pdf (accessed 8 January 2018) (archived at https://web.archive.org/web/20170913231647/www.eld.gov.sg/pressrelease/PreE2017/Press%20Release%20on%20Issue%20of%20Certificate%20of%20Eligibility%20and%20Malay%20Community%20Certificate%20 for%20Presidential%20Election%202017.pdf).

66 Chan Chun Sing (Minister, Prime Minister's Office), speech during the Second Reading of the Presidential Elections (Amendment) Bill, *Singapore Parliamentary Debates: Official Report*, 6 February 2017, vol. 94.

67 PEA (n. 7), s 8F(2).

68 *Ibid.*, s 8G(2)(b)(ii).

69 *Ibid.*, s 8J(2).

70 *Ibid.*, ss 8G(4)(b) and 8H(4)(b).

71 Teo, speech during the Second Reading of the Constitution of the Republic of Singapore (Amendment) Bill (n. 39).

72 For further discussion, see Jaclyn Neo's "Constitutionalizing minority representation: the reserved elections mechanism and politicization of ethnicity in Singapore", Chapter 5 in this volume.

73 Constitution (n. 5). Article 18(12) has the distinction of being a finality clause in a constitutional text, but apart from taking precedence over inconsistent ordinary legislation, it is submitted that there is no particular reason why it should have a different legal effect from a finality clause in such legislation.

74 PEA (n. 7).
75 A number of decisions have affirmed the effectiveness of ouster clauses, but arguably without fully considering relevant cases: see, for example, *Mohamed Yusoff bin Mohd Haniff* v. *Umi Kalsom bte Abas (Attorney-General, non-party)* [2010] 3 SLR 481, 488, [25] (HC); and *Cheong Chun Yin* v. *Attorney-General* [2014] SGHC 124, [2014] 3 SLR 1141, 1151–1152, [28]–[31] (HC).
76 [1999] SGHC 183, [1999] 2 SLR(R) 866 (HC).
77 [1968] UKHL 6, [1969] 2 AC 147, 171 (HL).
78 *Stansfield* (n. 76), 874, [21]–[22], quoting *South East Asia Fire Bricks Sdn Bhd* v. *Non-Metallic Mineral Products Manufacturing Employees Union* [1980] UKPC 21, [1981] AC 363, 370 (PC on appeal from Malaysia). The finality clause in question in *Stansfield* was s 14(5) of the Employment Act (Cap. 91, 1996 rev edn; now 2009 rev edn): "The decision of the Minister on any representation made under this section [for wrongful dismissal] shall be final and conclusive and shall not be challenged in any court." See also, to similar effect, *Re Application by Yee Yut Ee* [1978] SGHC 32, [1977–1978] SLR(R) 490, 494–497, [18]–[31] (HC), and *Attorney-General* v. *Ryan* [1979] UKPC 33, [1980] AC 718, 730 (PC on appeal from the Bahamas). In the latter case, the finality clause in the Bahamas Nationality Act 1973, s 16 ("[T]he decision of the Minister on any such application or order shall not be subject to appeal or review in any court"), was held not to prevent the court from inquiring into the validity of the Minister's decision on the ground that it was made without jurisdiction and *ultra vires*.
79 [2009] SGHC 154, [2009] 4 SLR(R) 92 (HC).
80 *Ibid.*, 100, [28], quoting Harry Woolf, Jeffrey Jowell and Andre Le Sueur, *De Smith's Judicial Review*, 6th edn (London: Sweet & Maxwell, 2007), [4–051]. See also *Tey Tsun Hang* v. *Attorney-General* [2014] SGHC 253, [2015] 1 SLR 856, 869–870, [44]–[45] (HC) (ouster clause upheld as matters relating to national policy best left to the Executive, and in any case the clause does not oust matters involving compliance with procedural requirements).
81 [1983] UKHL 1, [1983] 2 AC 237, 278 (HL).
82 [1992] UKHL 12, [1993] AC 682, 701–702 (HL).
83 *Ex parte Page*, *ibid.*
84 [2018] SGHC 112 (HC) (hereafter *Nagaenthran* (HC)).
85 *Ibid.*, [107].
86 *Ibid.*, [123].
87 [2015] SGCA 62, [2016] 1 SLR 1020 (CA).
88 *Ibid.*, 1048, [65] (original emphasis).
89 Li-ann Thio, "Law and the administrative state", in Kevin Y.L. Tan (ed.), *The Singapore Legal System*, 2nd edn (Singapore: Singapore University Press, 1999), 195. See *Chng Suan Tze* v. *Minister for Home Affairs* [1988] SGCA 16, [1988] 2 SLR(R) 525, 553, [86] (CA) ("All power has legal limits and the rule of law demands that the courts should be able to examine the exercise of discretionary power"), cited with approval in *Tan Seet Eng* v. *Attorney-General* [2015] SGCA 59, [2016] 1 SLR 779, 816–818, [97]–[99] (CA).
90 Chan Sek Keong, "Judicial Review – from angst to empathy: a lecture to Singapore Management University second year law students" (2010) 22 *Singapore Academy of Law Journal* 469, 477, [19]; Li-ann Thio, "The Judiciary", in *A Treatise on Singapore Constitutional Law* (Singapore: Academy Publishing, 2012) 538, [10.218]. In *Nagaenthran a/l K Dharmalingam v. Public Prosecutor* [2019] SGCA 37, [2019] 2 SLR 216 (hereafter Nagaenthran (CA)) at 248–249, [71]–[74], the Court of Appeal found it unnecessary on the facts of the case to reach a final decision on the matter, but expressed the view that a statutory clause which purports to oust the courts' power to review the legality of an executive decision, as opposed to its merits, will be regarded as "constitutionally suspect for being in violation of Art 93 of the Constitution as well as the principle of the separation of powers".

91 Cap 129, 2004 rev edn.

92 *Per Ah Seng Robin* (n. 87), 1049, [66].

93 *Ibid.*, 1049, [67].

94 *Chng Suan Tze* and *Tan Seet Eng* (n. 89).

95 Internal Security Act (Cap. 143, 1985 rev edn), s 8.

96 Criminal Law (Temporary Provisions) Act (Cap. 67, 2000 rev edn) (hereafter CLTPA), s 30.

97 *Chng Suan Tze* (n. 89) 563, [119]; *Tan Seet Eng* (n. 89) 808, [74]. As is well known, the Court of Appeal's ruling in *Chng Suan Tze* relating to the Internal Security Act was legislatively reversed by the Constitution of the Republic of Singapore (Amendment) Act 1989 (No. 1 of 1989) and the Internal Security (Amendment) Act 1989 (No. 2 of 1989).

98 [2011] SGCA 9, [2011] 2 SLR 1189 (CA).

99 Constitution (n. 5), Art. 22P(2).

100 *Yong Vui Kong* (n. 98), 1235, [82].

101 *Ibid.*, 1235, [83].

102 CLTPA (n. 96), s 30(2), inserted by the Criminal Law (Temporary Provisions) (Amendment) Act 2018 (No. 12 of 2018), s 3.

103 K. Shanmugam (Minister for Home Affairs and Law), speech during the Second Reading of the Criminal Law (Temporary) Provisions (Amendment) Bill, *Singapore Parliamentary Debates: Official Report*, 6 February 2018, vol. 94.

104 Although the Evidence Act (Cap. 97, 1997 rev edn), s 4(3), states that:

> [w]hen one fact is declared by this Act to be conclusive proof of another, the court shall, on proof of the one fact, regard the other as proved, and shall not allow evidence to be given for the purpose of disproving it,

the wording suggests that the provision does not apply to conclusive evidence clauses in other statutes: *compare Tun Datu Haji Mustapha bin Datu Harun* v. *Tun Datuk Haji Adnan Roberts, Yang di-Pertua Negeri Sabah & Datuk Joseph Pairin Kitingan (No 2)* [1986] 2 MLJ 420, 465–6 (HC, Kota Kinabalu, Malaysia) (Evidence Act 1950 (Act 56; Malaysia), s 4(3), which is identical to Singapore's Evidence Act, s 4(3), held not applicable to the conclusive evidence clause in the Chief Minister (Incorporation) Ordinance (Cap. 23; Sabah, Malaysia), s 5).

105 [1986] QB 1114 (CA).

106 *Ibid.*, 1169–70.

107 *Ibid.*, 1172, citing *Re Yolland, Husson & Birkett Ltd* [1968] 1 Ch. 152, 158 (Ch. D).

108 *Ibid.*, 1180–1.

109 Contrast *Tun Datu Haji Mustapha* (n. 104), 465–6, where the Malaysian High Court held that the Chief Minister (Incorporation) Act, s 5 ("A notification in the *Gazette* of the appointment of any person to hold or act in the office of Chief Minister, State of Sabah, shall be conclusive evidence that such person was duly so appointed"), was primarily designed to dispense with the need for detailed proof that a person had been appointed has the Chief Minister of Sabah by providing that production of a notification published in the *Government Gazette* sufficed. The notification was only conclusive as to the fact and procedural requirements of the appointment, and did not preclude a challenge to the validity of the appointment itself. The case was applied by the Federal Court of Malaysia in *Lombard Commodities Ltd* v. *Alami Vegetable Oil Products Sdn Bhd* [2010] 2 MLJ 23, 34, [26]–[28].

110 [2007] SGCA 14, [2007] 2 SLR(R) 568 (CA).

111 *Ibid.*, 575–8, [25]–[42]. See also *Galstaun* v. *Attorney-General* [1980] SGHC 17, [1979–1980] SLR(R) 589, 592–3, [16]–[18] (HC), citing *Syed Omar bin Abdul Rahman Taha Alsagoff* v. *The Government of the State of Johore* [1979] 1 MLJ 49, 50 (PC on appeal from Malaysia) (a statutory provision stating that a declaration that certain lands were needed for specified purposes was conclusive evidence of that

fact could be treated as a nullity if the public authority had acted in bad faith and misconstrued its statutory powers or specified a purpose not allowed by the statute); and *Eng Foong Ho* v. *Attorney-General* [2009] 2 SLR(R) 542, 555–6, [39] (CA), citing *Syed Omar* and *Teng Fuh, ibid.*

112 Constitution (n. 5), Art. 4.

113 See, for instance, *Teo Soh Lung* v. *Minister for Home Affairs* [1989] 1 SLR(R) 461 (HC), [1990] 1 SLR(R) 347 (CA), where a clause freezing the law governing judicial review of decisions made under the Internal Security Act (n. 95) as at a specified date and a finality clause in s 8B of the Internal Security Act were found to be constitutional.

114 For an example of the application of harmonious construction to constitutional provisions, see *Phang Chin Hock* v. *Public Prosecutor* [1980] 1 MLJ 70, 72, in which the Federal Court of Malaysia held that the basic structure doctrine did not apply to the Malaysian Constitution.

115 Cap. 185, 2008 rev edn. For the wording of s 33B(4), see the text to n. 120.

116 *Nagaenthran* (HC) (n. 84) [82].

117 *Ibid.*, [88]. In *Nagaenthran* (CA) (n. 90), 237–239, [47]–[51], the Court of Appeal found that s 33B(4) was not in fact an ouster clause but a clause immunizing the Public Prosecutor from suit. As such, it was not unconstitutional. (This judgment was released too late to be substantively examined in the main text.)

118 As is the case for the PEA (n. 7), ss 8C (certificates of eligibility) and 8J (community certificates).

119 William Wade and Christopher Forsyth, "Restriction of remedies", in *Administrative Law*, 11th edn (Oxford: Oxford University Press, 2014), 617.

120 *Cheong Chun Yin* (n. 75).

121 *Cheong Chun Yin* (n. 75) 1151–2, [31].

122 [2015] SGCA 53, [2015] 5 SLR 1222 (CA).

123 *Ibid.*, 1235–6, [35], citing *Law Society of Singapore* v. *Tan Guat Neo Phyllis* [2007] SGHC 207, [2008] 2 SLR(R) 239, 310, [143] (CA). While the latter case did not involve any finality clause, the Court of Appeal expressed the view that the rule of law entails that the exercise of prosecutorial discretion be subject to judicial review on the grounds of bad faith and contravention of constitutional protections and rights: *ibid.*, 313, [149].

124 *Constitutional Commission Report* (n. 2), [4.96].

125 The existing members of the PEC are the Chairman of the Public Service Commission, who serves as the Chairman of the PEC; the Chairman of the Accounting and Corporate Regulatory Authority; and a member of the Presidential Council for Minority Rights appointed by the Chairman of that Council: Constitution (n. 5), Arts 18(2)(a)–(c).

126 The recommendation was implemented by the Constitution, *ibid.*, Art. 18(2)(d).

127 *Ibid.*, Art. 18(2)(f).

128 *Ibid.*, Art. 18(2)(e): see the *Constitutional Commission Report* (n. 2), [4.92].

129 *Constitutional Commission Report, ibid.*

130 The PEC is also required to consult the Attorney-General if it desires advice on any question of law arising in the performance of its duties: Presidential Elections (Certificate of Eligibility) Regulations 2017 (n. 11), reg 33.

131 The Presidential Elections (Community Declaration and Community Certificate) Regulations 2017 (n. 56), reg 5(1)(d) provides that a Sub-Committee may "consult any person" when deciding whether a declarant belongs to a certain community. Under reg 5(2)(d), the CC may do the same when deciding whether to invite a declarant to submit another community declaration.

132 Presidential Elections (Certificate of Eligibility) Regulations (n. 11), regs 13–32 read with the Schedule, Form 1, Annex B5.

133 Thio, "(S)electing the President" (n. 14), 527.

134 Curiously, Article 19B(5) was not mentioned when the reserved election scheme was challenged for inconsistency with Article 12(2) in *Ravi s/o Madasamy* v. *Attorney-General* [2017] SGHC 163, [2017] 5 SLR 489 (HC). Instead, the High Court relied on, among other things, the fact that Article 12(2) prohibits discrimination "[e]xcept as expressly authorised by this Constitution": *ibid.*, 524–5, [81]–[84].

135 See *Lim Meng Suang* v. *Attorney-General* [2014] SGCA 53, [2015] 1 SLR 26 (CA), discussed in Jack Tsen-Ta Lee, "Equality and Singapore's first constitutional challenges to the criminalization of male homosexual conduct" (2015) 16 *Asia-Pacific Journal on Human Rights and the Law* 150, and Jaclyn L. Neo, "Equal protection and the reasonable classification test in Singapore: after *Lim Meng Suang* v. *Attorney-General*" [2016] *Singapore Journal of Legal Studies* 95.

136 That is, the qualifications set out in the Constitution (n. 45), Arts 19(2)(e) and (g): *ibid.*, Art. 18(12).

137 *Ibid.*, Art. 19(2)(d) read with Art. 45(1)(b) and (c).

138 Emphasis added. On the meaning of *Election Judge*, see the text to n. 27.

139 *Ezion Holdings Ltd* v. *Teras Cargo Transport Pte Ltd* [2016] SGHC 175, [2016] 5 SLR 226, 231–232, [18] (HC), citing *Tee Soon Kay* v. *Attorney-General* [2007] SGCA 27, [2007] 3 SLR(R) 133, 148, [41] (CA).

140 See generally the PEA (n. 7), ss 68–76, and the Supreme Court (Presidential Elections) (Application for Avoidance of Election) Rules (Cap. 322, R 7, 2007 rev edn).

141 *Ibid.*, s 8B.

142 *Ibid.*, s 8I.

143 *Ibid.*, ss 36A and 36C.

144 The maximum amount is S$600,000 or 30 cents per elector, whichever is greater: PEA (n. 7) s 50(1). Based on the number of electors as of 28 August 2017, the maximum amount for the 2017 Presidential Election was $754,982.40: "Campaigning Guidelines for the Presidential Election" (Elections Department website, Prime Minister's Office, 29 August 2017) [21] www.eld.gov.sg/pressrelease/PreE2017/Press%20Release%20on%20Campaigning%20Guidelines%20for%20the%20Presidential%20Election.pdf (accessed 9 September 2017) (archived at https://web.archive.org/web/20170909004737/www.eld.gov.sg/pressrelease/PreE2017/Press%20Release%20on%20Campaigning%20Guidelines%20for%20the%20Presidential%20Election.pdf) (hereafter Campaigning Guidelines).

145 Not to exceed 850 by 600 mm, except for posters on the day and at the site of any election rally held by a candidate: Presidential Elections (Election Advertising) Regulations (Cap. 240A, Rg 3, 2000 rev edn) (hereafter Election Advertising Regulations), regs 6(1) and (3).

146 Tessa Wong, "Tan Kin Lian: President should speak up publicly", *The Straits Times* (Singapore, 28 July 2010), A6.

147 Leong Wee Keat, "Candidates cross swords", *Today* (Singapore, 24 August 2011).

148 The Minister for Law relied on the Constitution (n. 5), Art. 21(1):

> Except as provided by this Constitution, the President shall, in the exercises of his functions under this Constitution or any other written law, act in accordance with the advice of the Cabinet or of a Minister acting under the general authority of the Cabinet.

and constitutional conventions applicable to the British monarch that Singapore inherited from the United Kingdom: see K. Shanmugam, "Speech by Minister for Foreign Affairs and Law, Mr K. Shanmugam, at the Institute of Policy Studies Forum on the Elected Presidency", Ministry of Law website (5 August 2011) http://app.2.mlaw.gov.sg/News/tabid/204/Default.aspx?ItemId=567 (accessed 7 April 2012); archived at https://web.archive.org/web/20120407001233/http://app.2.mlaw.

gov.sg/News/tabid/204/Default.aspx?ItemId=567; see also Teh Shi Ning, "The President's Role and Powers: Shanmugam", *The Business Times* (Singapore, 6 August 2011).

149 *Constitutional Commission Report* (n. 2), 130, [7.15].

150 *Ibid.*, 130–1, [7.16].

151 PEA (n. 7), s 9(3)(c)(iii).

152 Section B of Form P4 in the Schedule to the Presidential Elections (Forms and Fees) Regulations (Cap. 240A, Rg 1, 2000 rev edn), as amended by the Presidential Elections (Forms and Fees) (Amendment) Regulations 2017 (S 266/2017). The Presidential Elections (Certificate of Eligibility) Regulations 2017 (n. 11), r 35, states: "For the purpose of section 9(3)(c)(iii) of the [Presidential Elections] Act, the Returning Officer may provide explanatory material on the role of the President to a prospective candidate." During the 2017 Presidential Election, the Returning Officer issued a document titled "Explanatory Material on Role of the President under the Constitution of the Republic of Singapore", Elections Department website (1 June 2017) www.eld.gov.sg/Resources/Presidential/Explanatory%20Material%20on%20Role%20of%20the%20President%20under%20the%20Constitution%20of%20the%20Republic%20of%20Singapore.pdf (accessed 10 May 2018) (archived at https://web.archive.org/web/20180510081808/www.eld.gov.sg/Resources/Presidential/Explanatory%20Material%20on%20Role%20of%20the%20President%20under%20the%20Constitution%20of%20the%20Republic%20of%20Singapore.pdf).

153 Cap 211, 2001 rev edn.

154 *Constitutional Commission Report* (n. 2), 128, [7.12]–[7.13].

155 Campaigning Guidelines (n. 144), [14].

156 "Press Release: Presidential Election 2017", Elections Department website, Prime Minister's Office (28 August 2017) [9] www.eld.gov.sg/pressrelease/PreE2017/Press%20Release%20on%20Presidential%20Election%202017.pdf (accessed 8 September 2017) (archived at https://web.archive.org/web/20170908154526/www.eld.gov.sg/pressrelease/PreE2017/Press%20Release%20on%20Presidential%20Election%202017.pdf).

157 "Voluntary undertaking on campaigning by presidential election candidate", Election Department website, Prime Minister's Office, www.eld.gov.sg/Resources/Presidential/Voluntary%20Undertaking%20on%20Campaigning%20by%20Presidential%20Election%20Candidate.pdf (accessed 17 May 2018), also reproduced in Annex A of the *Presidential Election 2017 Candidate Handbook* (Elections Department, Prime Minister's Office 2017) 53 www.eld.gov.sg/pdf/CandidateHandbookforPresidentialElection2017.pdf (accessed 9 May 2018) (archived at https://web.archive.org/web/20180509113641/www.eld.gov.sg/pdf/Candidate%20Handbook%20for%20Presidential%20Election%202017.pdf).

158 Election Advertising Regulations (n. 145).

159 Pursuant to the PEA (n. 7), s 60AA(1)(b).

160 Election Advertising Regulations (n. 145), regs 1B and 1C(2).

161 *Ibid.*, reg 1C(1).

162 *Ibid.*, reg 1C(3).

163 *Ibid.*, reg 1D.

164 By the Parliamentary Elections (Amendment) Act 2010 (No. 10 of 2010) and the Presidential Elections (Amendment) Act 2010 (No. 11 of 2010), both in force with effect from 1 July 2010.

165 PEA (n. 7), s 60A(1).

166 *Ibid.*, s 60A(2)(c).

167 "Press Release: Cooling-off Day and Polling Day – General Election 2015", Elections Department website (9 September 2015) [5(f)] www.eld.gov.sg/pressrelease/ParE2015/Press%20Release%20on%20Cooling-Off%20Day%20and%20Polling%20Day.pdf (accessed 1 May 2017) (archived at https://web.archive.org/web/20170501231459/

www.eld.gov.sg/pressrelease/ParE2015/Press%20Release%20on%20Cooling-Off%20Day%20and%20Polling%20Day.pdf). Based on this information from the Elections Department, a similarly worded statement was published on the Government's website *Factually*: see "What happens on cooling-off day?", *Factually*, Government of Singapore website, (25 August 2015) www.gov.sg/factually/content/what-happens-on-cooling-off-day (accessed 31 March 2016) (archived at https://web.archive.org/web/20160331083504/www.gov.sg/factually/content/what-happens-on-cooling-off-day).

168 Parliamentary Elections Act (n. 38).

169 The Amendment Act was the Parliamentary Elections (Amendment) Act 2010 (n. 164).

170 By the Presidential Elections (Amendment) Act 2010, *ibid.*

171 K. Shanmugam (Minister for Law and Home Affairs), speech during the Second Reading of the Parliamentary Elections (Amendment) Bill, *Singapore Parliamentary Debates: Official Report*, 27 April 2010, vol. 87, cols 238 (emphasis added).

172 *Ibid.*, cols 285–6 (emphasis added).

173 Constitution (n. 5), Arts 19A(1)(c) and (d).

174 *Ibid.*, Art. 19(2)(f).

175 Campaigning Guidelines (n. 144), [17]. There does not appear to be any legislative backing for this advisory. The only persons expressly excluded from taking part in election activity are students attending primary or secondary schools; persons against whom orders of police supervision have been made under the Criminal Law (Temporary Provisions) Act (Cap. 67, 2000 rev edn), s 30(b); undischarged bankrupts; and non-citizens: PEA (n. 7), s 65(1). *Election activity* is defined as including "any activity which is done for the purpose of promoting or procuring the election of any candidate at any election other than clerical work wholly performed within enclosed premises": *ibid.*, s 65(8).

176 Thio, "(S)electing the President" (n. 14), 537–8.

177 *Constitutional Commission Report* (n. 2), 131–2, [7.18].

178 Thio, "(S)electing the President" (n. 14), 538.

179 *Nagaenthran* (CA) (n. 90): see the text to nn. 114–16.

8 Of Constitutional Commissions and expert-led interpretation during processes of constitutional change

Maartje De Visser

8.1 Introduction

In an 1816 letter, Thomas Jefferson expressed himself in favour of including a provision in the constitution that would prescribe its regular upkeep. "[E]ach generation", the Founding Father wrote, ought to be able to revise the constitution "every nineteen or twenty years", so it could "be handed on, with periodical repairs, from generation to generation, to the end of time."[1] As we know, his advice was not heeded: the U.S. Constitution is notoriously difficult to change, with the longest interval between two amendments running to slightly more than six decades.[2] Closer to home, the Singapore Constitution similarly does not mandate generational maintenance. The absence of any prescription to that effect, however, has not inhibited regular revision, occasionally at a pace that even exceeds the Jeffersonian idea. The amendment that forms the central focus of this volume sought to reform the Presidency about a generational interlude – 25 years to be exact – after it became a popularly elective office. When first announcing the prospect of changes to the institution of the Elected President, Prime Minister Lee Hsien Loong noted, in language evocative of that used in the 1816 letter, that "we need to continue to review and adjust the scheme regularly, to keep it functional and in good repair".[3]

Unlike the other chapters in this volume, this chapter will not explore the relative merits and remaining challenges attendant on the substantive changes that were made to the Constitution in 2016. Instead, it explores extra-legislative and extra-judicial processes along the route that led to its adoption. More particularly, this chapter critically examines the involvement of a Constitutional Commission in the reform process, it being only the second time since the country's independence that such a body was established to lay the groundwork for a constitutional revision.[4]

I seek to develop two claims in relation to the practice of relying on a Constitutional Commission when the formal procedure to amend the constitution is about to be initiated.

First, the use of a Constitutional Commission can infuse reform processes with greater popular credentials and may allow the resultant changes to take firmer root in the public's consciousness. This would be in line with the contemporary theme of fostering public participation in constitutional design,[5] traces of which can already be found in Jefferson's letter. In the case of the 2016 amendment process, however, the possible virtues of popular input did not materialize to the extent possible. This chapter suggests reasons as to why this may have happened and offers some policy prescriptions to improve future amendment trajectories that include a Constitutional Commission.

Second, a Constitutional Commission may bridge the distinction typically drawn between constitution-making and constitution-application. Adaptive interpretation is typically conceived as an alternative to formal constitutional revision.[6] In recommending the need for and proposed formulation of new formal constitutional rules, some thought will however inevitably have to be given to the meaning that should be attributed to these rules. As a body whose involvement is envisaged for the initial stages of the amendment process, a Constitutional Commission can contribute in a more or less significant manner to fleshing out the meaning that the suggested new constitutional rules should bear. This reality confirms the need for constitutional scholars to carefully study the entire process of making formal changes, especially in jurisdictions like Singapore that tend to shy away from "living instrument" or progressive interpretations of their Constitution.[7]

8.2 Constitutional amendment processes, democracy and technocracy

These are the heydays of constitutional change: empirical studies have shown that each year, multiple countries across the world replace or thoroughly revise their big-C constitution.[8] The manner in which a new constitution is made or an existing text is revised has begun to elicit a keen interest from academics and policy makers.[9] The reason is simple: the amendment process will at least in part shape the content of the eventual constitutional text as well as its subsequent acceptance by the recipient society. Constitutional change is not a value-free or neutral exercise. The range of rights to be protected, the kind of government structure to be created and the distribution of competences among State organs or levels often reflect the interests and concerns of those with a seat at the drafting table or otherwise able to make their voice heard.[10] Notwithstanding, or perhaps precisely because of, this reality framers and foreign advisers are increasingly urged to attempt to make the process inclusive by featuring the population in some way or another.[11] This is a reflection of the classic legal fiction that: "[a]s regards the constitution, 'We the people' is its author and font of legitimacy as well as its master and chief beneficiary."[12] Participation is further said to enhance involvement with the polity and render the outcome more palatable, which should lead to societal respect for and compliance with the new constitutional text.[13] This view is premised on the 'developmental citizen': individuals should have an active voice as regards fundamental legal changes that directly impact on their lives and human flourishing.[14]

Popular involvement in constitutional amendment procedures can take a variety of forms. Citizens may have the right to initiate the process by proposing an amendment, as in the Philippines or Thailand;[15] they may be able to elect the representatives that draft and debate the new text;[16] they may have the right to participate in the discussions, as in Canada;[17] or they play a part in ratifying the changes through voting in a popular referendum, as is for instance prescribed in Australia, New Zealand and Sri Lanka.[18]

At the same time, Ginsburg has astutely noted that the process of formal constitutional change:

> [I]s not only a competition among different actors, but a competition among *different forms of expertise*. Law competes with political science, economics and other disciplines; technocrats compete with interest groups to articulate their positions.[19]

While his focus was on constitution-making, it is submitted that Ginsburg's point applies *a fortiori* to amendments. When tinkering with only (a small) part of the text, there is a need for legal expertise to safeguard the constitution's internal logic and coherence; and when the proposed changes concern financial or procedural provisions, imbuing the amendment process with technical expertise should result in new constitutional arrangements that are workable and hence able to generate output legitimacy. It is moreover an open question whether citizens would even relish the opportunity to participate in the making of such amendments, notably if revisions are scheduled in relatively quick succession.

Now, participation and expertise are of course not mutually exclusive. On the contrary, processes of constitutional change will typically combine both democratic and technocratic elements. This is, among others, the case when preparatory Constitutional Commissions are used. Such commissions are usually composed of legally qualified persons and other experts, while simultaneously being charged to consult widely among the public. The extent to which the democratic potential of Constitutional Commissions is actually realized will depend on the manner in which the public is able to submit representations and how these are engaged with. Section 8.3.3 explores how Singapore's 2016 Constitutional Commission fared in this respect.

Before doing so, it is worth recalling the likely benefits attendant on using a Constitutional Commission as well as possible costs that will serve as a helpful reference point for the discussion to follow. The establishment and recommendations of a Constitutional Commission are typically picked up by mainstream media, thereby raising awareness among the general public about the prospect of constitutional reform and making the issues under study watercooler conversation topics. In addition, and as just mentioned, such commissions are expected to solicit views from within the citizenry. This happens, crucially, before the text of the amendment bill is drawn up and send to parliament for debate. Different from popular ratification, which only offers citizens a 'yay' or 'nay' vote on the end product, early consultation should accordingly allow for some public control over the eventual amendment. The fact that Constitutional

Commissions operate at arm's length of the Government of the day may further encourage active engagement with its work by the citizenry. On the other hand, citizens may experience reform fatigue, notably when amendments happen semi-regularly. People could become desensitized or disinterested in constitutional change, with fewer high quality contributions being received by the Constitutional Commission as a corollary. From an organizational perspective, the Government may face difficulties in finding qualified members to sit on such a commission. This holds true notably for countries with a smaller pool of eligible candidates, bearing in mind that seats are typically reserved for those holding citizenship. Finally, the Government and Parliament could point to the extensive preparatory work done by a Constitutional Commission as obviating the need for them to similarly dedicate significant time and resources to deliberations regarding the amendment.

In view of these considerations, it is unsurprising that there is no constitution that mandates the establishment of a Constitutional Commission as part of its formal amendment procedure. Establishing such a commission involves the exercise of unfettered discretion on the part of the Government. In Singapore, Constitutional Commissions have been a rarity, especially when compared to the number of times the Constitution has been amended. The first such commission was the Rendel Commission, named after its chair as per common practice, appointed by Governor Nicoll during the twilight years of colonial occupation.[20] Since independence, Constitutional Commissions have only been set up on two other occasions. In 1966, the Wee Chong Jin Commission was asked to consider how best to safeguard the rights of minorities[21] and in 2016, the Menon Commission was tasked to proffer recommendations on selected aspects pertaining to the Elected Presidency.[22]

In Singapore, it is common practice for the Government to keep the preparation of constitutional revisions in its own hands. This is a manifestation of a strong national tradition of expert-led governance, whereby citizens are conceived as relatively passive beneficiaries of State actions.[23] The preference for an elite-driven approach was set out in clear terms in the 1991 White Paper on Shared Values. This White Paper embraced the Confucian conception of "government by honorable men … who have a duty to do right for the people, and who have the trust and respect of the population."[24] As far as daily governance is concerned, significant confidence is placed in the State's strong bureaucracy. As Prime Minister Lee Hsien Loong said in a 2005 speech, in Singapore, "civil servants [are shielded] from political interference [and given] the space to work out rational, effective solutions for our problems … in Singapore administrative officers can practice public administration in almost laboratory conditions."[25] Think further of the existence of bodies like the Presidential Council for Minority Rights or the Council of Presidential Advisers[26] that must provide expert advice on designated topics or in specific circumstances, the unique category of Nominated Members Parliament[27] and the stringent eligibility criteria for the office of the Presidency.[28]

In this regard, Singapore is not unique. A study on constitution-making exercises in Asia has found that "there does not appear to be a pattern of popular participation in Asian constitution-making … [it] tends to be an elite affair."[29] Matters do not seem to be very different as far as amendments are concerned. The constitutions of the majority of ASEAN countries – with the exception of Myanmar, the Philippines and Thailand[30] – do not envisage any role for the people in the amendment process.

8.3 Commissioning Constitutional Reform of Singapore's Elected Presidency

8.3.1 The rationale for the 2016 Menon Constitutional Commission

The People's Action Party (PAP), which has ruled Singapore since independence, has tended to retain strict control over the drafting and adoption of constitutional amendments. The Government typically holds internal deliberations on the need for, and desired content of, an amendment and subsequently announces the outcome of these deliberations through a Prime Ministerial speech. As the PAP continues to hold more than two-thirds of the seats in Parliament – the required supermajority for constitutional revisions – the actual adoption of an amendment is all but guaranteed and usually accomplished with alacrity. As mentioned, in 2016, the Government however chose to make use of a Constitutional Commission. The opportunity thus created for early-stage popular input held out the promise of imbuing resultant constitutional changes with more social legitimacy. Whether that indeed happened is the main subject of this section.

The Government's intention to convene a Constitutional Commission was first made public in Prime Minister Lee Hsien Loong's speech, delivered in the wake of the President's annual address in late January 2016.[31] The main theme of that speech was the need to ensure that Singapore can stay abreast of new global and local developments – a familiar refrain that shows that even after the celebration of its golden anniversary, traces of existential angst and survival linger in the national psyche. A future-proof system, the Prime Minister noted, was not only to be a question of good policies, but also of good politics. It was the latter that he focused on, the logic being that systemic arrangements ought regularly to be investigated to preserve their effectiveness in the medium to long term: "it is this generation's responsibility to make sure that our political institutions and system continue to work well, well beyond the term of this [Prime Minister and Cabinet], and work well for future generations."[32] Three institutions were identified as warranting review and possible adjustment: the Non-Constituency Members of Parliament (NCMP); the Group Representative Constituencies (GRCs); and the office of the Elected Presidency. A common feature is that all have a bearing on the relationship between the incumbent political party and the available room for the opposition to partake in the exercise of government powers. Additionally, this selection signals a concern with minority race representation in the upper echelons of government: the official justification for the introduction of the GRC in the late 1980s was to guarantee the election of Malay and Indian candidates to Parliament[33] and a central reason to single out the Presidency for review was the perceived importance of keeping occupancy of this office within reach of minority candidates.[34]

Of particular interest for the purpose of this chapter is that only the third institution – the Elected Presidency – was deemed suitable for referral to a Constitutional Commission for study and recommendations. In relation to the NCMP and GRC schemes, the Government followed the typical approach to amending the Singapore Constitution: it had held internal Cabinet deliberations and used the Prime Minister's speech to announce the outcome thereof. This was because the Government believed that the underlying justification for having both institutions remained sound, meaning that all that was required was some tinkering around the edges. In the case of the NCMP scheme, the relevant constitutional provision would be revised to enhance the voting rights and increase the minimum number of NCMPs. No constitutional amendment would be pursued for the GRC scheme as the decision to have smaller GRCs could simply be implemented by the Electoral Boundaries Review Committee.

This begs the question why the Government decided to take a different tack for the evaluation of the office of the Elected Presidency. No answers are provided in the Prime Minister's speech, which merely announces the imminent creation of a Constitutional Commission without saying anything about the Government's intention or expectations. When speculating about its motivations, it is worth recalling that this is only the second time in Singapore's history that such a commission has been set up. A great many and arguably more radical changes to the Constitution – such as the creation of the NCMP and GRC schemes and the Elected Presidency itself – were effected without a Constitutional Commission being used to assist in the preparations.

So why now, and why for this institution only? A combination of rationales may be suggested. On the one hand, the PAP Government appears to have been concerned about the spectre of a 'freak election' in which its preferred candidate for the Presidency would fail to win the popular vote. This almost happened during the 2011 Presidential Election, when the PAP-endorsed candidate Tony Tan Keng Yam clinched the victory by a razor-thin margin of less than 1 per cent. It must be remembered that the choice to transform the Presidency from an appointed to an elected office and the simultaneous grant of veto powers to this office over annual budgets drawing from past reserves and key public service appointments was itself in response to the fear of a freak parliamentary election in which the PAP would lose its majority.[35] The Elected President was conceived as a bulwark against an incoming rogue government that would make nought of the country's financial and human resources. The prospect, however slim, of the intended custodian going rogue instead (or as well!) would be diametrically opposed to the very *raison d'être* of the office and as such ought to be pre-emptively addressed. Indeed, in his January 2016 speech, the Prime Minister emphasized the importance of ensuring that only qualified and competent individuals with a solid understanding of the responsibilities of the office would be able to be Elected President. This comes out clearly in his comments about the 2011 election: "Regrettably, during the last Presidential Election, those who did not understand [that the President has no executive, policy-making role] included some candidates. They campaigned for President *as if they were going to form an alternate Government*."[36] He added that this seemed to be a widespread misunderstanding that has persisted "even now [among] quite a number of people".[37] The hope may have been that the publicity about the role and powers of the Elected President likely to be generated by the work of a Constitutional Commission could help dispel such misunderstandings and hence, reduce the risk of a freak presidential election result. On this view, the Constitutional Commission would primarily be conceived as a useful tool for civic education.

A related though distinct rationale concerns the desire to safeguard racial minority representation.[38] In 1999, the then Senior Minister Lee Kuan Yew said that the Government would seek to achieve alternation among the various races by ensuring that its nominated candidates would be racially diverse over time and lending the strongest possible support for these candidates. The 2011 Presidential Election would have cast doubt on the sustainability of this tactic. Alternative methods for minority representation would likely involve some form of affirmative action that could be controversial among the general public, given Singapore's meritocratic ethos. Using a Constitutional Commission that would actively solicit feedback and engage with the public is clearly a better strategy to win societal support for a special minority scheme than merely debating the matter in Parliament in line with the normal procedure for changing the Constitution.[39] Furthermore, any suggestion to this effect would seem more palatable coming from a neutral and independent body as opposed to emanating from the Government itself.[40]

8.3.2 Mandate and composition

The Constitutional Commission was not be expected to perform a comprehensive review of the Elected Presidency. As with the NCMP and GRC scheme, the underlying premise was deemed sound: the office should remain a directly elected one. Instead, three specific and relatively technical aspects were singled out for evaluation: the eligibility criteria for those interested in running to become the Elected President; the election of minorities to the office; and the role and composition of the Council of Presidential Advisers (CPA). This is a marked contrast with the decidedly more generous mandate of the 1966 Wee Chong Jin Commission, which was asked to advise on the design of institutional, procedural and substantive constitutional safeguards to build a multiracial society. These broad Terms of Reference notwithstanding, the Wee Chong Jin Commission ended up making but a small contribution to Singapore's constitutional architecture, as few of its recommendations were accepted.

The 2016 Constitutional Commission was officially convened less than two weeks after the Prime Minister's speech and duly given Terms of Reference that mirrored those laid out in that speech.[41] Like its 1966 predecessor, it was headed by the Singapore Chief Justice. Alongside CJ Sundaresh Menon sat eight other members that can broadly be divided into two categories. Those in the first group held public office or have done so in the past. These were Justice Tay Yong Kwang, who has held various positions within the Singapore Judiciary and the Singapore Legal Service since the early 1980s; Eddie Teo, a career civil servant and current chairman of the country's strong Public Service Commission; Abdullah Tarmugi, whose political career comprised stints as the minister-in-charge of Muslim Affairs and Speaker of Parliament and who is presently a member of the Presidential Council for Minority Rights; and Chan Heng Chee, a professor in political science who also sits on the Presidential Council for Minority Rights.[42]

The second category of membership comprised prominent business executives, to wit, Chua Thian Poh, the Chair and founder of local real estate developer Ho Bee Land; Philip Ng Chee Tat, the CEO of Far East Organization, a family-owned property development and investment group; Peter Seah Lim Huat, Chair of the home-grown DBS Bank, among others; and Wong Ngit Liong, Chairman and CEO of technology-service provider Venture. Neither the Wee Chong Jin Commission nor the Rendel Commission included members who were appointed to represent the private sector and contribute commercial insights. Having such voices on the Menon Commission was arguably necessary given its brief to investigate the need to tighten the eligibility criteria for presidential hopefuls, in particular those coming from the private sector. As an op-ed written shortly after its establishment put it, having the

> head honchos of Singapore's largest corporations [on the Commission] suggests that this constitutional review is largely about addressing a human resource issue – determining the credentials for a financially astute leader – rather than issues of constitutionalism, which the Wee Commission faced.[43]

The decision to populate Constitutional Commissions with individuals that have extensive practical legal or other experience and tailor their make-up to fit the nature of the items included in their Terms of Reference confirms Singapore's proclivity for expertise-led governance. The presence of these persons on the Commission ensured that it had sophisticated 'in-house' legal expertise, including regarding the manner in which the existing constitutional framework should be understood. It would only be on that basis that the Commission would subsequently be able to recommend sensible improvements to the existing regime. The importance of members with a legal background was underscored in the ministerial statement announcing the creation of what became the Wee Chong Jin Commission: "The Government has decided that this Commission shall consist of legally qualified persons, who will know what is feasible and practical of constitutional guarantee."[44] (Former) public office holders moreover have a good grasp of the political realities that shape the actual functioning of State institutions. This is especially useful when the matters referred to a Constitutional Commission for study centre on the design of the rules pertaining to the branches of Government or their constituent parts, as in the case of the Menon Commission. At the same time, staffing the Commission with persons tied to the political establishment and very familiar with its political philosophy may lead a government to believe – justifiably or not – that the recommendations will be in line with its political preferences.

The approach taken in other jurisdictions is noticeably different, as these tend to be more amenable to reserve several spots on such commissions for prominent constitutional scholars. This was, among others, so in Australia, where two of the five members of the 1985 Constitutional Commission charged with conducting a fundamental review of the entire Constitution held professorships[45] as well as in Canada, where three of the five seats on the 1937 Rowell-Sirois Commission that successfully advised on federal-province relations were filled by academics, including the Chair.[46] Although the composition of both of Singapore's Constitutional Commissions was strongly oriented towards practical expertise, neither was deprived of more constitutional-theoretical insights. Academic perspectives were infused in the deliberations as a result of their outreach to the public for representations and it is to this participatory dimension of the Commission process that the chapter now turns.

8.3.3 "Do you hear the people?"

The Menon Commission took slightly more than half a year to complete its work: its report was submitted to the Government on 17 August 2016.[47] During that period, it convened seven formal meetings that were supplemented by informal exchanges among some or all Commission members. A significant portion of its time, however, was dedicated to engagement with contributions from the public, in line with the explicit instruction to that effect in its Terms of Reference. The remainder of this section explains how the Menon Commission has sought to enhance the democratic credentials of its eventual report. It will become clear that it should generally be commended for its approach, in particular the evident commitment to transparency.

At its maiden meeting, the members agreed that they would "benefit from inviting representations from the public".[48] The Commission duly issued a call for written submissions on the matters within its purview. This was done through the media about a week after its formal appointment, meaning that the Commission was able to capitalize on the publicity surrounding its establishment and presumably reach all those potentially interested in sharing their views. The consultation period ran for just over a month, from 18 February to 21 March 2016, and resulted in 107 written submissions being received.[49] With the exception of a handful of contributors desiring anonymity or having offered defamatory feedback, the names of all contributors were included in the final report as Annex A. This mirrors the approach taken by the Wee Chong Jin Commission and should be evaluated positively from an accountability perspective, as it reveals which interests or concerns may have shaped the Commission's deliberations and its eventual recommendations.

Two points are worth noting. First, a relatively wide range of individuals and entities took advantage of the opportunity provided to make their views known. As was to be expected given the nature of the reform, these included academics working in the field of (Singapore) constitutional law and sociology. Several lawyers and law students similarly sent in submissions. So too did leading local civil society organizations, such as AWARE (campaigning for gender equality) and MARUAH (advocating for the promotion of human rights). With the exception of the Eurasian Association, no memoranda were however submitted by any other community-based organizations. This is disappointing, given the Commission's task of considering how to safeguard minority representation in the Presidency. It is also in striking contrast to the experience of the Wee Chong Jin Commission, which received input from a vast number of such organizations like the Tamilian Association, the Sikh Advisory Board and the Indian Chamber of Commerce. The non-participation of community-based organizations detracts from the representativeness of the views obtained, which is particularly undesirable when minority interest questions are on the table for review. Future Constitutional Commissions may therefore want to actively solicit feedback from these kinds of organizations and explicitly note their effort in doing so in the report if their outreach efforts would not have the desired effect. A further category of respondents consisted of those with an overt political perspective, including opposition parties (the Workers' Party and the People's Power Party) and a former politician.[50] The two previous incumbents of the office under examination also shared their views at this early stage of the constitution-amendment process: outgoing President Tony Tan (2011–2017) and his predecessor Mr S.R. Nathan (1999–2011).

Second, different types of contributors appear to have focused on different aspects of the Commission's Terms of Reference, with few offering comprehensive feedback. For instance, the stringency of the eligibility criteria for the office of the Presidency primarily drew comments from legal academics, those with a business background devoted attention to the criteria for private-sector candidates and sociologists were keen to provide input on the question of minority representation. At the same time, some contributors commented on issues that were outside the ambit of the Commission's Terms of Reference. These were however not discounted in the subsequent deliberations and report, but in fact appear to have induced the Menon Commission to follow suit, as will be recounted in greater detail below.

Having discussed the written submissions internally, the Commission invited 20 of the 107 contributors to elaborate on their views during four public hearings in late April and early May 2016. The composition of the shortlist was motivated by the Commission's desire to hear from those whose written briefs had provoked questions that would benefit from oral elucidation as well as from contributors who had set out their thinking particularly carefully or comprehensively. When looking at the names of the invited contributors – that, too, were included in Annex A to the eventual report – it is clear that these categories notably comprised Singapore constitutional law scholars and sociologists. The

Commission furthermore intimated that it had wanted to ensure that the line-up "would reflect a broad cross-section of society, including civil society groups and young Singaporeans".[51] As such, AWARE, MARUAH, the Eurasian Association and several law students were given the opportunity to make representations during the public hearings. Only one contributor, the Workers' Party, refused the invitation to participate in the hearings as it preferred to air its views during the course of the parliamentary debate on the eventual amendment bill. This was arguably not unexpected: the Workers' Party has never been comfortable with the idea of casting the President as a check on the Government and has instead spoken out in favour of changing Parliament so that it can better fulfil its natural role as accountability forum. This option was, however, outside the Commission's Terms of Reference, making a submission on this wider, more fundamental point appear either futile or gratuitous. This shows how a tightly circumscribed mandate focusing on the details of a constitutional institution may have the – presumably unintended – effect of discouraging participation from stakeholders who query the continued merits of that institution or its role within the overall constitutional constellation.

Moving from process to substance, the report shows that the feedback provided through the public consultation process was treated seriously and exerted influence on the Commission's thinking on several occasions. At its most basic, and beyond recording the names of those who made written or oral representations, the report recounts the substantive arguments and concerns raised, with accompanying footnotes that identify the author. Again, this is commendable from a transparency and accountability perspective. More significantly, several suggestions made by contributors were endorsed by the Commission. These included the need to extend the duration of the tenure of the qualifying office beyond the current period of three years;[52] adding a requirement that the leadership experience of prospective presidential candidates must be current;[53] requiring the Presidential Elections Committee to give reasons when refusing to issue a certificate of eligibility to an interested candidate;[54] demanding that the President should publish her opinion whenever he exercises his veto power (and not only when she concurs with intended government action or proposed money bills);[55] and ensuring better and more public education about the role and powers of the office of the Elected President.[56]

Picking up on that last point, the Commission seems to have used the public hearings to a similar effect, albeit pitched at a high level. It was keen to initiate a real dialogue with those making oral representations that could result in them changing their views on the correct frame to apply when thinking about the Elected Presidency. A good example is provided by the exchange on the merits of having stringent eligibility criteria. As the report notes, "when the point was canvassed more thoroughly during the oral hearings, several of the contributors who originally raised concerns … agreed that comparison with the criteria applicable to the office of Prime Minister might not be appropriate."[57]

A further measure of the impact of the public feedback is the fact that the report includes an entire, separate chapter devoted to points brought up in the contributions that were outside the Commission's Terms of Reference. There was, obviously, no need for it to engage with these additional matters. That it decided otherwise seems to have been due to the perceived significance of the points raised, like the desirability of constitutionally entrenching the President's discretionary powers and the fundamental question as to whether it was better to return the office from an elected to an appointed one. Relatedly, and as confirmed by these examples, all the unsolicited points were closely connected to the three aspects that the Commission had requested feedback on. While they "did not", as the report notes, "fall *squarely* within the Terms of Reference",[58] they were not so far removed as to warrant accusations that the Commission was acting ultra vires by considering these.

The fact that the Commission actively engaged with or even endorsed the unsolicited suggestions[59] signals to members of the public that the members appreciated their willingness in being a junior partner in the preparatory stages for amendment-making and validates their efforts in this regard. As long as such suggestions are logically connected to the topics on which representations are explicitly invited, this is accordingly a good practice worthy of emulation in other times and in other jurisdictions. It is to be hoped that future Constitutional Commissions will adopt a similarly encouraging approach, assuming that any unsolicited suggestions would similarly be.

8.3.4 Aftermath: political reception and formal constitutional change

The Menon Constitutional Commission submitted its recommendations to the Government in mid-August 2016, to which the latter responded with a White Paper nearly a month later.[60] The main recommendations for the three aspects under review were all accepted. The Government agreed that the eligibility criteria for those interested in running for President should be tightened, in particular for individuals coming from the private sector. The Commission's suggestions to update the original qualifying office from Chairman or CEO to the more generic "holder of the most senior executive position" as well as raising the financial clout of the company in which the prospective candidate held this position from having $100 million in paid-up capital to $500 million in shareholders' equity were taken over. In relation to the second aspect under review, safeguarding minority representation, the Government endorsed the Constitutional Commission's "hiatus-triggered mechanism" whereby a presidential election would be reserved for candidates from a particular racial group if a member from that group had not occupied the office of the Elected Presidency in the five preceding terms. Finally, the Commission's recommendation that the scope of the President's obligation to consult the Council of Presidential Advisers (CPA) before the exercise of his discretionary control powers should be extended to all fiscal matters touching on the national reserves and all key public service appointments was also accepted, as was the proposal to expand the size of the CPA to reflect its enlarged responsibilities.

There were, probably inevitably, some points on which the Government and Constitutional Commission parted company. Most of these related to relatively technical or procedural points, such as the duration for which a prospective presidential candidate should have held the qualifying office or the disclosure of the voting results within the CPA. Arguably, the most significant disagreement concerned a matter that had not been included in the Commission's Term of Reference, but was nevertheless addressed in the report as it had been the subject of public feedback. This concerned the nature of the office of the Elected President. In line with the representations made to it, the Constitutional Commission expressed itself in favour of reverting back to the old system in which the President was appointed by Parliament and only exercised symbolic functions. The custodial powers bestowed upon the Presidency when it became a directly elected office in 1990 could be better entrusted to an appointed specialist body. The Government disagreed, taking the view in the White Paper that the custodial powers could be more vigorously exercised by an institution with a popular mandate. This stance was not unexpected, as the Prime Minister had indicated as much in his January 2016 speech that initiated the constitutional reform process:

> The President must remain an elected office. If the President is not elected, he will lack the mandate to wield his custodial powers. ... [Suggestions] to go back to the old system [are] most unwise. ... [We should] not abandon the project [of fine-tuning this institution] altogether and leave ourselves naked and defenceless against all the difficulties which the elected President enables us to avoid.[61]

These comments confirm the Government's belief that the Elected Presidency remains an essential check on a possible future rogue government. As such, this constitutional reform exercise should be about improving the likelihood of future presidents following the playbook and not going rogue themselves – hence the stricter eligibility criteria and enhanced role for the CPA.

The constitutional reform process continued to move apace after the publication of the White Paper. On 10 October 2016, a Bill setting out the proposed amendments to the Constitution was tabled in Parliament.[62] Its second reading took place in early November. After a three-day deliberation, the Bill was passed on 9 November with 77 votes to 6.[63] While space constraints prevent a full examination of the points canvassed during the parliamentary debate,[64] in keeping with the focus of this chapter a few comments are warranted about the procedure followed. In particular, no Select Committee for considering the Bill was set up nor were there other arrangements made by Parliament for public consultation. The thinking appears to have been that such would have been superfluous, as the Constitutional Commission would have catered to whatever demand for participation that existed within society. This comes out clearly in the White Paper's description of the consultation conducted by the Commission. We can read that its "wide consultation allowed a broad spectrum of views to be canvassed, *by all persons who had an interest in coming forward*".[65] Those who accepted the open invitation to contribute "represented a broad cross-section of society"[66] and those who did not would have heard about the tenor of those representations as the "public hearings were extensively reported in local media, and excerpts of the contributors' oral submissions were also broadcast on local television."[67] The impression thus created is that providing further opportunities for input during the parliamentary stage of the reform process would amount to an unnecessary duplication of efforts.[68] This view would have been bolstered by the substantial agreement between the recommendations made by the Constitutional Commission and the eventual amendments proposed by the Government.

Any assumption that the existence of an avenue for popular involvement through a Constitutional Commission obviates the need to also allow for public participation during the parliamentary stage may however be problematic, for various reasons. The submissions made to the Constitutional Commission and its resultant deliberations are not always comprehensive in their consideration of the topic. As these take place at the very early stages of a possible reform, the focus is on policy questions: the desirability of an amendment and perhaps the broad strokes of any constitutional regulation. By the time Parliament becomes involved, however, it will be clear which provisions will be revised (or added) and the likely phrasing thereof. This concretization can trigger concerns or insights that were not thought of earlier, such as those pertaining to the operationalization of the new provisions. Soliciting public feedback at the parliamentary stage would thus be complementary to the Constitutional Commission's consultation process, not a repetition thereof.

In a related vein, the voluntary character of the consultation conducted by the Constitutional Commission can detract from the representativeness of the views obtained through that process. Recall, for instance, that preciously few community organizations submitted memoranda to the Menon Commission, even though minority representation was a core aspect of the latter's mandate. A Select Committee would be able to send for individuals or entities to buttress the representativeness of the public views infused into the amendment process.

Consider further the scenario where the proposed amendments deviate significantly or in important respects from the recommendations made by the Constitutional Commission. While this did not happen with the 2016 Menon Commission, such a fate befell the findings made by the earlier Wee Chong Jin Commission, the bulk of which were rejected by the political establishment. It seems fair and proper, in such situations, to grant interested parties another opportunity to make their views known as their earlier comments would have been rendered moot by the different approach proposed by the Government and Parliament.

To be fair, there are financial and personnel costs involved in setting up a Select Committee or creating other avenues for public involvement before Parliament. It is further likely to lengthen the amendment process. Given that such a Committee comprises opposition MPs alongside PAP members, it may also be politically less appealing than relying only on a Constitutional Commission, the composition of which is decided by the Government. For the amendments to the Elected Presidency, the time factor would have been particularly relevant, as the Government was keen to ensure that the constitutional reforms were in place before the next election, scheduled for August 2017.

To be fair also, several ministers participated in town hall dialogues and reported having heard expression of support for the proposed changes to the Elected Presidency. Yet, the format of such meetings – with one minister facing dozens if not hundreds of people at once – is not conducive to a meaningful exchange of views between the governors and the governed. In reality, the town hall meetings were occasions for the Government to inform citizens about the changes afoot rather than occasions where the latter could have provided feedback and voice concerns in a truly dialogic fashion, as is more prone to happen during Select Committee hearings.

The preceding paragraphs have emphasized the instrumental value of more public participation: by combining additional insights from a wide range of stakeholders into the making of new constitutional rules, the provisions eventually adopted should be of a better quality. We should, however, not overlook the intrinsic values that can be generated through closer interaction: bolstering the social legitimacy of the upcoming constitutional changes, notably the introduction of the reserved election, and promoting constitutional literacy among the citizenry. The importance of the latter cannot be underestimated given the underlying concern to put in place safeguards against freak election results, rogue governments and irresponsible presidents as preventing such hazards cannot be guaranteed by legal rules alone.

8.4 Beyond textual change: Constitutional Commissions and constitutional interpretation

8.4.1 Blurred boundaries between formal and informal constitutional change

This chapter has so far examined the process that resulted in formal changes to Singapore's Constitution in relation to the office of the Elected Presidency. It is trite, however, that constitutions do not only change at the culmination of formal procedures specifically designed for that purpose. They also evolve in an organic or informal fashion.[69] That second variety of change is typically taken to refer to the practice of giving constitutional provisions a meaning different from that previously ascribed or easily deduced through classic textualism. In this process, the interpreter may 'read in' words or phrases or, conversely, 'read down' portion of the official text. The U.S. Supreme Court, for instance, has famously held that the "liberty" explicitly guaranteed under the due process clause extends beyond freedom in the economic realm.[70] This expression is understood as also affording citizens a general right of privacy, notably for choices that pertain to family, procreation, child rearing and sexuality.[71] In Japan, in contrast, the hallmark of its Pacifist constitution – Article 9 – has been virtually emaciated through interpretation. While explicitly proscribing the maintenance of armed forces, Article 9 has been construed as nevertheless allowing for the establishment of self-defence forces that may even participate in foreign military missions in what is considered an exercise of the country's collective self-defence power.[72] At the same time, it seems clear, even among those propounding a broad reading of Article 9, that the outer boundaries of what is possible by means of interpretation have been reached. This explains the contemporary push for a formal change of the Chrysanthemum constitution by the political establishment to solidify and further increase the competences of Japan's de facto military.

These examples highlight two dominant themes in our understanding of informal constitutional change. First, that courts are the principal agents of such alteration. One implication is that changes in the meaning ascribed to rules and structures come about in the course of constitutional adjudication and hence, in the wake of the making of – formal revisions to – the constitutional text, during which time non-judicial actors are in the driving seat.[73] The second, related, theme concerns the relationship between textual and interpretative change: these are typically seen as alternative paths for constitutional upkeep or at most as sequentially ordered.

The argument developed here is that formal and informal alterations may in practice be quite closely intertwined and can take place almost contemporaneously, involving courts as well as non-judicial actors. The following sections show how the Menon Report featured several instances of extra-judicial constitutional interpretation and discuss the possible effects thereof for both the addressees and guardians of the national constitution.

8.4.2 Expert constitutional interpretation in the courts

In *Tan Seet Eng*, the Court of Appeal affirmed that in Singapore, as in many other jurisdictions, it is for the Judiciary to "pronounce authoritatively and conclusively on the meaning of the Constitution".[74] This assertion of final interpretative authority does not, of course, prevent other State institutions from putting forward their (preferred) understanding of constitutional provisions. These however will not be attributed the same weight *de jure* as judicial interpretations. For that to happen, a court would need to officially endorse a non-judicial reading of a constitutional clause, in what would amount to the grant of derivative authority to such a reading. The typical scenario would involve a challenge to the validity of constitutional provisions or the measures taken in implementation thereof. To be able to rule on such a challenge, the court would have to construe the legal rules in dispute and in doing so, could decide to rely on materials other than the formal legal text as interpretation aids. In Singapore, the prospect of non-judicial interpretations, including those contained in a Constitutional Commission report, receiving validation by the courts along the lines just sketched are however at present dim.

The Constitution declares in Article 2(9) that its interpretation shall, in principle, be governed by the Interpretation Act.[75] This Act commands that written law should be construed in a manner that would promote its purpose and explicitly allows consideration of extraneous materials in doing so.[76] The use of extraneous materials is permissible to confirm the ordinary meaning of the written text or to determine the proper meaning when the text itself is ambiguous, obscure or produces an absurd result.[77]

The question of the approach to take when interpreting constitutional provisions, notably the weight accorded to extraneous materials such as the 2016 Constitutional Commission Report, was addressed by the Court of Appeal in *Tan Cheng Bock* v. *AG*.[78] The case involved a challenge by a 2011 presidential candidate regarding the constitutionality of the section in the Presidential Elections (Amendment) Act 2017 that had the effect of reserving the next election for the Presidency to candidates of the Malay race. As the appellant was of Chinese ethnicity, he would accordingly be precluded from running and would need to wait until 2023 to try again. In its decision, the court confirmed the inclusion of the Constitutional Commission's Report as *prima facie* within the range of eligible extraneous materials that can be relied on for the interpretation of constitutional provisions. Not only does this recognize that an ad hoc, independent body like the Commission will engage in constitutional interpretation, it also underscores the potential enduring relevance of the views expressed by a Constitutional Commission after it has completed its task and has ceased to exist.

At the same time, the court made it clear that "primacy should be accorded to the text of the provision and its statutory context [or the Constitution as a whole] over any extraneous material."[79] That was not to say that the latter were unimportant: such material could have a legitimacy-enhancing function by "assuring the governed that the court is applying the law in keeping with the policy imperatives for which it was enacted".[80] This would entail a discriminating approach to the available extraneous material: not everything said therein would be deserving of judicial consideration. Indeed, the court indicated further restrictions that would govern its use of extraneous materials beyond those set out in the Interpretation Act. First, the observations in the extraneous material should be clear and unequivocal. Second, and as a logical consequence thereof, these observations should not themselves become the subject of judicial interpretation. Third, the observations "should be directed to the very point in question to be especially helpful."[81]

In *Tan Cheng Bock*, the third condition proved fatal to the appellant's reliance on the Constitutional Commission's Report. As the court explained, the Commission had focused on evaluating mechanisms to ensure minority representation in the Presidency but had intentionally left the operationalization thereof to the political sphere. It accordingly held that "[t]o this extent, the Commission's Report [is] incapable of giving assistance in the relevant regard, and thus need not be considered."[82]

The court's formulation leaves open the possibility of a different outcome in future cases should the provision referred for review be one that the Commission *had* commented on. Indeed, the Report features several instances of extra-judicial interpretation of constitutional clauses by the Commission. Some of these resulted in the Government proposing to revise the constitutional text of those provisions in line with the Commission's interpretation, which duly happened. This suggests that the latter's statements will meet the threshold criteria for consideration of extraneous material.

The Government's acceptance of the Commission's interpretations concerned the eligibility criteria for presidential hopefuls. Article 19(2)(g)(iv) (old) required prospective candidates to have held a position of "similar or comparable ... seniority and responsibility" in an organization of department of "equivalent size or complexity" as compared to those that lead to automatic qualification. The Constitutional Commission posited:

> that "equivalent" in the latter context does not mean precise equivalence but in fact bears the same meaning as the expression "similar or comparable" used in the first clause. Although the words used are different, the Commission considered that it would be practically impossible to find two organisations that are precisely equal in size and complexity.[83]

This interpretation of the word "equivalent" seems straightforward, obvious even, which probably explains why it was tucked away in a footnote in the opening paragraphs of the relevant chapter in the Report. The Commission also did not think it necessary to call on the Government to amend the language of Article 19 accordingly. That this was a conscious decision becomes clear when considering its approach to another qualifying element for the deliberative track, that is, proficiency in handling financial matters. The Commission was concerned that in its current wording the clause could be read as favouring private-sector candidates as opposed to those from the public sector that do not benefit from automatic qualification. Here, the Commission urged a revision of the constitutional text that should clarify whether the apparent bias was inadvertent or intentional.[84] The White Paper not only heeded the explicit plea for clarification; it also picked up on the Commission's own elucidation, with the Government promising that it would "streamline the language [of old Article 19(2)(g)(iv)] to more accurately reflect the Commission's interpretation".[85]

In practical terms, though, even when statements by the Constitutional Commission are deemed to be clearly and unequivocally directed to the interpretational query before the court, the impact thereof on the judicial construction of the pertinent provision may not be significantly greater than in *Tan Cheng Bock*-like situations due to the primacy accorded to the formal text in constitutional interpretation exercises.

8.4.3 Extra-judicial interpretations, implementation and agenda-setting

While the prospect of Commission interpretations exerting influence in the judicial arena appear limited, they can generate effects in other ways. Civil servants and members of committees entrusted with operationalizing amended or new constitutional provisions can very well decide to consult the Constitutional Commission's Report and other *traveaux préparatoires* as they go about doing so. The interpretations set out therein may accordingly shape the manner in which new constitutional rules are understood and applied when first put into practice. Two examples will illustrate how this can play out.

To start with, the Constitutional Commission had proposed an increase in the duration for which a candidate should have held the position(s) that qualify her for the office of President from three to six years for the *prima facie* qualifying public- and private-sector offices.[86] For individuals seeking to use the deliberative track, it concluded that the number of years need not be spelled out "to accord the [Presidential Elections Committee (PEC)] greater flexibility in its deliberations".[87] At the same time, the Report provided guidance on the manner in which the PEC ought to exercise its discretion. The latter should measure the performance of the applicants using this route "over a sustained period of time", which ought to be "of comparable duration" to the six-year tenure proposed for the other tracks to ensure that they possess "comparable" experience and expertise.[88]

The Government declined to accept this recommendation, making the question of the impact of the Commission's interpretation in shaping the PEC's exercise of discretion this instance moot. It is however apt to note that *had* revisions been made to the length of qualifying tenure, the PEC would likely have followed the guidance provided in the Commission's Report. This would mainly be the corollary of the considerable overlap in the composition of the PEC and the Constitutional Commission respectively. Three of the latter's nine members served on the PEC that was tasked with assessing the candidature of individuals vying to compete in the 2017 Reserved Presidential Election, to wit: Mr Eddie Teo, who holds the position of PEC chair; Prof. Chan Heng Chee (in her capacity as a member of the Presidential Council of Minority Rights); and Mr Peter Seah (appointed by the Prime Minister as a representative of the private sector). The remaining three PEC members must include a (former) judge, who could for obvious reasons of familiarity, respect or comity also have been expected to take serious account of the views contained in a Report jointly authored by one of her colleagues on the bench.[89]

The second example concerns the conduct of campaigns by presidential candidates. Eager to ensure that the solemnity and symbolism associated with the office would not be wantonly imperilled, the Commission recommended the adoption of (sub)statutory rules to curb inflammatory and divisive speech as well as "[making] it an offence for candidates to make promises or to take positions that are incompatible with the office of President".[90] In what could be seen as a marker of the strength of its members' sentiments on the topic, it proceeded to interpret its proposed prohibition, mentioning that this would encompass promises to "promote wider healthcare or better public transport" or conversely the commitment "to oppose spending for such programs".[91] This suggestion has been heeded, with the Elections Department amending its Candidate Handbook & Advisory to include the following cautionary statement:

> Candidates should not make statements that may cause racial or religious tensions or undermine social cohesion. Candidates should also avoid negative campaigning practices based on hate or denigrating opposing candidates, and should not make false statements that allege corruption or that criminal offences have been committed. Egregious acts of negative campaigning could be in breach of the law.[92]

In deciding whether presidential hopefuls have comported themselves in the desired manner, it would be natural for the officials working at the Elections Department to consider the Commission's Report, all the more given that neither the White Paper nor the Parliamentary debates contained any guiding statements on this topic.

Two more general observations can be made. First, the greater the similarity in the composition of a Constitutional Commission and the State entity responsible for giving effect to the constitutional prescriptions that the former is advising on, the greater the influence on the latter's construction of those prescriptions, regardless of any formal legal obligation to this effect.[93] Second, some interpretative guidance will be explicitly incorporated in a Constitutional Commission's report, as in the examples above. This makes it possible to chart and comment upon the extent of its influence on the addressees of the constitutional requirements. Other interpretative influence will happen outside the public eye, as there will always be interpretations that are canvassed informally during meetings among Constitutional Commission members, but do not make it into the final report. Any hope to identify these instances will typically rest on the protagonists writing their memoirs or otherwise speaking candidly about their time in government service, in a vein akin to the musings by Sir George Rendel about his stint as Chair of the 1953 Constitutional Commission.[94] As such, studies of extra-judicial interpretation by Constitutional Commissions and similar preparatory bodies will almost inevitably paint only a partial picture of this phenomenon.

Beyond articulating its reading of specific provisions and situations, the Commission's Report also set out how the office of the Elected President and its place within the Singapore constitutional structure should be understood. In Chapter 2, the Report offered a chronological narrative of the evolution of the Presidency from which it distilled "guiding principles". The first of these was the symbolic role of the President as a unifying force and the incarnation of the nation in human form, which was how the office was historically conceived. Crucially, the Constitutional Commission postulated that this symbolic function remains the core of the Presidency. The transition of the office from an appointed to elected one and the vesting of custodial powers in the President, has "not in any way abrogated" or "displaced" the "principal [symbolic] role" and because "this is an important point which might tend to be overlooked", it "bears emphasising".[95]

This understanding of the role of the President became the lens through which the Constitutional Commission approached the matters referred to it for consideration. It was one of the reasons to defend strict eligibility criteria for prospective candidates: these should reduce the likelihood of a politicized and divisive election that could detract from the "eventual victor's ability to effectively discharge his historical role as a symbol of national unity."[96] It was the decisive argument in favour of ensuring periodical minority representation in the Presidency.[97] In a similar vein, it was used to oppose the stipulation of a minority presence for other State bodies or offices.[98]

The Commission's view on the quintessence of the Presidency may also explain why it decided to elaborate at some length and quite animatedly on two topics that were outside the scope of its Terms of Reference, but raised in the written and oral observations by the public contributors. The first of these concerned the conduct of campaigns by presidential hopefuls, as elaborated above. The second topic was whether the 1991 constitutional changes should come undone, with the Presidency reverting to a nominated office. In line with the Constitutional Commission's understanding of the symbolic role of the President as *primus inter pares*, it hinted in terms as clear as could be deemed appropriate, bearing in mind that this topic was outside its remit, that the President's custodial powers over Singapore's financial reserves and public service appointments should be transferred to a different institution. The Report again went further, sketching in some detail what such a body could look like and cleverly noted precedents for this idea in other Westminster systems. And for the avoidance of doubt, the Report spelled out the obvious advantage of divesting the President of his custodial role: the incumbent of the office would once more be able to "focus on his historical role of being a symbolic unifying figure".[99]

It should be noted that this was the last substantive point made by the Commission, which could accordingly be said to have come full circle in its Report, from fleshing out its understanding of the role of the President in the opening chapter to drawing the perhaps unavoidable inference from that interpretation in the penultimate chapter. Additionally, by making this observation where and how it did, the Constitutional Commission signalled to the Government that it ought to consider moving beyond a review of specific aspects of the Presidency to continuing a dialogue about the general conception of the institution and its role within the overall constitutional infrastructure.[100] Put differently, this can be seen as an instance of constitutional interpretation for wider agenda-setting purposes rather than for the performance of existing, specific legal duties.

As mentioned earlier, the Government's response to the Commission's unsolicited advice was, perhaps unsurprisingly,[101] muted. It rejected the latter's observations on assigning the custodial role to a specialist body, explaining that previous office holders had not faced any difficulties in discharging this role alongside their symbolic function. The Commission's views on Presidential Election campaigns fared slightly better: these were politely shelved for consideration at a future, not further specified, point in time.[102] Arguably more interesting than what the White Paper contained by way of reply is the fact that it addressed the suggestions in the reverse order in which they appeared in the

Commission's Report. The Government appeared to be uncomfortable with endorsing the Commission's veiled attempt to foster a dialogue on how the Presidency *qua* institution should be conceived, and instead wished to signal that the review exercise could safely remain confined to ancillary matters. The relatively critical reception of the amendments in online discussions and public forums suggests that the Constitutional Commission's reflections on the Elected President's role and functions may find a more welcome reception in the societal discourse,[103] where they can continue to germinate, perhaps finding their way back into the official debate if and when the review of the institution of the Presidency is once again placed on the agenda.

8.5 Conclusion

Buttressing popular involvement with the polity is decidedly democratic, and all the more to be commended when it comes to changes to the basic constitutional arrangements affecting the way citizens live and are ruled. In this regard, convening a Constitutional Commission as part of the formal constitutional revision process can be a useful strategy to enhance the democratic quality of the resultant amendments. In the particular context of Singapore, a Constitutional Commission's engagement with the general public could moreover offer a welcome correction on the technocratic tendencies typical of the country's style of governance. As alluded to earlier, this would also require the Government to display sufficient willingness to act upon any grassroots-inspired recommendations proffered by such commissions.

The proceedings of the 2016 Constitutional Commission have confirmed the parameters for public participation first used by the Wee Chong Jin Commission and improved on the transparency that the views received were dealt with in its Report. The result is a solid template for public consultation that future commissions can and should follow. Having said that, one important area for consideration and possible improvement concerns the range and identity of contributors to ensure that the public views considered when rendering advice to the Government are sufficiently representative of affected societal interests. Dependent on the political reception of the Report, Government and Parliament may need to continue the dialogue with the citizenry for reasons of legitimacy and improved constitutional literacy.

We have also seen that the reports of a Constitutional Commission may have an afterlife once the text of the constitution has been revised. The interpretations of constitutional provisions or institutions contained therein can shape the understanding of the same in the judicial arena, the civil service or social discourse. This places a premium on the quality of its proceedings and the report. Beyond public participation, this would require the Government to continue to think carefully about the membership of future Constitutional Commissions to ensure that they are populated by eminently qualified and respected individuals. Such Commissions should, accordingly, quite literally be designed for success.

Notes

1 Letter from Thomas Jefferson to Samuel Kercheval, 12 June 1816, reprinted in Adrienne Koch and William Peden (eds), *The Life and Selected Writings of Thomas Jefferson* (New York: Random House, 1944), 675.

2 The 12th Amendment, passed by Congress on 9 December 1803 and ratified on 15 June 1804, followed by the 13th Amendment, passed by Congress on 31 January 1865 and ratified on 6 December 1865.

3 *Singapore Parliamentary Debates: Official Report*, 27 January 2016, vol. 94 (Lee Hsien Loong, Prime Minister).

4 The first was the Wee Chong Jin Commission, appointed in December 1965. Its report was issued in August 1966.

5 See, among many others, Abrak Saati, "Participatory constitution-making as a transnational legal norm: why does it 'stick' in some contexts and not in others?" (2017) 2 *UC Irvine Journal of International, Transnational, and Comparative Law* 113; Vivien Hart, "Democratic Constitution-Making" (2003) 107 USIP Special Report; Cheryl Saunders, "Constitution-Making in the 21st century" (2012) 4 *International Review of Law* 1; Stefan Voigt, "The consequences of popular participation in constitutional choice: towards a comparative analysis", in Anne van Aaken, Christian List and Christoph Luetge (eds), *Deliberation and Decision: Economics, Constitutional Theory and Deliberative Democracy* (Aldershot: Ashgate, 2004); Justin Blount, "Participation in constitutional design", in Tom Ginsburg and Rosalind Dixon (eds), *Comparative Constitutional Law* (Cheltenham: Edward Elgar, 2011).

6 See, for example, Carlo Fusaro and Dawn Oliver, "Towards a theory of constitutional change", in Dawn Oliver and Carlo Fusaro (eds), *How Constitutions Change: A Comparative Study* (Oxford: Hart, 2011), 430.

7 See the chapters by V.K. Rajah, Li-ann Thio and Yap Po Jen in Jaclyn Neo (ed.), *Constitutional Interpretation in Singapore: Theory and Practice* (Abingdon: Routledge, 2017).

8 Most notably: Zachary Elkins, Tom Ginsburg and James Melton, *The Endurance of National Constitutions* (Cambridge: Cambridge University Press, 2009).

9 Among many others, see, for example, Xenophon Contiades and A. Fotiadou (eds), *Participatory Constitutional Change: The People as Amenders of the Constitution* (Abingdon: Routledge, 2017); Andrew Arato, *Post Sovereign Constitution Making: Learning and Legitimacy* (Oxford: Oxford University Press, 2016); Marco Bünte and Björn Dressel (eds), *Politics and Constitutions in Southeast Asia* (Abingdon: Routledge, 2017); Yaniv Roznai, *Unconstitutional Constitutional Amendments: The Limits of Amendment Powers* (Oxford: Oxford University Press, 2017); Richard Albert, "Constitutional amendment and dismemberment" (2018) 43 *Yale Journal of International Law* and the responses in the same journal by Carlos Bernal, David Landau and Yaniv Roznai; Denis J. Galligan and Mila Versteeg (eds), *Social and Political Foundations of Constitutions* (New York: Cambridge University Press, 2013); Xenophon Contiades (ed.), *Engineering Constitutional Change* (Oxford: Hart, 2011).

10 See, for example, Tom Ginsburg, Zachary Elkins and Justin Blount, "Does the process of constitution-making matter?" (2009) 5 *Annual Review of Law and Social Science* 5; Ran Hirschl, *Towards Juristocracy – The Origins and Consequences of the New Constitutionalism* (Cambridge, MA: Harvard University Press, 2007), arguing that elites expecting to lose power will establish constitutional review in an attempt to preserve their original hegemony.

11 See, for example, Guidance Note of the Secretary-General: United Nations Assistance to Constitution-Making Process (April 2009); Michele Brandt, Jill Cottrell, Yash Ghai and Anthony Regan, *Constitution-Making and Reform: Options for the Process* (Geneva: Interpeace, 2011), Part II, Section 2.

12 Chaihark Hahm and Sung Ho Kim, "To make 'we the people': constitutional founding in postwar Japan and South Korea" (2010) 8 *I·CON* 800, 800.
13 A general argument in favour of participatory democracy is provided by Jürgen Habermas, *Between Facts and Norms: Contributions to a Discourse Theory of Law and Democracy*, W. Rehq (trans.) (Cambridge, MA: MIT Press, 1996).
14 Cf. HLA Hart, *The Concept of Law*, 2nd edn (Oxford: Clarendon Press, 1994); John Rawls, *A Theory of Justice* (Oxford: Oxford University Press, 1973).
15 In the Philippines, the petition must have the support of at least 12 per cent of the total number of registered voters that represent each legislative district. Such petitions can only be submitted once every five years, Philippines Constitution Article XVII s2 and Article XVII s1 read together with s3. Thailand imposes a quantitative threshold of 50,000 eligible voters, with those signing the petition additionally having the right to address Parliament during the second reading of the amendment bill, Thailand Constitution s256(1) and (4).
16 Philippines Constitution Art. XVII(1) and (3).
17 Canada Constitution s 35(1).
18 Australia Constitution Art. 128; Ireland Constitution Art. 46(2); New Zealand Constitution s268; Sri Lanka Constitution Art. 83.
19 Tom Ginsburg, "Constitutional advice and transnational legal order" (2017) 2 *UC Irvine Journal of International, Transnational, and Comparative Law* 5, 29 (emphasis in original).
20 The Rendel Commission was set up in 1953 and submitted its report in February 1954.
21 See *Singapore Parliamentary Debates: Official Report*, 22 December 1965, at cols 429–30. For detailed analysis, see Li-ann Thio, "The passage of a generation: revisiting the Report of the 1966 Constitutional Commission", in Li-ann Thio and Kevin Tan (eds), *Evolution of a Revolution: Forty Years of the Singapore Constitution* (London: Routledge, 2014).
22 *Singapore Parliamentary Debates: Official Report*, 27 January 2016, vol. 94 (Lee Hsien Loong, Prime Minister).
23 Although today, there are more opportunities for the public to provide feedback on selected legislative proposals.
24 Singapore Parliament (1991) White Paper on shared values (Paper cmd 1 of 1991). See further Li-ann Thio, "Soft constitutional law in non-liberal Asian constitutional democracies" (2010) 8 *I·CON* 766.
25 Speech by Prime Minister Lee Hsien Loong at the 2005 Administrative Service Dinner (24 March 2005), at 6–8.
26 Cf. Singapore Constitution Art. 37D(2)(b).
27 Singapore Constitution Art. 39(1)(c).
28 Singapore Constitution Art. 19(2)–(5).
29 Justin Blount and Tom Ginsburg, "Participation in constitutional design: Asian exceptionalism", in Tom Ginsburg and Rosalind Dixon (eds), *Comparative Constitutional Law in Asia* (Cheltenham: Edward Elgar, 2014), 24.
30 Myanmar Constitution Article 436(a) (requiring endorsement with a simple majority vote in nationwide plebiscite); Philippines Constitution Art. XVII(4) (similar requirement with the addition that the referendum must be held within 60 to 90 days after congressional approval of the amendment); Thailand Constitution Ch. XV s256 (requiring a referendum for changes to constitutional provisions relating to the general provisions, king, amendment provisions, courts and independent organs).
31 *Singapore Parliamentary Debates: Official Report*, 27 January 2016, vol. 94 (Lee Hsien Loong, Prime Minister).
32 *Ibid.*
33 Cf. Singapore Constitution Art. 39A(2)(a).

34 On which, see Chapter 5 by Jaclyn Neo and Chapter 6 by Eugene Tan in this volume.
35 See Chapter 1 by Kevin Tan and Lam Peng Er in this volume.
36 *Singapore Parliamentary Debates: Official Report*, 27 January 2016, vol. 94 (Lee Hsien Loong, Prime Minister), emphasis added.
37 *Ibid.*
38 Cf. Ronald J.J. Wong, "Why a Constitutional Commission to review the Elected Presidency?", *The Straits Times* (Singapore, 17 February 2016).
39 More cynically, the Government would have the option of abandoning the idea of a mechanism to guarantee minority representation altogether if public opinion would be strongly against it.
40 Cf. the observations by the Deputy Prime Minister: *Singapore Parliamentary Debates: Official Report*, 9 November 2016, at 95: "[W]hy did the Prime Minister decide to set up an independent Commission? Because he did not want this review to end up being embroiled in partisan to-ing and fro-ing … We wanted an objective look at the issues."
41 See also Prime Minister's Office, "Constitutional Commission to review specific aspects of the Elected Presidency" (10 February 2016).
42 Chief Justice Menon is the present Chair of this Council.
43 Wong, "Why a Constitutional Commission" (n. 38).
44 See *Singapore Parliamentary Debates: Official Report*, 22 December 1965, at cols 429–30.
45 The Chair was a distinguished constitutional lawyer and former Commonwealth Solicitor-General and the other two members were former heads of government.
46 The other two members were a highly influential journalist and a prominent Canadian politician and jurist.
47 *Constitutional Commission Report 2016* (Singapore, 17 August 2016).
48 *Ibid.*, para. 1.3.
49 Submissions received after the deadline were also considered.
50 Mr Suppiah Dhanabalan, a former MP who had also served as Cabinet Minister in charge of several portfolios between 1980 and 1993.
51 *Constitutional Commission Report 2016*, para. 1.4.
52 *Ibid.*, para. 4.72.
53 *Ibid.*, para. 4.75.
54 *Ibid.*, para. 4.97.
55 *Ibid.*, paras 6.51–52.
56 *Ibid.*, paras 7.32–33.
57 *Ibid.*, para. 4.11.
58 *Ibid.*, para. 7.1 (emphasis added).
59 See the text after (n. 97).
60 White Paper on the Review of Specific Aspects of the Elected Presidency (Cmd 7, 2016).
61 *Singapore Parliamentary Debates: Official Report*, 27 January 2016, vol. 94 (Lee Hsien Loong, Prime Minister).
62 Constitution of the Republic of Singapore (Amendment) Bill 2016 (NoB28 of 2016).
63 *Singapore Parliamentary Debates: Official Report*, 9 November 2016, vol. 94.
64 But see Chapter 9 by Swati Jhaveri in this volume.
65 White Paper (n. 59), para. 25 (emphasis added).
66 *Ibid.*, para. 22.
67 *Ibid.*, para. 23.
68 Similar sentiments were expressed by the Prime Minister, Deputy Prime Minister and PAP-affiliated MPs when the Amendment Bill was discussed in Parliament: *Singapore Parliamentary Debates: Official Report*, 7 November 2016, vol. 94 at 52 (per Teo Chee Hean), at 77–8 (per Tin Pei Ling), at 31 (per Lee Hsien Loong) and (8 November 2016) at 54 (per Edwin Tong Chun Fai).

69 For example, Fusaro and Oliver (n. 6), 429; Craig Martin, "The legitimacy of Informal Constitutional Amendment and the 'reinterpretation' of Japan's war powers" (2017) 40 *Fordham International Law Journal* 427; Reijer Passchier, "Informal constitutional change: constitutional change without formal constitutional amendment in comparative perspective" (PhD thesis, Leiden University, 2017).
70 For example, *Lochner* v. *New York* 198 U.S. 45 (1905).
71 For example, *Griswold* v. *Connecticut* 381 U.S. 479 (1965); *Roe* v. *Wade* 410 U.S. 113 (1973); *Stanley* v. *Georgia* 394 U.S. 557 (1969); *Lawrence* v. *Texas* 539 U.S. 558 (2003).
72 For example, Hajime Yamamoto, "Interpretation of the Pacifist Article of the Constitution by the Bureau of Cabinet Legislation: a new source of constitutional law?" (2016) 26 *Washington International Law Journal* 111; Tomosuke Kasuya, "Constitutional transformation and the Ninth Article of the Japanese Constitution" (1986) 18 *Law in Japan*, 1 (Paul Stephen Taylor trans).
73 Although (prospective) judges too may have been involved in the initial drafting of the constitution, see further Rosalind Dixon, "Constitutional design two ways: constitutional drafters as judges" (2007) 57 *Virginia Journal of International Law* 1.
74 *Tan Seet Eng* v. *AG* [2016] 1 SLR 779 [90].
75 Interpretation Act (Cap. 1, 2002 rev edn).
76 *Ibid*., Art. 9A(1).
77 *Ibid*., Art. 9A(2) and see also (4).
78 *Tan Cheng Bock* v. *AG* [2017] SGCA 50; see also the minority judgement in *AG* v. *Ting Choon Meng and another* [2017] 1 SLR 373.
79 *Ibid*., para. 43.
80 *Ibid*., para. 49.
81 *Ibid*., paras 53–4.
82 *Ibid*., para. 115.
83 *Constitutional Commission Report 2016*, note 141.
84 *Constitutional Commission Report 2016*, para. 4.69.
85 White Paper (n. 59), paras 47 and 50.
86 *Constitutional Commission Report 2016*, para. 4.72.
87 *Ibid*., para. 4.73.
88 *Ibid*.
89 On a related note, the presence of a (former) judge and an individual with private-sector experience on the PEC has come about as a result of the Constitutional Commission's Report, which recommended doubling the PEC's membership so it would be "better placed to discharge its functions" (at para. 4.91).
90 *Constitutional Commission Report 2016*, para. 7.16.
91 *Ibid*.
92 Elections Department, "Advisory to Candidates for Presidential Election 2017" (29 August 2017), para. 6.1. Candidates may also voluntarily complete a form promising to conduct their campaign in a dignified and decorous manner that will be published alongside their nomination papers.
93 This assumes that the text does not outright prohibit the intended construction, that is, if the Government and Parliament were to decide against changing the wording of the constitution along the lines suggested by the Commission.
94 Sir George Rendel, *The Sword and the Olive – Recollections of Diplomacy and the Foreign Service 1913–1954* (London: John Murray, 1957), 331–40.
95 *Constitutional Commission Report*, para. 2.53, repeatedly in similar words in para. 5.4.
96 *Ibid*., para. 4.14; and see also para. 4.79.
97 *Ibid*., para. 5.5.
98 *Ibid*., para. 5.14 (Prime Minister, Chief Justice and Speaker of Parliament) and para. 6.37 (composition of the Council of Presidential Advisers).
99 *Ibid*., para. 7.52.

100 The word "continuing" is used to reflect that the opening salvo came from the public, initially in the form of op-eds in media outlets and subsequently by contributors who made submissions to the Constitutional Commission.

101 The Rendel and the Wee Chong Jin Commission had also offered suggestions on topics outside the ambit of their Terms of Reference, notably the establishment of a second chamber or expert-like body. In both cases, the Government and Parliament gave short shrift to these ideas.

102 As mentioned, this suggestion has since been incorporated in the Elections Department's Candidate Handbook & Advisory for presidential hopefuls.

103 See also *Singapore Parliamentary Debates: Official Report*, 9 November 2016, vol. 94 (per K. Thanaletchimi).

9 Reflecting on constitutional change in Singapore

The role of the Executive, Legislature and Judiciary

Swati S. Jhaveri

9.1 Introduction

The chapters in this volume have analysed different aspects of the amendments to the office of the Elected Presidency over time. This concluding chapter goes beyond the content of the amendments to consider what the process of change indicates about the nature of constitutional change in Singapore. Specifically, it considers the relative contributions of the different branches of government to the design and evolution of the office of the Elected President ("EP") and how this illuminates the distribution of the constitutional power of change in Singapore. The role of the Legislature, Executive and Judiciary during a period of constitutional change can reveal much about the distribution of constitutional power in a particular jurisdiction. The chapter will demonstrate that while the power to drive constitutional change is concentrated in the Executive, the 2016 amendment exercise was marked by changes in the level of engagement from the other two branches: Parliament and the Judiciary. This did not ultimately cause a significant shift in power. The amendments were passed by Parliament without substantial change and the challenges to certain amendments were successfully defended in judicial review proceedings. However, it opened the door for a more diverse engagement on questions of constitutional change in the future.

The formal rules of constitutional amendment in Singapore situate this power in the Legislative branch.[1] In practice, however, change is driven by the Executive branch of government. The latter drafts and introduces constitutional amendment bills in Parliament. Such bills require a two-thirds majority in Parliament to be passed – a majority which the incumbent government have comfortably held since independence in Singapore's Westminster parliamentary system. Various alternative amendment provisions have been mooted from time to time that would shift some power to the EP and to the citizens via the use of national referenda. However, these options, while introduced into the text of the Constitution, have not been brought into force.[2] Until they are, the power to amend the Constitution remains with the Executive – either *qua* executive in the initiation and design of changes or *qua* the majority that passes the amendments in Parliament. It is in this context that commentators have come to the conclusion that Singapore exemplifies a particularly strong form of political constitutionalism.[3]

The amendments to the office of the Presidency discussed in this volume provide a particularly apt context for assessing the balance of the power of constitutional change in Singapore. Once the Presidency was converted into an elected office, it became the subject of a significant number of amendments.[4] The Presidency has, in fact, been behind the majority of the amendments to the Constitution since it was first enacted in 1965.

This chapter considers the above power distribution in more detail. Section 9.2 breaks down the Executive's role throughout the 2016 amendment exercise. This includes its involvement in initiating the process; setting the agenda for change; and maintaining control over the agenda following the conclusion of the Constitutional Commission's public consultations. Sections 9.3 and 9.4 then go on to consider the role of members from opposition parties and Nominated Members of Parliament during the legislative debates on the amendments and the role of the Judiciary respectively. The discussions consider the nature of the constitutional issues that dominated discourse in those settings and, more importantly, the extent to which they were able to influence the eventual content of the amendments. The issues that did dominate are those that have been the subject of discussion elsewhere in this volume: the most prominent being the new reserved election mechanism.[5] This was the only aspect of the 2016 amendments that triggered responses from all three branches and therefore, provides a useful context for considering the inter-branch balance of constitutional power on questions of constitutional change.

It has been argued by the incumbent government that it is important to control the pace and scope of constitutional change in Singapore: this may explain their role thus far at the helm of the amendment process. However, this chapter argues that the 2016 amendment exercise also demonstrates the advantages of a more diverse engagement in the constitutional-political arena. The various proposals and arguments put forward by the other actors can have an important role to play in raising the profile of key issues, in prompting the further clarification and rationalization of key proposals and in shaping the agenda for future amendment exercises. Indeed, this has been the ambition of this volume of essays on the office of the EP.

9.2 The Executive: setting the agenda and managing public deliberation

In Singapore's Westminster-style parliamentary system, the Executive drafts amendment bills, introduces and supports them in Parliament and ultimately votes on them *qua* the majority political party.[6] The constitutional implications of this have already been the subject of discussion elsewhere.[7] The discussion here looks at the Executive's role outside of this formal legislative setting. First, in setting the agenda for change. For the 2016 amendment exercise, the Executive determined what would be the subject of amendment and the process that would be used to deliberate and design these amendments. Second, in redirecting the course of the amendments following recommendations made by the Constitutional Commission at the conclusion of the public consultation exercise. Finally, the discussion below also, briefly, looks at how public reactions to the introduction of the reserved election mechanism prompted a more involved civic engagement exercise by the Executive prior to parliamentary debates.

The 2016 amendment process was kick started by the Prime Minister in January 2016 with a speech in Parliament. This speech was used to set the course for change in a way that would have repercussions on the scope and content of the amendments down the line. First, the Prime Minister demarcated those items for amendment that would be the subject of deliberation within the Executive and those that would be deliberated on by a Constitutional Commission following a public consultation. For example, changes that would involve increasing the numbers and voting rights of Non-Constituency Members of Parliament ("NCMPs"),[8] and rebalancing the number of group representation constituencies and single-member constituencies in Parliament would be deliberated on and finalized by the Executive.[9] A Constitutional Commission would be set up to focus instead only on changes to the office of the EP. This included exploring modifications to the qualification criteria for candidacy for the office of the EP; the need for multiracial representation in the office of the EP and the powers of the Council of Presidential Advisers ("CPA") that advises the EP.[10] Second, the Prime Minister used the opportunity to set out the criteria that should inform any recommendations for change made by the Constitutional Commission. This included the need to ensure candidates for the office of the EP possessed the requisite technocratic credentials to discharge the custodial functions of the office.[11] In addition, the need to maintain stability in politics that may require enhancing the role of the CPA, especially in situations where the EP disagrees with the Executive.[12] And that any issue of minority representation needed to be handled with care – with the focus being on enhancing *multiracial* representation versus *minority* representation.[13] This detailing of the parameters for constitutional change dictated how far any alteration to the office of the EP could go. In particular, the amendment exercise proceeded on the assumption that the office of the EP was a fixture of Singapore's autochthonous constitutional set-up and that there was indeed a need to address the multiracial representativeness of the office. This prevented more fundamental root and branch or existential discussions on the office of the EP. Thus, in narrowly demarcating the territory of the Constitutional Commission, the amendment exercise could be contained to focus on what the Executive had identified as the areas in pressing need of change.

The speech, therefore, was also used to reiterate the need to maintain a conservative approach to constitutional change and democratic politics in Singapore. When the office of the President was first converted into an elected office, it was clear that this was motivated by concerns about the outcome of elections, as discussed in Chapter 1 by Kevin Tan and Lam Peng Er.[14] Once the office of the EP was established as such, the focus shifted to gradually and incrementally moulding the office. The Prime Minister expressed how the pace of change must be gradual and incremental given Singapore is constantly "[l]earning from experience, stretching and easing the old shoe, and adapting it to our needs and dealing with problems as new problems emerge, as we understand the difficulties and weaknesses."[15] Therefore, any amendments must work with the existing design of the office of the EP and the CPA versus proposing alternative design options for the discharge of the custodial and symbolic functions of the President. The Prime Minister also stressed the importance of maintaining a stable political system: while the Government must be responsive to changing circumstances, it is important to avoid disruptions that may arise as a result of a transient public mood at elections or an erratic government.[16] As further discussed in Section 9.3, this vision of gradual constitutional change and stable democratic politics was reinforced by the Executive during parliamentary debates to respond to criticisms that the changes did not go far enough and to turn down alternative proposals that went too far.

The Executive's role was apparent again downstream following the Report by the Constitutional Commission. Less than a month after the Report was issued, the Executive issued a White Paper in which it responded to each of the recommendations by the Constitutional Commission. This White Paper set the scene for the rebalancing of power – the Executive pushed back on a number of key proposals, especially those that would have been inconsistent with the above vision of constitutional change and democratic politics.[17] This included the Commission's proposal to remove the Accountant-General and Auditor-General from the public-sector qualifying track for the office of the EP, as well as, amendments that would enhance Parliament's capacity to vote to override the EP's decisions where the latter disagreed with the CPA.[18] In rejecting these suggestions, the Government emphasized the need for a more careful reflection on the proposals in the interests of maintaining stability in constitutional change and politics.[19]

Most significantly, the Executive rejected a proposal by the Constitutional Commission to decouple the symbolic and custodial roles of the office of the EP.[20] The Commission recognized that it was departing from its Terms of Reference in considering and proposing this option, but felt that it needed to for two reasons. First, this issue needed to be considered and discussed, given that it had been raised by contributors.[21] Second, the Commission independently noted the need for decoupling the two roles of the EP, outside of the recommendations from the public. It observed the "emergence of strains [in the office of the EP] rooted in the unavoidable tension between the President's historical and custodial roles".[22] While the Commission reiterated that the issue was eventually a question for the Executive to consider if and when it decides to undertake a more fundamental reconsideration of the office of the EP, it proposed a detailed solution for how this decoupling of the two roles may be done.[23] The Commission proposed reverting to a system where the President was appointed by Parliament and performed mainly symbolic functions. The first four Presidents of Singapore, prior to the conversion of the office to an elected one, were appointed by Parliament and were respectively members of the Malay, Eurasian, Indian and then Chinese communities.[24] The symbolic nature of the office was reinforced by a convention of rotating the office among the major ethnic groups in Singapore.[25] The custodial role would then pass to an appointed specialist body.[26] This 'council of experts' could form a second chamber of Parliament and would have the power to delay the implementation of financial measures by forcing a debate on them. Parliament could override any objections by the council by a super-majority vote in Parliament.[27] This was an important step by the Commission. First, it attributed some weight to the public in having a say on broader questions of design that were not part of an agenda set by the Executive. Second, the Commission leveraged on its own collective expertise in deliberating on and coming up with a design solution.[28]

The proposal was firmly rejected. In doing so, the Executive reiterated its view of the office of the EP and the way in which Singapore should approach multiracial politics and constitutional change. When the idea of the EP was first mooted, it was clear that the Government had considered alternatives and eventually settled on the EP as the institutional mechanism for the checking of the Government's spending of reserves.[29] Thus once settled on, any further changes to the office would be by minimalist intervention into existing structures. In addition, it was important to maintain a system where the custodial functions are exercised by an institution with a democratic mandate (which the proposed appointed body of experts would lack even if they are formally part of Parliament). The Executive emphatically reiterated its view that a "custodial President democratically elected in a national election remains the most workable and effective solution for Singapore".[30] In doing so, the Executive reclaimed control over the content and pace of the reform agenda, indicating firmly that any more fundamental changes were for another day. Even in the course of accepting the proposal for the introduction of a reserved election mechanism, the Executive reiterated its own views on why this was the optimal way of achieving the objectives it had set out at the outset. This included the fact that this new measure was temporally restricted with a natural sunset period. In addition, it did not compromise on meritocracy because any candidates standing in a reserved election would still need to meet the technocratic qualifying criteria. Finally, the mechanism was racially neutral in not preferring any particular race, but of benefit to all races.[31]

Following the White Paper and prior to the parliamentary debates on the amendments, the Executive was concerned to minimize misinformation or misunderstandings on the new reserved election mechanism. Such misunderstandings were seemingly apparent from public discussions that followed the proposal.[32] It therefore, did a considerable amount of work in coordinating public engagement on the proposed amendments. There were a number of public meetings and events facilitated by different Ministers aimed at informing the public of the changes and soliciting reactions to the amendments.[33] For the first time, there were also televised discussions with key members of the Executive on the amendments.[34] This was a much deeper political engagement with the electorate on constitutional issues than was the case with previous amendment exercises.[35] The reserved election mechanism generated a considerable amount of debate – in mainstream media as well as online. The Executive was therefore, prompted to join the discussions and create alternative fora where they could respond to and redirect discussions. It is clear that public deliberation and participation can imbibe a constitutional amendment process generally and the specifics relating to the changes with greater sociological legitimacy.[36] However, in this case the public engagement was aimed not so much at soliciting responses to modify amendments (which had been the aim of the earlier Constitutional Commission exercise). Rather, it was seen as part of a broader exercise in civic education and building support for the office of the EP prior to parliamentary debates.[37] This chapter turns to consider this next.

9.3 Parliament: the role of the opposition and nominated Members of Parliament

In a Westminster parliamentary system, the Executive is the originator of policy and legislation. However, Members of Parliament, through deliberation and debate, can be an important check and can inject important political legitimacy into executive-led law-making.[38] Commentators still doubt the real efficacy of Parliament as an independent check in Westminster systems.[39] This concern is not peculiar to Singapore, with reasons for doubt varying across jurisdictions.[40] For example, the composition of a legislature can impact the strength of Parliament's checking function. In the Singapore context, this concern may arise due to the particular political make-up of Parliament. Since independence, a single political party – the People's Action Party – has had a majority of seats in Parliament. Some mechanisms are in place for a guaranteed opposition and broader representation in Parliament through NCMPs (up to 12) and Nominated Members of Parliament ("NMPs") (up to nine).[41] However, the presence of these other members remains relatively small.[42]

The precise format chosen for vetting legislative proposals can similarly influence the nature of Parliament's checking function. For example, where a Constitutional Commission is not convened, the incumbent government generally introduce White Papers in Parliament detailing proposed amendments, followed by a parliamentary debate.[43] Sometimes a Select Committee is set up to consider some amendments in more detail. The Committee can sometimes have some influence on the outcome of the amendment exercise.[44] Depending on the diversity of its membership, it can also imbibe the deliberation with viewpoint diversity.[45] On most occasions, however, amendments are discussed directly in plenary parliamentary debate sessions on draft bills.[46] Here, the way voting is undertaken during these plenary sessions can determine how much influence Parliament can have on government business.[47] In Singapore, the presence of a strong majority from one party, the powers of the government whip and the fact that political parties observe strict rules of party discipline (with members of the ruling party voting to support party proposals versus their individual political preference) may mean that proposals put forward by the incumbent government are unlikely to be voted down.[48]

In this environment, Parliament's checking function will be dependent on the expression of a diverse range of views and questions from members during these plenary sessions, as opposed to resistance through a formal voting down of proposals.[49] What if there is an absence of such a diversity of views? On this, there are two possible conclusions. First, it could be argued that where there is little opposition and a clear, majority vote, we must doubt the outcome of legislative choice. What emerges from the legislative process may just be a question of who controls the agenda.[50] Conversely, it could be argued that the prevailing of a uniform or majority view does not necessarily undermine the legitimacy of the final result, nor the role of Parliament in rigorously deliberating over amendments.[51] On this latter view, "control" by Parliament is not only seen as altering or changing the final result, but a more elastic function which can include the ability to ask difficult questions freely. In answering such questions, the Government will be forced to confront difficult aspects of any proposal and either amend the proposal or overcome the criticisms through counter-debate. The latter elastic function may need to be the route of influence in Parliament in Singapore, given the current dominant majority held by a single party. This section looks into the parliamentary debates on the 2016 amendments to highlight the points of resistance that arose during the debates, particularly from the opposition members of Parliament (elected and NCMPs) and the NMPs on the issue of the reserved election mechanism. The discussion below compares the approaches of the NMPs and opposition members and concludes that the more measured strategy of the former may have had greater impact in forcing the Government to confront the problematic aspects of the reserved election mechanism.

During the debates, the following non-PAP MPs spoke most prominently on the reserved election mechanism: three NCMPs, five elected opposition members of Parliament and seven NMPs.[52] The latter group included: Mr Mahdev Mohan, Mr Azmoon Ahmed, Ms Chia Yong Yong, Mr Thomas Chua, Ms Kuik Shiao-Yin, Mr Kok Heng Leun and Ms K. Thanaletchimi. Out of this group, three raised fundamental issues with the reserved election mechanism. Chapter 5 by Jaclyn Neo and Chapter 6 by Eugene Tan highlight a number of these fundamental issues.[53] Of the three NMPs that raised core issues with the reserved election mechanisms, Ms Thanaletchimi queried how to deal with the issue of mixed-race parentage of candidates. Mr Kok Heng Leun and Ms Kuik Shiao-Yin questioned more fundamentally whether there was a need for the introduction of race into politics. Mr Kok queried whether the reserved election mechanism might end up amounting to a form of discrimination or tokenism. Ms Kuik stated that any race-based measures in politics must be done on the back of empirical information on how much race indeed matters in decision-making by voters. She also highlighted how this should not take away from the need for more systemic changes in the representation of races at lower level offices in politics. The remaining NMPs expressed concern with the issue of race being raised in the context of politics but accepted that it may be necessary.[54] The statements from the latter group mirrored, to a large extent, the views expressed by the ruling party. Of the 27 PAP MPs who spoke on the reserved election mechanism, all were in support with five raising queries related to the specifics of the implementation of the reserved election mechanism, for example, on the responsibilities of Community Committees[55] and on the issue of mixed-race parentage of possible candidates.[56]

The interventions from the NMPs can be seen as representative of the more 'elastic function of Parliament' – this is apparent from the various responses to their interventions. They prompted the Government to further explain and rationalize the proposed reserved election mechanism and address some of the difficult questions, especially those relating to mixed-race parentage of candidates. For example, Mr Chan Chun Sing responded to Mr Thomas Chua's concerns on mixed-race parentage by setting out that: "if a citizen whose parents belong to two different communities decides to run and decides to apply for a community certificate, the relevant community sub-committee should adopt an inclusive attitude toward his application."[57] Further, the concerns expressed by Mr Kok Heng Leun prompted a Member of Parliament from the ruling PAP party to observe that this highlighted how Singapore is not 'race-blind' and has 'pushed' everyone to think more about the issues.[58] Deputy Prime Minister Teo Chee Hean was also prompted to acknowledge the concerns about race and ethnicity expressed by Ms Chia Yong Yong, Ms Kuik Shiao-Yin and Mr Kok Heng Leun, and offer reassurance that this may be the best way to progress towards "the ideal of society where race is no longer a significant issue".[59] The range of questions from the NMPs, therefore, brought to the fore a broader discussion on how matters of race are perceived in Singapore and the need to address the matter at this stage. Through the clarifications on the operation of the scheme, the Government was also pushed to consider and set out their expectations on how it was going to work: through an inclusive approach to race-based classifications versus an exclusive one.

The approach of the NMPs can be contrasted with that adopted by the opposition during the debates. The Workers' Party – one of the main opposition parties in Parliament – adopted a different approach to the NMPs. One that was ultimately unsuccessful. The Workers' Party has long held the view that the office of the EP should be abolished.[60] This is on the basis that the EP undermines parliamentary democracy: the real focus of constitutional change should be to further enhance Parliament's capacity to check the Executive. A further concern is that the EP could inadvertently evolve into an alternative executive or legislative power centre causing political gridlock.[61] During the debates, the Workers' Party proposed the establishment of a Senate as an Upper House within Parliament to exercise the EP's custodial functions. It further proposed the reversion of the EP to an office appointed by Parliament to fulfil its symbolic role of multiracial representation. The input from the Workers' Party revived the question posed by the Constitutional Commission on the need to decouple the symbolic and custodial functions of the office of the EP. Indeed, the Workers' Party leveraged on the Constitutional Commission's proposal.[62]

This reference to the Commission was still insufficient for the proposal to gain traction during the debates. The main issue appeared to be that it was felt that the proposal was insufficiently articulated. The incumbent party identified a number of fundamental issues with the mechanics of the proposal. For example, the Minister for Law and Home Affairs asked the Workers' Party to clarify what the criteria for candidacy would be for election to the Senate, which it was unable to fully articulate.[63] A further, more fundamental, problem was that the proposal was inconsistent with the general philosophy of gradual and incremental constitutional change adopted by the ruling party.[64] The proposals by the Workers' Party and Commission differed in two respects. First, the Workers' Party suggested an elected Upper House, whereas the Commission had recommended setting up an appointed specialist body of experts. Second, the Workers' Party recommended that the issue should be put to a vote in a national referendum where the electorate decide on whether they prefer the Executive's proposals or the proposal to establish a Senate.[65] The Commission had, instead, recognized that the "choice of constitutional design and arrangements to achieve particular ends are quintessentially political questions … [they] should be left to the Legislature or, in extreme circumstances, the electorate voting in a referendum."[66] These two aspects – overall – made the Workers' Party's proposal a much more significant one to put on the table.[67] It was unlikely that a major proposal of this kind would have been accepted or precipitated changes to the Executive's own proposal.[68] It was further unlikely that the issue would be put to a national referendum, especially as the issue of change through referendum has been consistently parked every time the issue has come up.[69]

The Workers' Party renewed their efforts at addressing issues with the reserved election mechanism once the amendments were passed. Ms Sylvia Lim, an elected MP from the opposition Workers' Party, moved a motion in Parliament to clarify the Government's basis for counting the timing of the reserved presidential election cycle.[70] The Workers' Party choose to do this via an "adjournment motion" pursuant to Order 24 of the Standing Orders of Parliament. This is a motion debated after the call to end a parliamentary sitting, to raise additional matters of public concern. However, this right to raise matters via an adjournment motion is allotted to one Member of Parliament per sitting. Pursuant to Order 24(5), should there be more than one member claiming the right, the adjournment motion will be decided by ballot. There is always a need to strike a balance in parliamentary procedure – so that standing orders and rules do not unnecessarily limit the occasions for debate but also discourage obstruction of government and parliamentary business.[71] The motion was unsuccessful in being picked for debate during two prior ballots: and was only selected in a third ballot. This was unfortunately after the presidential election in 2017. When ultimately debated, the debate was brief and ultimately the motion was not passed.[72] This highlights a level of difficulty with getting issues on the parliamentary agenda for debate.[73] This, in turn, raises the question of whether the proposed motion would have met with more success had the opposition adopted an alternative process than an adjournment motion. For example, Orders 34 and

35 allow for the introduction of a private members' motion. This only needs to be backed by five supporters from Parliament in order to be introduced onto the agenda: there is no ballot, nor any restriction on the number of motions that may be allowed per parliamentary sitting. This type of motion could have been a more timely way of getting the issue on to the agenda: prior to the presidential elections. The next section looks more closely at the constitutional challenges, including a challenge to consider the same question raised in the adjournment motion.

The approach to politics and constitutional change set out in the Prime Minister's speech (discussed in Section 9.2) thus formed the benchmarks for discussions in Parliament. Significant counter-proposals for reform were unlikely to be pushed through or cause any significant deviation in the existing proposals. This suggests that alternative strategies may have been more useful for influence by the opposition: for example, in highlighting potential gaps in the Government's proposals (as was done by several NMPs on the issue of mixed-race parentage). Through posing questions on these issues, the relevant members were at least able to get clarity on the intention and purpose behind the various reform proposals.

9.4 The Judiciary: contributing to the constitutional narrative

These constitutional amendments triggered judicial challenges in Singapore.[74] This provides a unique opportunity to consider the role of *all three* branches during a process of formal constitutional change.[75] There were two separate challenges: *Ravi s/o Madasamy* v. *Attorney-General & Other Matters*[76] ("*M Ravi*") and *Tan Cheng Bock* v. *Attorney-General*[77] ("*Tan Cheng Bock*"). In *M Ravi*, the plaintiff challenged the stringency of the qualification requirements for candidacy to run as a President as well as the reserved election mechanism. In *Tan Cheng Bock*, the plaintiff challenged the constitutionality of the legislative provisions that implemented the reserved election mechanism.[78]

Both challenges were unsuccessful. This section analyses the two constitutional challenges and the different strategies used by the plaintiffs: one that relied primarily on the basic structure of the Constitution to challenge the amendments and the other that relied more generally on the interpretation of and inter-relationship between different provisions of the Constitution. The discussion demonstrates that the role of the courts, going forward, is unlikely to involve the striking down of constitutional amendments: the courts have indicated that this is not part of the constitutional tradition in Singapore.[79] The more likely role for the courts will be in articulating aspects of the basic structure and the nature of the Constitution that can and ought to inform political debates on matters of constitutional design and change.

This role for the courts is already manifest in and prior to the case of *M Ravi*. The plaintiff challenged the amendments to Article 19 and the newly introduced Article 19B of the Constitution on a number of grounds. First, he argued that the imposition of stricter qualification criteria to be eligible to stand for election as President constituted a violation of the right to equality in Article 12(1) and, in particular, amounted to an unequal protection of the "right to political participation".[80] Second, the reserved election mechanism constituted discrimination on grounds of race (in contravention of Article 12(2)). Finally, these amendments violated the 'basic structure' of the Constitution: the latter imposes substantive limits on the power of Parliament to amend the Constitution and the office of the EP.[81] The arguments based on the 'basic structure' were not clear from the plaintiff's submissions. However, they appeared to coalesce around a guarantee of representative democracy, the right to political participation and the right to stand for public office being components of the basic structure of the Constitution.[82]

The applicant was unsuccessful.[83] The court did not accept the applicant's reading of Article 12 to include a right to political participation and equal right to stand in elections.[84] Even if it did, any restrictions on these rights did not violate Article 12. The applicable test for deciding whether a particular differential treatment contravenes Article 12 is the "reasonable classification" test. Such treatment would fail this test if the classification is founded on non-intelligible differentia (where you cannot tell who is in and who is out of the class of individuals); and where the differentia bears no rational relation to an object that is sought to be achieved by the law in question. The court stated that the relevant provisions of the Constitution (Articles 19 and 19B) easily satisfied this test.[85] The argument further failed on the basis that Article 12(2) of the Constitution expressly states that the anti-discrimination barrier set out therein only applies in respect of differential treatment not "expressly authorised by this Constitution". In any event, the reserved elections mechanism in Article 19B did not discriminate against any particular ethnic group (it was racially blind).[86] In addition, it had been pre-vetted as constitutional by the Presidential Council for Minority Rights. Finally, it was in fact aimed at promoting multiracialism versus perpetuating discrimination.[87] This exemplifies the hurdles an applicant may face when challenging race-based alterations to the electoral set-up in Singapore. Provided the provision is race-blind, has been vetted by the Presidential Council for Minority Rights, and passes the relatively low threshold imposed by the unreasonable classification test, the courts will not interrogate the use of race further.[88]

On the basic structure, the defendant argued that, even if there was an identifiable basic structure to the Constitution – namely, certain fundamental principles underpinning it – these did not impose substantive limits on the powers of Parliament to amend the Constitution. It argued that this had not been recognized in case law in Singapore – as had been argued by the plaintiff.[89] To recognize it would, in any event, be 'retrograde' in preventing constitutionally progressive amendments aimed at further enfranchising citizens.[90]

In previous cases, the Court of Appeal has accepted that there was a recognizable 'basic structure' to the Constitution.[91] For something to be recognized as part of the basic structure of the Constitution "it must be something fundamental and essential to the *political system* that is established thereunder".[92] However, even if something was regarded as part of the basic structure, the courts have not stated unequivocally in previous cases whether recognizing something as part of the 'basic structure' of Singapore imposes a substantive limit on formal amendment powers.[93]

The court in *M Ravi* was not willing to accept that the "right to stand for public office" proposed by the plaintiff was an aspect of the basic structure of the Constitution that met this definition. The plaintiff had argued that this right comprised an "unqualified right of any citizen to stand for elections, not only for the office of the President, but for any public office".[94] The court held that such a broad right could not be regarded as fundamental and essential to the political system. An alternatively framed right may conceivably have been considered part of the basic structure by the courts. For example, while restrictions in standing for election for the office of the EP itself is unlikely to be considered part of the basic structure, any restrictions (direct or indirect) on the right to vote in elections for the office of the EP may violate the basic structure. This is a right that has been recognized as fundamental to the "concept of representative government and representative democracy" and, therefore, part of the basic structure in earlier cases.[95] In any event, in *M Ravi*, the court concluded that there was at best "minimalist" judicial support for a "thin" conception of the basic structure doctrine.[96] The "thin" conception was:

> no more than a broad restatement of the truism that the Constitution rests on an overarching principled framework embracing the precepts of the rule of law and the separation of powers … these overarching principles essentially served to inform the interpretation of the Constitution … a specific application of the general principle of purposive statutory interpretation … the amendments … would not conceivably offend this "thin" conception of the basic structure doctrine. These amendments did not involve any curtailment of the judicial power or any other incursions into the precepts of the rule of law and the separation of powers.[97]

It is on this latter point that the courts in Singapore can have input when it comes to constitutional amendments. For example, the "thin" conception of the basic structure – in particular, the "overarching principled framework" – can provide the courts with the power to "remedially" interpret constitutional amendments in a manner that is compliant with the basic structure. Indeed, the courts have utilized the basic structure in this way to consider *legislative* amendments.[98]

However, the potential for this use of the basic structure as an interpretive tool needs to be considered in light of the approach taken to constitutional interpretation in *Tan Cheng Bock*.[99] The latter approach places greater emphasis on the text of constitutional provisions and the specific intention of Parliament in enacting that provision.[100] In *Tan Cheng Bock*, the plaintiff challenged the constitutionality of the new Schedule to the Presidential Elections Act, which specified the presidential term that would be used to determine whether the time had come to designate a particular election cycle as reserved for a particular race.[101] Specifically, the plaintiff argued that the Schedule contravened provisions of the

Constitution. The latter provisions constrained the mode of calculating the timeframe for calling a reserved election. The challenge focused on the correct interpretation and interrelationship between two provisions of the Constitution: Article 19B and Article 164.[102] The former introduces the system of reserved election cycles, while the latter is a transitional provision empowering Parliament to specify the first of the five most recent terms of office to be used as a starting point. The plaintiff argued that Parliament's powers under Article 164 were constrained: it could only use the term of a popularly Elected President as the starting point for counting whether to designate a particular election as reserved. This was consistent with the general purpose behind Article 19B, namely, to deal with the problem of open elections not returning a minority candidate. Parliament had thus acted unconstitutionally in designating the second term of President Wee Kim Wee, who was elected by Parliament versus popular vote, as the relevant "first term" under Article 164.

The defendant took the view that the plain language of Article 164 gives Parliament the "full discretion" to specify any term of office of the President as the "first term". In addition, it was clear from the relevant parliamentary debates that President Wee's second term would be specified as the second term. Accordingly, the courts must give effect to this clear and specific intention of Parliament, as manifested in the text and parliamentary debates, over the general purpose argued for by the plaintiff.

The plaintiff was unsuccessful. The court set out the approach to constitutional interpretation in Singapore:

> It is common ground that the Constitution should be interpreted purposively. This follows from the fact that Art 2(9) of the Constitution provides that the [Interpretation Act "IA"] IA shall apply in the interpretation of the Constitution; and the IA, as we note below, mandates the purposive approach. That means it should be interpreted in a way that gives effect to the intent and will of Parliament. This intent will generally be reflected in the text of the enactment. The Constitution's words are to be read in their grammatical and ordinary sense and in their entire context, harmoniously with the scheme of the Constitution as a whole, and the relevant objects or intentions that may be gleaned from this. Additionally, the court may consider, in certain circumstances and subject to certain limitations, relevant extraneous material … The relevant Parliamentary intention is to be found at the time the law was enacted or, in some circumstances, when it subsequently reaffirms the particular statutory provision in question …[103]

Using this approach, the court concluded that the purpose of Article 19B(1) was to ensure periodic representation of the major communities in Singapore and the purpose of Article 164 was to allow Parliament to determine when the reserved election mechanism in Article 19B(1) was triggered. The ordinary meaning of the text of these provisions and the underlying purpose shows that Parliament can specify any of the five most recent terms of office as the first term under

Article 164 for the purposes of Article 19B. The Court of Appeal went as far as to say that "the purpose of the provisions in question clearly supports only one textual interpretation".[104]

This "one clear" interpretation of the text was possible given the court's approach to identifying the purpose of the relevant provisions. On this, the Court of Appeal held that extraneous materials could only be used to "confirm but not to alter the [clear] ordinary meaning of the provision".[105] The extraneous materials the court used would typically be restricted to the parliamentary debates. From those debates, the courts would generally rely on the speech made by the sponsoring Minister proposing the Bill and any other clear and equivocal statements directed specifically to the question of purpose. The courts would also be careful not to enter into a task of construing or interpreting statements made in Parliament and deviate, therefore, from the task of interpreting legislation. On this, the court noted the difficulties:

> the debates feature different statements by various MPs, from which the court must extract the collective will and intent of Parliament. As we earlier indicated, we must also carefully assess whether the Parliamentary statements relied on are directed to the point in dispute.[106]

Therefore, the parliamentary debates – questions and answers and statements from various MPs – need to speak to the collective will and intent before they are utilized by the courts.

On this basis, the Court of Appeal restricted itself to considering only those parts of the parliamentary debates that addressed the specific issue at hand: when the reserved election model was to take effect and the extent of Parliament's power when it came to specifying the first term under Article 164. This was found in one section of PM Lee's speech, which specifically stated that Parliament will start counting from Dr Wee Kim Wee.[107] Accordingly, the Court of Appeal did not accept the plaintiff's evidence based on the Constitutional Commission's Report or the White Paper that followed thereafter because:

> neither document addressed the question of when and how the hiatus-triggered model would commence. Instead, these documents pertain to the concept of the reserved election rather than to the specific question of when the count could start for the purposes of determining if an election would be reserved.[108]

This arguably made the broader constitutional narrative or purpose of reserved elections subservient to the specific intention of Parliament as manifested through specific statements during parliamentary debates – even where the latter may arguably be seen to undermine or under-serve the former.[109]

This also contrasts with the broader approach to purposive interpretation proposed by the High Court in *M Ravi*. While the court in *M Ravi* called the thin conception of the basic structure doctrine a "specific application of the general principle of purposive statutory interpretation",[110] it is clear that it methodologically differs from the approach to purposive interpretation set out in *Tan Cheng Bock*: which relies on parliamentary intent as apparent primarily from the text of a provision. The *M Ravi* approach to interpretation is instead informed by the meta-purpose of the Constitution: the broad principles of rule of law, the features of the political system and separation of powers. If the *Tan Cheng Bock* approach prevails, it will mean that courts cannot appropriate too much ground for themselves but will have to vest significant authority in Parliament to drive the way text is interpreted. The scope of the court's role going forward will, therefore, depend on how the courts eventually reconcile these two approaches to "purposive interpretation". It is the "thin conception" of the basic structure that provides the greater scope for judicial input on the interpretation and post-enactment operationalization of constitutional amendments.

9.5 Conclusion

The discussions in this concluding chapter demonstrate that the interventions by other actors – the Constitutional Commission, opposition and non-elected members of Parliament and the Judiciary – were ultimately unable to alter the course of the amendments. The chapter has considered, however, the capacity for a softer impact of the input from other actors at this stage of Singapore's constitutional evolution: in particular, the opposition and unelected members of Parliament and the potential impact from the Judiciary via the thin conception of the basic structure. It is possible that recent structural changes in the way the opposition organized themselves may also lead to enhanced input from this sector.[111] These alternative sites of constitutional deliberation have the potential to be important additional and different voices on important constitutional questions. A culture of constitutional polyphony can be an important advance in constitutional politics in Singapore: especially on critical issues like multiracialism.[112]

Ensuring a diversification of input on institutional design questions becomes ever critical as the Constitution develops. A major theme of the volume is the various trenchant tensions that have developed over time within the constitutional framework of Singapore and the task of managing and resolving them through constitutional design and redesign. In Chapter 2, Li-ann Thio observes that the ease with which the Constitution can be changed in Singapore (both through formal amendment and the organic development of soft constitutional law norms) has contributed to the creation of a number of tensions. As Li-ann Thio observes in her chapter, the focus of the various constitutional amendment exercises has then had to shift to resolving and managing these tensions.[113] The most recent amendment exercise sought to resolve the build-up of a number of strains in the system. The friction between electoral and multiracial representation was a significant source of debate during the 2016 amendment exercise. It is only the second time since Singapore's independence that the electoral system has been reconfigured to ensure a degree of multiracial representation.[114] These competing ideas of representation – electoral and racial – stem from another strain within the office of the President: that between the symbolic and custodial functions of the President. The former envisage the President as an embodiment of multiracial representation, whereas the latter require the President to also have a democratic mandate from elections. The natural sunset mechanism built into the reserved election mechanism is indicative of the discomfort with the current situation where racial representation is not possible through open competitive elections. It therefore is an expression of optimism that there will be a time when "free and unregulated elections produce presidents from a varied distribution of ethnicities".[115] The reserved election mechanism was seen as an optimal way of resolving this tension.[116]

The changes to the powers of Parliament to override a presidential veto sought to resolve another tension identified by Li-ann Thio: how much power should be accorded to the President? As highlighted by the Constitutional Commission, "inherent in the concept of checks and balances is the prospect of impasses arising. The ability of the Government to function effectively is critical and Singapore can ill-afford a logjam…"[117] The Constitutional Commission thus thought it necessary to reconsider the balance between the Government and the President.[118] This was to be achieved by augmenting the parliamentary override of the presidential veto by according greater weight to the collective views of the CPA.[119] This raised the secondary concern that augmenting the parliamentary override actually involves a shift in power from the President to the CPA (given Parliament would, in effect, be siding with the CPA in the case of an impasse). This needed to be done without unduly politicizing the CPA, especially given that the latter are unelected.[120] The precise scope of the custodial functions of the President therefore required a fine calibration between the following metrics: the need for a sufficient external check, this check must be done on the back of a democratic mandate, the check should not be at risk of politicization and the check must not cause 'logjams'.

It is not just the substantive aspects of the 2016 amendment exercise that exemplify tension. The 2016 exercise also demonstrated how the process for consulting and deliberating on constitutional amendments could itself embody a particular tension. How much should constitutional design be responsive to public consultation and input, as opposed to managed by the political branches? As Maartje De Visser discusses in her chapter, the involvement of citizens on questions of constitutional amendment can inject an amendment process with an important diversity of views and, ultimately, a sense of legitimacy. This chapter however, exemplifies how the Executive considered it equally important to maintain control over the agenda, scope and pace of constitutional change. This control is evident throughout the process: in initiating and setting up the Constitutional Commission as the fora for public deliberation, setting the Terms of Reference and agenda for change and in reacting to the proposals made by the Constitutional Commission's following its public hearings. The involvement of the public was important, but so was the need to manage the pace of reform. This pervades the approach to political and constitutional change generally. Most recently, this philosophy was reinforced in the context of the leadership transition within the People's Action Party. The current Prime Minister Lee Hsien Loong has already indicated he will be stepping down by 2021. This brings into question leadership transition within the party. Speaking on this, the Prime Minister emphasized the need for a "smooth and sure-footed" transition.[121] This point was reiterated by ex-Prime Minister and now Member of Parliament, Goh Chok Tong:

> It requires painstaking preparation and testing in all aspects – in policies and politics, in taking hard decisions, in fighting and winning elections, in winning the minds and hearts of people, in forging good relations with leaders of other countries and in bonding as a team.[122]

Balancing the need for change and evolution against the need for stability and endurance is clear in the new (yet to be brought into force) amendment provisions. For example, a bill seeking to abolish the Presidency could only be introduced in Parliament if the President concurs (or where the CPA had recommended to the President that he should concur) or the introduction of the bill is supported by a simple majority at a national referendum. Once introduced, the bill can be passed with a two-thirds majority in Parliament.[123] Amendments to provisions setting out the discretionary powers of the President would be subject to alternative amendment rules. For example, a bill that sought to alter the President's discretionary powers – but not remove them *in toto* – could only be introduced in the same way as a bill seeking to abolish the Presidency. However, there is an alternative procedure whereby it can also be introduced in Parliament if this is supported by three-quarters of the members of Parliament, thereby by-passing both the President and CPA.[124] All other constitutional amendment bills require a two-thirds majority in Parliament to be passed. Once passed and if the President withholds his assent to the bill on the ground that it actually does curtail his powers, the bill can still be passed if: (a) the CPA concur with the President, but either a simple majority at a national referendum or three-quarters of the members of Parliament override the President's withholding of assent; or (b) if the CPA had recommended the President to assent to the bill and a two-thirds majority of the members of Parliament override the President's veto.[125] These provisions highlight that each point of resistance in the process is always subject to an override aimed at unlocking any potential gridlock, in favour of change.

Given that the Elected Presidency has been the focus of the various alternative amendment provisions proposed over time, it is unsurprising that the suggestion by the Constitutional Commission to fundamentally alter the nature of the office was firmly rejected by the Government. The Commission had proposed decoupling the custodial and symbolic functions of the office, as a way of resolving the tension inherent in these two roles. The President could revert to being appointed by Parliament and perform symbolic functions, with the custodial functions being transferred to a "council of experts" that form a second chamber of Parliament.[126] This recommendation from the Commission came on the back of submissions from the public.[127] However, the Government's response was modest: this was too big a change, preferring the more modest race-blind reserved election mechanism with its natural sunset.[128]

Going forward, constitutional amendment and change will need to evolve to be a multi-event and multi-actor effort: starting upstream and *ex ante* through legislative debates on the legislation to downstream and *ex post* efforts in the discussion of those changes in courts and in participation in constitutional change by citizens. Thoughtful and considered interventions in parliamentary debates upstream can eliminate or minimize the possibility of tension developing in the Constitution. It can also have important secondary outcomes further downstream in setting out what the courts can then rely on to clarify grey areas in the course of constitutional interpretation; in providing the Executive with guidance on how to operationalize new provisions in new contexts; and indeed influence how the electorate debate and discuss issues of constitutional importance. The diversity of viewpoints expressed by the authors in this volume exemplify the advantages of debate and deliberation on core constitutional questions.

Notes

1 Article 5(2):

> A Bill seeking to amend any provision in this Constitution shall not be passed by Parliament unless it has been supported on Second and Third Readings by the votes of not less than two-thirds of the total number of Members of Parliament (excluding nominated Members).

2 The old Article 5(2A) and the new Articles 5A, 5B and 5C introduced in 2016 (but which have yet to be brought into operation). See "Entrenchment Framework": Deputy Prime Minister Teo Chee Hean, "Second Reading, Constitution of the Republic of Singapore (Amendment) Bill" (*Prime Minister's Office Singapore*, 7 November 2016) www.pmo.gov.sg/newsroom/speech-dpm-teo-chee-hean-2nd-reading-constitutional-republic-singapore-amendment-bill (accessed 31 August 2018).

3 Kevin Y.L. Tan, *The Constitution of Singapore: A Contextual Analysis* (Oxford: Hart Publishing, 2015) (Hereinafter referred to as "Tan"), Chapter 2; Li-ann Thio, "In search of the Singapore Constitution: retrospect and prospect", in Li-ann Thio and Kevin Y.L. Tan (eds), *Evolution of a Revolution: Forty Years of the Singapore Constitution* (London: Routledge, 2008), 355; and Michael Dowdle and Kevin Tan, "Is Singapore's Constitution best considered a legal or political constitution?", in Jaclyn L. Neo (ed.), *Constitutional Interpretation in Singapore: Theory and Practice* (Abingdon: Routledge, 2017), 365–72.

4 Informing the Executive's decision not to entrench the office of the Elected President through the commencement of more difficult amendment provisions: see Li-ann Thio, "Past imperfect, future tense: the Elected Presidency and the constitutional development of an 'ever evolving hybrid'", Chapter 2 in this volume, on the entrenchment of the President and the political conditions that make regular amendments to the Elected Presidency possible.

5 The new Article 19B provides that: "[a]n election for the office of President is reserved for a community if no person belonging to that community has held the office of President for any of the 5 most recent terms of office of the President." "Community" here means the Chinese, Malay or Indian/other minority communities in Singapore. Hereinafter referred to as the "reserved election mechanism".

6 Most bills are government bills introduced by the Minister concerned: there are very few instances where a private member can introduce a bill – see Tan (n. 3), 97–9. See also M. Russell and D. Gover, *Legislation at Westminster: Parliamentary Actors and Influence in the Making of British Law* (Oxford: Oxford University Press, 2017), Chapters 1 and 2.

7 J. Neo and Y. C.L. Lee, "Constitutional supremacy: still a little dicey", in Li-Ann Thio and Kevin Y.L. Tan (eds), *Evolution of a Revolution: Forty Years of the Singapore Constitution* (London: Routledge, 2010).

8 NCMPs are those members who were not directly elected but received the highest number of votes from the losing candidates in a general election.

9 This would involve changes to the Constitution (in the case of the number and voting rights of NCMPs). Changes to the designation of constituencies as single member or group representation constituencies would be done by the Election Boundaries Review Committee.

10 Terms of Reference, Constitutional Commission: Prime Minister's Office, "Constitutional Commission to review specific aspects of the Elected Presidency", *Prime Minister's Office Singapore* (10 February 2016) www.pmo.gov.sg/newsroom/constitutional-commission-review-specific-aspects-elected-presidency (accessed 31 August 2018). Maartje De Visser's contribution to this volume considers in detail the Terms of Reference and influence of the Constitutional Commission.

11 Prime Minister Lee Hsien Loong, *Singapore Parliamentary Debates: Official Record*, 27 January 2016, vol. 94 ("Debate on President's Address"). Reiterated at the 2016 National Day Rally by PM Lee: PM Lee Hsien Loong, "PM Lee Hsien Loong delivered his National Day Rally speech on 21 August 2016 at the ITE College Central", *Prime Minister's Office Singapore* (21 August 2016) www.pmo.gov.sg/national-day-rally-2016 (accessed 31 August 2018) (Hereinafter referred to as "2016 National Day Rally"): "the President makes critical decisions and it is here that we need the President to be competent, to be on top of the job, to be capable and that is why we need the most qualified person." See Eugene Tan, "Perfecting Singapore's system of political governance: privileging elites in the quest for good governance", Chapter 4 in this volume.

12 *Ibid.* Again this was reiterated during the 2016 National Day Rally, *ibid.*:

> When we designed the scheme, we designed it like that – you have a President, he is elected, but he does not act alone. He is advised by a council of wise men – the Council of Presidential Advisers. So, when he makes decisions, he will have the benefit of the experience and judgement of the CPA. We expected to improve the CPA and strengthen the CPA over time as it became more established. The arrangements have worked well and so, the changes being proposed are incremental and straightforward.

See also Select Committee, *Report of the Select Committee on the Constitution of the Republic of Singapore (Amendment No 3) Bill (Bill No 23/90)* (Parl 9 of 1990, 18 December 1990) (hereinafter referred to as "1990 Select Committee Report"), para. 31 – "*[over] time, [the CPA] should grow in importance, perhaps evolving into a Council of State*". See Eugene Tan, "Perfecting Singapore's system of political governance: privileging elites in the quest for good governance", Chapter 4 in this volume.

13 *Ibid.* Again reiterated during the 2016 National Day Rally: "We want a minority Singaporean regularly to become President, to represent what we feel about Singapore, and our ideal of a multi-racial society."

14 See Kevin Y.L. Tan and Lam Peng Er, "Looking back at the Elected Presidency: design choices and unintended consequences", Chapter 1 in this volume.

15 2016 National Day Rally, n. (13).

16 *Ibid.*

17 "White Paper on the review of specific aspects of the Elected Presidency", *Prime Minister's Office Singapore* (15 September 2016) Cwww.gov.sg/~/media/elected%20presidency/files/white%20paper%20on%20the%20review%20of%20specific%20aspects%20of%20the%20elected%20presidency.pdf (accessed 31 August 2018) (hereinafter referred to as "White Paper"): The Executive did accept a number of proposals – most importantly the reserved election mechanism. The White Paper still, however, exemplifies how the end point for questions of constitutional design is the Executive.

18 This would involve shifting more power to the CPA. See Eugene Tan, "Perfecting Singapore's system of political governance: privileging elites in the quest for good governance", Chapter 4 in this volume.

19 White Paper (n. 17), paras 35, 103–5.

20 *Ibid.*, paras 124(a)–(d).

21 Constitutional Commission, *Report of the Constitutional Commission 2016* (2016) (hereinafter referred to as "Report of the Constitutional Commission 2016"), para. 8.23.

22 *Ibid.*, para. 7.43.

23 *Ibid.*, paras 7.46–7.53.

24 Yusof Bin Ishak (1965–1970; prior to that as Yang di-Pertuan Negara from 1959–1965), Dr Benjamin Henry Sheares (1970–1981), C.V. Devan Nair (1981–1985) and then Wee Kim Wee (1985–1993), respectively.

25 Zuraidah Ibrahim and Irene Ng, "Good to rotate EP among races", *The Straits Times* (11 August 1999), 27.

26 *Ibid.*, paras 7.46 and 7.48.

27 *Ibid.*, para. 7.48.

28 See Maartje De Visser, "Of Constitutional Commissions and expert-led interpretation during processes of constitutional change", Chapter 8 in this volume for a discussion of the expertise of members of the Constitutional Commission.

29 See, Kevin Y.L. Tan and Lam Peng Er, "Looking back at the Elected Presidency: design choices and unintended consequences", Chapter 1 in this volume.

30 White Paper (n. 17), 125.

31 *Ibid.*, paras 82 and 83. See, Jaclyn L. Neo, "Constitutionalizing minority representation: the reserved elections mechanism and politicization of ethnicity in Singapore", Chapter 5 and Eugene K.B. Tan, "Squaring the circle: the President as a symbol of multiracialism and national unity", Chapter 6 in this volume.

32 A. Teng, "Questions raised about presidential election show that people want race to matter less: D.P.M. Tharman", *Straits Times* (Singapore, 21 September 2017) www.straitstimes.com/singapore/education/questions-raised-about-presidential-election-show-that-they-want-race-to-matter (accessed 31 August 2018).

33 There was, of course, popular exchange outside of these fora – non-executive led/spontaneous exchange online/via the media/blogosphere. The discussion above just highlights the presence of significant broader executive-led mobilized activities relating to the political and constitutional changes with the office of the Presidency.

34 This included a televised interview with the Prime Minister on 4 September 2016 on Channel News Asia and a televised roundtable on 11 September 2016 with the Minister for Law and Home Affairs, K. Shanmugan, NMP Azmoon Ahmad and academics from the Institute of Policy Studies (Ms Gillian Koh) and Faculty of Law at the National University of Singapore (Assistant Professor Cheah Wui Ling).

35 When the Elected Presidency was first introduced in 1991, this was done via White Papers, parliamentary debates and a Select Committee: see K. Tan, "The Presidency in Singapore: constitutional developments", in K.Y.L. Tan and Lam Peng Er (eds), *Managing Political Change in Singapore: The Elected Presidency* (London: Routledge, 1997).

36 Joel Colón-Ríos, "Introduction: the forms and limits of constitutional amendments" (1 July 2015) 13(3) *International Journal of Constitutional Law* 567–74. See also

See Maartje De Visser, "Of Constitutional Commissions and expert-led interpretation during processes of constitutional change", Chapter 8 in this volume.

37 Ron Levy, "Breaking the constitutional deadlock: lessons from deliberative experiments in constitutional change" (2010) 34(3) *Melbourne University Law Review* 805, 829.

38 A. Horne and A. Le Sueur, "Introduction", in A. Horne and A. Le Sueur (eds), *Parliament: Legislation and Accountability* (Oxford: Hart Publishing, 2016), 2; Henry M. Hart, Jr. and Albert M. Sacks, William N. Eskridge, Jr. and Philip P. Frickey (eds), *The Legal Process: Basic Problems in the Making and Application of Law* (New York: Foundation Press, 1994), 164; Jeremy Waldron, *Law and Disagreement* (Oxford: Oxford University Press, 1999) (hereinafter referred to as "Waldron"), 9–10; C. Hübner Mendes, *Constitutional Courts and Deliberative Democracy* (Oxford: Oxford University Press, 2013), 12; T.R.S. Allan, "common law constitutionalism and freedom of speech", in J. Beatson and Y. Cripps (eds), *Freedom of Expression and Freedom of Information: Essays in Honour of Sir David Williams* (Oxford: Oxford University Press, 2000); and D. Baranger, "Parliamentary Law and Parliamentary Government in Britain: Some Historical Remarks", in Katja S. Ziegler, Denis Baranger and Anthony W. Bradley (eds), *Constitutionalism and the Role of Parliaments* (Oxford: Hart Publishing, 2007), 18, 46.

39 P.J. Yap, *Courts and Democracies in Asia* (Cambridge: Cambridge University Press, 2018), 19. See also W.E. Gladstone, "The declining efficiency of Parliament" (1856), 99 *The Quarterly Review* 529.

40 See A. Le Divellec, "Cabinet as the leading part of Parliament: the Westminster Model in Europe", in Katja S. Ziegler, Denis Baranger and Anthony W. Bradley (eds), *Constitutionalism and the Role of Parliaments* (Oxford: Hart Publishing, 2007) (hereinafter referred to as "A. Le Divellec").

41 NMPs are non-partisan members drawn from different sectors of society (Arts, Business, Education etc) and are appointed by a Select Committee versus elected into Parliament: see Articles 39(1)(*c*) and 44(1) and the Fourth Schedule of the Constitution.

42 The current make-up of Parliament is: 101 seats (with 89 MPs (out of which nine are elected opposition party members); three NCMPs and nine NMPs, that is, 20.1 per cent of the Members of Parliament are not from the dominant party. The "guaranteed opposition" in Singapore is thus far from the shadow opposition arrangements present in other Westminster parliamentary systems.

43 See, for example, *Singapore Parliamentary Debates: Official Report*, 29 July 1988, vol. 51, col. 478 (Constitutional Amendments to Safeguard the Financial Assets and the Integrity of the Public Services) and second White Paper: The President of the Republic of Singapore *Safeguarding Financial Assets and the Integrity of the Public Services: The Constitution of the Republic of Singapore (Amendment No 3) Bill* (White Paper, Cmd 11, 1990) in Parliament on 27 August 1990.

44 See, for example, the Select Committee on Article 5(2A) on some aspects of the entrenchment framework: *Report of the Select Committee on the Constitution of the Republic of Singapore (Amendment No. 3) Bill (Bill No. 23/90) (Parl 9 of 1990, 18 December 1990)* at [20] and [21]. It was not successful, however, in pushing through the commencement of the alternative entrenchment framework (at [73]; see Prime Minister Goh Chok Tong, *Singapore Parliamentary Debates: Official Report*, 3 January 1991, vol. 56, col. 722 (Constitution of the Republic of Singapore (Amendment No. 3) Bill). Membership of select committees – a spread across different categories of members of Parliament – is therefore important.

45 See, for example, on the introduction of the Elected Presidency scheme: *Report of the Select Committee on the Constitution of the Republic of Singapore (Amendment No. 3) Bill (Bill No. 23/90) (Parl 9 of 1990, 18 December 1990)* and more recently *Select Committee on Deliberate Online Falsehoods – Causes, Consequences and Countermeasures* (2018).

46 Tan (n. 3), 100–1.
47 N. Barber, "Prelude to the separation of powers", *Cambridge Law Journal* 60(1) (March 2001), 59–88, 84.
48 See Tan (n. 3), at 109. Again, these concerns are not unique to Singapore: see, A. Le Divellec (n. 40).
49 This is true here and elsewhere: Meg Russell and Daniel Glover, *Legislation at Westminster: Parliamentary Actors and Influence in the Making of British Law* (Oxford: Oxford University Press, 2017), Chapter 10 (Parliamentary Power and the Legislative Process).
50 W. Riker and B. Weingast, "Constitutional regulation of legislative choice: the political consequences of Judicial Deference to Legislatures", *Virginia Law Review* (1988) 74(2), 373–401.
51 Waldron (n. 38), 13–15.
52 This is across both debates – on the Constitution of the Republic of Singapore (Amendment) Bill (7–9 November 2016) and the subsequent debates on the implementing legislation, the Presidential Elections (Amendment) Bill (6 February 2017).
53 Including the politicization of ethnicity and the inadvertent introduction of group-based affirmative action into politics: see Jaclyn L. Neo, "Constitutionalizing minority representation: the reserved elections mechanism and politicization of ethnicity in Singapore", Chapter 5 and Eugene K.B. Tan, "Squaring the circle: the President as a symbol of multiracialism and national unity", Chapter 6 in this volume.
54 A powerful example is the speech by Ms Chia Yong Yong who observed that:

> I used to look at anything that we do that highlights differences in race as the institutionalisation of racial differences. For that, for many years, I had reservations and I could not in good conscience support a lot of initiatives. But I am coming to realise that when we talk about minority representation, it is a recognition of differences and when we institutionalise that in the Office of the President, we are respecting the differences. This is not new to have the rotation of different races in the Office of President. Switzerland has it. New Zealand has it. And I do not know why Singapore cannot have it.

Ms Chia Yong Yong, *Singapore Parliamentary Debates: Official Report*, 9 November 2016, vol. 94 (Second Reading of Constitution of the Republic of Singapore (Amendment) Bill.).
55 These Committees issue "community certificates" to certify that a particular applicant belongs to the community to which the election is reserved: Presidential Elections Act, Part III.
56 The PAP MPs who asked questions on the specifics of the reserved elections mechanism included: Vikram Nair, Rahayu Mahzam, Louis Ng Kwok Hang, Ang Wei Neng and Joan Pereira. For example, Mr Vikram Nair had queries on the mechanics relating to the appointment and setting up of the Community Committees (that certify membership of a particular race during a reserved election) and the issue of mixed-race parentage and the issues associated with classifying such individuals but generally supported the reserved election mechanism: Mr Vikram Nair, *Singapore Parliamentary Debates: Official Report*, 6 February 2017, vol. 94 (Second Reading, Presidential Elections (Amendment) Bill) This is in line with the vision for parliamentary politics in Singapore – where everyone must come together for the good of Singapore: see PM Lee – Toh Yong Chuan, "High-quality debate shows how Parliament should work: PM", *The Straits Times* (Singapore, 5 March 2017) www.straitstimes.com/singapore/high-quality-debate-shows-how-parliament-should-work-pm (accessed 31 August 2018).
57 Mr Chan Chun Sing, *Singapore Parliamentary Debates: Official Report*, 6 February 2017, vol. 94, 58. See Jack Tsen-Ta Lee, "From eligibility to election: the mechanics of the presidential poll", Chapter 7 in this volume for a further discussion on the role of the community committees.

58 Madam Rahayu Mahzam, *Singapore Parliamentary Debates: Official Report*, 9 November 2016, vol. 94, 74.

59 Deputy Prime Minister Teo Chee Hean, *Singapore Parliamentary Debates: Official Report*, 9 November 2016, vol. 94, 104.

60 See Submissions by Workers' Party to the Constitutional Commission Secretariat, 21 March 2016: Workers' Party, "The Workers' Party's Submission to the Constitutional Commission Secretariat on the Elected Presidency", *Workers' Party* (21 March 2016) www.wp.sg/the-workers-partys-submission-to-the-constitutional-commission-secretariat-on-the-elected-presidency/ (accessed 31 August 2018).

61 The concern that the elections for and the office of the EP would become politicized – with the office being seen as one that could 'confront' the Government of the day – was raised during the Constitutional Commission hearings, especially in light of 2011 Presidential Elections. The Government again reiterated that the issues could be resolved in a much more modest way than decoupling the office in the way suggested by the Workers' Party. It could be done through the regulation of elections: see Jack Tsen-Ta Lee, "From eligibility to election: the mechanics of the presidential poll", Chapter 7 in this volume.

62 See, for example, Mr Leon Perera, *Singapore Parliamentary Debates: Official Report*, 6 February 2017, vol. 94, 70.

63 Mr K. Shanmugam, *Singapore Parliamentary Debates: Official Report*, 8 November 2016, vol. 94 (Second Reading of Constitution of the Republic of Singapore (Amendment) Bill)).

64 As reiterated by Deputy Prime Minister Teo Chee Hean during the debates on the Workers' Party's proposal: *Singapore Parliamentary Debates: Official Report*, 8 November 2016, vol. 94, 110.

65 Ms Sylvia Lim, *Singapore Parliamentary Debates: Official Report*, 7 November 2016, vol. 94 (Second Reading of Constitution of the Republic of Singapore (Amendment) Bill)).

66 *Report of the Constitutional Commission 2016* (n. 21), para. 8.36.

67 See Maartje De Visser, "Of Constitutional Commissions and expert-led interpretation during processes of constitutional change", Chapter 8 in this volume.

68 Again, this contrasts with the approach of the NMPs. Mr Mahdev Mohan had commended the Commission's recommendations in his speech to the Executive, recognizing the potential of the proposed council of experts to serve as a 'stabilizer'.

69 With various provisions to allow referenda being introduced into the text but not brought into force.

70 Specifically they queried:

> on the Parliamentary debates, and one aspect only of those debates. What did the Government tell Parliament was the basis for counting Reserved Presidential Elections under the hiatus triggered model, and was what the Government told Parliament accurate? To cut to the chase – did the Prime Minister, Deputy Prime Minister Teo Chee Hean and Minister Chan Chun Sing make misleading statements to the House that the question of which President to count from was a legal question? Did the Government all along make a policy decision itself to count from President Wee Kim Wee? Did the Government merely use the AGC's advice as a cover to avoid full Parliamentary debate on why the count was not starting from President Ong Teng Cheong?

Ms Sylvia Lim, *Singapore Parliamentary Debates: Official Report*, 3 October 2016, vol. 94 (Motion on Counting From President Wee Kim Wee or President Ong Teng Cheong for Reserved Presidential Election – Policy Decision or Legal Question?).

71 T. Erskine May, "The machinery of parliamentary legislation" (1854) (January) *Edinburgh Review* 244, 282; D. Limon, W.E. McKay, G. Cubie *et al.* (eds), *Erskine*

May's Treatise on the Law, Privileges, Proceedings and Usage of Parliament, 22nd edn (London: Butterworths, 1997), 5.

72 See www.parliament.gov.sg/docs/default-source/default-document-library/v-p-3oct17.pdf.

73 Katja S. Ziegler, Denis Baranger and Anthony W. Bradley (eds), *Constitutionalism and the Role of Parliaments* (Oxford: Hart Publishing, 2007), 36, 45 on the absence of neutrality in the rules of procedure in parliament – the rules tend to allocate control over parliamentary agenda to the ruling party in a Westminster-style government.

74 The focus of the challenges was the reserved election mechanism. There could have been other challenges, for example, on the issue of the timing of the presidential election in 2017. This was ultimately held on 13 September 2017. Article 17A of the Constitution and Section 6(1) of the Presidential Elections Act specify when the election should be held: within six months after the office of the President becomes vacant before the expiration of a term of office or, in all other cases, not more than three months before the office of the President becomes vacant. President Tony Tan served the duration of his office, which became vacant on 1 September 2017. The writ of election was issued on 28 August 2017 for the election on 13 September 2017, that is, after the expiry of the term of office of the incumbent President: there thus could be an argument that the election was void for not complying with the provisions. However, the Government took the view that this was permissible under Article 22N of the Constitution: Mr Chan Chun Sing, *Singapore Parliamentary Debates: Official Report*, 6 February 2017, vol. 94 (Second Reading of Presidential Elections (Amendment) Bill).

75 Courts, of course, contribute to the organic evolution of a constitution through its interpretation of constitutional provisions and constitutional adjudication over time: see Swati S. Jhaveri, "The role of courts in advancing constitutional moments: constitutionalising the constitution in Singapore and Hong Kong", in Richard Albert, Menaka Guruswamy and Nischal Basnyat (eds), *Constitutional Creation and Reconstruction: Founding Moments* (Oxford: Hart Publishing, 2019, pp. 33–52).

76 [2017] 5 SLR 489.

77 [2017] 5 SLR 424 (High Court) and [2017] 2 SLR 850 (Court of Appeal).

78 Section 22 the Presidential Elections (Amendment) Act 2017; the new Schedule to the Presidential Elections Act.

79 See Swati S. Jhaveri and Jaclyn L. Neo, "The many facets of constitutional dialogue: the case of Singapore" (2017) 18(1) *Australian Journal of Asian Law*, 1–14. The position in Singapore resonates with that adopted in other common law jurisdictions.

80 This is not an explicit right – the applicant extrapolated this right from the right to vote which was recognized in earlier cases (*M Ravi* (n. 68), para. [29]).

81 *Ibid.*, 8–10, 14–15 and 29.

82 The court was similarly unclear and chose to extract the applicant's submissions in the judgement at great length due to this lack of clarity – *ibid.*, paras [29]–[30]. See also court's comments at para. [53,] on the lack of clarity in the applicant's arguments.

83 This was also due to his lack of standing. The applicant commenced proceedings in his "personal capacity" as a "public interest litigator": *ibid.*, para. [3], [43]–[53]. The rules of standing in Singapore are tightly drawn and would definitely exclude the application: Swati S. Jhaveri, "Advancing constitutional justice in Singapore: enhancing access and standing in judicial review cases" (2017) *Singapore Journal of Legal Studies* 1–24.

84 Article 12 states:

> (1) All persons are equal before the law and entitled to the equal protection of the law, (2) Except as expressly authorised by this Constitution, there shall be no discrimination against citizens of Singapore on the ground only of religion, race,

descent or place of birth in any law or in the appointment to any office or employment under a public authority or in the administration of any law relating to the acquisition, holding or disposition of property or the establishing or carrying on of any trade, business, profession, vocation or employment.

See *ibid.*, at [76].

85 The deferential nature of the test has been well documented: see, for example, B. Ong, "New approaches to the constitutional guarantee of equality before the law" (2016) 28 *Singapore Academy of Law Journal*, 320; Jaclyn L. Neo, "Equal Protection and the Reasonable Classification Test in Singapore: After *Lim Meng Suang v. Attorney-General*" (2016) *Singapore Journal of Legal Studies* March, 95; and P.J. Yap, "Section 377A and Equal Protection in Singapore: Back to 1938?" (2013) 25 *Singapore Academy of Law Journal*, 630–40.

86 In argument, the defendant made the point that, in any event the Constitution was not intended to be 'race-neutral': Article 152 of the Constitution specifically imposes a duty on the Government to care for the interests of racial and religious minorities: *M Ravi* (n. 68), para. 42.

87 *Ibid.*, [81]. Pursuant to Articles 78(2), 79(2) and 80(2) of the Constitution, the Presidential Council for Minority Rights considers all bills or subsidiary legislation for the presence of any differentiating measures. Article 68 defines "differentiating measures" as "any measure which is, or is likely in its practical application to be, disadvantageous to persons of other such communities, either directly by prejudicing persons of that community or indirectly by giving advantage to persons of another community".

88 See Yap Po Jen, "Section 377A and Equal Protection in Singapore: Back to 1938?" (2013) 25 *Singapore Academy of Law Journal*, 630; Jaclyn L. Neo, "Equal Protection and the Reasonable Classification Test in Singapore: after *Lim Meng Suang* v. *Attorney-General*" (2016) *Singapore Journal of Legal Studies*, 95–117 on issues with the reasonable classification test.

89 The plaintiff's position was based on the Indian "basic features" doctrine: *Kesavananda Bharati* v. *State of Kerala* AIR 1973 SC 1461 where it was held that: "every provision of the Constitution can be amended provided in the result the basic foundation and structure of the Constitution remains the same" (para. [316]). See also *Minerva Mills Ltd and Ors* v. *Union of India and Ors* AIR 1980 SC 1789 where the court held that the limit on absolute power was a fundamental feature of the Constitution – therefore any constitutional amendment which sought to further enlarge the amendment powers of Parliament and limit judicial power to review that was unconstitutional.

90 *M Ravi* (n. 76), para. [40]. The respondent also argued that it was not supported by the legislative history of Article 5 of the Constitution which envisaged repeal of provisions and in this way differed from the parallel Indian provision on the basis of which the Indian Supreme Court had introduced the basic features doctrine (Article 368 – which did not allow repeal of provisions but only amendment implying the possibility of a ceiling on amendments).

91 *Yong Vui Kong* v. *Public Prosecutor* [2015] 2 SLR 1158 relying on *Mohammad Faizal bin Sabtu* v. *PP* [2012] 4 SLR 947, [11]–[12], where the court held that the separation of powers was part of the basic structure of the Constitution.

92 *M Ravi* (n. 76), para. [71] citing Calvin Liang and Sarah Shi, "The constitution of our Constitution, a vindication of the Basic Structure Doctrine" (August 2014) *Singapore Law Gazette* 12, [38] and [46]. The Court of Appeal held that this included the right to vote: referring to its earlier decision in *Vellama d/o Marie Muthu* v. *AG* [2013] 4 SLR 1 (hereinafter referred to as "*Vellama*").

93 Which remain unresolved following the most recent discussion of the basic structure in *Wong Souk Yee* v. *Attorney-General* [2018] SGHC 80 (pending appeal). See generally,

A. Harding, "Does the 'basic structure' doctrine apply in Singapore's Constitution? An inquiry into some fundamental constitutional premises" and K. Tan, "Into the matrix: interpreting the Westminster model constitution", in Jaclyn L. Neo (ed.), *Constitutional Interpretation in Singapore: Theory and Practice* (Abingdon: Routledge, 2017); and The Honourable Senior Judge Chan Sek Keong, "Basic structure and supremacy of the Singapore Constitution" (2017) 29 *Singapore Academy of Law Journal*, 619.

94 *Ibid.*, 54 and 69.

95 *Vellama* (n. 92).

96 *M Ravi* (n. 76), para. 65. See also Jaclyn L. Neo, "Towards a 'thin' basic structure doctrine in Singapore", 17 January 2018, at: www.iconnectblog.com/2018/1/towards-a-thin-basic-structure-doctrine-in-singapore-i-connect-column/.

97 *Ibid.*, 66.

98 *Mohammad Faizal bin Sabtu* v. *PP* [2012] 4 SLR 947.

99 It is already used as a tool for interpreting legislative amendments (*Mohammad Faizal bin Sabtu* v. *PP* [2012] 4 SLR 947) and constitutional provisions (*Vellama d/o Marie Muthu* v. *AG* [2013] 4 SLR 1).

100 Relying on *Attorney-General* v. *Ting Choon Meng & Anor* [2017] 1 SLR 373. See also Yap Po Jen, "Uncovering originalism and textualism in Singapore", in Jaclyn L. Neo (ed.), *Constitutional Interpretation in Singapore: Theory and Practice* (Abingdon: Routledge, 2017).

101 The plaintiff also made an argument in his written submissions that Article19B encroaches on the rights to stand for election of persons who are not from the community for which an election is reserved. However, the plaintiff did not pursue this in oral argument.

102 Article 19B(1): An election for the office of President is reserved for a community if no person belonging to that community has held the office of President for any of the 5 most recent terms of office of the President. Article 164(1)(a): The Legislature must, by law specify the term of office of the President to be counted for the purposes of deciding whether an election is reserved under Article 19B.

103 *Tan Cheng Bock* (n. 77), para. [35].

104 *Ibid.*, [105], [106].

105 *Ibid.*, [106].

106 *Ibid.*, [118].

107 *Ibid.*, [119].

108 *Ibid.*, [109].

109 Interestingly, in the debates on the motion by the Workers' Party following the decision in *Tan Cheng Bock*, the Minister for Home Affairs and Minister for Law stated that:

> … the Government has been always very clear and upfront on the policy objectives of his hiatus-triggered elections framework … .our challenge was how to achieve both meritocracy and multi-racialism where qualified candidates from different races can regularly be elected to be our Head of State … the Government has always been clear that when it comes to the counting, it is a policy matter for Parliament to decide.

– it is a policy decision versus a legal question on when the Government "ought" to start counting as a matter of law: Minister K. Shanmugam, *Singapore Parliamentary Debates: Official Report*, 3 October 2017, vol. 94. (Motion on Counting From President Wee Kim Wee or President Ong Teng Cheong for Reserved Presidential Election – Policy Decision or Legal Question?).

110 *Tan Cheng Bock* (n. 77).

111 With opposition parties in talks to form a coalition of varying sizes: see Yuen Sin, "7 opposition parties discuss forming a new coalition, invite former PAP MP Tan

Cheng Bock to be leader", *The Straits Times* (Singapore, 28 July 2018), www.straitstimes.com/singapore/seven-opposition-parties-discuss-forming-a-new-coalition-invite-former-pap-mp-tan-cheng (accessed 31 August 2018); and Tham Yuen-C, "Opposition parties Democratic Progressive Party, People's Power Party, Reform Party to sign resolution on unity", *The Straits Times* (Singapore, 24 August 2018), www.straitstimes.com/politics/3-opposition-parties-to-sign-resolution-on-unity (accessed 31 August 2018); and the setting up of new political parties: Rachel Au-Yong, "Tan Cheng Bock applies to form new Progress Singapore Party", *The Straits Times* (Singapore, 18 January 2019), www.straitstimes.com/politics/tan-cheng-bock-applies-to-form-new-progress-singapore-party (accessed 6 May 2019); Choo Yun Ting, "Tan Cheng Bock's new party formally registered; party symbol to follow", *The Straits Times* (Singapore, 2 April 2019), www.straitstimes.com/politics/tan-cheng-bocks-new-party-formally-registered-party-symbol-to-follow (accessed 6 May 2019).

112 Dimitrios Kyritsis, "A moral map of constitutional polyphony", in *Where Our Protection Lies: Separation of Powers and Constitutional Review* (Oxford: Oxford University Press, 2017), Chapter 2.

113 See Li-ann Thio, "Past imperfect, future tense: the Elected Presidency and the constitutional development of an 'ever evolving hybrid' ", Chapter 2 in this volume.

114 The first time being the introduction of the Group Representation Constituency Scheme in 1988: see Jaclyn Neo, "Navigating minority inclusion and permanent division: minorities and the depoliticisation of ethnic difference" (2017) 17 *Jus Politicum*, 607–27.

115 *Report of the Constitutional Commission*, para. 5.36; *White Paper on the Review of Specific Aspects of the Elected Presidency*, para. 82: there will only need to be a reserved election if a particular race has not been represented in the past.

116 See Jaclyn L. Neo, "Constitutionalizing minority representation: the reserved elections mechanism and politicization of ethnicity in Singapore", Chapter 5 and Eugene K.B. Tan, "Squaring the circle: the President as a symbol of multiculturalism and national unity", Chapter 6 in this volume.

117 *Report of the Constitutional Commission*, para. 6.5.

118 *Report of the Constitutional Commission*, paras 6.1; 6.4–6.7.

119 *White Paper on the Review of Specific Aspects of the Elected Presidency* para. 96, 103.

120 *Report of the Constitutional Commission*, para. 6.1.

121 Royston Sim, "Singapore leaders striving for smooth transition", *Straits Times*, 9 November 2018. This is said to be manifest in the subsequent changes to leadership within the party: Royston Sim, "Heng Swee Keat picked as PAP's first assistant secretary-general, indicating he will be next PM", *Straits Times*, 23 November 2018.

122 *Ibid.*

123 Article 5A of the Constitution of the Republic of Singapore.

124 Article 5B of the Constitution of the Republic of Singapore.

125 Article 5C of the Constitution of the Republic of Singapore.

126 *Report of the Constitutional Commission*, paras 7.46–7.53.

127 *Report of Constitutional Commission*, para. 7.46 – citing the oral representations of Dr Loo Choon Yong and Loo Choon Hiaw (Transcripts for 6 May 2016 at p. 86) and Associate Prof. Eugene Tan (Transcripts for 18 April 2016 at p. 21). Kevin Tan had also recommended reverting back to an appointed President in his written and oral submissions (para. 7.35). The Workers' Party made a similar suggestion during the parliamentary debates on the amendments (discussed further in Chapter 8 by Maartje De Visser and Chapter 1 by Kevin Y.L. Tan and Lam Peng Er in this volume).

128 *White Paper on the Review of Specific Aspects of the Elected Presidency*, paras 82, 83 and 125.

Index

Page numbers in **bold** denote tables.

For Product Safety Concerns and Information please contact our EU representative GPSR@taylorandfrancis.com
Taylor & Francis Verlag GmbH, Kaufingerstraße 24, 80331 München, Germany

www.ingramcontent.com/pod-product-compliance
Ingram Content Group UK Ltd.
Pitfield, Milton Keynes, MK11 3LW, UK
UKHW020015200926
475702UK00014B/1903
* 9 7 8 1 0 3 2 0 8 2 6 2 2 *